A Celebration of Rare Breeds

Volume II

by

Cathy J. Flamholtz

OTR PUBLICATIONS

P.O. Box 481

Centreville, Alabama 35042

Versatility plus! This Curly-Coated Retriever is Best in Show winning Ch. Summerwind's Charles Dickens CD, WC, owned by Michael and Sue Tokolics and Debbie Wales.

OTR

PUBLICATIONS

PRESENTS

A Celebration of Rare Breeds

Volume II

A CELEBRATION OF RARE BREEDS, VOLUME II

ISBN 0-940269-06-6

Printed in the United States of America

10 9 8 7 6 5 4 3 2 1

Drawings by:

Amy Fernandez
100 Greenway South
Forest Hills, NY 11375

Library of Congress Cataloging-in-Publication Data

Flamholtz, Cathy J.
    A celebration of rare breeds

        1. Dog breeds.   2. Rare breeds.   I. Title
SF426.F586 1986   636.7   87-117404
ISBN 0-940269-00-7 (v. 1)

Although the author and publisher have extensively researched sources to ensure the accuracy and completeness of the information contained in this book, we assume no responsibility for errors, inaccuracies, omissions or any inconsistency herein. Any slights of people or organizations are unintentional. Readers should consult individual breeders or organizations for specific information on individual breeds.

OTR PUBLICATIONS
P.O. Box 481
Centreville, AL 35042

DEDICATION

To my parents, Wilson Henry and Evelyn Durr Vail
I hope they would have been proud

American, Canadian Champion Bertschires Jesse James CD, a son of the famous Champion Mantayo Bo James Bolingbroke. (Photo courtesy of Vernon Vogel)

Preface

Welcome back! I can't quite believe that it's been five years since the publication of the first volume of *A Celebration of Rare Breeds*. My, how time flies. Forgive my informal tone, but I've come to think of all you folks, who read the initial book, as my friends. I've received encouraging and heartwarming letters from so many of you. In fact, the response was so overwhelming that, regrettably, I couldn't answer all your letters. My apologies. A great deal has happened in the intervening years. I've gone on to author three other books and a baby has been added to the Flamholtz household (after eighteen years of marriage!). I am sure that you've been busy, too. There have probably been many litters whelped, new champions finished, and budding working and show dogs started on the path to success.

Much has happened in the rare breed movement, too. "Perhaps, in another ten years, some of the breeds listed in this book will have faded from view," I wrote in the preface to *A Celebration of Rare Breeds*. "However, many will have become a firm part of the purebred world in this country." It's my great pleasure to report that none of the breeds included in that first volume have faded from view. Four of the breeds, in fact, have gone on to achieve American Kennel Club recognition. Several others stand poised on the brink of achieving that goal. A number of the breeds have now been recognized by the United Kennel Club. There have been other breeds, too, who have grown in popularity, while their owners held to their beliefs that recognition is not in their breed's best interest. Though controversial, I included several breeds which had not yet been introduced to the United States. Today, all of these breeds can be found in this country.

The growth of the rare breed movement, in the past five years, has been nothing short of phenomenal. In fact, my fellow rare breed fanciers, we are forcing changes in the dog world. Both the A.K.C. and the U.K.C. have had to reexamine their requirements for registrations of breeds. I am sure that more changes will come, for the interest in rare breeds shows no sign of abating. Every month, it seems, we open a dog maga-zine to discover that a new breed has made its debut in America.

"Perhaps it will be possible, in the coming years, to celebrate with a second volume," I wrote in concluding the preface to *A Celebration of Rare Breeds*. I penned those words almost as an afterthought. I never dreamed that there would be so many letters encouraging me to write a sequel. I thank you all. What astounded me most, though, were the many letters from people desiring information on the rarer A.K.C. breeds. They complained of the short shrift these fascinating breeds received in most dog books. As you will see, I have indeed included coverage of some A.K.C. breeds in this volume. Normally, writers address the top breeds on the A.K.C. roster. Not me. I've drawn from the bottom of the A.K.C.'s list for this book.

As those of you who've been to a bookstore recently know full well, the costs of publishing have skyrocketed in the last five years. In order to allow me to discuss, in greater detail, the histories and personalities of all these breeds, my publishers have made a decision. They will be releasing the third, and final, volume of this work during the coming year. Dividing the current work into two volumes has enabled them to keep costs down. *A Celebration of Rare Breeds, Volume III* will include a number of A.K.C. breeds and a whole slew of as yet unrecognized breeds.

Once again, my sincere thanks go to the many rare breed owners who have generously shared their information with me. They have dipped into their scrap books and patiently fielded all my questions. I've been truly touched by their love for and dedication to their breeds. They really are the inspiration for this work.

My best to you and your dogs. May you have much success in the coming years. If you know of another rare breed, not covered in the first two books, please drop me a line. I'll be most grateful. Thanks again.

Cathy J. Flamholtz
September, 1991

The New Guinea Singing Dog is one of the world's rarest breeds. Jaya is owned by Phil Persky, of New York City. (Tara Darling photo)

Table of Contents

This lovely headstudy of an Affenpinscher is byaward-winning artist Amy Fernandez

Chapter 1

The Affenpinscher

"Often people outside the breed refer to Affen-pinschers as funny looking," writes long time breeder Sharon Irons Strempski, in the December 1978 issue of *The American Kennel Gazette*. "Of course, they're ab-solutely wrong! Part of the appeal of the Affenpinscher is that pert monkey-like face. They've burning eyes, shoe button noses, and expressive ears that move to signal their thoughts. How anybody could see that as strange is beyond me."

The Affen, as the breed is often called, is a charming little character who adds joy to his owners' lives. "Affenpinschers are very affectionate, perhaps more so than any other breed," says Mrs. Strempski, in the above cited article. "Unless you've owned an Affen-pinscher, you really couldn't understand the amount of devotion one can give. It's a five minute walk down and back to my mailbox," the Danbury, Connecticut breeder says, "and my little Affens greet me like a long lost rich relative when I return from collecting the mail."

Anne Skaggs, of Liebig Kennels, in Amanda, Ohio, is an ardent admirer of the breed. "Affens are willing to share any adventure and, in fact, may add a spark of spunk that turns a mere outing into an adven-ture." Anne should know. Back in the 1960's, she and her Affen, Henna, set out on one such adventure. The duo, accompanied by an aging Great Dane, hitchhiked from New York to Alaska. "Henna's interesting looks and comic personality could get a few extra miles out of a ride that had originally contracted for a lift to the next intersection." In fact, the little Henna added much to the trip. "Alaska would have been an adventure without Henna, but the old prospector would never have shown me his claim if he hadn't fallen in love with her."

Those who are fortunate enough to be "owned" by an Affenpinscher will find that the little dogs return their love with an incredible sense of devotion. Writing in *The American Kennel Gazette*, Sharon Strempski cites one example of the breed's fidelity. "One year when I was confined to bed for two weeks with pleurisy, my favorite bitch was permitted to stay with me. She had to be forcibly removed to be exercised. If I so much as sniffled in pain, she was there to lick my hand with a worried look upon her face."

Affenpinschers bond closely with their owners. They are not one man dogs, but adopt an entire family as "theirs." If the family has a sedate lifestyle, prefering quiet hours inside the family home, the Affen will be more than happy to accomodate them. However, if outside adventure is their cup of tea, that's fine with their little dog. "Affenpinschers can adapt themselves to their owner's level of activity," Mrs. Strempski writes in the *Gazette*. "I recall a pet Affenpinscher who divided his time among the family members. Part of his day was spent sitting next to the elderly grandmother while she sewed and watched television and another part was spent romping with a six-year-old boy when he came home from school. Affenpinschers are content to do as much or as little as their owners. The only thing that matters to them is being with their people."

For those with an active lifestyle, like Anne Skaggs, the Affenpinscher more than fits the bill. "Most Affens love to hike and camp and get into anything they can," the Ohio breeder says. "About half will chase a stick into the lake...but, because of their short faces, they have great difficulty bringing it back. Their short faces can make extremely cold weather a little hard on them.

For this reason, they don't get to go on long hikes in weather below 20°. They don't mind snow, as long as it is dense enough to walk on top of. Their hard coats are very burr resistant—a great asset for living in the country."

D. V. Gibbs and Tobin Jackson, in their 1969 book, *How to Raise and Train an Affenpinscher*, speak of the special joys of treking with the breed. "...A walk along a wooded lane with an Affenpinscher is sheer delight. Nothing escapes his attention, and everything must be thoroughly investigated. He will dance along in front of you or behind you—but rarely out of sight or earshot. For unlike the hounds, his real pleasure is in sharing any curious mystery with his master or companion."

One of the special delights in owning these dogs is their inherent playfulness. Indeed, they seem able to delight and entertain both their owners and themselves. Talk with Affen owners and they'll regale you with stories of the breed's playfulness. Most Affens take special delight in their doggy toys. They are masters at manipulating their dexterous front paws. Often they'll balance on their hind legs while tossing their toys skyward with their front feet. This game, often played for hours on end, delights their owners as much as it does the dogs. It has earned the breed it's oft heard description of "comically serious." Most owners find that it's difficult not to laugh at an Affen's antics. "A show off?" ask Gibbs and Jackson, in *How to Raise and Train an Affenpinscher,* "Indeed, yes. One has only to show curiosity or interest in what the Affenpinscher is doing for the little showman to pull out his bag of tricks for your approval and applause."

One of the favorite times at Anne Skaggs home is twilight. It's then that her Affenpinschers join together to serenade the closing of the day. "A group of Affens loves to sing. Get five or six of them together at around 7:00 p.m. Pretty soon heads will tilt back, and a choir will rehearse for ten to fifteen minutes."

One of the Affenpinscher's inherent traits is his absolute fearlessness. He may be a toy dog, but you'll never convince him of that. The Affenpinscher has supreme confidence in his courage and ability. Writing in *The Complete Book of Toy Dogs,* C.G.E. Wimhurst states, "The Affenpinscher is certainly a dog of character—there can be no question about that. Small it may be, but it stands upon its dignity and is quite fearless in the defense of its owner and its home. This does not imply that the breed is noisy. Usually an Affenpinscher is quiet and well behaved, but it can become extremely excited when aroused, and any intruder is left in no doubt as to its intentions." Indeed, most owners praise the breed for its capability as a watchdog.

The Affenpinscher considers it his duty to protect those he loves and is rather territorial in his attitude.

Anne Skaggs found this out on her New York-Alaska adventure. "One otherwise peaceful morning was pierced by a vehement demand for something to leave Henna's territory." The intruder turned out to be a large Grizzly bear. "...Henna was determined that this smelly creature would leave," Anne laughs. "Perhaps her ridiculously small size in combination with her fearless bark convinced it that the berries were easier to come by on the next ridge."

Due to the breed's fearlessness, owners must exercise a degree of caution in overseeing their Affens. An Affenpinscher is not likely to be deterred by a threat from a large dog and must be protected before he gets himself into a precarious situation. One of Anne Skagg's dogs was injured when he challenged a full grown stallion. It is not only with other dogs and animals, however, that the breed demonstrates its fearlessness. Puppies have been known to leap from high sofas or chairs resulting in injury. "Their fearlessness can sometimes be a pain," Anne Skaggs confides. Her dogs have been known to climb fences to sit on the toprails.

Like many German dogs, the Affenpinscher can be stubborn, at times. This will vary from dog to dog. Some dogs are quite dominant, while others are more laid back. Don't be surprised in your Affen challenges you, always testing the limits. In their excellent 1949 book, *Know Your Dog,* authors John Hickey and Priscilla Beach say, "The Affenpinscher is a proud, haughty little rascal, winning in his personality and smart as a whip. He has a refined, gentlemanly manner, but in his eyes there is an impertinent gleam which seems to say, 'I'm *your* dog, but you're *my* servant!' and he proves this by getting his own way. For his eyes just melt you and make it impossible to say no..." But, say no, you must. Consistency is the key to effectively raising an Affenpinscher. It's best to approach the training of this breed with firmness, tempered with patience and understanding. The rewards will be great.

Where did this charming rogue, this fearless spitfire, this absolutely adorable toy dog come from? The breed, undoubtedly, originated in Germany. Dog writers in that country say with pride that the Affen is a pure German breed. Originally, the small, wiry-coated, somewhat scruffy appearing dogs became popular fixtures around country homes. These early dogs earned their keep as ratters, ridding both the stable and home of vermin. We do not know precisely when the Affenpinscher came into being. Some fanciers believe that the breed dates back to, at least, the 15th century, when a dog of this type was depicted in an Albrecht Dürer woodcut. Undoubtedly, the dogs of this early period were larger than today's toy breed and came in a variety of colors.

By the 1700's and 1800's, toy dogs had become popular on the Continent. It was probably during this

This cute Affen puppy belongs to Anne Skaggs, of Amanda, Ohio.

time that the stable ratter was ushered into the house. Often seen as the companions of noble ladies, it's likely that the little terrier was bred down in size during this period. The breed's jaunty air must have captivated and intrigued owners. But, the dogs were not mere ornaments. They earned their keep by serving as able watchdogs.

By the early 1900's, the breed appears to have been well established. It's difficult to tell how popular the Affenpinscher of that day was. Emil Ilgner in his 1902 book, *Gebrauchs-und Luxushund*, states that the breed was neglected, as interest in pet dogs had waned. We do know, however, that there were some stalwart breeders. Ilgner identifies one Georg Goeller as a breeder. The first volume of the PZ (the studbook of the German Pinscher-Schnauzer Klub) includes an illustration of two dogs, Affi and Pitti, owned by Gräfin Larisch, of Munich. We also know that two Frankfurt breeders maintained Affen kennels. Records indicate that Heinrich Schott, of Affentor Kennels, and George Riehl, of Dornbush, were early breed fanciers.

We also know that the little dogs had spread to other countries. Count de Bylandt, in his great work on dogs, misspells the breed name as "Offenpinscher." He says that this toy terrier was, at one time, exceedingly popular on the Continent. English dog lover, Will Hally, writing in 1918, indicates that the breed was known in Great Britain. He tells of "the little Affenpinschers which a few of us youthful enthusiasts used to import from Germany in the days before the quarantine laws."

The Affenpinscher was to achieve lasting fame for his contribution to two more popular breeds. Most authorities concede that the Miniature Schnauzer originated as the result of a cross between the Standard Schnauzer and the Affenpinscher. Indeed, in some early Swiss studbooks, littermates are registered, some as Affens and some as Mini Schnauzers. This cross seems logical, since we know that several early Miniature Schnauzer breeders also bred Affenpinschers. Interestingly, in 1935, England's Kennel Club changed the name of the Miniature Schnauzer to the "Affenschnauzer." This decree lasted only a year. The name was changed back to the present one when the Germans vehemently protested.

The Affenpinscher also played an important role in establishing the Brussels Griffon. Many authorities contend that the little Griffon resulted from a cross of the Affenpinscher and the little street dog of Belgium. Marjorie Cousens, in her 1960 book *The Griffons Bruxellois*, states, "Sifting these various theories, I have been able to evolve a theory of my own...That there has always existed a breed of small rough-haired dogs, as early as the fifteenth century or before, and that those were the forerunners of the Affenpinscher. And that it was the Affenpinscher, which was kept in the back streets of Brussels in the mid-nineteenth century...and which, crossed later with...other breeds..., eventually produced the Griffon Bruxellois."

The breed first came to the United States in the early 1930's. The American Kennel Club granted official recognition in 1936. *Nollie v. Anwander* would earn fame as the first AKC registered Affen. She was not alone, though. In all, 27 Affenpinschers were registered in 1936. The breed began to appear at shows. Illinois breeder Mrs. Bessie Malley exhibited her *Otto von der Franziskusklause* and other dogs in the Chicago area. Henrietta Proctor Donnell, a toy breed enthusiast and owner of Nollie, showed her dogs in the New York area. All in all, the breed seemed headed for a bright future.

Then came the war years. With the mounting troubles in Europe, it was impossible to secure further breeding stock. With the advent of World War II, the breed was endangered in its homeland. German breeders struggled valiantly to save the little dogs. D.V. Gibbs and Tobin Jackson explain how critical the situation had become, in *How to Raise and Train an Affenpinscher*. "After World War II, German breeders were appalled to discover that only a handful of really good specimens had survived those devastating war years. With the sanction of The Pinscher Schnauzer Klub, Brussels Griffon crosses were used to strengthen the breed. The resulting shorter nose caught the fancy of the breeder and public alike and remains characteristic of the modern Affenpinscher. In using only Brussels Griffon blood, the Affenpinscher may be said to have remained essentially pure and uncontaminated, for...the Brussels Griffon...drew heavily from the more ancient Affenpinscher..."

After the war years, interest in the breed revived in the U.S. Mrs. Evelyn Brody, of Cedarlawn Kennels, finished the imported Ch. Bub v. Anwander. Arthur and Mary Harrington began their famous Aff-Airn breeding program and Mr. and Mrs. Walter Kauffman launched the Walhof Kennels. It was tough going for these early breed pioneers. We owe them our gratitude for maintaining the breed and keeping it in the public eye. Finally, in 1965, the American Affenpinscher Association was formed. Today, Affenpinschers are more popular than ever before. Many are capturing the eye of group and best in show judges.

The Affenpinscher has long been known by the nickname "Monkey Dog." Many writers have proclaimed that the breed's unusual appearance accounts for this appellation. Others point out, truthfully, that the breed bears little actual resemblance to this primate. Some owners think that the term stems from the breed's agile playfulness. In researching the breed's background, however, I have come to a different conclusion. I believe that the "Monkey Dog" term was probably first applied in the 1800's. We know that performing animal acts were popular throughout Europe in that period. Monkeys were the featured stars in many of these acts, but dogs were also popular participants. Organ grinders often set up shop on street corners to entertain passersby. Those who could not afford a more costly monkey, often employed dogs. Photos from the 1890's, in France, clearly demonstrate this. One particular shot shows a dog of decidely Affen type, decked out in a darling costume. He wears the same waistcoat, pants and cap that the more familiar organ grinder's monkey frequently wore. Balanced on his paws is a little wand. Surely this dog must have delighted the crowds with his antics. An 1860 German engraving entitled "The Showman of Augsburg and His Dogs," pictures a performing canine troop. One dog leaps through a hoop, one balances on his front paws and two little dogs dance gleefully about. One of the group, although with an undocked tail, is clearly of Affen type. Interestingly, in a *Dog World* article, "Affenpinschers and their Fans," Darlene Arden quotes current breeder Sharon Irons Strempski, on her family's introduction to the breed. Mrs. Strempski's love for the breed began with her mother-in-law. "She and her husband were over in Germany," she told Ms. Arden. "She was serving on a displaced person's commission and saw an Affenpinscher in a night-club act. She had to have one." Who knows, perhaps in Germany, the intelligent little Affen is still performing, winning hearts and gaining loyal followers for the breed.

The Affenpinscher is a sturdy, terrier type toy dog. The breed's distinctive head is one of its hallmarks. The skull is domed and the forehead rather prominent. The bristly whiskers and bushy eyebrows give him a unique look. The muzzle is short and rather pointed. Those oh-so expressive rounded eyes should be black and brilliant. His body shape is square with a slight tuck-up. The body ends with a natty docked tail which is carried high. A toy dog, the Affen should not exceed 10 1/4 inches in height. The average weight of the breed is about seven to eight pounds.

The wiry coat, with it's neck ruff, is one of the breed's essential characteristics. Coat quality is extremely important and varies somewhat within the breed. In *How to Raise and Train an Affenpinscher,* the authors divide the coat into two types: rough and smooth. The term "smooth" is relative and should not be mistaken for the sleek coat found in other short-haired breeds. In the Affen, this type has smooth, glossy hair on the back and hindquarters, with little rear leg feathering. Dogs of this type have feathering on the front legs and a profuse ruff about the neck. The smooth coat, they report, is slower in developing and may not reach its full glory until the dog is two years or older. The longer and denser "rough" coat is the most common type within the breed. This type is slightly softer in texture and often produces more abundant feathering. The authors fully concede, however, that many Affen coats fall somewhere between these two extremes.

The standard states that black is the preferred color for the breed. Indeed, most Affenpinschers come in this color. However, black and tans, grays and reds (which may vary from wheaten to brown) also delight fanciers. Whites or very light colors are faults.

Though still rare, the Affen is gaining an ever growing following in this country. Top wins, in recent years, have done much to stimulate interest in the breed. Still, it is his winning ways at home that earn him his loyal following. "If you haven't observed an Affenpinscher close up in a home situation, you really wouldn't believe how gay and fun loving they are," writes Sharon Irons Strempski, in the December 1978 issue of the *Gazette.* "....Affenpinschers are perfect in every way. I may be a wee bit prejudiced, but I think I'm right. Ask any Affenpinscher owner!"

Chapter 2

The American Water Spaniel

Writing in *The Complete Guide to Bird Dog Training,* well-known sporting dog writer, John R. Falk, says "The American Water Spaniel comes about as close to genuine versatility as any breed can..." In his earlier work, *The Practical Hunter's Dog Book,* Mr. Falk describes the breed as "the embodiment of utility personified....this little gun dog shows a penchant for hunting virtually any small species that swims, runs, hops or flies. If I exaggerate, it is only slightly; few, if any, American Water Spaniels hunt fox, bobcat, coon or possum. But, trail hound duties form about the only blank spot in this tiny tyro's hunting repertoire."

In his 1964 book, *The Hunting Dogs of America,* Jeff Griffen sings the breed's praises. "As far as I'm concerned, the American Water Spaniel is one of the most overlooked dogs on the American hunting scene. He's ideal for the man who wants everything a spaniel can do on land plus more powerful water work, but doesn't want as much dog as a retriever. Why the breed has not become more popular in recent years is one of those unexplainable things...I recommend him highly for inland water work and upland game hunting of all kinds."

Though still considered rare, this all-American native has thrilled sportsmen for more than 100 years. We do not know precisely how or when the American Water Spaniel originated. Breed history is mostly a matter of oral tradition. Some old-timers like to say that Columbus brought over the first pair. While colorful, this legend is, of course, inaccurate. Most authorities believe that the American sprang from an admixture of the English Water Spaniel, the Curly-Coated Retriever and the Irish Water Spaniel. However, Dr. F.J. Pfeiffer,

the great breed pioneer, strongly and loudly proclaimed that the Irish Water Spaniel had never been used in the formation of the breed.

The best bet for the breed's ancestor appears to be the now extinct English Water Spaniel. Indeed, this breed figures prominently in the formation of the Curly-Coated Retriever, too. There are many, many similarities between the now vanished English Water Spaniel and the American Water Spaniel. In Vero Shaw's 1879-1881 work, *The Illustrated Book of the Dog,* he quotes a description of the English breed penned by A.W. Langdale. Mr. Langdale says the breed should stand 19 inches at the shoulder and should never exceed 40 pounds. "His ears may be fairly long, and covered all over with curl, also the body, not the close curl of his Irish brother (the Irish Water Spaniel), but one somewhat looser and more straggly; his head is broad and long, with a piercing eye; his legs are well feathered in behind as well as in front..." In color the breed was either liver or liver and white, although the solid colored dogs seem to have been preferred. One is struck by the amazing similarity between this description and the current standard for the American Water Spaniel. True, present day Americans should be solid colored, but white markings are permitted, indicating that they were probably more prevalent in earlier days.

Is it probable that the English Water Spaniel made its way to America? The rare 1891 work, *The American Book of the Dog,* edited by G. O. Shields, certainly bears this out. The esteemed dog writer William Bruette, who wrote the chapter on the English Water Spaniel, was familiar with the breed. "By many the old English Water Spaniel is considered extinct, but

John Barth holds a pair of American Water Spaniel puppies. (Ned Vespa photo)

this claim I can not allow, for scattered throughout Great Britain, as well as in a few instances in America, are perfect specimens of the breed, in the hands of sportsmen who know their true worth, and who use them extensively in their private shooting. Were the good qualities of this dog better known, they would be very popular among our inland duck hunters...

"I have found the English Water Spaniel extremely intelligent, particularly fond of water, which he will enter by choice in all weathers," Mr. Bruette continues. "His powers of swimming and diving are immense; he works through mud, rice and weeds seemingly with as much ease as on land, while his keen nose enables him to scent the dead or wounded duck at marvelously long distances. He will work out the hiding place of a wounded bird with a perseverance and intelligence that can only be born of a genuine love of the sport. He requires little if any training, and seems to have inherent a desire to please his master as well as to gratify his own love of the sport. He will frequently mark the approach of the wild fowl before the hunter sees it; will crouch down till he hears the report of the gun, when he is all animation to mark the fall of the dead

or wounded duck....(he) makes an excellent companion at home as well as in the field."

Such observations, penned more than 100 years ago, must surely strike a familiar chord to all those familiar with the American Water Spaniel. Is it possible that the breed we see today is the living ancestor of the famed old English Water Spaniel, first described by Dr. Johannes Caius in the 1500's? Could today's American be the breed closest in type to that venerable old dog, so important in the evolution of modern retrievers? The answer appears to be a resounding yes.

In the early to mid-1800's, a few intrepid American pioneers began to venture westward. There, they found a wild and untamed land which abounded in game of all kinds. We believe that they brought with them their sporting dogs. Life in those days was incredibly hard. Hunting was not a sport, but a necessity. Meat was needed for the table and to put by for the harsh winter months. These early hunters needed an all-around dog, one who could plod through a marsh or dive into frigid waters to retrieve a duck, lope through the fields in search of grouse or pheasant or give chase to the prolific rabbit. If he was small enough to fit inside the boats or canoes used in duck hunting, so much the better. But, these were not his sole duties. On the homefront, he had to serve as a watchdog and companion to the children. The dog they developed was commonly called simply the Water Spaniel or the Brown Water Spaniel. Some hunters named him the American Brown Spaniel. His current breed name pays homage to these earlier appellations.

By the late 1800's, the breed was well established. He was particularly popular in Wisconsin. Hunters along the Fox and Wolf River Valleys, in the central-eastern portion of the state, especially prized the breed. While he was still primarily a personal hunting dog, market hunters began to use the American Water Spaniel, too. The hardy, rugged little dog made quite a name for himself.

With the advent of the new century, the fate of the little brown dog would change. Though a club devoted to the breed had been established in 1881, interest in the American Water Spaniel dwindled. Now, American hunters were interested in more specialized breeds. They used Pointers and Setters or flushing spaniels for upland game. When duck hunting season came around, they turned to the larger retrievers. And, if it was furred game that was wanted, well, that was a hound's job. True, the American Brown could still be found, but his place was fast being usurped by these specialists. Environmental factors, too, would play a part in the breed's decline. A severe drought, in the 1930's, devastated the waterfowl population in Wisconsin.

One individual, however, came to the breed's

rescue. Dr. Fred J. Pfeiffer obtained his first American in 1894, when he was still a boy. He and the little dog enjoyed many happy hours afield. He attended medical school and hung out his shingle in New London, Wisconsin, in 1909. An avid hunter, Dr. Pfeiffer continued to use the breed, but was concerned with their declining numbers. He decided to establish a kennel devoted to perpetuating the all-round hunter. His Wolf River Kennels became the driving force in saving the breed.

Fred J, Pfeiffer was not content to just enjoy his dogs, though. He became an advocate for the breed, singing its praises at every opportunity. He genuinely believed that sportsmen in this country would appreciate the American Water Spaniel, if only they knew of his existence. In the 1920's, he approached the United Kennel Club and persuaded them to recognize the breed. In the 1930's, he teamed with other fanciers to re-establish a club devoted to the breed. He approached the American Field, asking that the breed be admitted to the Field Dog Stud Book. They worked with him to prepare a standard and officially recognized the breed in 1938. Two years later, the American Kennel Club followed suit. Dr. Pfeiffer's own *Curly Pfeiffer* would be the first dog registered. The breed gained momentum and was no longer endangered. By 1967, when Dr. Pfeiffer died, he was able to reflect on the long hard road and see the great progress the breed had made.

While paying tribute to Dr. Pfeiffer, there were others who contributed to the breed's resurgence. John and Celestine Scofield, of Ozark Kennels, in Jonesburg, Wisconsin, have long been active in the breed. John obtained his first American Water Spaniel, Rex, in 1927 and still owns several of the breed. He was an early club secretary. Driscoll Scanlon, of Nashville, Illinois was a driving force in the 1930's, and Karl Hinz, of Milwaukee, Wisconsin, was also a devoted follower of the breed.

Thomas Brogden, of Rush Lake, Wisconsin, was an avid fancier "I had my first American Water Spaniel in 1891 and have owned and bred them more or less since, extensively since 1930." His Ch. Rush Lake Navigator earned top ring honors, finishing his championship undefeated, in only four shows. During the 1940's, Mr. Brogden had this country's largest kennel of American Water Spaniels.

The title of largest kennel, these days, goes to John and Mary Barth's Swan Lake Kennels. John first became acquainted with the American Brown when he was a boy. He spent many happy hours duck hunting with the dogs in the LaCrosse area. In 1967, he obtained his first pair and they became the foundation of Swan Lake. The kennel is located in Pardeeville, near the breed's original home along the Fox and Wolf Rivers. John avidly trains and hunts his dogs.

The American Water Spaniel is an attractive and distinctive breed. Those who read the first volume of *A Celebration of Rare Breeds,* will note the breed's resemblance to the Boykin Spaniel. This is no accident, for the American was the primary breed used in the Boykin's formation. The American stands 15 to 18 inches at the shoulder and weighs 28-45 pounds. He has a rather broad skull and medium length head. His spaniel type ears are set on above the eyeline and, when stretched forward, come to the end of the nose. The eyes should be dark or hazel in color. Yellow eyes are a disqualification. This is a good rule as light eyes, once they slip into a strain, are hard to eliminate. The American's tail curves in a "slightly rocker shape," and is carried low.

The breed's most distinctive characteristic is its coat. The standard calls for a solid liver or dark chocolate coat. Some breeders liken their dog's color to that of a Hershey bar. Small white markings are permitted on the chest and toes. The standard says, "The coat should be closely curled or have marcel effect and should be of sufficient density to be of protection against weather, water or punishing cover, yet not coarse." The hair on the American Water Spaniel's forehead is short and smooth. A dog of this breed should never have the topknot seen on the Irish Water Spaniel. The ears and the tail are covered with close curls. For those too young to remember the "marcel" hairstyles, once so popular, the standard may seem a trifle confusing. Named after a French hairdresser, the marcel style featured a series of even waves. This "permanent wave" effect can often

An American Water Spaniel hits the water at Swan Lake Kennels. (Ned Vespa photo)

been seen in the American's slightly oily coat. Moderation is desirable in the coat. It should never been too tightly curled, too fine nor too straight.

"My first experience with the American was as a kid of twelve or thirteen," recalled John Scofield, in Eugene V. Connett's 1948 book, *American Sporting Dogs*. "I was invited along on a hunting trip to carry the game, and I had some game to carry. The dog on this trip was a Water Spaniel, and I shall never forget the way he worked and hunted. He was a marvel. Not an in-or-outer, he was as mechanical as a machine. I had rabbits and quail and squirrels. Late that afternoon we chanced on some mallards on a creek; eight were shot, and he was in and retrieved them all. Not a piece of game was lost because of that Spaniel, and from that day on there was only one breed of dog for me."

Indeed, it is the American Water Spaniel's all-around capabilities that thrill sportsmen. Australian sporting dog trainer, Roy Burnell, speaks glowingly of the breed in his *Gundogs for Field or Trial,* published in 1972. "The breed is phenomenal at marking the fall of game and is very staunch. Frequently a dog may be kept under control until four or five rabbits or ducks have been dropped, and then, when sent, he will invariably make for the wounded one rather than for the nearest dead one. Such sagacity is all part of a real gundog...to many people the breed would look a rather rough type of dog, but those who have seen him work would have nothing but admiration for this bustling, energetic, merry all-rounder who gives such a good account of himself on pheasants, quail, grouse, rabbits or ducks."

One of John Barth's dogs practices retrieving. (Ned Vespa photo)

The American Water Spaniel earns high marks for his water work. Retrieving is the breed's forte and this has made the American particularly popular with wildfowlers. He is noted for his swimming abilities and most dogs take readily to water. Icy waters and a long day of hunting do not deter him. He will enter the water willingly and cheerfully for as long as the hunter wishes.

"In water, he works just like a retriever, handles himself better than any of the other spaniel breeds, loves to ride the prow of a skiff through marshes, fetching in mallards, teal, pintails, whatever such sneak hunting produces," says Jeff Griffen, in his 1964 book *Hunting Dogs of America*. "In a duck blind along a river or in a wheat field, where the birds will settle to feed, he blends in perfectly with the surroundings, learns almost immediately to sit still at the approach of the birds and has great ability at marking falls. The little fellow is a highly intelligent and skillful dog with a flypaper memory. Hence he adapts easily to a variety of situations. Though game as any retriever alive, he is a little light for coastal waters, and this is probably the reason he was developed as an inland dog and has so remained."

As in the days of old, the American Water Spaniel is the perfect companion for hunting from a small boat or skiff. He doesn't take up much room and can readily dive into the water without capsizing the craft. There's also less water in the boat when he returns and shakes off. While the breed is often recommended for duck duties, some experts claim that he's too small to handle geese. John Barth disagrees. He owns property near Portage, Wisconsin's Pine Island, a popular goose shooting locale. He has successfully used his Americans on geese, with no problems. However, he does point out that goose hunting is only for the well-seasoned dog. "A wounded Canadian can work a dog over severely with beak and wings," Barth says. "The big birds have been known to ruin a dog permanently for future retrieving use." Therefore, only his most experienced dogs are used on these big honkers.

While a splendid water dog, it would be wrong to ignore the American Water Spaniel's accomplishments as an upland hunter. It's true that the breed is not as fast or stylish as a Springer Spaniel, but many average hunters don't need a big running dog. The breed has a very keen nose and a methodical, yet merry way of working. In upland field work, the American operates like other sporting spaniels. He quarters the field, within range of the shotgun, in his quest for game. John Barth uses a check cord, during early training, to teach the dog an acceptable range. The American often employs a combination of both body and foot scent in his search, and quarters the field from side to side. His frantically wagging tail usually signals a find of game. He flushes any birds he finds, forcing them into flight, at an easy

An American wades ashore at Swan Lake Kennels, in Pardeeville, Wisconsin. (Ned Vespa photo)

have been several cases of young children training their own dogs in short order.

Like all spaniel breeds, the merry little American makes a wonderful companion. One must deal with him with patience and praise, however. Harsh methods do not suit this breed at all and will kill his spirit. He bonds closely with his family and it is for them that he reserves his best performances. In fact, this is the main reason that the breed is not often sent for professional field training. Most Americans perform much better when trained by their owners. He has a calm, loving way with children and enjoys rough housing with them. At home, he is a docile, well-behaved gentleman and a very good watchdog.

distance from his master. He has wonderful retrieving skills and a soft mouth. It's true that his coat sometimes picks up burrs in close cover, but it also provides protection from briars. While his coat color would seem to be a disadvantage for upland work, since he works close to the gun, this presents few problems.

"The American Water Spaniel has a way of winning your confidence, of saying to you with his eyes and actions, 'I want to please you; I hope to be one of your friends or perhaps one of your family if you will allow me,'" writes John Scofield. Indeed, it's the breed's easy going, pleasant demeanor that endears him to owners. "I like their dispositions better than anything else," John Barth says. "They're friendly and easy to train." Indeed, this eager to please breed is very easy to work with and fun to have around. The few dogs that have been exhibited in obedience, have been quite successful. In field work, the American Water Spaniel requires much less training than other breeds. There

The American Water Spaniel is rarely seen in show rings. While not flashy, there have been a couple of group placings. Most breeders are intent on preserving the breed's hunting instincts, and tend to shy away from conformation competition. This seems a shame. Certainly, the little American will never be so popular as to lose his hunting status. Many specimens are to be found who are solid, sound moving dogs, excelling in breed character. It's a shame more show goers and judges don't have the opportunity to see the breed and appreciate his merits. The breed has been shunned by field trial enthusiasts, too. This is not surprising, for the breed has not the spectacular style and dash to compete with other more specialized breeds. This, however, is to the breed's benefit for those who love the American Water Spaniel want to see him continue as the fine, versatile, all-around hunter that he is. It would be a shame if he were modified to comply with current field trial demands.

Ch. Al Hara's Hima in motion. This regal bitch is owned by Ingrid Aigeldinger, of Switzerland. (Photo courtesy of The American Azawakh Association.)

Chapter 3

The Azawakh

"At a show in Vienna in 1975, I came across my dream hound, full of aesthetic grace and charm. This was a red Tuareg hound with white stockings, very proud bearing, floating past with long strides without a lead, ignoring everything around him. This proud, almost arrogant manner made a deep impression on me. My first thoughts were...Primaballerina, miniature Arabian horse...Verdi...Bellini...Rossini...I ask forgiveness for such a comparison, but I have never seen anything like it before, and I was overwhelmed. My skin was all in goose bumps, as always happens when something touches me deeply. Of one thing I was sure, this was the breed to accompany me throughout my future." These eloquent and stirring words from noted Swiss breeder Ingrid Aigeldinger, describe her first encounter with one of Africa's most intriguing sighthounds...the Azawakh.

The Azawakh (Ahz-ah-wok) bears the name of a valley in northeastern Mali, where the breed was first discovered. Originally, it was thought that the dogs were exclusive to this area. However, travelers have confirmed that the breed is found throughout the southern Sahara, in western Africa. It is believed that his range may extend not only throughout Mali, but also eastward into Niger, westward into Mauritania and southward into Burkina Faso.

"The Azawakh is like a phoenix rising from the ashes, if we consider how and where it lives and under what conditions," writes Hedi Meier-Hospenthal, of Switzerland. "The Azawakh is...in his homeland, the true companion of the Tuareg Bedouins, the 'sons of the wind.'" While other tribes may also have owned the breed, it is from the Tuaregs that we have learned most about these dogs.

The Azawakh appears to have served this Berber tribe in a variety of ways. Naturally wary of strangers, the dogs helped to guard the possessions and livestock of their nomadic owners. They were also companions and playmates to the children of the tribe. However, it was their prowess at hunting that made the breed such a treasured prize.

The Azi, as the breed is known, starts to hone his coursing skills at a young age. Three month old pups begin to chase rats. When the puppies become proficient on these, they graduate to rabbits and other small game. Only the mature dogs are allowed to pursue the fast moving and evasive jackal, gazelle, or antelope. Gazelles are now protected in several African countries, but the old ways die hard and doubtless some dogs are still used on this prey. "The Azawakh has such a penchant for the chase," says Debra Rookard, of Dacula, Georgia, "that he will course anything that is put in front of him."

The Tuaregs practice a very primitive style of hunting that is suited to the hostile land in which they reside. When hunting big game, the dog sits on horseback, in front of his master. When game is spotted, the Azi springs from the horse and pursues the fleeing animal. The dog's objective is to closely trail the animal using his extraordinary eyesight, driving him on until he reaches total exhaustion. This incredible feat requires a dog of superb speed and stamina, who has the intelligence to outfox his opponent. The duel between adversaries may last for hours (hunts lasting six hours have been observed) and speeds of 43 miles per hour have been reported.

When the Azawakh finally overtakes the prey, he cripples the animal. His strong jaws clench the flanks or legs, hamstringing the prey. Then, the Azi guards his disabled opponent until his master arrives. Unlike other sighthounds, this breed must never actually kill the game. This is a very important point and shows how the Azawakh is peculiarly suited to his environment. At this final moment of the chase, the dog is usually some distance from the human hunter. In the blistering sub-Saharan sun and on the scorching sand, meat spoils quickly and vultures wait for any sign of a meal. Therefore, the Azi waits patiently for his master to make the final kill.

The Tuaregs use no firearms or bows and arrows in their primitive hunting style. Instead, animals are killed swiftly, with a knife, and their bodies bled out and gutted immediately. The faithful dog is given the meat from around the kidneys as a reward for his success. The carcass and the dogs are loaded on horseback and returned to the encampment.

Small wonder that the Azawakh is such a cherished treasure of the Tuaregs. A bedouin's status is measured by the animals he owns. His camels, goats, horses and his dogs are an intimate part of his life and essential to his standing in the community. The quality of his "oskas," the Berber word for a beautiful Azawakh, are very important to him and he treats his dogs as members of the clan. The dogs sleep inside the tents, in the special partitions reserved for men only. They often lie next to their masters, sharing their blankets. Dogs eat the same food served to people, namely camel or goat's milk, dates and couscous. Dogs are often adorned with amulets or talismans, which provide protection and insure success in the hunt. Decorative strings of shells sometimes encircle the dogs' necks.

In the Tuareg encampments, Azawakh breeding follows a curious ritual. Litters are rigorously culled and a number of superstitions have evolved surrounding the selection of dogs. Pups with white markings on the end of the tail, the chest and the paws, are highly desired. The Tuaregs like to see at least one black toe nail. The small moles that dogs have, called "warts" among the nomadic tribe, are greatly esteemed and the dog must have five of these...two on each cheek and one under the chin. Interestingly, only males are kept by the Tuaregs, as they are believed to be the most proficient hunters. An occasional female is allowed to live to perpetuate the line. Lastly, the Azawakh is never sold or traded. The only way to acquire one of these dogs is as a gift and, because possession of the dogs is so cherished, they are only given as a great honor.

The true beginnings of the Azawakh remain a mystery. Some say that the dogs have existed in the region for thousands of years. "Petroglyphs found in Egypt confirm this is a very old...breed," says Swiss

A lovely head study of Ch. Reckendahl's Kanishka, owned by Gisela Cook-Schmidt.

owner Heidi Meier-Hospenthal, "which has existed for 3,000 years. These dogs were used at that time to hunt ostrich, mufflon (sheep) and antelope." Gervais Coppé, a socioeconomist whose specialty is the development of pastoral societies in western Africa, spent fifteen years living and working in the region. He agrees that the Azawakh is an ancient breed. The frescos of the Tassili 'bovidienne' dating from 4,000 years ago, he observes, show the Peul ancestors accompanied by their Azawakhs.

The relationship of the Azawakh to the other members of the sighthound family has not been established. "These questions are difficult to answer...," says Gisela Cook-Schmidt. "Large segments of the populace in these regions of Africa have been migrational since time immemorial." Some fanciers believe that the Azi was brought to northern Africa by Arab conquerors and found a home with the Tuaregs. Debra Rookard, President of the American Azawakh Association, and others believe that the breed is a "pure African sighthound, different from other Oriental sighthound breeds." Does the Azawakh share a common lineage with the Sloughi? Perhaps it did thousands of years ago, Gervais Coppé says, but the breeds became isolated and each developed along very different lines. We may never be able to pinpoint the breed's exact origins, but obviously the Azawakh of today is a unique and distinctive breed all its own.

Our thanks go to the French and Yugoslavians for introducing the breed to Europe. The dogs of Dr. Picar, a Yugoslavian envoy to the Ivory Coast and Burkina Faso, first brought the breed to the attention of European fanciers. He first saw them at an African leader's home and was enthralled with their beauty. Eventually, Dr. Picar was presented with an outstanding male, whom he named Gao. The dog became his beloved companion and he was intent on obtaining a mate for Gao. As we've discussed, few bitches are left alive and those that survive are destined for breeding. There seemed no one willing to honor Dr. Picar with such a gift. The resourceful man, however, would not be stopped. Dr. Picar had heard of a tribe of Tuaregs that was being terrorized by a rogue bull elephant. An avid big game hunter, the Yugoslavian tracked and killed the animal, delivering it's dead body to the chieftain. As thanks for his services, he was given a bitch. Interestingly, it was the offspring of these two desert-bred animals that Ingrid Aideldinger saw at that Vienna show in 1975.

Meanwhile, Monsieur and Madame Parigi returned to France with several of the breed. These, along with the Yugoslavian imports, account for most of the Azawakh in Europe, today. "At present these are the two main Azawakh lines in Europe," says Gisela Cook-Schmidt. "Both lines are highly inbred and consist only of reds and browns in different shades with the usual white markings."

Recently, other imports have arrived in France from Africa. A German couple imported several dogs.

The majestic beauty of Gisela Cook-Schmidt's Reckendahl's Isesi.

And, when Grevais Coppé returned from his sojourn in Mali, he brought several of the hounds with him. In an interview for *Le Figaro*, he recounts, "At that time, my dogs represented the umbilical cord that joined me to the Africa I love. In caressing my companions, in

seeking to know their identities better, I kept up my dream to return to the Sahel." Though his knowledge of dogs was limited, Monsieur Coppé has established a breeding program. Doubtless, this new unrelated stock will benefit the breed.

The road to recognition for the Azawakh has not been an easy one. When the first dogs were introduced, little was as yet known of their origins. The Federation Cynologique Internationale classified them as Sloughis, despite the differences in their physical type. When one looks at a map, it's easy to see how this mix up occurred. The Sloughi hails from the region known as the Maghreb. This encompasses the present countries of Algeria, Tunisia, Morocco and a portion of Libya. The range of the Azi is directly south of this area and has about the same breadth. This inaccurate recognition allowed for the interbreeding of the Sloughi and the Azawakh. Fortunately, most breeders recognized the F.C.I's error and continued to maintain their respective lines.

Finally, on January 1, 1981, the F.C.I. accorded separate breed status to the Azawakh. Unfortunately, the problems of the breed did not entirely end. In an effort to weed out any potential Sloughi crosses, the color brindle (very common to the Sloughi) was disqualified in the show ring. This seemed little cause for concern at the time, as a majority of European Azawakh came in shades of red or brown. As our knowledge of the breed has increased, however, we have learned that brindle dogs exist in the Tuareg camps. Indeed, some think that they are the most valued of all colors. In 1987, Mrs. Ursula Arnold traveled extensively throughout the Sahel and recorded her observations of color. Her list of Azawakh colors include: "light red to mahogany; light sable; all shades of brown, even chocolate; white, with light to dark brown patches." She describes the brindles as "black to dark brown brindle on red background; black or gray brindle on sable background." She reports that white trim, often with a white facial blaze, may be found in all colors. "Questioned which color was favored," Mrs. Arnold wrote in *Der Windhunde*, "the nomads always pointed to the hounds they owned. I was under the impression as if the comparatively rare brindles were favored, in the case of a brindle puppy occurring in the litter, it was always the one kept alive." One can only hope that this confusion will soon be rectified and we will see in the show ring the full range of Azawakh colors. The American Azawakh Association recognizes the brindle color.

The Azawakh is relatively new to the American scene. German born Gisela Ina Cook-Schmidt, of Twenty-nine Palms, California, is credited with introducing the Azawakh to the U.S. Gisela first saw the breed at a European show. "In 1986, I purchased my own foundation bitch, *Al Hara's Hiba,* from Ingrid

Aigeldinger, in Switzerland," Gisela says. "This is a bitch from the French line." Hiba was boarded at Al Hara Kennels until she came into season. "In 1987, she was bred to a male from the Yugoslavian line, Ch. Faysal Ushi of Silverdale, bred by M. Roder-Thiede in Germany." The pregnant Hiba soon arrived in the U.S. "On Halloween eve, 1987, the first litter of Azawakh was born in the United States," Gisela says. "Hiba has also whelped a second litter...by a dog imported directly from Africa to Germany." It was Gisela's hope that this would "enlarge the very restricted gene pool."

Several other dogs have since been imported and the breed is attracting the attention of many American sighthound enthusiasts. In 1980, the American Azawakh Association was formed. A standard was agreed upon and a studbook established. "From this we hope to maintain a future for the Azawakh in this country," Gisela says. Several Azawakh owners have been involved with other sighthounds. They have begun to run the breed in practice coursing trials throughout the country. "As one would assume from the shape of these long-legged creatures, they are excellent coursers. Not only are they extremely competent, they are also breathtaking to watch," Gisela confides. "They skim above the ground, ceaselessly searching for prey. If there is no more worthy opponent, they will even course lizards." The Azawakh can compete in rare breed events, States Kennel Club shows and, of course, shows sponsored by the F.C.I.

The Azi is the epitome of elegance. His body is somewhat longer than tall and fairly ripples with muscles. The breed has a long, graceful neck which blends into

Ch. Al Hara's Hima epitomizes the "sighthound extraordinaire. (Photo courtesy American Azawakh Assn.)

a level topline. The hip bones are quite pronounced and should, according to the standard be "almost as high or higher than the shoulder point." He has the characteristic sighthound deep and narrow chest and extreme tuck up. Males stand 25-29 inches tall at the withers, while females measure 23 1/2 to 27 1/2 inches. This gives the dog a decidedly long legged, yet sturdy look. The standard describes the ideal Azi head as "long, dry and distinctly elegant....with very little stop." The ears hang close of the skull and should never be rose shaped, like those of the Greyhound. In order to fulfill his job as a hunter, the Azi must have strong jaws. His "cheeks are flat with no flewing." The nose should always be dark. A long, slender tail completes the picture. In an alert dog, the slightly curving tail is carried in high, gay fashion. White tipped tails are preferred. The Azawakh's smooth taut skin is covered with a short silky coat. The American standard allows for a lovely array of colors: "cream to dark red, also to include white, chocolate, black, brindle, grizzle and parti." White markings are frequently seen.

"The temperament of this breed is unlike any other sighthound," Debra Rookard observes. Hedi Meier-Hospenthal describes them as true "individualists." While the Azi needs a chance to exercise, cavort and run daily, they are rather quiet individuals in the house. "They prefer relaxing in elevated places," says Debra Rookard, whose dogs can often be seen lounging on the sofa, "after a bout of effusive and exuberant play with anything and everything that will join in the fun." Heidi Meier-Hospenthal says "The Azawakh is exactly the right dog for someone who dislikes noise and wild demonstrations of affection....the Azawakh will place its beautiful head trustfully in its owner's lap and use its expressive eyes to carry on a silent dialogue. The Azawakh will be a loving, quiet (indoors), faithful and alert companion for someone who can understand its nature (this understanding does not come overnight, which enhances the pleasure when it finally arrives)." Indeed, this understanding thrills those who know the breed. Debra Rookard says that the breed "is a joy to behold...one that is well suited to life with the family. As pups, they bond immediately with their owners and seem to live only to delight their people with their loving and charming demeanor."

The Azi seems particularly well suited to homes with children and other dogs. "The breed's great love for children deserves special mention," Heidi Meier-Hospenthal says. "I know this from relationships between our female, *Nayama Al Hara,* and our four sons. Woe to anyone who would appear to threaten our children. The love for children assumes, of course, that the children treat the dog with respect and love and not view it as a toy."

From a very early age, the Azawakh bonds to his family. "This bond is the most critical feature in ownership of this hound," says Gisella Cook-Schmidt. "The Azawakh is his master's dog. He bonds very early in life and grows up in tune with his master and family, often almost to the exclusion of anyone else. In rearing an Azi, one must put great emphasis on as much socialization as possible, to avoid a dog which might be unfriendly to every visitor. Even so, the Azi is never a dog to greet a stranger like his long lost friend. Being a dog with the need for a strong bond with his master, the Azi will, for this reason, never do well in a kennel situation. Lacking the communication with someone who is his, he might turn in on himself, becoming quite unfriendly and hard to manage. As a product of the desert, the Azi knows inherently that life can be extremely hostile. By nature he is a very cautious dog." Debra Rookard agrees, saying that the breed's cautiousness is "instinctually generated self protection, learned over centuries of survival in the Sahara." Great care must be taken to socialize the Azi, particularly if you intend to show your dog. Ms. Rookard believes that this tendency to avoid strangers is so inherent, that the dog should not be penalized in the show ring if he doesn't wish to stand for examination.

Those who own the breed, say that the Azi is more amenable to obedience training than other sighthounds. Gisella Cook-Schmidt believes that this stems from the breed's close bond with his owner. "The Azi," Debra Rookard says, "is very trainable in obedience and other work...They take direction well and are easily trained on hand signals....The Azawakh takes happily to obedience training on a *wide* choke collar, and responds well to a praising voice. A harsh hand should never be used as the dog will refuse to work." Heidi Meier-Hospenthal agrees. "Force and severity produce nothing; in fact, quite the opposite. Effective instead are love, perseverance and consistency."

The Azawakh shows more protective instinct than many other sighthounds. Debra Rookard says they have more "backbone" than other coursing breeds. "As a rule, the Azawakh is a quiet and settled dog, but will report any approach made toward their home by strangers, be they two or four legged," Ms. Rookard says. "While it is true that they will protect what is theirs, or their master's, they don't display unreasonable aggression of any sort and will freely accept those whom the master has welcomed."

Interest in the Azawakh appears to be growing steadily both in America and in Europe. This may prove to be a critical point in the breed's survival. Continuing drought, the destruction of the desert habitat and a terrible plague of locusts, have all devastated the breed's sub-Saharan home. When Gervais Coppé first began traveling to Africa, some twenty years ago, the breed was still widespread. On a recent trip, he saw only fifteen dogs. "In the face of nature's caprices," explains Gervais, "man panicked. The families splintered and the dogs followed the people through hell. This explains the incredible degradation of the Azawakh breeding in their region of origin. The dogs that are born today...are smaller than their ancestors." As we can see, the situation for the Azawakh in his homeland is particularly bleak. "Africa is now in a time of great unrest and change," Gisella Cook-Schmidt laments. "Several of the African breeds, including the Azawakh, are caught in these changes. This might well spell the extinction of them in the land of origin. To ensure their survival, outsiders will have to assume more responsibility for the future of these special hounds." Indeed, many breeders hope they will be able to keep the breed alive and, one day, return a few individuals to their African homeland.

Those interested in a sighthound would do well to consider the exotic Azawakh. The breed is hardy, easy to care for and long lived. "Anyone who has ever seen one of these magnificent dogs gliding over a meadow, will forever lose his heart, as I have, to such splendid animals," says Swiss owner Heidi Meier-Hospenthal. "It is a joy to experience them in action and will deeply affect anyone who loves beauty, nobility and harmony." American owners familiar with the breed will surely understand when Debra Rookard describes the breed as "a sighthound extraordinaire!"

A family portrait from Carillon Bedlingtons. (From left to right) Three month old Absolutely Positively Carillon and four month old future champion New Improved Carillon pose with their grandmother, Ch. Claremont Lana. All are owned by Lucy A. Heyman.

Chapter 4

The Bedlington Terrier

If you want to meet people, take a walk with a Bedlington. They are real attention getters and sure fire conversation starters. What first catches the eye, of course, is the startling lamb-like visage. Beneath the stunningly elegant exterior, you'll find an outgoing dog of great charm. But, the lamb-like countenance is quite deceptive for it cloaks a dog with the veritable heart of a lion. The Bedlington, you see, is a true terrier, through and through.

There has always been a good deal of dispute about the Bedlington's origin. Undoubtedly, he shares a kinship with the Dandie Dinmont Terrier. In the late 1700's and early 1800's, the breed was known by a host of names. Dubbed variously the Rothbury and Rodberry Terrier, he was also known as the Northern Counties or Northumberland Fox Terrier. It's said that he originated in the Hannys Hills, a mecca for sporting terrier enthusiasts. The present name comes from the mining shire of Bedlington, located in England's Northumberland County.

Joseph Ainsley, of Bedlington, is credited with stabilizing the breed and fixing type. It is said that, in 1820, Ainsley acquired a bitch, Coates Phoebe. Bred to a dog named Anderson's Piper, she produced, in 1825, Ainsley's Piper. He was to become quite famous and was the first dog to bear the official name of "Bedlington Terrier." A sporting paper, dated 1870, included a letter supposedly written by Ainsley himself, which talked of Piper. "With regard to the doings of Piper, it would take a volume to contain them; but I may mention that he was set on a badger at eight months old, and from that time until he was fourteen years old was constantly at work, more or less, with badgers, foxes, foulmarts,

otters, and other vermin. He drew a badger after he was fourteen years old, when he was toothless and nearly blind, after several other Terriers failed."

Naturally, news of Piper's exploits spread throughout the north country. He, and with him the Bedlington, became immensely popular in the region. Piper sired many of the early dogs in this newly emerging breed.

That the dogs became popular, there can be no doubt. Vero Shaw, in one of the most entertaining passages in his 1879 *The Illustrated Book of the Dog,* speaks of the local preference for the breed. "Though the breed may not be so popular as others with 'doggy' men throughout the country, it is nevertheless certain that in its own district its merits meet with due recognition. In Newcastle and its environs almost every man has a 'poop,' and that 'poop' is certain almost to be a Bedlington. In the company of his trusty tyke, the miner when off duty is supremely happy. They hunt or poach together, fight together, sleep together, and not unfrequently drink together; it is no uncommon sight to enter the tap-room of a north-country public-house and see as many dogs as men in the room, and all apparently equally interested in the evening's proceedings. The greatest insult which can be put upon such a master is a reflection upon his dog's appearance or gameness; and as for ill treating them, a stranger had better injure 'Geordie' than hurt his dog. 'If thau poonch ma dog, 'arl poonch thee' is proof of the miner's love for his Bedlington, and it is no uncommon threat in the neighborhoods where this breed is mostly found."

As Shaw mentions, the Bedlington was used for a variety of purposes. In traditional terrier style, he was put to all manner of vermin. The breed displayed its gameness and sporting talents on everything from badger and otter to fox. With his speed and agility, he was also well equipped for rabbit hunting. The Bedlington also performed remarkably well in the rat pits.

In one of the breed's sadder moments, the Bedlington was pressed into service as a pit fighter. His owners often waged great sums on his gameness. Sometimes he was pitted against fellow Bedlingtons and, at other times, his opponent was another terrier. While not inherently quarrelsome, these men knew that, once challenged, the Bedlington would never quit.

The breed's show career began in 1869 when two dogs were exhibited at a London show. They created a sensation. By 1870, British shows were offering classes for the breed. In 1877, a club was established for the little terriers.

One of the leading breeders to emerge was Thomas J. Pickett, of Newcastle-on-Tyne. His involvement with the breed began during boyhood. "Whilst a schoolboy I recollect one day wandering in the woods of the Brandling estate of Gosforth, in Northumberland, gathering primroses," Pickett wrote in an 1877 issue of *The Livestock Journal*, "when I met a woodman named David Edgar, who was accompanied by a Northern Counties Fox-terrier, and who gave me a whelp by his celebrated dog Pepper. This whelp was the first of the breed I ever possessed. Being an ardent admirer of this description of dog, I followed up the breed, and have seen as many of them as most people...."

Obviously, Pickett's knowledge of the breed paid off for he was a very successful breeder. Most notable of his dogs were the trio Tyne, Tear'um and Tyneside. A show in Bedlington, in 1870, pulled an entry of 52. Tear'um topped the breed. It's said that the judge was none other than Joseph Ainsley.

By 1905, there were three English specialty clubs to support the breed. The breed's first major triumph came in 1906 when Mr. Harold Warnes' Ch. Cranley Blue Boy captured a Best in Show at Ipswich. Blue Boy's victory foretold an illustrious show future for the breed and that it certainly has had.

The Bedlington was first recognized by the American Kennel Club in 1886. By 1890, there were a few specimens of the breed that had been imported from England. One of the earliest fanciers was Mr. W. H. Russell, of New York City. Writing in G. O. Sheilds 1891 book, *The American Book of the Dog,* Russell's devotion and love of the breed is obvious. Since this is such a rare volume, I thought readers might enjoy seeing a few of his remarks.

"Good specimens of this breed (I speak from personal experience)," Mr. Russell writes, "resemble one another even more mentally than they do physi-

Cynthia Cook's twin daughters, Paige and Rachel Pruitt, pose with their pal Wally (alias Serendipity Showstopper).

cally. There is always the same alert interest in outdoor matters, with the ever-present *penchant* for hunting and excavating. These energies can, of course, be misdirected, and one's chickens or cats may become the unwilling objects of the dog's pursuits; and, if not watched, one may even find the house-walls undermined. Young dogs may, however, be taught to conduct themselves so as to meet with general approbation, even respecting their owner's flowerbeds.

"These dogs are happiest when taken for an outing with their master, searching about at a gallop for anything that runs wild...

"They have, in good specimens, something of the appearance of a thorough-bred race horse, and when animated show a fiery energy that illumines them. It is this over-flowing vitality and sporting instinct in the field that has such a charm for the man who loves what is all about him in nature as she is found in field, wood and stream, and who appreciates a sympathetic canine friend....

"There is a consensus among writers on the Bedlington that he is of the highest courage, and instances are adduced to show his desperate gameness. It was said when he first became generally known that he was quarrelsome. This has been repeatedly contradicted in print by good authorities. The idea may have arisen from the fact that he was kept by a certain class of men as a fighting dog, and because of his undoubted pluck.

However, when not trained by this species of cannibalism, he has been found peaceable when abroad. A brave man may be either a hero or a desperado. Being a dog capable of strongest attachment to his master, he is likely to be blindly jealous, and will 'bear no rival near the throne.' At home he will usually not tolerate the intrusion of strange dogs. This can hardly be called a peculiarity of the Bedlington, dogs not being inclined, as a rule, to show hospitality to visitors of their own species..."

Though the breed has never been popular, interest in the Bedlington did continue to grow. The Bedlington Terrier Club of America was founded in 1932. The breed received nationwide attention, in 1948, when Ch. Rock Ridge Night Rocket won Best in Show at Westminster. Today the Bedlington is seen at most shows and one of the delights of watching the terrier group is catching sight of the springy stepping Bedlington.

"A Bedlington is all flowing curves with no right angles," says Lucy A. Heyman, a breeder from Brownsville, Texas. The standard calls for a "graceful, lithe, well-balanced dog with no sign of coarseness, weakness or shelliness. In repose the expression is mild and gentle, not shy or nervous. Aroused, the dog is particularly alert and full of immense energy and courage."

The Bedlington's head is rounded and deep, yet narrow and capped with a profuse topknot. His almond-shaped eyes should never tear or water. His triangular shaped ears are set low and rounded at the tips, which end in a little silken tassel. Nose and eye color coordinate with the shade of the coat.

The Bedlington is indeed all curves, a striking departure from the angular lines found in most terriers. Indeed, his well muscled body is more reminiscent of the sighthound family. He has a deep chest, flat ribs, an arched loin and a pronounced tuck-up. Slightly longer than tall, the Bedlington is remarkably flexible. His distinctive tail is set low and shaped like a scimitar. The breed is moderate in size, generally standing about 15-18 inches at the shoulder and weighing about 17-23 pounds. The breed's movement must truly been seen to be appreciated. Bedlingtons move with a light, airy, springing gait, that never fails to thrill. At the gallop, they move with all the sinewy grace, power and flexibility of a sighthound.

One of the breed's most unique features is, of course, it's coat. Breeders say it is extraordinarily soft. "The closest analogy," veterinarian Cynthia S. Cook, says "is to dryer lint." A special appeal of the breed is that the Bedlington does not shed, making it a suitable breed for those allergic to dog hair. "The non-shed coat is terrific around the house, as is the Bedlington's odor-free nature," says Lynn Hall, of Elkader, Iowa. He has no "doggy odor, even when wet," Lynn says.

Bedlington colors run to either blue or liver, but there are many variations. The standard allows "blue, sandy, liver, blue and tan, sandy and tan, liver and tan. In bi-colors the tan markings are found on the legs, chest, under the tail, inside the hindquarters and over each eye, the topknot of

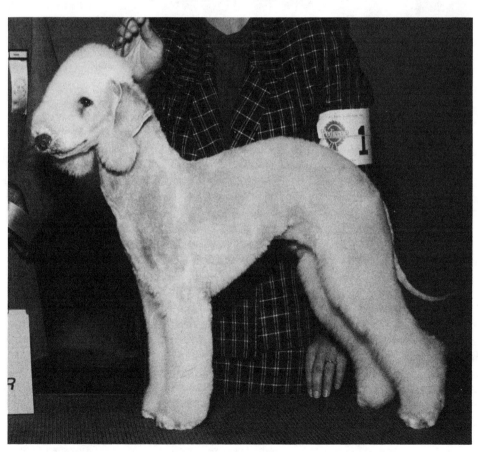

The lovely Ch. Carillon Salsa Serendipity, owned by Lucy A. Heyman, Carillon Bedlingtons, Brownsville, Texas.

Best in Show and Multiple Group winner Ch. Claremont Anchor Man, owned by Lucy A. Heyman, relaxes on a glass table.

all adults should be lighter than the body color."

Lucy Heyman, of Carillon Bedlingtons, says that one of the "truly fascinating things about this breed is that they are ever evolving and ever changing, a living art form, if you will. They are born solid black or solid brown and begin to show signs of 'clearing' color as their eyes are opening. The color in males and females change and vary with age and the seasons. In the case of females, changes in hormonal level will result in color changes. Many young adults can be an undesirable 'stone white' color for a while, before the mature coat and color get established. Of course, they never revert to the solid dark colors of early puppyhood."

To achieve that wonderful lamb-like appearance, the Bedlington's coat needs routine trimming. Regular combing will prevent matting. While it does require some practice to turn out coats on show dogs, pet owners can easily learn the technique themselves. Some, however, elect to have their dogs trimmed regularly at a grooming parlor. The Bedlington Terrier Club of America offers instructions on grooming the breed. "The grace and beauty of the dog's lines can be enhanced and changed with the stroke of a scissors," Lucy Heyman says,"and changed again with a little hair growth."

By and large, Bedlingtons are vigorous healthy dogs. There is one particular condition, however, that all new owners should be aware of. Who better to describe the breed's health problems than a breeder and veterinarian. Cynthia Cook, of Half Moon Bay, California, has volunteered. "With regard to health problems specific to the breed, there are several which have been described including: congenital polycystic kidneys, patella luxation and ocular conditions including retinal dysplasia and cataract. However, because of its incidence, the condition of most significance to the Bedlington is Inherited Copper Toxicosis. This is a disease in which affected animals are unable to eliminate excess copper which then accumulates in the liver. Although exact statistics are not known, a large proportion of the breed is affected by this disease. Affected individuals may not exhibit symptoms until seven to eight years of age (or even later) by which time they may have already contributed extensively to a breeding program. This disease is inherited in an autosomal recessive fashion so that two unaffected animal (who are carriers) may still produce affected pups. To date, the only effective method of diagnosis involves analysis of a piece of the liver tissue (obtained by liver biopsy, a relatively simple surgical procedure) for copper content after an animal is at least one year of age. Affected animals may be successfully treated with agents to bind to the copper in the liver and remove it. This treatment is lifelong and in order to be effective, must usually be initiated prior to an animal exhibiting clinical syptoms of liver disease. Because of the prevalence of this disease in the Bedlington, it is recommended that only animals which have been biopsied and found to be free of the disease be used for breeding. Unfortunately, there are only a minority of Bedlington breeders who follow these breeding practices."

Most of the Bedlington breeders I spoke with seemed very responsible and conscientious with regard to Copper Toxicosis. If you are interested in the breed, you should definitely inquire about the status of the parents before purchasing a puppy. "Responsible breeders test their dogs before breeding from them and breed only from biopsied normal animals," says Lynn Hall. "Buyers should ask to see copies of the biopsy reports before buying a puppy. Responsible breeders are happy to provide this proof."

"The personality is...hard to describe in a believable manner," Martha McVay writes in the November 1979 issue of the *American Kennel Club Gazette*. "You could tell hundreds of incidents where the Bedlington calculated, acted, tricked, loved, protected, fooled, read your mind and outwitted you. All for just your love and entertainment..."

Indeed, Bedlingtons are charmingly docile in the home, eminently lovable and sure to delight you with their sense of humor and penchant for tricks. "They are very outgoing and people oriented," Cynthia Cook observes, "without being submissive, clingy or fawning." Lucy Heyman agrees. "They are really terrific and very lovable with people."

Lynn Hall, an author of children's books, is an enthusiastic supporter of the breed. "My first attraction to the breed was based on their woolly lamb-like appearance, the softness of the coat and the mild humorous expression. I wanted dogs to love and the Bedlingtons seemed to offer that kind of affection. They are indeed among the most loving of breeds....They are serious professional huggy-bears who want to be in the closest possible contact with people."

Bedlington owners agree that the breed makes a good companion for children. "They are superb with kids," Lucy Heyman says. "They seem to take special delight in them." Lynn Hall says, "Most Bedlingtons are excellent with children and love to be included in all family activities."

Owners should be aware that this breed, like so many other terriers, has a proclivity toward digging. "They can be bad about digging holes in lawns," Lynn Hall notes, "but are not destructive by nature. Mine are left along in the house for long periods with nothing more than an occasional excavated wastebasket to answer for."

The breed is known for its great intelligence.

Am. Mex. International Ch. Magic Mist Sir Blue, owned by Lynn Hall, of Touchwood Bedlingtons, shows the Bedlington's lamb-like appearance.

"They housebreak very easily and most take happily to obedience or other forms of training," Lynn Hall remarks. "Besides conformation showing, my Bedlingtons compete successfully in obedience and agility and seem to love it. They learn quickly and enjoy showing off." Cynthia Cook praises the breed's intelligence and eagerness to please, but adds that, like many terriers, the Bedlington can be a mite stubborn. "Although they are very intelligent and can certainly be obedience trained, it requires an extra dose of patience on the part of the trainer."

The breed earns high praise as a watchdog. "This singular canine gentleman is also one of the most alert of dog breeds," writes Elinore Young, in the 1966 book, *How to Raise and Train a Bedlington Terrier*. "He is quick to advise whether a strange sound is a cause for investigation and will announce the presence of guests before they get near the doorbell."

Stories of the past often criticized the Bedlington Terrier for his penchant for fighting. Does this hold true for the modern dog? "Temperaments vary tremendously in this regard," Lucy Heyman says. "Some Bedlingtons are more easy going than others with dogs. The Bedlington is not at all a quarrelsome dog. However, while they don't pick fights, they will not stand to be challenged. They will, indeed, fight to the death. Many breeders have bred specifically to quell this nature, but I feel that it's an intrinsic part of the breed. All the historical writings mention it. I know there are many that will disagree with me, but I work to preserve this as well as the breed's hunting instincts."

Cynthia Cook adds that the breed has an "assertive nature with other dogs. This particularly applies to two individuals of the same sex—when provoked, a Bedlington can be a formidable adversary and will not retreat from a fight."

"Some Bedlingtons can be aggressive toward other dogs," Lynn Hall says, "but they are in the minority and, in my experience, they usually object only to other Bedlingtons of the same sex. A sharp Bedlington might not combine well with a toy dog with a high-pitched voice, because of their terrier instincts." In Lynn's opinion, "Bedlingtons are the mildest, most laid-back of the terrier breeds. Overly aggressive Bedlingtons are not good Bedlingtons and should be avoided," she adds, "but they are a small minority."

"I am constantly amazed that the Bedlington has not become more popular," Cynthia Cook says. Why indeed? This breed has much to recommend it and these "woolly woofers," as Lynn Hall calls them, are the ultimate in loving, playful companions. Perhaps, in the future many others will learn the delight of living with one of these dogs. As Martha McVay says, "There is just no way to describe the joy of living with a Bedlington!"

Chapter 5

The Belgian Malinois

The Belgian Malinois (pronounced Mal-n-wa) is growing in popularity. His gains have been made the hard way—he's earned them! Until recently, the breed has been little known in this country. While the long haired Belgian Sheepdog and the Belgian Tervuren have steadily attracted attention and new fanciers, interest in the Malinois has been minimal. This is a shame ,for in his native homeland the Malinois is the most popular of all varieties. Things are beginning to change, though. The breed's performance in European style working competitions have commanded new respect from trainers. The Malinois is being lauded by both amateur and professional trainers alike. He's now seeing duty, in this country, as a police and military dog and he's receiving rave reviews. Indeed, Americans are discovering what the Belgians have long known: the Malinois is one of the world's most versatile and adept working breeds.

The breed has been hampered, somewhat, because of its superficial resemblance to the German Shepherd. I can well recall watching, in the early 1970s, a superb obedience performance, in the Open class, by a dog of this breed. As the audience applauded, the person next to me sighed. "It's too bad that dog is such a nondescript looking German Shepherd," she said. As the dogs stepped forward to receive their awards, I looked closely at this extraordinary worker. There was a poise, an elegance and a grace to the dog that singled him out. His head was decidedly different, on close inspection, from that of the German Shepherd. He was leggier, more finely boned, with more upright pasterns and lacking the extreme angulation now seen in the German breed. His keen expression and overall counte-

nance screamed class. I rifled through the pages of the catalog and soon had my answer. Here was the Belgian Malinois, one of the rarest of the Working group (I hate to date myself, but this was in the era before the herding dogs were separated from the Working group). I made it a point to seek out the dog's owner and asked if I could see her Malinois. "I can't believe it," she exclaimed. "You mean there's someone at this show who actually knows he isn't a German Shepherd!" Until recently, such was the lot of the Malinois owner. What few realized was that this breed has a long and illustrious heritage.

We don't know precisely when the various varieties of Belgian sheepdogs first emerged. Some say they date back to the Middle Ages. Before our modern age, the majority of Belgians lived self-sufficient lives on farms. All the Belgian sheepherding varieties were all-round farm dogs. These versatile dogs herded livestock and protected the family and their property. Since they worked closely in association with man, intelligence, trainability and companionship developed to a remarkable degree.

In the late 1800s, a proud spirit of nationalism erupted in Belgium. Other Europeans were working to protect and develop their national breeds and the Belgians were interested in this, too. In 1891, the *Club de Chien de Berger Belge* was formed. Farmers and shepherds wanted to determine if there was a national sheepherding breed, indigenous to Belgium alone. Adolphe Reul, a professor at the Belgian School of Veterinary Medicine, was called upon to assist these fanciers. He contacted veterinarians in all of nine of Belgium's provinces, seeking their assistance in making a survey of the sheepherding dogs used in the country.

In 1891, at Cureghem, on the outskirts of Brussels, the first breed survey was held. A total of 117 dogs were present to be examined by Professor Reul and a panel of judges. All the experts agreed that the dogs presented were anatomically identical. The only differences noted were in the length, texture and color of coats. Similar exhibitions were held in the remaining provinces. The results were all the same. The dogs were remarkably similar in type, but varied widely in coat. After reviewing his survey of the dogs, Professor Reul determined that the Belgians did, indeed, have a national shepherd breed. Sorting out the mishmash of colors and coat types, though, was the problem. He suggested that the breed be subdivided into different varieties and that only certain coat types and colors would be allowable. Then, while maintaining type and ability, breeders could concentrate on standardizing coat and color.

The Belgian import, Lison des Deux Pottois, is owned by Robert Felcher, of Fiddletown, California.

Initially, the Belgian Shepherd was subdivided into six distinct types, based on coat and color. (Some authorities hold that there were originally eight types.) Only four survive to the present day. In Belgium, all are shown together under the general classification of "Belgian Shepherds." As we shall see, it is only in the United States that the varieties have been divided into distinct and separate breeds. The long-haired black dogs, known in this country as "Belgian Shepherds," are referred to in their native land as "Groenendael." The American Kennel Club also recognizes the short-haired Malinois and the long-haired Tervuren. Those who have read *A Celebration of Rare Breeds, Volume I,* will already be familiar with the rough-coated Lakenois.

The Malinois was the first of the varieties to be uniform in type. According to Adrienne A. Pagel, Professor Reul found a dozen of the short-coated dogs, of pure Belgian type, in the town of Oosterhout, in Holland. The dogs were most common, however, in the Belgian town of Malines, and it is from this locality that the variety takes its name. So famous did the dogs of Malines become that other short-haired Belgian Shepherds were referred to as "other than Malinois." Professor Reul was obviously impressed with these dogs for, in subsequent years, he bred and owned this variety. One of his most noted dogs was the important stud, *Mastock.*

The breeders and dogs of Malines became quite famous in those early days. Dog fanciers in the the area took great pride in training their dogs. In the late 1800s, they formed a club and held exhibitions to showcase their dogs talents. The dogs performed in a variety of fields, from circus type acts to more traditional uses like sheepherding. In 1903, the Malines club held one of the earliest police dog trials ever staged on the Continent. Photos exist of this early outing showing the remarkable ability of the Malinois. Dogs are seen scaling ten foot ladders and jumping over trenches filled with water. The event was even covered by the Belgian magazine, *Chasse et Peche,* which lauded the dogs and their owners. As the new century dawned, the Malinois was pressed into service in police and border patrol work.

We gain a picture of the breed, during the first World War, from Captain Max von Stephanitz, the father of the German Shepherd. In his massive work, *The German Shepherd Dog in Word and Picture,* von Stephanitz tells of his travels throughout Belgium, as a member of the Kaiser's army. It is clear, though, from his writings, that the Captain knew of the Belgian sheepherding dogs before he was posted to Belgium. "There are shepherd dogs in large numbers, in proportion perhaps more than in Germany," he writes. "Owing to the great popularity of the shepherd dog in Belgium, it is not to be wondered at that the German shepherd dog was found comparatively rarely...."

In 1914, von Stephanitz traveled to western Flanders. "I could still see shepherd dogs everywhere being used as yard dogs," he says, "Almost in every farmyard they have built for him a hive-shaped brick kennel. In the towns, the short-haired variety prevailed; in the Brussels area, on the other hand, the black, long-haired kind were found...."

Things were to change, though. By the next year, 1915, von Stephanitz was hard pressed to find a single dog working in the traditional manner. Large numbers of all varieties of Belgian Shepherds had been pressed into service for the military. "Already as early as 1915 I saw no dogs in Belgium being used with the flocks-but this may have been due to the war." In the final days of the war, many dogs had entered the service. "Among the Walloons, south of the Maas, through which the closing stages of the war...led me, the dogs had already been appropriated throughout the district to be trained for the Intelligence Service. The people where I was billeted recognized my dog as being a shepherd dog."

Von Stephanitz both commends and condemns the Belgian breeders. "The Belgians are clever and zealous breeders," he says. At the same time, he totally rebukes them for forming the various varieties based on coat and texture. He says that "with the shepherd dog they entirely overlook the question of utility and emphasize the importance of external appearances, which, after all, is only of secondary importance. Shape of head, carriage of ears, tail, hair and, above all, color, weigh with them." And, he adds, with typical Aryan arrogance, "Everything in hair and color that does not sufficiently fall in with what any of these paltry little Societies consider as ideal in the race, is considered not pure." He categorizes their principals as "narrow-minded." It seems so contradictory that the founder of the highly regimented German system should offer such criticisms. He predicted that this method would lead to disintegration. Time, however, has proven him woefully wrong.

Von Stephanitz, who pioneered the use of German Shepherds for police work and was an advocate of working trials, also found fault with Belgian training methods. He did concede that they were very skilled at training. "They are as keen trainers as they are breeders," he reports. But, he did not approve of the Belgian working exhibitions. "...They lay stress...on matters which are entirely beside the point, such as external features, trivialities, and circus acts. They develop, for example, jumping powers to a remarkable degree, but they are of no practical use. The Belgian breeders scarcely ever busy themselves with the all-important consideration of training the powers of scent."

We can only assume that von Stephanitz would have been surprised to see present day German Shepherds attempting to scale ten foot high walls, just like their Belgian cousins. And, as to scent training, the Belgians did begin to place emphasis on it, and their versatile dogs proved quite adept at tracking. One can only wonder if he might be a bit chagrined to see the outstanding performances of current Belgian Malinois, who regularly place over the German Shepherd in working competitions.

Americans appear to have gotten wind of the Malinois performance in the 1903 trials in Malines. A few years later, several Malinois were imported to work with police departments in both New York and New Jersey. The departments were, of course, only interested in their dogs abilities and never sought to register them in this country. All records of these early imports have been lost.

It was in 1911 that the American Kennel Club first granted recognition to the Belgian Sheepdogs. They followed the European plan, simply registering the breed as "Belgian Sheepdogs." We do know that, of the original four imports, two were Malinois and two were Groenendaels. In the period from 1911 to 1939, several other Malinois were imported and bred in this country. They came, we are told, from some of Europe's top kennels and had illustrious pedigrees. But, there appears to have been little effort to actually promote the breed. Only breeder Walter Mucklow, working in the 1920's, seemed to take an interest in publicizing the breed. He was an enthusiastic fancier and attempted to trace the breed's history. He penned an article for *The American Kennel Club Gazette* on the Malinois. Despite his enthusiasm, the breed failed to take hold. By 1939, the Malinois was extinct in this country.

There would not be another Malinois registered until 1950. In that year, several dogs were imported. At the 1951 Specialty, long dominated by the black, long-haired Groenendael, spectators were stunned when a Malinois captured Reserve Winner's Bitch. Breed numbers, however, remained low.

In 1959, the A.K.C. made a momentous decision. It divided the varieties of Belgian Sheepdogs into three separate breeds. Breeding between the respective varieties was outlawed. This proved a problem, particularly with imported dogs from Europe and Canada. Malinois breeders would occasionally find a Tervuren, or long-haired fawn puppy, in their litters. Before 1959, and to this day in Europe, this puppy could be registered as a

Tervuren while the remainder of the litter would be registered as Malinois. No more. Such odd puppies were just considered Malinois with a disqualifying fault.

With the AKC's decision to split the varieties, they allowed the black Groenendael to retain the name Belgian Sheepdog. It was by far the most popular of the varieties and the one most often seen in the show ring. The Tervuren had a number of extremely dedicated advocates and it too entered the Working Group. (The Herding Group had not yet been formed.) But, what of the rare Malinois? The AKC decided to remove the breed from regular competition and placed it in the Miscellaneous Class. It was a unique situation, because although the breed could not compete in regular classes, dogs were still registered, as before, in the AKC stud books.

Support for the Malinois continued to grow, slowly but surely. By 1965, there was sufficient interest for the AKC to once again fully recognize the breed.

This beauty is Robert Felcher's Dutch import Xorca-Marel v.d. Morgenhoeven. Xorca makes her home at Bob's Malinois O'Oberwager.

From 1963 to 1973, a total of 107 Malinois were registered. Since that time, there have been importations from France, Belgium and Switzerland. From 1974 to 1982, a total of 329 Malinois were registered in this country. While still rare, the breed has continued to grow steadily.

With the Belgian Malinois, what you see is what you get. His elegant, upstanding, proud look is not obscured by the profuse coat found on so many other herding dogs. He is strong, well-muscled and agile, with a keenly alert expression. He is strongly built, but never bulky. His is moderately well boned, but should never appear cumbersome. In this breed, sex differences are readily apparent. Males are larger and more impressive, while bitches have a distinctly feminine look. His body is approximately square. The tail is carried low when the dog is relaxed but, when he moves, the tail is raised and ends in a slight curl at the tip. This should never, though, form a hook. Males stand 24-26 inches at the withers and bitches are 22-24 inches.

The ideal Malinois head is clean cut and strong. He carries his head proudly and his expression clearly shows an incredible alertness, indicating a dog that's always ready for action. He seems to gaze intently at his master, as if awaiting his next command. He has stiffly erect ears that are triangular in shape. The eyes are slightly almond-shaped and brown, the darker the better. The nose is always black.

Some have described the Malinois as having "half a coat." By this, they mean that it is too long to be considered smooth, yet too short to be considered long. In comparison to the other varieties of Belgian sheepdogs, however, it is short. The Malinois has a double coat with a dense undercoat which provides protection from the elements. The hair is longer on the neck and shoulders and forms what breeders call a "collarette." This is most pronounced in males. The coat is also longer on the tail and backs of the thighs. The color ranges from a rich fawn to mahogany with an overlay of black. The underparts of the coat are a lighter fawn, but should never appear washed out. This variety always has a black mask and ears, one of their identifying characteristics. A little white on the chest and tips of toes is permitted.

As I said, in beginning this chapter, the Malinois is earning his growing reputation the hard way. It is not the breed's elegant appearance nor his illustrious heritage, but his intelligence and character that are winning friends. Americans are learning that the Malinois is incredibly responsive to his handler and learns very rapidly. This breed makes an impressive obedience competitor.

It is the Malinois' performance in schutzhund and European-style ring sport competitions that has really captivated dog fanciers. "American 'dressage' trainers are discovering what the Belgian and French trainers have known since the 1903 Malines trial," writes Adrienne A. Pagel, in the article "Viva la Difference," published in the November 1986 issue of *The American Kennel Gazette.* "The Malinois is an ardent and precise worker. In the past few years, American Malinois have placed either first, second or captured both places, at the National NASA...trials—thus joining ranks with French Malinois who consistently win the Coupe de France, and with Belgian Malinois who are a staple of European working championships."

The breed has been used, for years, as a military and police dog in Europe. In the past few years, the breed is increasingly used, for such purposes, in this country. During the recent Desert Storm conflict, several Malinois accompanied the troops to the Persian Gulf.

The McAllen, Texas, sector of the U.S. Border Patrol Service has been using Malinois successfully for the past several years. They search cars crossing the U.S.-Mexican border to detect drugs and illegal aliens. The Border Patrol imported several Malinois and one Malinois/Airedale cross from Holland to work with their team of human handlers. The dogs received their initial training in Holland and had their final training in Texas. They have proved to be superior workers who win high praise from their handlers. In less than a year, two of the dogs, Rocky and Barco, detected 187 shipments of illegal drugs. The heroin, cocaine and marijuana they found has an estimated street value of over $130 million dollars. In fact, Rocky and Barco have proved so successful that drug smugglers have placed a $30,000 bounty on each dog's head.

"The Malinois is something new to dog handlers," Juan Garcia, Assistant Chief Patrol Agent told Cle Francis for an article published in the July 1988 issue of *Dog World.* "...Here in the U.S., most handlers work with German Shepherds, Labradors, and a few other breeds. But I've seen their dogs perform and I've seen ours and I'll stick with the Malinois. They outlast other breeds in terms of time on the job." Indeed, the dogs' endurance and excitement for their work has impressed all of the Patrol Service agents. "Our dogs really enjoy their work and they need only about fifteen minutes to half an hour break," Agent Garcia told Ms. Frances. "During that time they just lie down, sleep a bit, and then they can continue working. We don't

overwork them, but they have been known to wear down their handlers! In fact, our patrol agents have lost weight trying to keep up with the dogs."

Why did the Border Patrol pick this rare breed? "We decided on the Malinois because of their intelligence and temperament," Agent Garcia says. "They work very well around people and that was one of our primary considerations. We didn't want a dog with an aggressive temperament; one which might bite. Our dogs are trained to be petted by children, since they are also an important part of our successful educational program, 'War on Drugs.'" The dogs have proved so successful, in fact, that other Border Patrol stations are interested in using Malinois, too.

While he's proving quite successful in military, security and police work, the Malinois still retains his traditional herding instincts. Those who use the breed for herding applaud his speed, agility and incredible endurance. In the past decade, there has been a proliferation of herding trials in the U.S. Many of the participants are show advocates, who want to insure that their dogs maintain their original heritage and instincts. Malinois breeders are finding that the breed is a keen competitor. One dog Ch. Crocs-Blancs My Dagan N'Me TT, HIC, STDS has proven his versatility. In the show ring he is a specialty winner and group placer. He has

The stunning Ch. Croc Blancs Gentlmn Jim, owned by Barbara Huitt, of Rio Hondo, Texas.

also received his temperament testing certification, his Herding Instinct Certificate and earned a Started Trial Dog on Sheep certificate.

Those who have owned Malinois are unstinting in their praise for the breed. "The Malinois is a wonderful obedient pet," one owner says. "You have to really live with the breed to appreciate their deep loyalty and affection for their family. They have a delightful sense of humor and a unique originality. I am often amazed at the ingenuity of my dogs.

"They are gay, happy dogs with a wonderful spirit. While they are super friendly and affectionate, they're also rather possessive. They crave human attention and companionship and really insist on having it. They are naturally suspicious and wary of strangers, which makes them great guard dogs. Unlike some other breeds, like the German Shepherd, they are very sensitive to their handler's mood. You cannot be too harsh or rough with this breed. They take a light touch."

Socialization is an absolute must with the Malinois. With proper exposure, this breed develops into an alert, poised, self-confident dog who, unless specifically discouraged, makes friends easily. I have, however, seen a few Malinois who were not given any socialization. They turned into shy, skittish creatures who tucked their tails between their legs. This is never acceptable in any breed, but seems particularly appalling in the case of the courageous, assured Malinois. In buying a puppy, purchasers should ask if the dogs have been thoroughly socialized.

After years of being the least popular of the Belgian varieties recognized in this country, the Malinois' star appears to be rising. It's no wonder that Americans are finding much to admire about the breed. He combines beauty, elegance and a rugged naturalness, with intelligence and, most important, versatile utility. The Belgian Malinois is a breed to watch.

Chapter 6

The Bolognese

For centuries, the delightful Bolognese has charmed his way into the hearts of a host of loyal owners. One of our oldest breeds, the Bolo, as he's called, has long been associated with Europe's royal families. In fact, the list of Bolognese patrons reads like a veritable roll call of European rulers. A companion *par excellence,* he has shared his owners' political triumphs, comforting them in times of turbulence and war. What wonders these little dogs could disclose, if only they could tell us about their history.

The Bolognese is a member of the celebrated "Bichon" group. Noted for their extraordinary companion qualities, the Bichons are among the most glamorous individuals in all of dogdom. The Maltese and the Bichon Frise (formerly the Bichon Teneriffe) are the most recognizable of these breeds and the only ones currently registered with the American Kennel Club. In recent years, however, the remaining members of the family have made their way to America. Those of you who have read the first volume of *A Celebration of Rare Breeds,* will already be familiar with the Havanese and the Lowchen, or Little Lion Dog. In this book, we will cover the two remaining members of the group—the Bolognese and the Coton de Tulear. The little Bolognese is the final member of this family to be introduced to the United States, and still the most rare.

The precise origins of the Bichon group remain a mystery. It seems certain that the dogs developed in the area surrounding the Meditteranean Sea. The Bolognese and the Maltese appear to be the oldest of this family of dogs, but it's impossible to tell which is more ancient. Clearly, the Bolo has long been identified with the city of Bologna, from which it takes its name.

Bologna has always been an important locale. Settled by the Etruscans, it became a Roman municipality in 192 B.C. In 1183, it was recognized as a free state. A succession of important ruling families dominated the city and it became a mecca for academics and art. A prestigious university was founded and scholars from all over the Continent flocked to study with the world's most learned men. Small wonder that, with the patronage of the nobles, word of the Bolognese spread throughout Europe.

Flavius Biondi (1388-1463), who wrote under the pen name Blondus, gives us our first information about the Bolognese. The breed was highly prized by the breeders of Bologna and great care was taken in breeding and raising the dogs. While white was the preferred color, black dogs could also be seen. Small specimens of the breed were sought after and many measures were taken to control size in breeding. Great attention was paid to the diet of the dogs, taking care to provide them with small portions of delicate food. "People enjoy these little dogs to such an extent," Blondus reports, "that queens gave them the small portions of their own food in golden vases."

Another writer of the period, Albertus, gives us a glimpse of the breeding practices employed during those early times. Breeders, he said, will go to any lengths to get puppies, because the dogs are extremely sought after and command high prices. Stimulants were even used to induce the dogs to breed. Evidently, coat was a great part of the breed's appeal. Superstitions abounded on the way to induce greater coat, or as Albertus says, to make the dogs "more hairy." Whelping places were often strewn with the wool of cattle or sheep, for it was felt that seeing hair about the bitches would cause them to whelp pups with more profuse coats. Some provided their treasured bitches with ram skins to lay upon throughout their pregnancies.

The breed has always been linked to the great ruling families that predated modern Italy. The Bolognese was the dog of choice in the luxurious Florentine courts of the Medici. This royal family ruled in the 1300s and their patronage did much to stimulate interest in the breed. Records indicate that Cosimo de Medici sent eight Bolognese, by royal courier, to his friend Colonel Alamannui, in Belgium. He requested that the little dogs be given, in his name, to several wealthy and influential families in Brussels. The date of this introduction of the breed to Belgium is often given as 1668, but this is wholly inaccurate. We are unable to precisely date the story for there were several Cosimos de Medici and none ruled in the 1600s.

By the 1400s, the little dogs had become closely associated with all the noble Italian families. Famous Renaissance artists, who often survived on royal pa-

tronage, were quick to include the breed in their paintings. No doubt this delighted their patrons. Depictions of the Bolognese may be found in the paintings *Tobias and the Archangel Raffele, The Angel Raphael and Tobias* and *The Three Archangels and Tobias*.

The Bolognese was closely associated with the Bentivoglio family, who dominated the city of Bologna, in the latter half of the 1400s. They carefully cultivated a series of alliances and became one of the most wealthy and powerful families in all of Italy. Their lavish courts were frequented by a host of talented writers and artists. The Bolognese was the treasured companion of the Bentivoglios and many of the pampered dogs could be seen at their courts. While the family had made many contributions to the culture and beauty of Bologna, this came to an abrupt end during the rule of Giovanni II. Giovanni and his sons earned a reputation for their scandalous and wanton exploits. In 1506, Pope Julius II, with the help of the French, drove them from power. He ordered that they be exiled, never to return to their native home. Most of the family members retreated to Malta, taking their beloved Bolognese with them. *Hutchinson's Dog Encyclopedia* notes: "there they introduced the Bolognese, which, crossed with native dogs of small size, produced the Maltese, of a somewhat smaller size than itself." A number of the residents of Malta, Hutchinson tells us, eventually emigrated to South America, landing in Argentina. Their dogs accompanied them on their voyage. The pure white dogs became popular and emerged as a new and slightly larger breed...the Jessamine. Sadly, this member of the Bichon group is now believed to be extinct.

It is to Ulisse Aldrovandi, a true "Renaissance man," that we owe credit for much of our information on the Bolognese. Born in 1522, in Bologna, Aldrovandi was orphaned at the age of six. A wealthy bishop took him in as a page. He became a doctor in 1553 and was appointed inspector of drugs and pharmacies. He later compiled one of the world's first pharmacopias.

Not content to rest on his laurels, Aldrovandi turned his attention to the study of botany and natural history. It was in this capacity that he was to achieve his greatest fame. For more than thirty years, he worked, with dogged determination, to compile the world's most extensive book on natural history. The money received from his position as professor of natural history and logic was all used to achieve this aim. He collected specimens from all parts of the world and personally hired artists and engravers to record their likeness. The first four volumes of the book were completed before his death in 1605. In tribute to him, the senate of Bologna University voted to underwrite completion of his work. His students prepared an additional ten volumes, but this was not the full extent of his

The impressive Berdot's Alfredo, owned by Bert and Dorothy Goodale, of Montrose, Colorado.

This is the first litter of Bolognese born in the United States. The litter was whelped at Berdot's Kennels.

research. Sadly, much of his original manuscript was never published.

Only a small portion of Aldrovandi's work pertains to dogs. A fair amount of this section is devoted to the little dogs of Bologna. It was Aldrovandi who gave us the reports of Blondus and Albertus. He was doubtless well acquainted with the Bolognese. He says that the dogs were extremely popular and sold for high prices, often 400 Italian lira. Their ownership, he reports, was not limited to Bologna alone. They could be seen in many Italian cities. In some places the little ones had quite a reputation as watchdogs and were called "botoli." Despite their small size, he tells us that the Italians considered them ferocious and irascible, like the little venemous toads known as "botas." Aldrovandi, however, did not share this opinion. He found the dogs to be gentle and aristocratic, if somewhat overbred and delicate. This, no doubt, reflects their pampered existence. The Italians of the day, he says, viewed the Bolognese as exotic.

These exquisite creatures from Italy were to travel to other European countries. In the 1500's, Poland's King Sigismund I married a noblewoman from Milan. She made it her mission to introduce the joys of the Renaissance to her new homeland. Italian architects were summoned to design an extraordinary castle on Wawel Hill, in Krakow. When completed, it was said to be the highest monument to Renaissance art north of the Alps. Eager to introduce all the treasures of her homeland to Poland, Queen Sforza purchased a Bolognese. The little dog became her cherished companion and must have reminded her daily of her native Italy.

In the 1600s, word of the dogs had even spread to England. Topsell, writing in 1607, refers to the white Italian breed, which he knew as the *Bottolo*. "They are of pleasant disposition and will leape and bite without pinching, and bark prettily," he says, "and some of them are taught to stand upright, holding their forelegs like hands to fetch and carry in their mouths that which is cast unto them."

It's difficult to imagine the reverence with which these dogs were treated in Italy. In *Dogs: Their History and Development,* Edward Ash relays the story of Mrs. Hester Piozzi, who visited Italy in 1786. Mrs. Piozzi witnessed first-hand the kindly treatment and careful care accorded to lap dogs, although she does not describe the breed. She says a man informed her "yester morning, that his poor wife was half broken-hearted at hearing such a Countess's dog was run over; 'for,' said he, 'having suckled the pretty creature herself, she loved it like one of her children.' I bid him repeat the circumstance, that no mistake might be made; he did so; but seeing me look shocked, or ashamed, or something he did not like, 'Why, Madam,' said the fellow, 'it is a common thing enough for ordinary men's wives to suckle the lap-dogs of ladies of quality;' adding that they were paid for their milk, and he saw no harm in gratifying one's *superiors.* As I was disposed to see nothing *but* harm in disputing such a competitor, our conference finished soon; but the fact is certain."

In the 1700's, the breed would journey to France, where it probably contributed to the development of the Bichon Frise. Giovanni Maria Flipponi specialized in bringing Bolognese to Paris. He carried the little dogs in crates strapped to the backs of mules. Louis XIV was always given first choice of his dogs, and many of the breed made their home at his court at Versailles. The King, it is reported, paid handsomely for any dogs that caught his fancy. Flippponi continued bringing the dogs to France for a dozen years or so. Those not purchased by the monarch were eagerly snapped up by other royals.

The breed also travelled to Russia's imperial court. Catherine the Great, who ruled for 34 years, was a Bolognese owner. This remarkable woman, of surprising intellect, had a very unhappy marriage. Her husband was described as a weakling and an imbecile, and it was said she tolerated him only as a vehicle to power. Her many love affairs were the talk of Europe. When he died, she assumed the throne. It was her objective to make Russian society every bit as cultured as that of Paris. The hard working Queen avidly read French books, including Buffon's 1777 book *Historie Naturelle et Particuliére,* in which the term Bichon is first used and the dogs are described. She procured a Bolognese, who became her trusted companion. So fond was she of the little dog, that it shared her bed.

Perhaps the most ardent Bolognese admirer, though, was Queen Maria Theresa, ruler of the vast Austrian Empire. A member of the Hapsburg family, she is credited with converting the Empire from a feudal to a centralized state. We do not know precisely when she acquired her first Bolognese. Her love for the dog, however, is certain. Heartbroken when her little Bolo died, she enlisted the Empire's top taxidermist to mount his body. This way, she said, the dog would remain with her forever. To this day, the little body can still be seen in the Museum of Natural History in Vienna.

The breed has long been popular with the Belgians. No doubt, Queen Maria Theresa's fondness for the breed contributed to this. She instituted great reforms in Belgium. In fact, she was the only foreign ruler ever to be remembered with great public affection. It is

Bert Goodale holds two of the pups from the first litter born in this country. He and wife, Dorothy, were the first to import this breed.

not surprising then, that when Umberto II (1896-1947), of the House of Savoy, married Marie José of Belgium, he presented her with a Bolognese. Perhaps the little dog was a comfort to them when, in 1946, the monarchy was terminated. To this day, the Belgians remain confirmed supporters of the breed.

Dogs in all the European countries fared badly during World War II. The Bolo almost became extinct. Italian and Belgian breeders rallied to the breed's defense. Thanks to their efforts, the breed survived and prospered. Today, the Bolognese enjoys great popularity in Europe and is frequently seen at shows on the Continent. Now, finally, this charming dog has been introduced to the United States.

Those who have read the first volume of this book, will recognize the names of Bert and Dorothy Goodale. The Montrose, Colorado, couple have been most active in promoting the Havanese. With more than thirty-five years of experience in dogs, they obtained their first Havanese sixteen years ago. It was through their work with that breed that the Goodales became acquainted with the Bolognese. While I was interviewing Dorothy for the Havanese chapter, she excitedly told me that she had made contact with Bolo breeders in Europe and was hoping to soon import her first dogs. The little dogs arrived in 1987, with the first American litter making its debut at the Goodale's Berdot Kennels. Bert, Dorothy and other fanciers promptly established the Bolognese Club of America, which maintains the stud book for the breed in this country.

The Bolognese is a sturdy toy breed. According to the standard, males are to stand 10-12 inches at the shoulder, while females should be 9-11 inches. Weight averages from 8-13 pounds. Slightly longer than tall, the breed has an elegant neck (the standard calls for it to equal the length of the head), a straight topline and a tail which curves over the back. The last is an essential characteristic and judges must see the tailed carried properly when the dog is gaited. For his size, the Bolognese is well boned, with a straight front and moderately angulated rear. The chest is deep and the ribs are well sprung.

The ideal Bolognese head is broad, medium in length, with a moderate stop. Dorothy Goodale says that the head should be "neither too blunt nor too long." The dark eyes are round, larger than normal and should convey a lively intelligent expression. Dark black pigmentation is essential. According to Bert and Dorothy the "dark halo rims add much to the breed's beautiful expression."

The Bolognese is essentially white in color and must give an all-over white impression. However, touches of champagne color, usually found on the ears and occasionally along the back, are permissible and not to be faulted. The standard says that the "hairs are long, in locks, without sticking tightly to the body. That is to say they appear raised. They cover each part of the head, body and limbs, and appear shorter only on the forehead." Dorothy Goodale describes the coat as falling in "fluffy/flocky ringlets."

Because the coat is nonshedding, the dogs do require frequent grooming to prevent matting. A sensible program of regular bathing and brushing will keep your Bolognese looking presentable. The coat is far easier to care for than that of the Maltese and does not require the skilled scissoring of the Bichon Frise.

The Bolo has a pleasing disposition. The standard describes them as "highly intelligent, quick to learn and completely devoted to their masters." Nancy Holmes, of Penrose, North Carolina, imported her first Bolo in 1988. "I own Havanese and Lhasa Apsos, and have raised and shown dogs for years," Nancy says, "but this Bolognese breed is really quite different. If I was given the choice of only one breed, I would have to take the Bolognese. While they are all nice breeds, I think the Bolognese has it on brains and lovability."

Nancy is impressed with the breed's intelligence and desire to please. "A little praise works much better than a scolding with this breed," she says. "They like their outdoor rowdy playtime, but are well behaved in the house. They also enjoy well behaved children and will play with them for hours on end." Dorothy Goodale is also enthusiastic about the breed's personality. "They will devise their own games to entertain themselves and are truly a delight to own."

Owners stress that, first and foremost, the Bolognese is a house dog. "Their primary purpose down through the centuries has been as companions and lap dogs," Dorothy Goodale stresses. "They do not make good kennel dogs," Nancy Holmes says. "They must know where their people are at all times. They prefer to be at your feet or in your lap. They can almost be considered 'pesty' in this regard. Yet, it's hard to think of them like that, because they are so loveable. The breed has a definite need for people. The Bolognese is not a dog you can ignore. They do not seem to single out a particular person as their favorite. They're devoted to anyone who will love and play with them. The family that gets a Bolognese needs to have time and love to give, or this breed is not for them. They *demand* your attention." Indeed, all Bolo owners are impressed with the breed's loyalty and devotion. "They are at their best as full members of the family," Dorothy Goodale says.

The Bolognese gets along well with other breeds. By nature, they are very non-aggressive. They do, however, make quite suitable watchdogs. "They are a friendly breed, but at the same time make a very discriminating little watchdog," the Goodales say. "They are wary of strangers and watchful of their owner's interests." Nancy Holmes agrees. "They are naturally wary, but with proper socialization during puppyhood, they will be friendly with strangers."

The Bolognese should have a bright future in the U.S. They are a very healthy and hardy breed, not prone to medical problems. In addition, they are known for their longevity. These qualities coupled with the breed's glamorous appearance and endearing disposition have helped to make them favorites in Europe. Hopefully, the latest of the Bichon group to enter this country will win a host of loyal admirers. "Although all of the Bichon breeds are related...and have a similarity one to the other," Dorothy Goodale says, "still there is a distinct individualism to each one of these breeds."

Rough-coated Border Collie Fly in action at John H. Weikel's Highland Farms, in Mount Vernon, Indiana.

Chapter 7

The Border Collie

"There is no good flock without a good shepherd and there is no good shepherd without a good dog," a wise man once said. While there are many herding breeds, the world over, the one peerless representative of the art of herding is the Border Collie. He is different, in his working style, from all other breeds. Only those breeds that have dipped into the Border Collie well, have acquired his unique "eye" and style. In the view of countless shepherds, he is the preeminent example of the working sheepdog.

It may seem odd to include the Border Collie in this book. Clearly, the breed is not at all rare. If this dog were registered by the American Kennel Club, the Border Collie would certainly rank, in popularity, among the top twenty-five breeds. You'll find Border Collies aplenty in most rural areas of this country. Still, for city folk or those acquainted only with the A.K.C. line-up, the Border Collie remains a mystery. I hope that, some day, they will have the opportunity to see these dogs in action. It's a remarkable experience, one that will remain etched forever in their memories.

I had such an opportunity, several years ago, on our acreage in the beautiful mountains of northern Alabama. The neighboring pasture had been rented by a cattle rancher. The man lived many miles away and came by infrequently to check on his stock. Access to the property was through a rickety, tumble-down, homemade gate that opened onto our pasture. On several occasions, the cattle had escaped and my dog (a non-herding breed) and I had managed to guide them back to their pasture. I'd suggested to the owner that such problems would be avoided by the installation of a new gate. "I'm not spending money on someone else's

property," was his only reply.

One morning, I awoke to find the cattle spread over our land. Some had trampled down the little fence surrounding my garden and were eagerly devouring my sweet potatoes. I tried shooing them away, but they merely ambled over to the squash and melons. Honeydews and cantaloupes exploded beneath their plodding hooves. Another group had descended into our newly constructed pond. In the process they'd broken down a section of the bank and feasted on the newly seeded grass cover. A third group had ensconced themselves at the front of the house, munching blithely on my newly planted annual flowers and shrubs. With cows everywhere, there was little chance that I could round them up.

I placed an irate call to the rancher. "I was going to move them to a new pasture anyway," he said. "I'll get my truck and be right over."

He arrived shortly, accompanied by a helper. But, there was a problem. Recent downpours had turned the lower portion of our pasture into a mucky bog. It was conceivable that they might bring the truck to the cows, tearing up our pasture in the bargain, but they'd never get the loaded vehicle out again. Clearly, we would have to bring the cattle to the truck. We needed a dog to gather and move them.

"My neighbor has an Australian Shepherd we can borrow," the helper said.

"I could get my son and his Border Collie," the rancher replied.

"Naw," the helper reflected, "a Border Collie's fine for sheep, but for cattle you need a harder dog, like an Aussie."

"You haven't seen this Border Collie work. She can herd anything that moves. Why, she once brought home a herd of deer."

The conversation continued with each man lauding the merits of the respective breeds. The accounts grew more impressive with each detail. To hear the men talk, you'd have thought that each of these dogs was a phenomenal worker. I was having difficulty sorting fact from fiction. As amusing as this "my dog is better than yours" repartee was, it was getting us nowhere.

"Please get the Border Collie," I chimed in. I hoped, in this way, to speed the process along. In truth, my suggestion was really self-serving. I'd often seen and marveled at the skill of Aussies, but I'd yet to see a Border Collie in action.

The dog and her owner arrived shortly. The rancher's son, Jake, was a rugged looking sort, his skin leathery and tanned from years outdoors. He had twin-

kling blue eyes which betrayed his stern countenance. He was obviously a no-nonsense sort and it was easy to see that he did not suffer fools gladly, be they of the two-legged or four-legged variety. A dog leaped from the truck to his side. She was a small attractive dog, unassuming in looks. Her black and white coat was sprinkled with dew which glistened in the early morning sun. Her name was Jill and there was a bright look in her brown eyes. She looked at her master, waiting for direction, as she wiggled in excitement.

"There's work to be done, old girl," Jake said quietly. Jill wagged her tail. They walked off in the direction of the cattle, with me struggling to keep up. Jake gave a quiet command and Jill suddenly arced around the herd. I lost sight of her for a moment as she disappeared behind the stock. Then she stopped, opposite us. She had given the animals a wide berth and had moved so quietly that the cattle were oblivious to her.

She paused, crouching down, but one could plainly see that she was ready to spring at a moment's notice. Her eyes surveyed the scene. You just knew that she was sizing up the situation and deciding on a course of action. There was no doubt that this was a thinking dog.

Stealthily, she crept forward, ever so slowly, her body more crouched now, her tail held low. At first glance, her stalking reminded me, for all the world, of a big cat. A steer saw her first. His nostrils flared and his ears twitched. Soon the whole herd turned to stare at this disturbing interloper. With snake-like stealth, Jill crept closer. Then she froze, as immobile as any bird dog on point. She fixed the leader of the group with the famous Border Collie "eye." Until you've seen this, first hand, you'll never be able to grasp the intensity of that penetrating stare. I felt the hair on the back of my neck rise. It was hypnotic in its intensity. Surely some wild animal, facing a wolf, must have seen this same riveting gaze.

All the cattle were quiet, mesmerized and intimidated by Jill's power. That is, all the animals save for the lead cow. She stamped her foot in indignation, lowering her head and shoulders. I knew she would make a move. She started to a pre-emptive run at Jill, although in truth her lunge was more of a test than an outright attack. I found that my natural impulse was to move back slightly, even though I was far removed from the encounter. Jill was more experienced than I. She stood her ground and the cow pulled up short.

The tension built and I felt myself sweating. Then, slowly, the cattle turned and moved to-

A lovely head study of Serendipity CD, owned by Kathy Kemper, Border Corner, in Everman, Texas. (Kathy Kemper photo)

ward us. At first they were bunched together, but as they walked briskly, the mass evolved into a single file. The military precision with which they marched would have gladdened the heart of any sergeant. Jake whistled a command, but I had no idea what it meant. Jill followed the herd at a discreet distance. While they occasionally looked over their shoulders, to make sure she was there, she stayed far enough behind so as not to panic the flighty animals. Her eyes, though, didn't miss a thing.

As they approached the truck, Jake prodded the first of the animals aboard. The others followed, but one made a break for it, leaping off the ramp. In a split second, Jill was there. She swung to the side and, crouching, approached him. I marveled at her power. There was no doubt that she'd give him a strong nip if he didn't board. He decided not to test her.

In ten minutes (less time than it had taken the men to decide on which dog to secure), all three groups of reluctant cattle were safely loaded in the truck. I looked at Jill with an enormous measure of respect. The term "working dog" is bandied about in dog circles so often that it almost loses its meaning. In that moment, Jill seemed to epitomize the term for me. Here was a true farm dog, a partner, a helpmate in the day-to-day chores one encounters in the country. There was a grace and nobility about the dog that I hadn't noticed before.

"Well done," Jake said. What an understatement, I thought, still under the spell of this Border Collie's performance. Jill's tail wagged and she yipped her pleasure. Jake pulled a soiled tennis ball from his pocket and tossed it into the air. Jill leaped, her body twisting to catch her favorite toy. She returned to her master, nudging the ball into his hand. He threw it again and chuckled.

"She just loves to play ball," he smiled. "She'll retrieve anything. She begs my son to throw a frisbee for her. She could chase it for hours, never missing, and she never tires of it. She's the designated right fielder for the neighborhood softball team," Jake said with pride. "Well, we gotta go. I have some sheep to move to a new pasture." Jill immediately headed for the truck, leaping into the open window to take up her command post on the front seat. I wouldn't have been surprised if she'd cranked up the engine. "Hope we've been of some help to you," he said in parting.

In most ways, Jill worked in typical Border Collie fashion. Most dogs of this breed work quietly and gently. They will use force if they must (often a necessity with hogs or cattle), but generally they rely on strategy. The Border Collie is what's called a "heading," rather than a driving, stockdog. Instinctively, he runs wide around the flock or herd (trainers call this the "cast" or "outrun"), trying not to disturb them and ends up opposite his handler. He then pauses to assess the

Nant Chip, owned by Sandra Holmes, of Meridian, Texas. (Kathy Kemper photo)

situation. Trainers call this brief respite the "lift." He then drops his tail, crouches, creeps or "claps" (a down position) the ground.

The most famous attribute of the Border Collie is, of course, his legendary "eye." This keen, intense gaze is an inborn characteristic which can be seen even in young puppies. It intimidates the stock and causes them to move to avoid the uncomfortable stare. It's a juggling act for the dog. If he moves too quickly and darts too close, the animals are apt to panic and flee. Some dogs have what's termed an "over-strong" eye. They dominate the stock, causing them to become nervous or rebellious. Indeed, some "over-strong" eyed dogs clap to the ground, fix the animals with their stare and never succeed in actually getting them to move. Also shunned are "loose-eyed" dogs, who lack the intensity and concentration to move the stock.

Most Border Collies show evidence of their potential at an early age. Some want to herd from the time they are weaned, while others may wait until one year of age to show their talents. "Young pups and older dogs who have not been exposed to livestock often try to herd anything that moves from blowing leaves to automobiles," says a brochure prepared by the Border Collie Club of America. "The dog will 'eye' these moving objects just as it would livestock, and in many cases will even try to circle or head the object off." Indeed, some owners report that their puppies eye and attempt to herd cats, other dogs and even chipmunks and squirrels.

Another Border Collie trait is the breed's remarkable intelligence. Most farm families can tell a tale or two about the time their dog's quick thinking averted danger or tragedy. The breed is eminently trainable which is, of course, why Border Collies have been used for such a variety of purposes. During World War II, this breed was used extensively for rescue work and message carrying. Their crouching, creeping style was said to be invaluable in messenger work as the dogs could stealthily move from trench to trench without being detected. Some of the dogs were even trained for aggression work and they gained a reputation for their hard-biting enthusiasm. Hearing these stories, some present day owners have worked their dogs in schutzhund competitions. They have often earned the admiration of owners of the more traditional guarding breeds. Several U.S. dogs have earned degrees including the advanced Schutzhund III.

In England, Border Collies are regularly used for bomb and drug detection. In recent years, they are being used for the same purposes in this country. Some owners have employed their Border Collies as gundogs. They report that their dogs use their "eye" to pinpoint the location of birds. And, in New England, the breed has been increasingly used in sled dog racing.

The Border Collie is a top competitor in obedience circles. I can recall, many years ago, seeing J.C. and Hazel Thompson's extraordinary Rex, U.D.T. At the time, Border Collies were a rarity in obedience rings. There was always a buzz among enthusiasts when Rex arrived. Scores of people crowded around the ring to watch this incredible worker. And what a competitor he was! During his career, he wracked up hundreds of first place and High in Trial awards. Indeed, his superlative performances won many friends for the breed. A great number of American Border Collies have earned obedience degrees and many are Obedience Trial Champions. In England, where the Border Collie is recognized, the breed has come to dominate obedience rings. Competitors often complain that the breed has taken over the sport. Some authorities contend that fully 90% of English awards go to Border Collies.

In his 1937 book, *Heather Jean, The Working Sheep Dog,* Luke J. Pasco calls the Border Collie "always a friend." Most fanciers would agree with that simple assessment. Most dogs of this breed are loving and affectionate. The Border Collie has an alert, curious, always inquisitive nature. Nothing escapes his attention. The dogs make wonderful playmates and companions for children. In fact, many people obtained their first Border Collie after watching the rapport shared by Laura Ingalls and her dog on the *Little House on the Prairie* series. While the breed can be reserved with strangers, most properly socialized Border Collies are quite friendly. Don't be fooled by the guise, however. Should danger threaten, they are very able protectors.

The adorable six week old "Skye," owned by David and Kathy Crockett. (Kathy Kemper photo)

"The qualities of the Border Collie are such that they make an ideal house dog and companion," Luke Pasco wrote. "They are faithful to the end and a true shepherd and master will rarely or never part with his favorite dog." Indeed, Border Collies are uncommonly devoted to their masters. Human contact is essential to the making of a well-balanced dog, be he a worker or a companion. Border Collies are just plain happier when they can share their lives with people. "Once a Border Collie has chosen a favorite person," writes Janet Larson in her 1986 book, *The Versatile Border Collie,* "he will follow him or her like a shadow, offering protection with his life if necessary." By loving your dog and treating him with kindness, you will win a lifelong friend. "A good dog is faithful to his master under all conditions, regardless of hunger or trouble," Mr. Pasco says, "for he seems to place duty above all else."

By nature, the Border Collie is a sensitive dog. Like all herding breeds, he must be treated with kindness. Firm, consistent discipline, coupled with love and respect, are the best tactics to use when dealing with this breed. The Border Collie can't take harsh discipline. Some dogs will wilt under such handling, while others will become sullen and uncooperative. In training this breed, one must always consider their intelligence. Once a Border Collie understands what you want, his eagerness to please makes him more than happy to accommodate you.

Those interested in the breed should be aware of certain facts. The Border Collie has been bred, for centuries, as a working dog. He's very active and energetic. He has an innate desire to work and a bored dog can present problems. If you don't provide him with something to do, he's apt to seek his own diversions, and a bored Border Collie can quickly become a canine juvenile delinquent. One family discovered this when they decided to retire from farming. They sold off their stock and their loyal dog no longer had any work to do. Bored and restless, he began herding neighboring farmers' livestock and ushering them home. Finally, the couple had to give the dog to a new owner. Many bored Border Collies become car chasers *par excellence*. It's very difficult to break your dog of this habit once it has begun. If you plan on purchasing a dog of this breed, be sure to provide some means for the dog to channel his abundant energy. Most breeders strongly recommend obedience training. Obedience provides a logical and satisfying release for your dog.

"Without him," James Hogg (1772-1835) said of the sheepdog, "the mountainous land of England and Scotland would not be worth sixpence. It would require more hands to manage a flock of sheep and drive them to market than the profits of the whole are capable of maintaining." Indeed, sheepdogs have existed in the British Isles for centuries. In 943 Hywel Dda, King of Wales, declared that a good sheepdog was equal in value to a prime ox. Sheep herding dogs are again mentioned in Johannes Caius' 1500 work, *English Dogges.*

Writing in the 1700's, Thomas Bewick, in his *The General History of Quadrapeds,* speaks of a "rough coated Collie, black with white tail tip...this breed of dog appears at present to be preserved in the greatest purity in the Northern parts of England and Scotland, where its aid is highly necessary in managing the numerous flocks of sheep in these extensive wilds and fells." He included a woodcut which closely resembles the modern Border Collie.

Indeed, it is from the border areas of Scotland and England, that the breed takes its name. It is a misty country of hilly farms where sheep raising is a way of life. Rain occurs often and sudden, unexpected snow storms are wont to happen. The farms of the region are small and unfenced. Dogs were an absolute necessity for keeping the sheep from wandering. The sheepdogs of the area are no-nonsense workers able to brave the rain or snow. The breed most certainly shares common ancestors with the show type Collie. However, as those dogs were taken up by show exhibitors, and altered to suit their purposes, the Border type Collies remained down on the farms.

It was the start of sheepdog trials that really put the humble Border Collie on the map. The first of these exhibitions was held in 1873 in Bala, Wales. The winner was Tweed, a sheepdog from Scotland. Few people realize that a conformation show, of sorts, was also held at this first outing. The prize for best type of sheepdog also went to Tweed. So popular did that first trial prove, that soon sheepherding trials were being held throughout the hill country.

In 1893, a dog was born who was to change both the look and working style of the Border Collie. His breeder, Adam Telfer, of Northumberland, England, christened the dog Hemp, but he would become known later as "Old Hemp." He was just a youngster when he attended his first trial, but he captivated the crowd. In his career, he compiled an incredible record and was never beaten. He remains the only dog, in the history of the breed, that can boast such a feat. He worked in what we now know as typical Border Collie style. Spectators marveled at his quiet intense style, his use of eye and his speed. "Hemp was so successful at making a difficult course look simple," says Janet E. Larson, in *The Versatile Border Collie,* "that the usually taciturn Scots described him as 'bluidy marvelous.'"

Talented photographer Kathy Kemper caught two dogs working in concert. These smooth-coated Border Collies are "Gem," owned by Claudia Frank, and "Tru," owned by Casey Fogt.

Indeed, Old Hemp's dazzling performances caught the eye of many shepherds. He was widely in demand as a stud dog. He is said to have sired more than 200 sons, many of whom became famous trial winners in their own right. Fortunately, he proved remarkably predominate for both his looks and talent. All modern Border Collies trace back to this legendary dog.

The sport of sheepdog trials took a giant step forward, in 1906, with the formation of the International Sheep Dog Society, in Haddington, Scotland. Their aim was to improve the breeding of sheepdogs and provide financial assistance, when necessary, to shepherds and their widows. This they did by instituting a stud book and holding trials. The first dog entered in the books was Old Hemp and the first bitch was Old Maid.

The first Border Collies made their way to the United States in the late 1800's. There was a steady stream of ships bringing cattle and sheep to this country from Scotland. While selecting their stock, Americans had a chance to see the Border Collie in action. Often the addition of several of these dogs clinched the deal. In some cases, shepherds accompanied the flocks and they some of their dogs with them. Shortly before the outbreak of World War I, however, the price of cattle and sheep dropped in this country. Exchange rates were also high and the large scale importation of livestock all but ceased. A few Border Collies continued to ply their trade on farms, but no concerted effort was made to perpetuate the breed.

The situation was to change in the 1920's, though. A number of sheepdog owners, including Sam Stoddart, Grover Tobey, Guy Hilton and Luke Pasco, banded together to form a group in New England. They imported a number of Border Collies and began holding the New England Sheep Dog Trials. It was not easy to get good dogs from Scotland. "Even to this day it is difficult to acquire a real high class working Border Collie," Pasco wrote in his 1937 book, *Heather Jean, The Working Sheep Dog*. "The true hill shepherds, regardless of how badly they need the money, are very reluctant to part with a good dog....The owner of a true sheep dog really becomes so attached to the dog that the friendship is permanent. There are Scotch shepherds so attached to their dogs that they would not part with them for a king's ransom. It is for this reason that one can hardly buy a first class, well-trained sheep dog...." Indeed, some of these Americans did pay nearly a "king's ransom" for dogs. Spot, the winner of a 1923 trial, in Scotland, fetched $1,000, an extraordinary sum in those days. For the most part, however, the Americans had to content themselves with acquiring puppies from Scotland's top winners.

Luke Pasco did much to popularize the Border Collie in this country. In 1932, he visited P.V. Ewing,

the editor of *The Sheep Breeder*, an industry magazine. A shepherd at Fillmore Farms, Mr. Pasco had a proposal. He would travel to fairs and shows around the country, demonstrating the remarkable skill of his dogs. In return for paying his expenses, he would represent the publication. The Border Collie, he explained, was a sensational working dog, possessing great intelligence, and could contribute much to the industry in this country. *The Sheep Breeder* accepted his offer.

During the next several years, Mr. Pasco crisscrossed the country. His dogs performed at state fairs and livestock exhibitions in Kentucky, New Jersey, Maryland, Louisiana, Michigan, Virginia, New York, Iowa, Pennsylvania, Montana, Illinois, Ohio, Indiana and South Dakota. Thousands of people were thrilled by the performances. By 1936, he was having to turn down bookings because his schedule was so crowded. The response to his dogs was tremendous. Among his star performers was Heather Jean, after whom his book is named. He dedicated the book to Jean, as she was called, "whose intelligence, friendliness and natural ability has endeared her to the hearts of all sheep dog lovers and revived a national interest in the Scotch Border Collie." Jean excelled in sheepherding trials, too. She was the 1932 and 1933 American Outdoor Champion and the 1933 American Indoor Champion. Our gratitude goes to Mr. Pasco and those other pioneers for firmly establishing the breed in this country.

As befits an active herding dog, the Border Collie is strong and agile. Soundness is a must as the dog is meant to work from sun-up to sundown. His body is longer than tall with a level topline and a well-angulated, muscled rear. The head is raised when standing, but carried level with the back when moving. The Border Collie's tail is set on and carried low, but may be raised when excited. It should never, though, be carried over the back. Type and size vary considerably since the breed has long been bred for working purposes only. Heights may vary from 17-26 inches, but 19-22 inches is considered the average for dogs, while bitches usually stand 18-21 inches. Weights may range astoundingly from 25-65 pounds. However, the average is 30-50 pounds.

The typical Border Collie skull is broad with a box-like shape. There is a moderate stop and a blunt muzzle. Ear carriage may vary from prick to drop. Most Border Collies, however, have either erect or semi-erect ears. The eyes are expressive and intelligent. Eye color conforms to coat color. Black and white dogs usually have medium brown eyes. The red and red merle shades have amber eyes and blue or blue merles may have one or both blue eyes.

Coat length also varies. The rough coat is the most popular. Dogs of this type have a short, soft

Border Corner's Tess, owned by Kathy Kemper, is an excellent sheepdog trial competitor. (Kathy Kemper photo)

undercoat, topped by a moderately long outercoat which may be straight, wavy or curly. There's a pronounced ruff, or mane, about the neck, breeching and feathering on the legs and a nice brush to the tail. Smooth coated dogs are covered with a short, smooth, dense topcoat.

Black and white is the most common color with tri-color (black, white and tan) next. White markings may consist of a full or partial ring about the neck, a trim on the chest and belly, a blaze on the face and a white tail tip. Blues, which may be any shade of grey, and blue merles (a base of grey with irregular broken patches of black) are also seen. Reds, which vary from fawn or light red to chocolate, and red merles (base color of fawn or light red with irregular broken patches of chocolate) can also be found. Sable and white dogs are sometimes seen. Also found are "mottled" dogs. These may be black or red with white spotting or speckling which creates a roan effect. All white or predominately white dogs are shunned by most breeders. Shepherds believe that these dogs are not respected by sheep.

In general, Border Collies are healthy, hardy dogs. There are, however, a few conditions that potential purchasers should know about. Hip dysplasia has been found in the breed and you should insure that the breeder x-rays his stock. Two eye conditions, Collie eye anomaly and Progressive Retinal Atrophy, are also found in the breed. Both traits are inherited and responsible breeders have their stock examined by certified veterinary ophthalmologists.

Bring up the question of A.K.C. recognition, at a gathering of Border Collie owners, and a heated discussion is sure to ensue. Most fanciers are vehemently opposed to recognition and fear it will destroy working instincts. They agree with Luke Pasco's 1937 view: "We must bear in mind that the purpose of the Border Collie is for work. It does not matter how homely or deficient in type he is if he is a true worker. When one has an exhibition to give before an audience of 50,000 or more people, he must have a dog with sufficient intelligence to do his bidding, a dog that is dependable, a willing worker and one that will do his stuff. When one has a carload of lambs to drive he is not interested in the appearance of the dog so much as in the dog's ability to bring up the sheep while the shepherd goes ahead to the car or pen as the case may be. Of course, other things being equal, it is desirable to have the most approved type, but certainly working ability always comes first..."

Others hold that the Border Collie is a truly versatile dog and should be able to compete in all activities, including the show ring. Some have a more moderate view. They would endorse A.K.C. recognition *if* the A.K.C. would require working certificates before a dog could qualify as a champion. Working certificates are awarded by the International Sheep Dog Society, the North American Sheep Dog Society and the Border Collie Club of America.

The breed is recognized in England, Australia, New Zealand and South Africa, and may be registered with the United Kennel Club. Most dogs are registered with the American Border Collie Association, the American-International Border Collie Registry, The North American Sheep Dog Society or the International Sheep Dog Society. The Border Collie was, long ago, admitted to the A.K.C.'s Miscellaneous Class and can compete in obedience and tracking.

"The super-intelligence of the Border Collie makes the breed an ideal friend and companion," Luke Pasco wrote. "They simply worship their master and always watch carefully to see if they cannot be of service." Indeed, in a few lines, Mr. Pasco has summed up the essence of the breed. Intelligence, fidelity, a desire to please and an unquenchable thirst for work. These are and always have been the hallmark of the Border Collie. May it always remain so.

The impressive group winner Dalton. (Photo courtesy of Beth Cepil)

Chapter 8

The Bourbonnais Pointer

One of the most exciting aspects of the rare breed movement is the opportunity it affords us to learn more about foreign breeds. Recently, Americans have begun to take an interest in the many and varied hunting breeds from France. Several of the French hounds, including the Petite Basset Griffon Vendéen (see *A Celebration of Rare Breeds, Volume I*), are gaining a following in this country. And now, the French "Braques," or "Pointers," are attracting attention. The first of these pointing breeds, the Braque du Bourbonnais, or Bourbonnais Pointer, has made his debut in the United States.

There are several French pointers. The *Braque Français* comes in two sizes: the Grand (or Large) and the Petite (or Small). The larger size, once known as the *Braque du Pays,* or Native Pointer, was the original. The smaller version was bred down in size. The traditional home for the Français is the region near the Pyrenees Mountains. At one time, this breed was nearly extinct but is now enjoying a resurgence of interest.

France is also home to the stunning *Braque d'Auvergne,* sometimes known as the *Bleu d'Auvergne.* This breed was developed in the province of Auvergne in central southwestern France. The region is not far from Gascony, noted for its great, blue mottled hounds. Because of the similarity of coat pattern, many authorities speculate that the hound breed, the *Grand Bleu de Gascogne,* may have played an important part in the breed's origin.

The *Braque Dupuy* stems from a cross between the Braque Français and the Sloughi (see *A Celebration of Rare Breeds, Volume I*). Gamekeepers Homere and Narcisse Dupuy are said to have crossed their Français bitch, "Miss," with the Sloughi, Zidar. One can still see the sighthound influence in the rare Braque Dupuy.

The elegant and flashy *Braque Saint-Germain* boasts both French and English lineage. France's King Charles X was an avid hunter. In the early 1800's, he was presented with a pair of imported lemon-and-white English Pointers. The male died and so the bitch was mated with a native dog. The breeding produced seven puppies which formed the basis for the breed. The bright orange and white color is the hallmark of the Braque Saint-Germain.

One of the most distinctive of all the French pointers is the Braque du Bourbonnais. Many authorities believe that it is the oldest of the French sporting breeds. They point to a woodcut in Aldrovandi's 1580 book, *Natural History,* showing a speckled, bob-tailed dog chasing a bird. These two traits remain key characteristics of the Bourbonnais Pointer. The breed takes its name from the province of Bourbonnais in central France. In early days, the dogs were most popular in that area.

In the late 1800's, many foreign sporting dogs were brought to France. The breeds from the British Isles proved particularly popular. As the French enthusiastically embraced these new imports, interest in the old native dogs diminished. By the turn of the century, the Bourbonnais and other native pointers had almost disappeared.

The Allied victory in World War I was to have a positive effect on French breeds. France was justifiably proud of the part it had played in the war and a wave of patriotism swept the country. French sportsmen took a renewed interest in their native breeds. Bourbonnais breeders banded together to ensure the breed's survival. By 1937, there were a number of top dogs who had successfully competed in both field trials and bench shows. Sadly, as with all French breeds, the Bourbonnais suffered a set-back during World War II.

Breeders resumed their activities at the end of the War. A new standard was crafted, but it was to have disastrous consequences. The standard had strict requirements for coat and tail. In order to be purebred, the standard said, all Bourbonnais Pointers must be born with a naturally short tail. Dogs were also required to have a "faded lilac" color. "In the old standard, the dog was only considered purebred if it wasn't spotted but rather had a mottled wine-coloring that actually was caused by several small spots of wine color mixed in together," says the Club du Braque du Bourbonnais. "As well, its tail was not to be down or mid-thigh."

These stringent specifications eliminated many otherwise fine dogs from breeding and competition. The small gene pool became even further restricted. Many complained that the emphasis should be on hunting ability and overall conformation, rather than such trivial points. But the zealots prevailed and many owners abandoned the breed.

The turning point came in 1970 when Michel Comte was elected president of the Club du Braque du Bourbonnais. A new, more sensible standard was drafted. Since that time the breed has grown in popularity. While still considered rare, the Bourbonnais is definitely making a comeback. Recently, the breed has been imported to Greece, Germany, Belgium, Italy, South Africa and the U.S.

The Bourbonnais is a newcomer to our shores. As of this writing, there are only about 10 dogs here and only one litter has been produced. Beth Cepil, of New

Brio de la Benigousse is ranked as one of France's best male Bourbonnais Pointers.

Tripoli, Pennsylvania, is a proud owner of this exclusive rare breed. She and her husband have long been interested in sporting dogs. They always dreamed of eventually raising one of the sporting breeds. But, Beth says, "we got sidetracked into the working breeds." The Cepils acquired several Rottweilers which they exhibit in obedience. Their introduction to rare breeds came with the acquisition of a Fila Brasileiro (see *A Celebration of Rare Breeds, Volume I*).

It was a fellow rare breed enthusiast who first told them of the Braque du Bourbonnais. The Cepils were intrigued and asked their fellow fancier if he would help them obtain one of these rare dogs. Soon, their male, Debrouillard, had joined the Cepil household. "Brou," as he's known, has been professionally field trained and is Mr. Cepil's personal hunting companion. Beth plans to breed, but only if there is sufficient interest in this country. "It is very important to us that this rare and beautiful dog not be popularized at the risk of sacrificing temperament and hunting instinct," Beth says.

Hunting is a popular pasttime in France. The French are passionate in their love of *venerie*. Shooting preserves dot the countryside and this is where the Bourbonnais demonstrates his prowess. He is primarily an upland bird dog used for grouse, partridge and pheasant. An enthusiastic and energetic hunter, the Bourbonnais is blessed with a keen nose. Owners report that he is particularly adept at searching out cripples. The French also say that the Bourbonnais is a proficient retriever. French sportsmen expect their dogs to deliver birds to hand and prize this breed's soft mouth. The dogs are sometimes used for water work with hunters reporting that they are good on ducks and geese. However, the short fine coat prevents their use in icy waters.

French hunters report that the Bourbonnais adapts readily to all types of terrain. Due to his short coat, however, he is best suited to open country. He should perform well in the U.S., where we have many open fields. Like so many of the other Continental breeds, the Bourbonnais is slower paced than his British cousins. He is not a big running, horizon busting dog, but stays within shotgun range. The French say that the "best performance is obtained when he is aware that he is working in unison with his master."

The Bourbonnais thrills hunters with his stunning style. He is firm, staunch and intense on point. Pointing style appears to vary somewhat. Some dogs freeze with a high head, *a la* the English Pointer, while others extend their necks lower in true European style. Beth Cepil says the breed's hunting style is more reminiscent of the German Shorthaired Pointer.

The breed's inherent natural instinct and easy trainability is prized by French sportsmen. Some say

Bourbonnais Pointers Happiness Ukauge and Happiness Camel, both owned by Bernard Martin, of France.

that the breed is "born trained." While this a bit of an exaggeration, it is a fact that amateur hunters routinely train their dogs to a high level of skill. Furthermore, once taught, the Bourbonnais retains his lessons well.

With his dramatic and unique coat color and pattern, the Bourbonnais Pointer is an eye-catching canine. He's a well balanced, strong and muscular dog with a square (or just slightly longer) body. His thick neck is on the short side and may show some dewlap. The topline is level with a slight arch over the loin. A moderate tuck-up is desirable. The rear is well angulated with a marked degree of muscle mass. A substantial, sturdy dog, the Bourbonnais Pointer nevertheless has a look of elegance. Females are more refined than males. Males stand about 20-22 1/2 inches and weigh approximately 40-55 pounds. Females measure about 19-22 inches and weigh about 35-48 pounds.

The Bourbonnais has a distinctive head, quite different from other pointing dogs. The skull is rounded and the muzzle is equal to or a little shorter than the skull. The Bourbonnais has a slight stop. The ears are attached at or a little above eye level. The eyes are large with a soft expression. Eye color coordinates with coat color, being either hazel or dark amber. Nose color also coordinates with the coat and a black nose is disqualified.

The Bourbonnais tail is a key feature and, at one time, the breed was known as the "tailless pointer." The tail is set on rather low. Many pups are born with a naturally bobbed tail and some with no tail at all. The early standard required that tails be naturally short and not exceed three inches in length. The present standard allows for a longer appendage and permits docking.

Those unfamiliar with the breed are usually intrigued by the Bourbonnais' unique color and pattern. The coat is short and fine, although it is sometimes a little longer and thicker on the back. The French standard describes color thusly: "Shades of 'faded lilac' and 'wine' are achieved by the overall effect of maroon-colored spots and lines blended in together to give a mottled effect. There is a streaked appearance. In 'fawn' dogs, a lot of brown spots and lines blend in together to achieve the shade of 'peach blossom.' Colored spots are permitted, symmetrical or not, as long as they do not dominate over the coat color or are too prevalent. If a spot appears on the face, one spot cannot cover both eyes." Black spots or a solid maroon or fawn coat are disqualifications. Early writers often described the wine color as *lie de vin,* or the shade of wine dregs. In describing the patterning, some have said that the Bourbonnais is "dressed like a trout." This is an obvious reference to the prized speckled trout and an attempt to describe the spots sprinkled on the coat.

The French report that the Bourbonnais has a delightful personality. The dogs are very sweet and affectionate. A well-adjusted, stable dog, the Bourbonnais is eager to please, easily trained and quite obedient. Adequate socialization will help to ensure a confident, self-assured dog. The French standard includes disqualifications for fearfulness, timidity, excessive nervousness and dogs who are easily alarmed.

"They are extremely sweet, docile and affectionate," Beth Cepil writes. "We raised Brou in the house and he was calm and easily trained." After field training, Brou took up residence in the kennel and then, Beth says, his "energy peaked." This is typical of the European bird dogs. Dogs kept in kennels are apt to become rowdy. For this reason, most breeders suggest that these dogs be kept in a home environment where they are happier, calmer and more responsive.

"The charm of all its qualities makes this dog a continuous pleasure for the owner," writes a French Bourbonnais fancier. With his stylish good looks, his zest for hunting and his winning personality, the Bourbonnais Pointer is sure to delight American owners, too. We hope we will be seeing more of this striking French breed in the coming years.

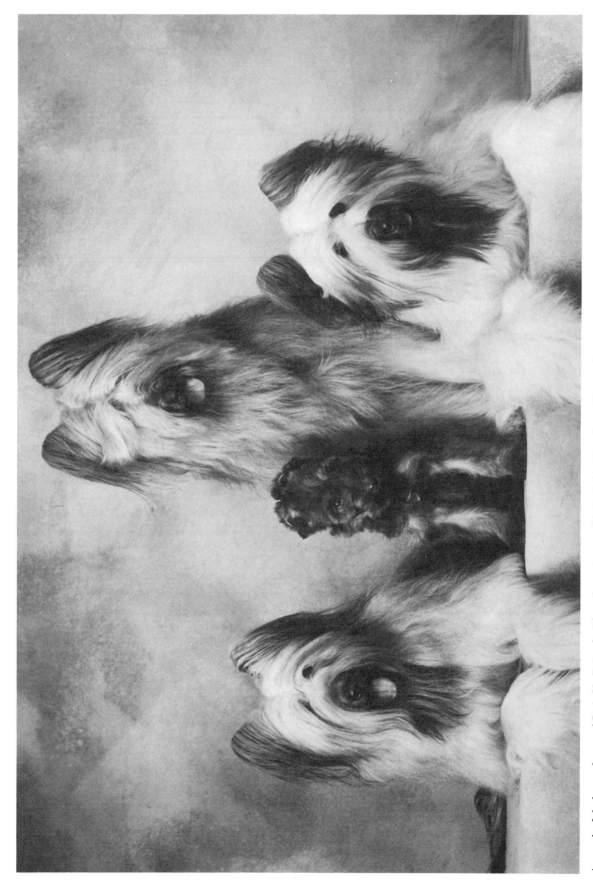

A wonderful photo of several Deja Vu Briards. These beauties are Ch. Deja Vu Woodbine Cheap Thrills, ten week old Deja Vu Four Leaf Clover, top winner Ch. C'est Bonheur Woodbine Tinsel HT (Herding Tested) and Ch. Deja Vu Deck the Halls HT. All are owned by Terry Miller, of Cleveland Heights, Ohio. (John Goldy photo)

Chapter 9

The Briard

"Briards have a winsome way of working themselves into the hearts of their owners. Their nice traits of staying at home—for which the French have nic-named them 'Mat Dog'—is a great comfort, as you know that you can count on their protection day in and out." So wrote Mrs. George Jacobs, this country's foremost 1930's Briard breeder, in a 1934 issue of *The American Kennel Gazette*. French actress Gaby Morlay summed up her love for the breed more succinctly. "My Briard?" she said. "He's a heart wrapped in fur."

Without a doubt, the Briard is one of the most glamorous and elegant of the A.K.C. recognized herding breeds. He's also a charming and beguiling companion...devoted, hard working, demanding, giving, eager yet willful, affectionate, intelligent, alert, protective and an irrepressible clown. With all these sterling attributes, you may ask, why isn't the Briard more popular? The answer eludes those who know the breed. However, they are not at all unhappy with the situation. As they frequently point out, the Briard is not the breed for everybody. They feel very protective toward this French native and would rather he not become too popular.

The Briard is a very old breed. The Emperor Charlemagne is believed to have owned the breed in the 8th century. In French tapestries, he's pictured with several of the dogs at his feet. An early historian, Einhard, tell us that, "In summer the animals are put out to pasture on fallow lands preserved for this purpose. One or more herders tend them with shepherd dogs, guarding against thieves by day and against beasts by night." Indeed, during the early days, the Briard was used primarily as a livestock guardian to defend flocks against wolves and poachers.

The breed appears to have made the transition to a herding dog about the time of the French Revolution. The great estates were broken up into small unfenced holdings. A herding dog was needed to keep the flocks within their boundaries and the Briard proved adept at the task. In Abbot Rozier's 1809 book, the *Course of Agriculture*, he observes, "In the country of the plain, the open hills and in the daily paths of sheep, the ancient Chien de Brie is employed....It is not his beauty which gives him merit, it is his perfect instincts, his obedience, his activeness and his industry...His charges are made to obey by his voice and movements combined, not by his biting...."

The first French dog show was held in Paris in 1863. A Briard, Charmante, was chosen best of all the sheepdogs exhibited. In 1888, the great French cynologist Pierre Mégnin penned the first precise description of the breed. In 1893, French fanciers began to make a distinction between the Chien Berger de Brie, or Briard, and the Chien Berger de Beauce, or Beauceron (see *A Celebration of Rare Breeds, Volume I*). Thereafter, separate classes were offered for each breed.

In 1896, *Le Club Français du Chien de Berger* (or French Herding Dog Club) was formed. The following year, they drew up standards for both the Briard and Beauceron. In 1907 a club specifically for the Briard, *Les Amis du Briard*, was formed. It would continue until the first World War when it was, of necessity, disbanded.

The breed gained international fame for its extraordinary performance during World War I. The Briard's tremendous intelligence, easy trainability and hardy ruggedness enabled him to be used for a variety of tasks. Many dogs were used as patrol dogs or sentries

Mother, Ch. C'est Bonheur Woodbine Tinsel H.T., owned by Terry Miller and J. Odom, and Daughter, Ch. Deja Vu Woodbine Cheap Thrills, owned by Terry Miller. Tinsel was the top winning Briard in 1988 and 1989. She holds the breed record for the most group placements. This three-time Westminster winner recently won the National Specialty from the Veteran's Class.

at outposts. They also served as liaison dogs, carrying messages from trench to trench. Briards often backpacked food and supplies and sometimes strings of carbine clips were wound round their bodies to be taken to the front lines. These dogs were also used frequently to pull carts, but this proved to have terrible consequences. Their eagerness to please caused the Briards to work without regard to pain or exhaustion. The dogs simply would not quit and many literally worked themselves to death.

The breed's most heroic use, however, was as an adjutant to the medical corps. After each battle, Briards fanned out into the infamous trenches, performing a type of battlefield triage. The dogs were said to be remarkably adept at discerning which soldiers were wounded and in need of aid and which were beyond help. Often, a wounded soldier's first sight was of a mud-covered, shaggy dog, who gently removed his handkerchief or helmet. To many, the Briard seemed a savior. The dog carried the object back to the first-aid tent and led medics, with stretchers, to the wounded. The performance of the breed made an indelible impression on both French and foreign soldiers.

While the extraordinary exploits of the Briard earned the admiration of all, it was to have a devastating impact on the breed. Untold numbers of Briards per-

ished during the conflict. There were justifiable fears that the breed would become extinct. But a few French breeders rallied to save the Briard. In 1923, they regrouped, picked up the pieces and again revived the club *Les Amis du Briard*. In 1925, they crafted a more detailed standard for the breed. We owe our thanks to these hard working people for saving these wonderful dogs.

The Briard made an appearance in America at an early date. In 1784, Thomas Jefferson was appointed U.S. Minister to France. He had a keen interest in everything relating to agriculture and is responsible for introducing many plants and animals to this country. He was most interested in French sheep and the dogs who tended them. With the aid of Lafayette and Pierre du Pont, he arranged to have a Briard shipped to his Virginia farm, Monticello. In 1879, he purchased a pregnant Briard bitch. Later, he imported several other dogs. His journals indicate that he was enthusiastic about the breed and gave a number of dogs to his friends. Despite such illustrious patronage, the Briard did not become a permanent fixture on farms in this country.

The breed would not be seen again until after World War I. American soldiers, who had seen the heroic breed in action, were impressed. Several adopted Briards and brought their beloved dogs home with them when they returned. The first litter was born in this country in 1922, before the breed had been recognized. In 1925, New Yorker Mrs. Frances Hoppin imported the black Briard, Dauphine de Montjoye. This dog would become the first registered Briard when the A.K.C. conferred recognition in 1928. Another black import, Ch. Regent de la Pommeraie became the first champion in 1931.

While the Briard has been used in many capacities, his traditional role is as a herding dog and home guardian. "We have, here in France, the presence of a working dog par excellence, the Chien Berger de Brie," wrote Louis de Lajarriage, in the late 1800's. "The shepherd dog is the first minister of the shepherd. He executes all orders. He maintains the sheep within the limits which have been set, he punishes the delinquents into order, and warns with his voice when necessary. He is the perfect minister, perfect policeman, and the perfect keeper of the flock. To be good at all these functions, it is important that he be intelligent. We find this quality immensely developed in the Chien de Brie..."

The French shepherd was a practical man who did not tolerate slackards, be they two- or four-footed.

His dogs had to be hardy, rugged, industrious and able to earn their keep. The Briard satisfied all of these needs. These dogs herd with a "heading" style, often nosing, nudging and prodding the stock with their powerful head and shoulders to get the animals to move. Current owners see the same traits in their dogs, even those far removed from their sheep tending ancestors. To attract attention, a Briard will often give his owner a nudge; ignore him and he'll bump harder. Owners also report that their dogs will frequently circle children, as if trying to herd them, and will press their shoulders against the kids if they veer too near the street.

The herding instincts were so strongly ingrained that little training was necessary. This quality, undoubtedly, endeared the breed to French shepherds. "The Briard scarcely needs any training at all," wrote Sédir, in *Le Berger de Brie,* posthumously published in 1926, "but they must understand clearly what is expected of them. For guarding man,...children, the house, the poultry yard...the flock, they can manage very well by themselves...." Sédir believed strongly in maintaining working ability. "It is good for the Briard to work. He enjoys the effort and likes to be useful. It gives him zest and develops his body and his intelligence."

"Lively, friendly and sometimes even mischievous as a puppy, the mature Briard is the epitome of loyalty and devotion, making him the ideal companion..." writes Mary Lou Tingley, in the 1964 book *How to Raise and Train a Briard.* "He is never too old to play; he loves to be included in family activities, especially when this includes trips in the car or long walks on a warm spring morning. He considers children in the family his own. He will play with them, guard them and actually play nursemaid to them. At other times he is content to lie at (or on) his master's feet, relaxed and content with this silent communion."

It's a little difficult to accurately describe the Briard's temperament. Dogs of this breed are quite individualistic and breeders report that no two are quite alike. All agree, however, that the Briard bonds very closely with the family and needs love and attention to thrive and develop fully. When he receives such attention, he is kind, friendly, loving and devoted. The Briard can also be a delightful and amusing clown. The French describe the temperament as "sage-hardi," meaning that the breed combines the quality of steady wisdom with fearlessness.

Briards are true homebodies and they are happiest when close to their owners. "My Champion Marquis de Montjoye, now four years old, has never been off the place," wrote Mrs. George W. Jacobs, Jr., in 1934. "If he is down in the woods with a companion on the luring trail of rabbits, the ring of the farm bell brings him scampering back to the house with a 'what can I do for you' manner. He delights in service, as they all do. (He)

Ch. Phydeaux Take the Money N Run, owned by Terry Miller, Deja Vu Briards.

always brings me the mail and the paper. (He) announces dinner each night, watching the setting of the table, and not until my man lights the candles, does he come for me."

A very intelligent dog, the Briard is eager to please and easily trained. Some dogs, however, are quite independent and apt to decide things on their own. This is a thinking breed that often reasons things out. Because of this, it is essential that the dog clearly understand what's expected of him. Breeders are honest in saying that the Briard is not an instantly obedient dog who works with military precision. He will be your companion, not your slave.

Like all herding dogs, the Briard responds poorly to harsh handling. "Training, such as used for a police dog, spoils the character of the Briard," wrote Sédir. "It annihilates his initiative. This is especially true of the German training methods. In order to obtain the most from Briards, it is necessary to be extremely kind, gentle, friendly and to talk a great deal to them as soon as they can understand." Mrs. George Jacobs certainly agrees. "They are so easy to train. Never punishment, just a 'nice dogs don't do that' in a shocked voice, is all they require, for they are so eager to please."

The Briard is apt to be diffident and reserved with strangers. He is an excellent and vigilant guardian and he takes his duties seriously. Many owners report that their dogs will not relax until all family members are home for the night. Some Briards insist on sleeping just inside the door at night to guard against intruders. Clearly, this is why the French dubbed the breed the "Mat Dog."

It is absolutely essential that Briard puppies be

well socialized. They must be exposed to strange people and situations from an early age. Only with such exposure will the breed mature into an impressive and self-confident dog. I've seen several Briards, raised in kennel situations, that were extremely shy and cringing. I've also heard of dogs who became overly aggressive. Neither of these postures is correct for the breed. Once you've seen a wonderfully alert, supremely confident Briard, you won't be able to settle for anything less.

Breeders stress that the Briard is not for everyone. This breed requires a great deal of commitment on the part of owners. In order to develop fully and flourish, you simply must shower your dog with love and attention. He must be treated in the same way that you would a child. Kind firm discipline and oodles of love, body contact and verbal encouragement will start you on the right track. "The potential for a grand relationship is always there, inherent in the breed and is directly in proportion to the effort given," writes Charles Child, in Diane McLeroth's 1982 book *The Briard.* This volume should be required reading for anyone contemplating the purchase of a Briard. It's a truly bold and remarkable book, jam packed with fascinating information. In fact, in my opinion, Ms. McLeroth has written one of the best breed books around.

The Briard is glamorous and elegant. But don't be deceived by outward appearances. Beneath the glorious coat, you will find a well-boned, strong and sturdy dog. His square body combines strength and power with agility. Size varies considerably with males standing 23-27 inches, while bitches measure 22-25 1/2 inches. Weight can vary from about 65 pounds to 100 pounds. The well-feathered tail is carried low and terminates in a hook, or "crochet," which resembles the letter "J." Soundness is of utmost importance for we must remember that this is a herding dog. Breeders describe the Briard's movement as "quicksilver," meaning that he's adept at springing starts, sudden stops and abrupt turns. He glides across the ground, with cat-like grace, his feet barely skimming the surface.

In true French tradition, the Briard *must* have two dewclaws on each of the rear legs. These should be placed quite low on the foot. Ideally, they form full functioning toes. The desirability of dewclaws has long been a hotly debated issue. The initial call for such appendages is rooted in superstition. The French shepherds believed that dogs exhibiting this trait were smarter and better workers. While current day fanciers acknowledge that this belief is preposterous, they've chosen to retain the characteristic as a bow to the breed's heritage.

The Briard's head gives the impression of length. The large expressive eyes are black or very dark brown. The ears are attached high and may be either cropped or uncropped. Natural ears lie flat against the head. The majority of Briards, in this country, have their ears cropped, which lends a very distinctive appearance. The shell type crop employed is unique to the breed. Only the

An uncropped Briard, English import, Am. Mex. Ch. Abbeywater Allante (Benny), is owned by Dawn Gould, of Alpine, California.

tips and a little width are removed, leaving a full "bell" at the ear's base. A Briard puppy's ears are cropped at an earlier age than most breeds. Breeders usually prefer to perform the procedure at about six weeks. The head is covered with abundant hair which should never be so profuse as to obscure the outline and totally cover the eyes. Most of the hair lies flat, but the eyebrows arch up and out, providing a light veil which protects the eyes.

One of the Briard's glories is his coat, which is long and lies flat. The coarse coat is hard and dry to touch and makes a rasping sound. The French say it resembles the hair of a goat. The Briard is double coated with a soft fine undercoat and a long, slightly wavy outercoat. The coat is profuse, particularly on the neck and shoulders. Dogs come in a variety of colors. Under the American standard, only white is excluded. Blacks, tawnys and grays are the most common colors. Black may range from a pure jet black to a slate color while grays may very from a very light shade to a deep blue/gray. Tawnys may range from a light golden shade to a deep chestnut. No matter the color, each should be uniform in appearance.

We see in the Briard probably the oldest of the French sheepherding breeds. His elegant, majestic appearance is wonderfully impressive. But, to those who know the breed best, this is merely the icing on the cake. The breed's true beauty lies in his remarkable, sterling character and his willingness to give his all for his owner. The Briard has endured through many hard times. He's made the transition from a livestock guardian to a herding dog. He's weathered battlefield rigors and managed to survive unchanged. Present day breeders bear the responsibility of preserving his unique traits for the next generation. If their devotion is anything like that given by the dogs, the Briard will always claim a place among the breeds known round the world.

Chapter 10

The Cane Corso

"I first saw a photo of the breed, some years ago, in a dog book," says Michael Sottile, of Montgomery, Alabama. "I was intrigued. Five years ago I made a trip to Sicily. While there, I attended the wedding of a friend. On the way to the ceremony, we drove along a road in the country. I just happened to see a farmer in a field with his cows. Working among the animals were these impressive dogs. I asked my friends to stop the car and I called out to the farmer. There we stood, on the side of the road, dressed in tuxedos. We must have looked really funny," Mike laughs.

"The dogs turned out to be Branchiero Sicilianos, the same dogs I'd seen in that book. I explained to the farmer that I was very much interested in these dogs and would like to purchase stock for show and breeding. 'Do you have cows?' he asked me. When I said, 'no,' he asked why I would want to breed these dogs. This is a common view," Mike says. "In Italy, this breed is thought of as a utility dog. Most farmers consider them as purely working dogs and can't imagine why else anyone would own them. It's only recently that they have come to be appreciated as show dogs."

Breed names are apt to be confusing, since these dogs have been known variously as Cane Corso, Branchiero Siciliano, Cane Corso di Puglia and Mastino Corso. Michael Sottile helped us to sort out the differences. "In Sicily, the breed is known as the Branchiero Siciliano, but on the mainland it is known as the Cane Corso. Those working to have the breed officially recognized use the term Cane Corso."

It should come as no surprise that Mike and his wife, Kathy, were interested in this Italian breed. They are best known, in rare breed circles, for promoting the Neapolitan Mastiff. Indeed, the dynamic couple has chalked up an impressive 21 Neo champions, to date. In fact, owning Neapolitan Mastiffs is a long standing tradition in Mike's family. Members of the Sottile clan have owned this massive breed for over 400 years. Mike's grandfather first imported the dogs, to this country, in 1902. Now the Cane Corso has come to the duo's Alaric Kennels.

Italian authorities believe that the Cane Corso is one of two breeds which stem directly from the Roman Molossus. They say that, in ancient times, the historic Molossus gave rise to two quite different breeds. One dog was very massive and became the progenitor of the Neapolitan Mastiff. The other was a taller, lighter and less cumbersome dog, known for his quickness and agility. From this very athletic Molossus sprang today's Cane Corso.

"I believe that they probably crossed coursing hounds with Mastiffs to get the Cane Corso," Mike Sottile says. "We have friends who have run these dogs with their Greyhounds. They are not as fast as the Greyhounds, of course, but they aren't far behind. And, when the Greyhound fades, the Corso is still going. They combine speed with great endurance."

In medieval times, the Cane Corso was used as a big game hunter. His power, courage and agility made him especially valuable on wild boar. It is also reported that he was used on stag and bear. Italian fanciers of the breed say, proudly, that the Corso is "the only true coursing mastiff." Doubtless, owners of other breeds will contest this assertion, but it does pay tribute to the Corso's past. "The word *cane* means 'dog' in Italian," says Mike Sottile. "*Corso* has several meanings, but the

The impressive Ch. Duro di Alaric, owned by Michael and Kathy Sottile, of Montgomery, Alabama.

with the Border Collie. Border Collies are farm dogs here and the Cane Corso is used similarly in Italy. This is a very old, somewhat primitive breed. It is unspoiled and we'd very much like to keep it that way."

According to Italian writer Ettore Frassinetti, the breed was in danger of becoming extinct. "A few years ago, Count Giovanni Bonalti, an authority and historian on the Molossus, gave the the alarm that there was an imminent danger that the Cane Corso could become extinct," he writes. "He made known where some purebred Corsos were to be found in the Mid-Central region of Italy. This outcry was the salvation of the breed. Some skillful and caring dog lovers acquired as many specimens as possible and began the selective breeding of the Cane Corso."

Fanciers joined together to form a breed club. Soon they had formulated a standard and were holding specialty shows for the Corso. Because Italian breed standards are so complex, it was necessary to take detailed measurements and compare the virtues and faults of all dogs present. The results of this survey was turned over to the E.N.C.I. (the Italian Kennel Club), which then granted the breed temporary acceptance. Full recognition is expected shortly.

most apt seems to be to 'run a race or course.' This is testament to the breed's great athleticism, which survives to this day."

With the decline in big game hunting, the Corso found a home with Italian farmers. He was often used as a drover, moving animals to market or to the slaughter house. On the farm, he protected the livestock from both human thieves and animal predators. He also doubled admirably as a guard dog for the home. Indeed, to this day, he can still be seen throughout rural Italy performing these old duties.

"In Italy, the breed is still very much a farm dog," Mike Sottile says. "They are considered valuable, all purpose dogs. It's akin to the situation in this country

The Cane Corso is a large, powerful dog. Males stand 24-28 inches at the shoulders and weigh 100-140 pounds. Females generally stand 22-27 inches and tip the scales at 80-100 pounds. The head is quite massive with a broad skull and wide, square jaw. Unlike his cousin, the Neapolitan Mastiff, the Cane Corso does not drool. When presented naturally, the Corso's ears are pendulous. However, most dogs are cropped with a short cut which forms a triangle. Uncropped ears are considered a serious fault.

A good Cane Corso is a dog with massive bone. His body length is a little longer than tall. The chest is broad and deep, while the hindquarters are moderately angulated and very muscular. The Cane Corso's tail is docked to one-third of its natural length. "Most important is that the dog appears balanced and athletic," the standard states.

The breed has a short dense coat which comes in a wide range of colors. The standard allows "black, black and tan, red, chestnut, fawn blue or any of these colors with brindling." White markings may appear on the chest, neck, chin and the tips of the toes. White on any other part of the body, including the face, is a disqualification. Eye color corresponds to coat color and may range from black to hazel.

But, what is the Cane Corso like to live with? "They're great dogs," Mike Sottile says. "Although they are superb protection dogs, they are quiet around the house. They're not at all noisy. They love their family and need lots of personal hands-on attention. There's a lot of eye contact with this breed. I'm very impressed with their intelligence. They always seem to be thinking. It's like you can just see the wheels turning. They are so eager to please that they are usually at your side just waiting for your next command.

"Despite the breed's size, they make excellent house dogs. The Cane Corso definitely needs socialization and we strongly urge that owners obedience train their dogs. Properly raised and trained, the breed is suspicious of strangers, but wonderful with the family. When raised correctly, the dog should be submissive to all members of the family.

"This breed gets along very well with children. They are protective, yet gentle. The Cane Corso has a very stable temperament," Mike observes. Ettore Frassinetti says that the breed "devotedly loves his owners, his family and in particular children with whom he behaves delicately and gently."

"Despite their large size, they are very athletic dogs," Mike Sottile says. "Because of this, they do need exercise. Here, we run our dogs with our horses to keep them in shape. In the house, though, they that he'd be badly injured. With one of the kicks, he went flying about twenty feet through the air. We really held our breath and feared the worst. However, he got up, shook himself off and came back to us. I was positive that there would be broken bones or some injury. Except for a little coat missing on his side, he was absolutely fine. What impressed me most, however, was that the whole experience didn't seem to faze him at all. That's what I mean when I tell people that these dogs are tough. They have a high tolerance for pain.

"The Cane Corso is a great guard dog. He has a very protective nature and yet seems to be able to discern a friend from a foe." Ettore Frassinetti says that "given the right circumstance, he instinctively knows how to become a terrifying defensive protective dog for his owners, his grounds, the house and the whole family."

A head study of eight month old Sansone di Alaric. "Soni" is owned by Barbara Baldan and Kathy Sottile.

The two year old Italian import Alaric Bullo Orso, an outstanding Cane Corso, is owned by Michael and Kathy Sottile, of Alaric Kennels.

This breed gets along, very well, with other dogs. "On Italian farms, these dogs are worked in groups,"

Mike Sottile says. "They must be able to get along with other dogs. Of course, they are strong dogs and will not run away from a fight, but they are not aggressive with other dogs.

"We are trying our best to preserve this inherent working ability. At our home, the dogs are expected to get along with horses, cats and other dogs. We have encouraged people to use them with cattle, in the traditional manner. All of the dogs that we've imported come from pure working stock and we're trying our best to preserve those qualities. We'd like to see them remain an all-round working dog."

Mike and Kathy Sottile have been showing their Alaric Cane Corsos since 1989. Several of their dogs have completed their championships and the breed is fast becoming the dog to beat, at rare breed shows. Their Ch. Duro di Alaric first went Best in Show at only one year of age. Since then, he has captured a total of six Bests in Show, in competition with both rare and A.K.C. breeds. "They are outstanding show dogs," Mike says. "They are so athletic and inherently sound. It's just a joy to watch these dogs move. They also have a very proud, self-confident air about them. They are extremely muscular and very impressive. I think they have a great future as show dogs."

The Cane Corso has come a long way in a short time. From a chance meeting in a field on an Italian country roadside to American Best in Show honors, the Corso has rapidly moved from obscurity to center stage. A loyal house dog, inherent protector, valuable farm dog and illustrious show dog, the Cane Corso would seem to offer much to dog lovers in the U.S. The Sottiles have our thanks for introducing us to this impressive Italian breed.

A beautiful three month old blue brindle puppy. Owners are Sandy and Ted Freeman and Kathy Sottile.

Chapter 11

The Caucasian Ovtcharka

As the rare breed movement has grown, we've learned about many breeds. Part of the excitement of attending rare breed events, is having the opportunity to look at a "new" breed. Dogs from Europe, Asia, South America, Australia, even little known North American breeds delight spectators. Dogs from the Soviet Union, however, are rarely in evidence. With the advent of *glasnost*, though, and the rapidly changing events in the Soviet republics, the Iron Curtain has tumbled and a few dogs from that region have made their way to this country. Much to the delight of American dog lovers, we are beginning to learn about the fascinating breeds which hail from this vast and diverse country. A few Karelian Bear Dogs (see *A Celebration of Rare Breeds, Volume I*) have recently been imported. And now, one of the most intriguing of the Soviet breeds, the Caucasian Ovtcharka, has made its debut.

Russell and Stacey Kubyn, of Painesville, Ohio, have undertaken the task of introducing the Caucasian Ovtcharka to Americans. The Kubyns are unlikely rare breed pioneers. They owned a German Shepherd and a Rottweiler, two of this country's most popular breeds. But the livestock guardian dogs had long fascinated them. They considered purchasing a Kuvasz, but fate intervened. A Russian emigree told the couple about the Caucasian Ovtcharka and they were fascinated. The possibility existed, he told them, that the dogs might finally be available for export.

Luck has been with Russell and Stacey from the beginning. They initially made contact with a Russian authority on the breed, who personally selected breeding stock for the Kubyn's Esquire Kennels. Among the dogs they received was the stunning male, Soviet Cham-pion Topush. "Toppy," as he's known, has become Stacey's much loved companion and friend. But, when their elderly Soviet contact died, the Kubyns thought they would be on their own. They had become so intrigued, with the dogs, that they desperately wanted additional knowledge.

Lady Luck again smiled on the couple. They were fortunate in making contact with esteemed Russian breeder/judge Elena Kuleshova. A graduate of the University of Leningrad, with degrees in biology and zoology, Elena is an official with the State Kennel Association. She carries the impressive title, "Specialist of Methodological Education," and concentrates on the working breeds. She is advisor to several working dog clubs, in Leningrad, and is licensed to judge all working breeds. The Kubyns were delighted to discover that she's a long time breeder of both Rottweilers and Caucasian Ovtcharkas. Recently, Elena arrived in the U.S., specifically to visit the Kubyns. She came armed with photographs and material on the breed, as well as four new dogs from Leningrad's top bloodlines. She's agreed to serve as advisor for the Caucasian Ovtcharka Club of America (COCA).

To the Kubyns, meeting Elena was like hitting the motherlode. They had become increasingly alarmed at some of the dogs, purported to be Caucasians, which had surfaced in this country. Though the dogs arrived with papers, they differed radically in type from those imported by the Kubyns. The couple also had many questions on the breed's origin and history. The scant written material available contained conflicting information. Clearly, the Americans needed the assistance of an expert. Elena provided the answers and helped to sort

Nart of Esquire is an outstanding three month old puppy imported by Russ and Stacey Kubyn, Esquire Kennels, Painesville, Ohio.

out the discrepancies. She, along with other Leningrad breeders, has taken a special interest in efforts to launch the breed in this country, and they have all volunteered their help. My thanks go to Elena for answering my many questions and to Stacey Kubyn for her generous assistance, in helping to bridge the language gap. My gratitude also goes to The Caucasian Ovtcharka Club of America, for supplying me with an article penned by breed expert and judge Marina Kuznetsova. This extraordinary article was prepared specifically for the COCA and I appreciate the opportunity to quote from it.

In recent years, we have learned more and more about the ancient livestock protection breeds. Indeed, a whole string of these dogs have appeared, spanning a geographical line from the mountains of Asia to those of Europe. Wherever old world, mountain shepherds have tended sheep, goats and other animals, they have relied on these dogs as invaluable deterrents against predators. From Tibet to Turkey, from Yugoslavia to Hungary, from Czechoslovakia to Poland, from Italy to France and from Spain to Portugal, these dogs have assisted their owners. Indeed, the presence of these dogs seems to parallel man's migrations on both continents.

Now, thanks to the Kubyns, we have one more piece of the intricately woven puzzle. The Ovtcharka ("sheepdog" or "shepherd" in Russian) hails from the Caucasus, that great range of mountains that is generally considered the dividing line between Europe and Asia. Russian authorities believe that the breed is more than 2,000 years old. According to Russian texts, the breed is very closely related to the Tibetan Mastiff. Opinions vary as to whether the breed is descended from the Tibetan dog or whether both breeds sprang

from a common Tibetan ancester. "The first reference about this dog was made before the second century A.D. in a manuscript of antiquity of the Armenish people," writes breed authority Marina Kuznetsova. "In the Azerbaijan mountain area I have seen pictures carved in stone of dogs drawn very tall and powerful. In addition, folk tales and folk legends often make mention of the large shaggy dogs which saved their owners from various dangers."

Ms. Kuznetsova has traveled extensively, in the Caucasus, and offers us an invaluable glimpse of the duties performed by the dogs. The breed is, of course, used as a flock guardian. Wolves are a constant threat to the sheep and the Ovtcharka is quite capable of dispatching a full grown wolf. Most shepherds keep five or six dogs to assist them. Males are greatly preferred and there are usually four males and one or two females to tend the flock. Survival of the fittest is definitely the rule of the day and this has resulted in extremely hardy and rugged dogs. Shepherds rarely provide food for the dogs and so the animals hunt for rabbits and other small game to sustain themselves. Females come in season only once a year and, generally, whelp in fall or early winter. Bitches dig dens for the occasion and whelp alone without assistance. All male puppies are kept and one or two females are allowed to survive. Mothers provide food for their young, until they are old enough to fend for themselves. Naturally, considering the primitive conditions, the mortality rate for dogs in very high. Only 20% of most litters survive.

Dogs destined to be livestock guardians must be, Martina Kuznetsova says, "steady, hardy," and "not spiteful to people and domestic animals...." Due to the demanding conditions, most shepherds keep all of the puppies. Even adult dogs don't live long and replacements are constantly needed. Occasionally, a dog may be presented to a close friend, but selling dogs is unheard of. "Some herders try to breed the best males and some of them know the pedigrees of males in their heads," Martina says.

Dogs were also kept as home protectors. Such dogs bond closely with their families and are fully under the control of their owners. They are, however, extraordinary protectors of their home property and will attack any stranger who enters. "However, outside the protected area," Martina reports, "the dogs can be walked off leash and are usually not aggressive with non-threatening strangers."

It will surprise many to learn that the Caucasian Ovtcharka is also kept for fighting purposes. Large sums are wagered on the bouts and only the wealthy can afford to own fighting dogs. "Caucasian mountain people are very superstitious and they keep this dog under lock and key. You can get puppies from these dogs or you can look upon their dogs at home only if you are close friends with the owner. I have seen none photographed because of the superstition of the 'evil eye' that the dog will fall ill and die."

Elena Kuleshova is quick to point out that, despite the different uses for the dogs, they were all the same breed. There were no specialized strains developed for one purpose alone. All of these gene pools overlapped. There are, however, some regional variations within the breed. The dogs which hail from the republic of Georgia are large, powerful, well-boned dogs. They have impressive "bear type" heads and longer coats. Some very good specimens also come from Daghestan. Generally, these dogs are a little rangier and lighter in bone than the Georgian representatives. Leningrad breeders have had excellent results in combining these two types. The small republic of Azerbaijan is home to two types of Caucasians. The dogs from the mountainous areas are heavy, rugged dogs with wide, deep chests and longer muzzles and bodies. Those found in the steppe regions are smaller boned, leggier and have squarer bodies. There are also Kangal type dogs from the Soviet-Turkish border region. Russian breeders are not enamored of this type and do not use them often in breeding programs. Elena Kuleshova dismisses the Kangal type as mere "yard dogs." It should be understood that all Caucasian Ovtcharkas are bred to a single standard and the type differences are not clear cut. Elena points out that there is often an overlap between the types and that all of them fit within the standard.

The breed was largely confined to the Caucasus Mountains until World War II. Sadly, the Caucasian has played a part in one of the most shameful periods in Soviet history. In 1919, the Soviet Union established prison camps, or "corrective labor camps," in Siberia. Anyone who disagreed with State policy, might be interned in the Gulags. By 1940, twelve million people were housed in such camps. By the end of World War II, however, this number was to rise dramatically. Stalin, in his increasing reign of terror, singled out large groups of people for imprisonment. Soviets who had been deported by the Nazis, to work in Germany, returning Prisoners of War, writers, Jews, intellectuals, political refugees who'd fled Germany to escape the war, dissidents, the devoutly religious...the list went on and on. Anyone who might question Stalin's unrivalled power, was likely to be sent off. It was not until Krushchev came to power, in the mid-1950s, that the system was partially dismantled.

Prisoners traveled on the great Trans-Siberian railroad to the Gulags. They were put to work, often felling trees in the vast Siberian forests, which were then loaded aboard the railway for use in places to the west. The climate was brutal and many people died in the camps. The short summers were oppressively hot. In winter, the temperatures could dip to more than 50 degrees below zero. While regulations called for men to be excused from labor when the thermometer dipped below minus 40 degrees, many commandants ignored the rules.

Dogs played an integral role in maintaining order in the Gulags. The Soviet aim was to find an imposing breed, tough enough to face the elements. They wanted intelligent dogs, who were naturally aggressive, to serve as a deterrent. In the years before World War II, the security forces experimented with a number of breeds. Clearly, the short haired guard dogs, such as the Doberman and Rottweiler, could not endure the severe climate. The Soviets tried using the German Shepherd, but found that this breed, too, could not cope with the extremes. They tried crossbreeding German Shepherds with various longhaired Russian hunting dogs, but these

This impressive male Caucasian from Leningrad is an excellent example of the Georgian type.

were also found to be lacking. Finally, they experimented with the Caucasian Ovtcharka. Georgi Nikoleavich Vladimov, writing in *Faithful Ruslan, The Story of a Guard Dog*, translated by Michael Glenny, says that "in time it was found that the most suitable breed was the *Kavkazskaya ovcharka* or Caucasian sheepdog, so that from World War II onward only this type of dog was bred for the prison service and frontier patrolling." Elena Kuleshova questions this and believes that the use of German Shepherds was more widespread.

The Gulags were encircled by a double barbed wire fence. The security forces were divided into two groups. The internal security guards were responsible for keeping order within the camps. It was the duty of the external guards to escort the prisoners to their designated work areas, oversee them during such hours and safely return them to the camp at day's end. If a prisoner, or group of detainees, broke from the work detail and attempted to flee into the forest (as often happened), the dogs would be sent to attack and stop them. The escort work was, by far, the more important, demanding and perilous chore. Each external guard was issued a sub-machine gun and assigned a specially trained dog to assist him.

Dogs destined for camp duties were raised in State run kennels. Naturally, the Caucasians' association with the Gulags stymied breed popularity. The breed did not come into general ownership, outside the Caucasus, until the 1960's. To this day, the mere sight

Soviet Ch. Topush of Esquire, owned by Russ and Stacey Kubyn, is typical of the Daghestan type..

of the breed strikes fear in the hearts of some citizens and refugees. Russian emigrees have even phoned and written Stacey Kubyn, to question how she could dare to introduce these dogs to the United States.

Sadly, the Caucasian has suffered in recent years in the Soviet Union. In the republic of Georgia, Caucasians have been extensively crossbred with German Shepherds and Great Danes. Authorities believe that only 20% of the remaining Georgian Caucasian Ovtcharkas are truly purebred. In Daghestan, where the dogs are still employed as flock guardians, few breeders pay close attention to breeding. We don't know much about the current breed status in Azerbaijan, or what effect the current political turmoil pitting Azerbaijanis against Armenians, will have on the future of the breed.

The situation in Russian cities is not encouraging either. In many of the largest cities, such as Moscow and Leningrad, Caucasians were, at one time, bred largely in military and "factory" kennels. Dogs from factory kennels were destined to guard warehouses and industrial sites. In recent years, however, many of these sites have installed modern security systems, which are used in lieu of dogs. Many of these breeding programs have been abandoned.

In Moscow, the situation is very distressing. Many Muscovite breeders, including the famed Red Star military operation, became interested in producing a larger dog. They bred their Caucasians to Saint Bernards and Newfoundlands. The resulting "Moscow watchdogs" were included in the Soviet's Experimental Breeds Group. These dogs are generally taller and heavier than purebred Caucasians and have inherited the jowly look of the Saints and Newfs. They also tend to have soft and wavy coats, and most Caucasian breeders feel that temperaments have suffered. In a practice that Americans would find deplorable, these dogs receive papers. If the offspring of one of these crossbreedings resembles a Caucasian, he is given papers identifying him as a purebred Caucasian. If the dog looks more like a Saint Bernard, he is given papers stating that he is of that breed. Dogs which look like a cross between these two breeds are identified, on official papers, as "Moscow Watchdogs." Caucasians have also been crossed with other breeds, including Tibetan Mastiffs. Many dedicated Caucasian breeders are appalled at these practices. Elena dismisses these dogs as "mutts," and Marina says that "in my estimation they were unsuccessful in creating anything of value!" It should be clearly stated that not all Moscow breeders engage in such practices.

In recent years, dog breeding has become a popular activity in the Soviet Union. Many of these dogs are destined for the black market. Caucasians commonly make an appearance at the Moscow Pet Market.

"Every Saturday and Sunday it is thronged with pigeon fanciers, fish breeders, peasants from the countryside with rabbits, hamsters, canaries...and other creatures," writes Michael Binyon.

"Dogs are not officially meant to be sold in the market, but there are plenty around," Mr. Binyon continues. "Usually their owners hang around the entrance, carrying large baskets covered with a blanket from which you occasionally see a wet, black nostril poking out. Big dogs sit on the ground under the trees, looking rather forlorn, especially in midwinter when only a bit of straw or old newspaper is put down for them on the snow. Many sellers, on the lookout in case they are moved on by the police for trading without a licence, keep their puppies tucked inside their jackets. As you walk past, they flash open their coats, with a furtive 'psst' like dirty postcard sellers, to reveal a trembling, furry face."

Naturally, the best dogs do not end up in such a place. They are common hangouts for what we would call backyard breeders and are also frequented by brokers and dealers. Reputable Russian breeders scathingly refer to people of this ilk as the "Dog Mafia." It should be noted that many of the dogs come complete with falsified papers, bearing the offical State Kennel Club stamps.

Sadly, many of these dogs have made their way to European countries, such as Germany, Poland, Austria, etc. Despite high prices, many dogs prove not to be of good quality. It's nearly impossible for a westerner to import really top quality dogs, says Elena Kuleshova. Most breeders simply won't part with their good dogs and they frequently pawn off inferior dogs on foreigners. While poor quality dogs and crossbreds have been readily available for export, it has always been the practice that top notch dogs remain in the country. Customs officials are often hesitant to allow their export.

Top quality dogs fetch high prices, and it's no wonder that such animals are so expensive. Elena says that American breeders have no idea how fortunate they are. There is no commercial dog food in the Soviet Union, and obtaining sufficient protein for the dogs is difficult and expensive. It's also very hard to get the routine vaccinations readily available in this country. Vaccines are often unavailable and, when obtained, may be ineffective. Parvovirus claims the lives of many Soviet dogs. Some Russian breeders loose 50% of their litters to diseases that are easily prevented in this country. Small wonder that Russian breeders treasure their top quality dogs.

In the past, all breeding was overseen by organized breed clubs. The best of these established criteria that had to be met before a dog could be bred. Dogs were required to be shown twice (one before the age of two

Debra Riesling, of Fontana, California, poses proudly with five month old Tri Satin's Gita of Esquire.

years and once after) and earn "excellent" or "very good" ratings before qualifying to be bred. According to Elena, about five years ago, the rules began to fall apart. The policies of the past are still maintained in the best breed clubs, but many independent groups have sprung up. There, the rules are either lax or nonexistent. It's a situation that alarms concerned, long-time breeders. "I am so sad that in general, breeding in the U.S.S.R. has no professional basis," Marina Kuznetsova writes. "People who do not understand the breed, casual breeders and those with only a commercial interest to sell puppies are responsible for this. If somebody has dogs with major faults and is prohibited from breeding in one club, these people go to another club with lower standards and they breed in this club and produce garbage. Excuse me please for these words about people from my country but it is very shameful and it hurts me when you have in dog shows in another country and in America abominable Caucasians and you get a bad opinion about the breed when you see these dogs."

Naturally, with the confusing situation in the Soviet Union, it's almost impossible for an outsider to obtain a good quality Caucasian. Your only hope, Elena Kuleshova advises, is to rely on a conscientious breeder who is affiliated with an esteemed breed club. A scrupulously honest breeder, she says, can help guide you to the best dogs.

Considering all the pitfalls, Russell and Stacey Kubyn have had remarkably good fortune. Working to establish the Caucasian Ovtcharka in this country has been an expensive, frustrating, demanding, yet rewarding endeavor. "It's been tremendously exciting," Stacey says. Progress has certainly been made. Stacey has exhibited her dogs at several rare breed outings. The Caucasian Ovtcharka Club of America has also grown. The Club is establishing contact with several kennel clubs and has kept busy dispensing information on the breed. They have enacted a code of ethics for owners. The Club has also made contact with the Orthopedic Foundation for Animals (OFA). Hip dysplasia can be a problem in the breed, but no one knows how widespread the condition is. Russian breeders don't have an opportunity to x-ray their dogs. For instance, in the city of Leningrad, home to six million people, only one x-ray machine is available. Of necessity, many Russian breeders have become well schooled in the practice of palpatation. Stacey has begun x-raying the dogs she's imported. She hopes that, by working with the OFA, dogs with bad hips can be eliminated from breeding programs.

There is much work to be done. "For now we battle mixed breed and low quality imports, unscrupulous brokers, greedy puppy millers hoping to cash in on a new breed, and those who believe the Caucasian should maintain its unsocialized 'ferocity' here in the United States," Stacey writes. "Wish us luck."

The Caucasian Ovtcharka is a large, powerful dog. The preferred height for males is 27 to 35 1/2 inches at the withers. Ideally, bitches should be 25 1/2 to 29 1/2 inches. While these dogs are obviously quite large, they should still have an active, athletic build. They should never have the ponderous look of a Saint Bernard. The Caucasian has a short, powerful neck and a deep, broad chest. Dogs should always be well-boned and muscular. The topline is level and the body is slightly longer than tall. The highset tail is long, reaching to the hock or below. The tail is carried down when the dog is at rest, but when excited or on the move, the tail is raised over the back in a ring or sickle-shape.

Caucasians have large impressive heads. The skull is broad and massive, with a slight stop separating the shorter length muzzle. The nose is usually black, though white or light fawn dogs may have brown noses. Soviet breeders have continued the age-old shepherd's

practice of cropping ears. These are cropped quite short, in the traditional manner, using a blunt, horizontal cut. The oval shaped eyes are dark and deeply set.

One of the Caucasian's most striking features is his lovely double coat. A soft dense undercoat is topped by straight, coarse textured guard hairs. Coats come in three lengths, all of which are acceptable. The long coats are the most popular. Long coated dogs sport a pronounced mane, or ruff, about the neck and profuse feathering on the hindlegs, known as "pants." Long coated dogs have richly furred tails. Dogs with intermediate coats have less pronounced manes and pants and less feathering on the tail. Short coated Caucasians are rare. Such dogs lack manes, pants and tail feathering. They still retain a thick double coat. The Caucasian comes in a whole range of colors from gray to red, fawn, white and tan. Brindle and piebald dogs are seen, too. The gray shades are common. "Typically the coat is agouti patterned," Stacey Kubyn explains, "each hair has varying shades giving the dog a sort of striated or salt/pepper appearance—very striking." Solid black, black and tan, and solid brown coats are disqualified. Also excluded are dogs with "St. Bernard red and white" coloration.

A thorough brushing, once or twice a week, will keep the Caucasian's coat in good condition. The dogs do blow their coats once a year. At that time, it's best to strip out the old coat. This will keep the dog looking neat, enable the new coat to come in more quickly and save wear and tear on your vacuum cleaner. If you don't, you will have drifts of snowy white hair all over the house.

"Caucasians are ideal family dogs and guardians," says Stacey Kubyn. "They are very steady and even tempered. I've found them to be very laid back in the house. They are exceptionally sweet, loving and docile dogs. They have a great deal of charm and bubble over with personality. We get lots of tailwags around here. Caucasians get along well with children and cats. I've found them to be very trustworthy. In fact, they are the most beautiful and cleanest house dogs I've ever owned."

Caucasians bond very closely with their families and it's best if they are allowed to be full family members. Like the livestock guardian of old, the dog adopts the human family and their property becomes "his" territory. "They do bond very closely," Stacey Kubyn says, "but they don't fawn or pester you."

They are very intelligent and very faithful dogs, Elena Kuleshova says. "They are more independent in personality than other working dogs, such as the German Shepherd. Elena makes a point of emphasizing that Caucasians are kindly to people they know and should always be completely trustworthy. These are qualities she selects for in her breeding program.

"These dogs respect an alpha figure," Stacey says. "They take a firm, but not a heavy hand. It's best to 'induce' the dogs to do what you want rather than manhandling them. They need a patient hand."

Elena Kuleshova describes the Caucasian as a very well balanced, stable dog. One of the key characteristics of the breed, she reports, is their inherent resilience. Nothing seems to phase these dogs. They rarely spook at anything. Even when they are temporarily perplexed by a strange new situation, they bounce back very quickly.

Another characteristic, according to Elena, is the Caucasian's phenomenal memory. Elena has placed puppies in new homes at three or four months of age. She hadn't seen the dogs again until they were adults, yet they still remembered her. Elena reports that this is a typical Caucasian trait.

The breed has gained fame as an outstandingly effective guard dog. The standard says that the Caucasian's "faithfulness, protectiveness and ferocity when provoked is legendary." It also describes the breed as having "well developed defensive reactions" and specifies that "suspicion and aggressiveness toward strangers" is inherent in this breed.

Like all the livestock guardian breeds, the Caucasian is naturally wary of strangers. But this Soviet breed appears to be bolder than many of the livestock protectors already known in this country. "It's amazing to see these dogs in action," Stacey says. "All I have to say is 'What's that?' and the dogs will spring into action. They growl and charge in the direction I'm looking. If they perceive no threat, they calm down very quickly. It's a very unique behavior."

"It's important for people to understand," Stacey says, "that these are not just vicious dogs." Recently, Stacey received a 14 month old bitch from Leningrad. "Hema," as she's known, had some initial training before leaving Russia. "She simply will not allow a stranger to get through the door," Stacey says. "She's quite ferocious looking. She's ten times more aggressive than a Rottweiler." However, Stacey has seen for herself how controllable the breed can be. Hema had

seen a visitor a few times and still would not allow the man into the house or yard. Stacey took her to the man's home, so that Hema would be out of territory she's used to protecting. "She was kind and loving to him," Stacey reports. "The next time he came to the house, she had accepted him. He was in the backyard when I let her out and she ran to him, gave him a big bear hug and tried to kiss him." This appears to be typical Caucasian behavior. "While our German Shepherd and Rottweiler will bark at anyone who comes to the fence," Stacey says, "the Caucasians bark only when it's a stranger."

This dog is an excellent, extraordinary guardian, Elena Kuleshova says, but they should never be vicious. In the standard it speaks of how ferocious they are. Soviet breeders understand that the dog acts this way when he is "on duty." Elena fears that Americans might misinterpret the standard's meaning.

While socialization is important in all breeds, it is particularly so with the Caucasian. "I believe this breed needs the maximum in socialization," Stacey Kubyn says. "We have worked very hard on that. All of our dogs live as pets. They are not relegated to a kennel. They see people everyday. They know our neighbors and their children and are very accepting of them. We feel that our emphasis on socialization will prevent problems." Indeed, socialization is stressed in the breed standard. "Characteristic aggressiveness should be tempered by careful socialization and training without suppressing natural instincts to guard and protect. Behavior in the show ring should be controlled, willing and adaptable. The dog should be trained to submit to 'Hands On' examination. *Only the handler shall show the mouth.*"

Conscientious Russian breeders have tried to retain the Caucasian Ovtcharka's natural qualities, both in physique and temperament, while producing sounder dogs. One of the breed's primary appeals, according to Marina Kuznetsova is its "beautiful character." One hopes that Americans will work concertedly to preserve this extraordinary breed. "Treat your Caucasian with love and patience," Marina advises, "and you will get the best friend and protector, fearless and faithful, who will stand by you through anything and everything."

A group of Charts Polski in Poland.

Chapter 12

The Chart Polski

"Supremely elegant," is the way Betty Augustowski, of Severn, Maryland, describes the Chart Polski, Poland's native sighthound. "It's difficult to explain just how beautiful and elegant they are to those who haven't had the opportunity to see the breed. Their sense of presence in the ring, their inherent showiness and their outstanding movement, must be seen to be appreciated. My involvement with the Chart Polski has truly been a magnificent experience."

Those who have read the first volume of *A Celebration of Rare Breeds,* will recognize the names of Kaz and Betty Augustowski. They have been this country's premier promoters of the Polish Owczarek Nizinny Sheepdog, or PONS. Both Betty and Kaz are of Polish ancestry. One day, while leafing through the American Kennel Club's *The Complete Dog Book,* the couple realized that no Polish breeds were included on the A.K.C. roster. They wondered if there were any breeds native to Poland. Shortly thereafter, they saw an advertisement for Polish Lowland Sheepdogs (another name for the PONS) and soon the first of what would be many Polish Owczarek Nizinnies took up residence at the couple's Elzbieta Kennels. To date, eleven of the Augustowski's dogs have earned States Kennel Club championships and several are now International champions. "I still love the PONS and plan to continue my breeding program, hoping to improve on our record," Betty says. "The work with the PONS has been hard at times, but very rewarding. I must admit, however, that my involvement with the Chart Polski has been pure fun."

It was through the couple's involvement with the PONS that they first became acquainted with the Chart Polski. In 1985, Kaz and Betty were invited to Poland,

as guests, to attend the international dog show, held in Poznan. The night before the show a customary dinner was held for dignitaries and guests. That evening, there was a tribute to all of the native Polish breeds. One of the special features was an enormous display of old paintings and some photographs of a dog called the Chart Polski. Polish breeders had been hard at work reviving this ancient sighthound and were hoping to gain Federation Cynologique Internationale acceptance for the breed. "The paintings and photographs were simply breathtaking," Betty recalls. "The dogs were so gorgeous that I couldn't wait to see them in the flesh."

Anxious to see the Chart Polski, Betty was ushered to the benching area at the next day's show. "It was love at first sight," she confides. "I was in awe of the dogs. They were just so beautiful. They reminded me of magnificent Greyhounds, but their heads were very different. It was somewhat reminiscent of a Borzoi. I began to call the dogs 'Polish Greyhounds,' for the word 'Chart' is translated in Polish-English dictionaries as 'Greyhound.' The breeders quickly corrected me. They wanted me to know that the Chart Polski is a distinctive breed all its own.

"I watched them being judged and they were so very elegant. I've just got to have one of these dogs, I thought. I went to see my first litter and we almost took one home. Kaz and I discussed it, though. At the time, we had our hands full trying to get the PONS known in the U.S. and we were afraid that having another breed might hinder our progress. Kaz suggested that we wait and see what happened with F.C.I. recognition. I was heartbroken that I didn't return with a puppy. In retrospect, however, it was probably for the best."

Over the next three years, Betty Augustowski

carefully watched the progress of the Chart Polski. "The whole time, I kept writing, asking how the breed was doing." In due course, the Chart Polski was, indeed, recognized by the F.C.I. "I just couldn't get those long legged creatures off my mind," Betty recalls. "In 1988, we received another special invitation to come to Poland. We discussed the possibility of bringing at least one Chart Polski home with us and I was really looking forward to the trip. A few weeks before we were ready to leave, I received a letter from a good friend in Warsaw. There's a show quality bitch available, if you want her, he said. I immediately told him to hold her for me. "

Betty and Kaz were at ringside to watch the judging of the breed. "This was an international show and there were 17 of them in the ring. I took a video camera along to tape them. I saw this magnificent male, named Rosochaty, that I just couldn't take my eyes, or the camera, off. He was entered in what would be our Junior Class." Although he was the youngest dog en-

tered, he teemed with quality and his muscular appearance coupled with superb type, captivated the Americans. "Under F.C.I. rules, he was too young to earn his championship, but he sure caught the eye of the judge. He was awarded a gold medal."

When the Augustowskis returned from their trip, they were accompanied by the puppy bitch, Troska Celerrimus. Better known as "Peepcha," this first American Chart Polski has gone on to make history. She became the first International Champion for the breed and also has earned her South American, Puerto Rican and States Kennel Club championships. In addition, she has consistently placed in and topped the group, attaining these awards over top A.K.C. champions.

"Peepcha is a real dream," Betty says. "She is affectionate, intelligent, fast, obedient, beautiful, elegant and independent enough to be mysterious. In short, we adore her!" Peepcha has impressed others, too, and Betty was frequently asked when she planned to breed. "There's been tremendous interest from other sight-

The absolutely stunning International, South American, Puerto Rican and States K.C. Ch. Troska Celerrimus, owned by Kaz and Betty Augustowski, of Severn, Maryland.

Five dogs assemble at Poland's famed Celerrimus Kennel.

hound people. Peepcha is extremely showy and she just loves being in the ring and meeting people." So impressed was Betty with her first Chart Polski, that she imported a male, who has since finished his States Kennel Club championship. They have also added another bitch to their kennel.

In 1990, the Augustowskis again traveled to Poland. It was to be a momentous visit, in more ways than one, and one of the great surprises and thrills of Betty's life. "We stayed with a veterinarian friend in Warsaw," she says. "The President of the Poznan Kennel Club kept calling to find out when we'd arrive in Poznan. When we got there, the President and Vice President of the Club were waiting at the train station for us. They presented us with flowers and handed me a box of candy. They took us to the hotel, registered us, got the key and took us up to a suite. I was beginning to feel a little like Queen Elizabeth." Both Betty and Kaz were surprised by their reception. On past visits, Polish officials had been warm, but the Americans hadn't been accorded such royal treatment. "I think they're just being nice," Kaz said. "They know that we have these International champions and have been doing so much with the Polish breeds. This must be their way of saying thanks."

As usual, Kaz and Betty attended the pre-show dinner on Friday evening. "All these dignitaries were there. Because it was an International show, they had judges from all over the world," Betty says. "The first thing I noticed was the American flag up front. In the past, all the other countries were represented with flags, but never was the Stars and Stripes displayed. On previous visits, I'd been carefully warned not to say anything that might be considered political. It was a real surprise to see the American flag right next to the Polish flag.

"As the meeting progressed, they made a speech. It was in Polish so I couldn't catch what was said. They translated part of it for me and it said that the Polish Kennel Club wanted to thank the ambassadors from the United States for all the help that they had given Polish breeds. Then, they walked over and handed me a huge bouquet of roses. Everyone clapped and I, of course, was smiling. Then, they returned to the podium and continued with a long speech. They announced that we would receive gold medals and that we were the first Americans to receive an honorary lifetime membership in the Polish Kennel Club." Betty and Kaz were dumbfounded. "I must have looked like a real fool," Betty says. "I just couldn't stop crying. All the work of

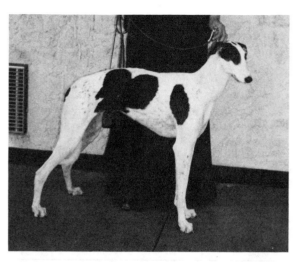

Elzbieta Kennel's lovely International, South American, Puerto Rican and States K.C. Champion, "Peepcha" has won many friends for the breed.

the last ten years, all the sleepless nights, all the dumb Polish jokes, all the work entailed in introducing a new breed to this country...I suddenly thought that it all had been worth it!"

Along with the medal, Betty was presented with a little leather bound book which looked something like a passport. "To tell you the truth, I didn't know what it said," Betty laughs. "I could see my name, but that was all." Later, Betty learned that the document said, "The Polish Kennel Club Board of Directors voted on October 20, 1990 to give Betty Augustowski a gold medal award and honorary membership for lifetime in the Polish Kennel Club." It was signed by the Board of Directors. On the opposite side of the page, the document reads: "This medal must be worn on the right side (of the body). The design of the medal and the regulations connected with this award have been approved by the Minister of Internal Affairs." Seeing the signature of this government official was a surprise and reflects the changing political climate in Poland. To Betty's delight, she learned that the award conferred other privileges. With this document, Betty can automatically get a visa to enter Poland, whereas in the past she had needed an invitation before securing a visa.

Surely, this would have been an incredible thrill for any dog lover. The Maryland duo had made dog history. But, further delights awaited the Augustowskis. "The next day we were personally taken to the dog show. They made sure that we had prime seats at the Chart Polski ring. I was sitting there with my video camera, when the judge saw me. He walked over, lifted up the ring rope and insisted that I step into the ring so I could have a better view of the dogs," Betty laughs. "I felt really foolish. Everyone was staring at me. I just

stepped off to the side and and tried to stay out of the way.

"As I watched the dogs in the ring, I spied this male. I couldn't quite believe it. It was Rosochaty, the dog I'd seen in the Junior class several years ago. He had matured now and he was truly magnificent. I later learned that he was one of Poland's top show dogs. That's quite an accomplishment since they don't have that many shows. In passing, the judge glanced at the dog, who immediately responded, wagging his tail enthusiastically. I just couldn't believe how gorgeous he was and his showiness thrilled me." Two days later, Kaz and Betty Augustowski became the proud owners of Rosochaty. Their purchase of the dog created quite a stir among Polish dog fanciers.

"I've really been having a ball showing this dog. His love for the ring, his superb type and his wonderful movement are winning many friends for the breed." In late 1990, Rosochaty made his debut in an American show ring. The famed Polish winner garnered a Group One and was pulled out, along with four other dogs, for the Best in Show consideration. He has since earned his States Kennel Club championship and Betty will be exhibiting him in International shows this year.

"It's really fun to show these dogs," Betty says. "From the minute we walk into the building all eyes turn. In Poland, the dogs win gold medals when they compete. Rosochaty has fifteen gold medals and they are traditionally worn on a chain around the neck. So, when he walks, all you hear is clank-clank-clank. In the ring, these dogs throw back their heads, like show horses, and fairly scream 'Look at me, I'm here.' When judges approach, they wag their tails with delight. It really makes them a pleasure to show."

Little is known of the Chart Polski's origins. In 1505, Roski Dymitir Samozwaniec introduced the breed to Russia. According to Thomas Borkowski, D.V.M., the first written mention of the breed dates back to 1600. The book, *La Natura*, published in 1825, describes a visit made by Prince Constantine the Great, to France, and gives some information on his short-haired sighthounds. In 1892, Sabaniejew, a Russian, gave a detailed description of the breed in *The Hunter's Calendar*. He describes the dogs as 29 to 31 1/2 inches tall and says that they were black, grey, blue or rusty red striped. They also sometimes had patches of color. Rarely, he says, were the dogs white. Whatever the exact origins may be, the breed has long been known, in his homeland, for his prowess in hunting wolf, fox, deer and rabbit. It was not until the beginning of the 19th century, that the name "Chart Polski" was applied to the breed.

The most important picture of the breed, however, emerges in the glorious paintings of noted Polish artists. Juliusza Kossaka, Jozefa Brandta and Alfreda

A beautiful head study of a Chart Polski, taken in Poland by Betty Augustokski.

Wierusz-Kowalskiego included the breed in their paintings. Depictions can also be seen in the sketches of Siemienski and Norblina. It was Julius Kossaka's wonderful portrayals of the breed, hunting with mounted Polish nobles, that have proved most enlightening to modern fanciers. Among authorities on Polish horses, Kossaka has a reputation for strict anatomical authenticity. When Polish fanciers began to revive the Chart Polski, they closely examined the works of Kossak to ensure that they maintained correct historical type.

In recent times, the Chart Polski almost ceased to exist. "The stormy history of Poland, its loss of independence and many social and political changes made it difficult to breed the Chart Polski," Dr. Borkowski writes. "Despite everything, some of the Chart Polski survived until contemporary times, mainly in the Eastern Region of Poland...also in the Kieleckiem Region around the town of Oleszna, on the former estate of Conrad Niemojewski."

In 1981, the Board of Directors of the Polish Kennel Club voted to open an introductory stud book for the Chart Polski. Critical work began to reactivate this old breed. In preparation for preparing a standard, H. Lipinska carefully analyzed the dogs shown in Kossaka's paintings. He said, "Kossak's great Hounds are tall, strong and muscular....The dogs behave with eminence and independence, without accompanying the person on the basis of partnership." Finally, after much study and years of work, the Chart Polski was officially recognized by the Polish Kennel Club. Although still rare, they are gaining quite a following in Poland.

The standard for the breed describes "a large muscular dog, clearly stronger and less slight of figure than other short haired sighthounds." It is important, however, that the Chart Polski never be so heavy as to be cumbersome or lose the impression of elegance. The preferred height of males is 28-32 inches, while bitches should be 27-30 inches at the shoulder. "Chart Polski larger than this are also desirable," the Standard says, "as long as they retain the proper proportions...Chart Polski smaller than the ideal are acceptable if they are otherwise well proportioned."

The ideal head, which Betty Augustowski likens to that of the Borzoi, should be lean, long and connote strength. A small "nose hump" is desirable and the skull should be flat with a barely noticeable stop. The almond-shaped eyes coordinate with the color of the dog, although dark eyes are most desirable. The standard says that their color may vary from "dark beer to amber." The expression of the eyes is one of the key features of the breed. "An outstanding feature of the Chart Polski is 'piercing eyes'....ever watchful, alert and vigilant."

The Chart Polski comes in a beautiful and interesting array of colors. Under the breed standard, all colors are permissible and none is given preference. Eye rims and nose should be black, although a slightly lighter shade is permissible in conjunction with such coat colors as blue or beige.

The breed standard describes the breed's temperament thusly: "The Chart Polski is a good tempered dog. It is loyal and normally reserved. It displays great courage under fire. During a chase, besides being extremely fast, the Chart Polski is also a very skillful and persistent hunter. It reacts quickly and confidently."

Betty Augustowski describes the breed in more personal terms. "They are very, very loving and incredibly affectionate. They love to go out and run, but they are very quiet and well-mannered in the house. In fact, mine could be considered real couch potatoes. They're incredibly obedient for a sighthound. At this point, Rosochaty only understands Polish. I've learned a few Polish commands over the years. If I say, 'Rosochaty, sit,' no matter what he's doing, he'll stop and obey me. This surprised me for I know that his owner's gave him absolutely no formal obedience training.

"I sometimes think sighthounds get a bad rap when it comes to obedience. Their sight is so incredible that they notice things that other dogs don't. Therefore, they can be more easily distracted. When we were obedience training one of our bitches, we performed a little test just for fun. We gave her the 'down' signal from over 100 feet away and she dropped immediately. Their eyesight is just incredible."

With their winning personalities, intriguing elegance and natural showiness, the Chart Polski should win a host of loyal admirers in this country. Betty and Kaz have imported outstanding stock to begin a breeding program and look forward to the first American litter. "I feel that we now have a very good basis for beginning the breed in the United States. I hope others will have as much fun as I have had with my Charts."

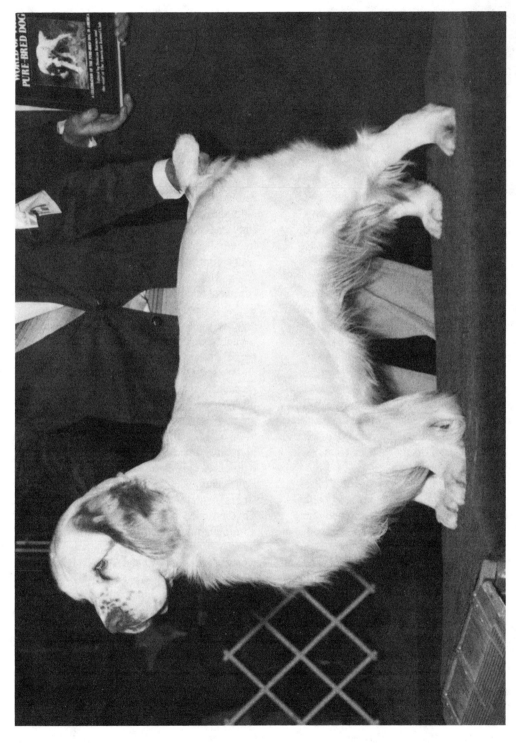

The beautiful group winner American, Puerto Rican, Dominican, Los Americas and South American Ch. Topjay's Pina Colada, owned by Ruth Gardner, of Ponca City, Oklahoma.

Chapter 13

The Clumber Spaniel

I have a confession to make: I love Clumber Spaniels. I suppose dog writers should stand back and dispassionately discuss the breeds they are describing. I find that this approach is an absolute impossibility when it comes to the Clumber. All pretense of objectivity goes right out the window when talking about this grand old dog.

I know the breed has been described as dignified, even pensive, but it's hard for me to think of the Clumber in those terms. That great massive head with the kind, gentle, oh so loving eyes, just melts my heart. The merry "woof, woof" greeting, coupled with the rapidly wagging tail (no, that's not right: the whole rear end of the dog wiggles in excitement) and the inevitable ball, sock or toy, held in its mouth, never fails to bring a smile to my lips. Sit yourself down on the floor beside a Clumber and he's likely to heave his massive body right into your lap, for his greatest pleasure in life is to be near you. And, on a colorful autumn day, to be afield with a Clumber; his nose twitching as he scents the air, his white coat the perfect foil to nature's fall display, and his tail twitching from side to side...well, life doesn't get much better than that.

There's been some debate about the Clumber's origin. Most authorities believe that the breed originated in France and was then introduced into England. All trace of the Clumber has mysteriously disappeared from France, though, and the French categorize the breed as purely British. James Farrow, in his 1912 book on the breed, took great pains to prove that the Clumber was entirely British, descending from the old Blenheim Spaniel. There seems little to support this, however, for it fails to explain some of the unique type differences

which set the Clumber apart from other British spaniels. Such nationalistic pride has often caused British writers to ascribe a homebred origin to their favorite breeds (the case of the Pug springs immediately to mind). Patriotism aside, the breed does seem to have originated in France. However, it is to the Brits that we owe the lion's share of gratitude for today's Clumber Spaniel. Without their diligent work, the breed would have become, as so many others have, a mere historical footnote rather than a thriving, useful and unique breed.

The story goes that a French sportsman, the Duc de Noailles, maintained a pack of largely white hunting spaniels. With the coming of the French Revolution, the aristocracy rightly feared for their lives. Mobs, unhappy with the excesses of Louis XVI and his followers, began to gather. In this charged atmosphere, the Duc must have had an inkling of the upheaval that would befall his country. Unwilling to sacrifice his dogs, he packed them up, lock, stock and barrel, and sent them across the Channel, to a fellow hunting enthusiast, Henry Clinton, who two years later would become the second Duke of Newcastle. Perhaps the Duc hoped that, when the terror had passed, he would again be able to claim his dogs. But it was not to be. The Duc de Noailles went to the guillotine, in 1789, and Henry Clinton became the sole owner of this spaniel strain.

The future Duke of Newcastle welcomed the dogs to his estate, Clumber Park, in Sherwood Forest. That the Duke treasured his newfound hunting companions, there can be no doubt. He jealously guarded the strain and tried to keep them as his and his alone. He placed William Mansell in charge of breeding, rearing and training the dogs. For thirty years, Mansell oversaw

Ruth Gardner's impressive Ch. Dappledown Stonewall is the sire of 24 champions.

the Duke's kennels and he, according to Idstone, "made it his study to produce this race of dogs unmixed..." So closely guarded were the dogs of Clumber Park, that they became known only as the Duke's or Mansell's breed. The 1807 issue of *Sporting Magazine* proclaimed that "The Duke's (or Mansell's) breed is still held in higher estimation than any other spaniel kind."

The English have always been known as a nation of dog lovers. Noblemen frequently had their portraits painted with their much loved dogs. The Duke was no exception. In 1788, he commissioned Francis Wheatly to paint a picture of him and his favorite dogs, engaged in his passion...hunting. The resulting portrait depicts the Duke, Mansell and a friend, Colonel Litchfield, as they pause for a respite from the day's hunt. Featured prominently in the foreground, are three early Clumber Spaniels. It is believed that these three dogs were among the original French imports. Wheatly's painting has proven, therefore, to be an invaluable aid to Clumber historians, showing them, in detail, what those early dogs looked like. Though undoubtedly smaller than modern Clumbers, the dogs clearly show many of the characteristics that survive today.

It was folly to believe that a hunting dog as talented as the Clumber could remain a purely private strain. Those who came to hunt with the Duke were impressed with the new spaniel's prowess. Some were fortunate enough to receive a gift of one of the Duke's treasured dogs. Gradually, Clumbers spread throughout the vast estates around Robin Hood's old stomping grounds. This lovely bastion of the aristocracy was known as "The Dukeries" and in the hunting fields, which surrounded the region's castles, the Clumber was *the* dog to own. Indeed, a list of Clumber enthusiasts of the time reads like a veritable roll call of the British gentry.

Game abounded in the woods and fields which comprised Sherwood Forest. The wealthy sportsmen

could afford to maintain large kennels of dogs and they employed huntsmen or gamekeepers to attend to the dogs' care and training. Clumbers were often hunted in packs of six or more dogs for the battué type hunting that was the style of the day. A line of Clumbers would set out before the men with their guns to beat or flush any game from their hidden coverts. They worked slowly, thoroughly and methodically, with little escaping their keen noses. Their white coats glinted in the sun and their silent method of hunting did not alarm the game. Some owners, though, preferred to attach bells to the collars of their Clumbers to aid them in driving the game forward. The rougher the going became, the denser the cover, the more hedgerows in which the prey could escape, the better the Clumber liked it. He proved an unerring finder of game, be it birds or rabbits. Clumber training was intensive and, fortunately, the dogs proved to be apt pupils, taking readily to the early training methods. Some packs of dogs hunted with an almost military precision. When a bird took flight, the dogs were trained to drop immediately to the ground or perhaps the hunter preferred to have them gather about him. One or two dogs, particularly proficient retrievers, were sent to reclaim the fallen birds. These they presented, with great pride, to the hunter. Sadly, this grand style of hunting was to fall from favor. Human beaters replaced the canines and there was little need to employ a huntsmen and maintain large kennels.

It was inevitable that the Clumber Spaniel would come to the attention of the general public. They, too, heard the glorious reports of the breed's achievements in the field. By the mid-1800's, a few Clumbers began to be seen outside the estates. The British gentry had always taken great pride in the excellence of their dogs. Litters were regularly culled to ensure top quality. It was probably due to this practice that the Clumber spread beyond the Dukeries. Clandestinely, gamekeepers would report that a puppy had been destroyed. Instead, it had secretly been whisked away and sold to an eagerly waiting public. Gamekeepers found that they could supplement their incomes, quite handsomely, through the sale of surplus puppies. It was because of this practice that Vero Shaw reported, in his 1879-81 work, *The Illustrated Book of the Dog,* that "indifferent Clumbers fetched very high prices when in the market. Of recent years, however, dogs of this variety can be more readily procured, and their value has sensibly diminished."

Though excited by the recommendation of noble sportsmen, the Clumber had to prove his worth to the average hunter. This he did with resounding success. "The Clumber has always been a popular Spaniel with sportsmen," Vero Shaw observes, "and his character fully entitles him to the respect which he has won from the highest in the land.

"In addition to his aristocratic associations, the Clumber Spaniel has much to recommend him to the general body of sportsmen, who...are more inclined to value a sporting dog on account of his own intrinsic merit than because he has been the recipient of patrician patronage. In covert shooting...the Clumber is almost unsurpassed by any breed...single specimens can readily be broken to retrieve and take water, which naturally increases their value very considerably in the sportsmen's eyes...It is not many sportsmen, however, who are in a position to work with a team of Clumbers, as few kennels contain a sufficient number to enable them to do so, but....a single Clumber Spaniel is a valuable assistance to the sportsman engaged in covert shooting."

The Clumber had made the transition. No longer was he just the sporting companion of the aristocracy, who could afford to employ full time trainers with no duties other than turning out polished field dogs. He was embraced by the single hunter, who was more concerned with filling the pot than just having a pleasant day in the field. The Clumber Spaniel had proven to be a valuable all-rounder. Easy to train, inherently birdy, keen nosed, soft mouthed and useful on both land and water. What more could a hunter ask for?

Though the Clumber had been adopted by the ranks of general sportsmen, he continued to be a favorite with the wealthy, too. Prince Albert, who married Queen Victoria, in 1840, was swept up in the great tide of Clumber Spaniel popularity. In fact, when he received his first dog, he was to start a grand family tradition of devotion to the breed. His son, King Edward VII, shared his father's love of sport. An ardent admirer of the breed, he spent many happy hours hunting with the family Clumbers. But, it was his son, King George V, who was to become the world's most famous Clumber enthusiast. At the family estate, Sandringham, the King could often be found in the field with his dogs. He is said to have proclaimed that the Clumber was the greatest and most reliable of any breed of gundog. His dogs were meticulously trained and reported to be superb hunters. The King was known far and wide for his love of hunting and was an excellent shot. He expected the best from his dogs and seldom was disappointed. So fond was he of his dogs and proud of their abilities, that at the end of the day's hunt, he stooped to pet and personally thank each dog for giving it's all. King George's great passion for the Clumber Spaniel stayed with him throughout his entire life. Many are the tales of the aged King, hobbling about the field with his beloved companions. In later years, this portrait of the old King and his dogs would work to the Clumber's detriment. The notion arose that the breed was only fit for use by "old men on shooting sticks." It's more likely, actually, that the dogs geared their hunting style to suit the needs of their royal master.

But, things were to change on the British sporting scene. There were new breeds...specialists...and the popularity of the all-rounder diminished. Spaniel devotees wanted dogs with more speed and style. They preferred a breed with dash rather than the slow, meticulous work of the Clumber. As the world wars came, they changed the lives of the Clumber's wealthy patrons, too. Though now known to the general public, the kennels of the gentry had remained the strongholds of the breed. No longer could the aristocracy afford the luxury of vast estates, with a battery of servants and large kennels, staffed with attendants and specialized trainers. The golden age of the Clumber Spaniel was declining. Brian Ghent and Eric Gillibrand, in their charming 1953 book, *That's a Good Dog,* speak poignantly of the changes which came. The Clumber, they say, "stands for an era, for a way of life which is slipping away, for the days of the gentry in Britain. And as the big estates shrink, and the housing estate thrusts its way into what was once pleasant parkland, so does the Clumber's domain pass from his reach."

The Clumber Spaniel was an early participant in British dog events. He made his show ring debut, in 1859, in Birmingham. These days we're apt to think of the Clumber strictly as a show dog, but that was not always the case. As Colonel R. Claude Cane points out, in Robert Leighton's 1921 work, *The New Book of the Dog,* "The Field Trials have, no doubt, had a great deal to do with the largely augmented popularity of the breed and the great increase in the number of those who own Clumbers. For the first two or three years after these were truly established no other breed seemed to have a chance with them; and even now, though both English and Welsh Springers have done remarkably well, they more than hold their own." The Clumber proved successful both in the field and on the bench. "A good many have, I am pleased to say," Colonel Cane reports, "won prizes both at Field Trials and in the show ring." Indeed,

A litter of three week old puppies, owned by Ruth Gardner.

81

many owners proudly displayed their dogs in British show rings. In 1934, King George joined the ranks of Clumber exhibitors. He selected three dogs, from his kennel of fourteen Clumbers, to be exhibited at a show.

While the Clumber has never regained the fame and popularity it had, during those halcyon days of royal patronage, he has retained a loyal following in Great Britain. Diehards have staunchly maintained their Clumber breeding programs, jealously guarding their bloodlines with all the fervor of William Mansell, in the 1700's. They continue to take their Clumbers out into the fields in order to ensure that hunting abilities are maintained.

The Clumber Spaniel was one of the earliest breeds to come to North America. Indeed, it was one of the ten breeds originally recognized by the American Kennel Club when it was formed, in 1884. The first imports appear to have made their debut in Canada. In 1842, Lieutenant (later Major) Venable was sent, with Her Majesty's 97th Regiment, to the garrison in Halifax, Nova Scotia. Accompanying him were several Clumber Spaniels. The dogs proved quite popular with the military men who spent their spare hours hunting. Locals were impressed with the Clumbers' performance, too. Soon, new imports joined the Venable dogs. For years, the Clumber would remain a popular hunting dog with folks in the region. Writing in 1891, Mr. F.H.F. Mercer declared that "Halifax now undoubtedly numbers more Clumbers in its canine population than any other city on the continent."

Mr. Mercer began a one-man public relations campaign to champion the interests of the Clumber Spaniel. "Of ancient and high lineage, useful, strong, enduring, faithful, watchful and beautiful—surely the Clumber Spaniel is deserving of popularity," he wrote. "It is therefore most gratifying, to those of us who know

Eighteen month old Clumgi's Maxwell McClumber. Max was bred by Freda Rountree and is owned by Patricia Farnsworth, of Ely, Nevada.

and love this noble dog, to observe that he is becoming more and more popular in America every year; that he is being sought after to-day by sportsmen who a few years ago either knew or cared nothing for him; that good specimens of the breed now sell readily for prices that a few years ago would have been thought by every American exorbitant. It is gratifying to know that...each year's entry of this breed at our bench shows indicate that the Clumber is a coming dog, and it is safe to predict that in time he will become almost as numerous and as generally popular in this country as is the Setter to-day."

Despite Mr. Mercer's optimistic prediction, the Clumber did not achieve great popularity in either Canada or the U.S. Statistics compiled by the Clumber Spaniel Club of America (CSCA), show how scant show ring appearances were until recent years. "Their appearance at shows was sporadic until 1903 when two new exhibitors...created a revival of interest, but competition was still somewhat scattered. From 1876-1931, 19 Clumbers attained the title of champion in this country. 1935 to 1942 saw 26 more finish....In the next 25 years, only 4 Clumber Spaniels got a ch. in front of their names..."

But, 1968 would prove to be a turning point for the breed. Several fanciers took up the cause of the Clumber, importing top notch stock from England. Soon, the dogs began appearing in shows around the country. During the early and mid 1970's, there were several Clumbers who regularly topped the sporting group and strutted their stuff in Best in Show rings. The massive dogs, with the flashy white coats, caught the eye of many knowledgeable dog people. Soon, there were new Clumber enthusiasts and breeders had waiting lists for their puppies. "Well over 100 Clumbers have attained the title of Champion in the U.S." the C.S.C.A. says, "and the majority have been after 1968." This statistic, compiled in 1977, is now out of date. The number of Clumber champions, since that time, has risen dramatically.

Among the Spaniel clan, the Clumber is truly a standout. Those seeing the breed for the first time, are apt to pause, let out a whistle and mumble "magnificent." Like the Basset Hound, the Clumber is a large dog on short legs. His low-slung massive body fairly screams power. And a powerful dog he certainly is. While males stand only 19-20 inches at the shoulder, they carry a hefty 70-85 pound weight. Females are only slightly smaller, standing 17-19 inches and tipping the scales at a solid 55 to 70 pounds. The Clumber has a broad deep chest and a wide body which ends in an endlessly wagging docked tail. With his wide body and short legs, Clumbers have a slightly rolling motion when they move out.

The Clumber's distinctive head has a well defined stop, heavy brow and pronounced occipital protuberance. When the ears are alertly raised, the Clumber has a somewhat frowning expression, often described as "thoughtful." The muzzle, when viewed from the side, has a square look. The soft, deep set eyes are dark amber in color. In some specimens, the haw may show. The nose comes in shades of brown, from beige to rose or cherry. A distinctive breed characteristic are the vine-shaped ears.

One of the breed's loveliest qualities is its coat. The Clumber's primarily white color makes him stand out in the sporting group. Clumbers often have lemon or orange markings and the muzzle and front legs are often freckled. Generally, the fewer markings on the body, the better. The soft coat is straight and lies flat. In these days, when spaniel coats are extensively shaved and thinned, the Clumber's natural appearance is refreshing. Clumbers are never shaved and the only the feet and tail are trimmed to present a neater appearance. The white coat seems to shed dirt easily and a weekly brushing, with special attention to the area behind the ears, will keep this breed looking presentable. Those interested in the Clumber should be aware that this breed does shed. "You tend to have white hairs everywhere," says Ruth Gardner, of Ponca City, Oklahoma. "The hairs are rather static in nature and this makes them difficult to brush off. I used to love wearing navy blue before I got my Clumbers. But, no more. Still, while annoying, it's a small price to pay for the joy of sharing your home with Clumber Spaniels."

In this country, most Clumbers are kept as companions and show dogs. The breed, however, can still earn its keep in the field. Like all true spaniels, the Clumber flushes his game. He has proven adept on quail, woodcock, pheasant, dove and grouse. He's particularly useful in dense thickets, ditches and hedgerows. As in days of old, thick covert is the breed's forte. The Clumber's white coat allows him to be easily seen by the hunter. The Clumber is often criticized for being slow in the field, but this pace suits him well in heavy cover. He keeps within shotgun range, a boon to those who prefer to hunt on foot. And, those who expect to see a ponderous, slow, lazy dog in the field, may find themselves surprised by the energy and industriousness of the Clumber. Dogs of this breed also have a fine reputation for being soft-mouthed and for their prowess at retrieving. Most Clumbers love the water and will readily retrieve wildfowl, adding another dimension to the hunter's enjoyment.

The Clumber's chief asset, however, is not his appeal as a show dog nor even his laudable enthusiasm in the field. It is his personality and great charm that endears him to owners. "Once a Clumber owner, always a Clumber owner. Few breeds return the same amount of loyalty a Clumber gives an affectionate owner,"

Clumgi's Dear Abby, owned by Freda Rountree and Jo Goldstein, sits at the table, while Clumgi's Duncan Dugud, owned by Freda Rountree, of Cordova, Tennessee, relaxes on the table.

states the booklet prepared by the CSCA. "His jingle bell personality and perceptive intelligence make him a much loved member of the family."

Always affectionate with their owners, Clumbers can vary in their response to strangers. Some are outgoing extroverts who rush to meet every new person as a long lost friend. Others are more reserved with outsiders, preferring to sit back and size a person up. "In general, they are a very laid back breed," says Ruth Gardner. "They are not at all aggressive and will do well in a home with other dogs." Ruth obtained her first Clumber after her husband died. "My daughter raised Cockers and really wanted me to have one," she recalls. "But Cockers were her breed and I wanted something different. I went to a show and it was there I saw my first Clumber. I fell head over heels in love with that dog. I decided then and there that I simply had to have one. In those days, Clumbers were quite rare. It took me over a year to finally get my first one. While they're more numerous today, you may still have to be patient and wait to get a Clumber puppy."

All Clumber Spaniels love attention. "The affectionate nature is one of the Clumber Spaniel's endearing qualities," writes Mrs. C.W. Marion, in the April 1977 issue of *Pure-Bred Dogs, The American Kennel Gazette.* "His foremost desire is to be loved and actually hugged in your arms. Our Clumbers are happiest when we sit right down on the floor with them and let them crawl up by our legs and cuddle as close as they can get to us, actually curling their head around our neck if allowed....The Clumber Spaniel...really can't get enough petting and sometimes I kiddingly will call one of ours a pest while they keep on nuzzling to get more attention. I love every minute of it."

You'll never doubt, for a single moment, where you stand in your Clumber's eyes. "Upon return home, a Clumber owner can pretty much count on an ecstatic welcome from his pal," Mrs. Marion writes. "Actually any separation from your dog, however short, may bring on this demonstration. The dog usually won't jump up and down, but he will wiggle back and forth almost touching his tail to his nose." The Clumber Spaniel Club of America would certainly agree with this assessment. "Many Clumbers will wag their whole back ends while bending their long bodies so that the head almost touches the rear—all the while dancing a little jig. It is quite unique and captivating."

"His greeting isn't only 'body language,' there is also a verbal hello," Mrs. Marion reports. "He seems to blow up his lips while making a noise that is sort of a cross between a growl and human talk. It is anything but a growl. It is the Clumber Spaniel's way of saying, 'hello, I'm so glad to see you and that you are here with me.' In our family, it is a special language familiarly referred to as 'Clumberese.' Not all Clumbers speak it but most do, some more fluently than others. It is their way of giving or trying to get attention."

The Clumber is a natural born retriever and dogs will often greet people by presenting them with some favorite object. "This seems to be an inherent Clumber trait," Ruth Gardner says. "They love to carry things about. When a stranger approaches my fence, my dogs will often go and get a ball and carry it to the visitor in greeting." Mrs. Marion agrees. "They constantly want to bring some object to their master. I don't mean just a bird in the field, which is of course their first love, or the dumbbell in obedience exercises. Everyday life in a Clumber home sees wash cloths, socks, potholders, or whatever happens to be at hand, or probably better said 'at mouth,' proudly brought by the Clumber to his owner. The dog's head is carried high, he is so pleased with himself, you take it away from him, replace it to its proper spot and your heart is warmed."

With his affectionate nature and extreme desire to please, the Clumber Spaniel is an easy to train dog, whether for field work or as a home companion. New owners must realize, however, that the Clumber is most definitely a spaniel. Like all spaniels, he simply will not respond to harsh treatment. When treated thusly, the Clumber's likely to plant his feet and simply refuse to budge. No amount of tugging, pulling or yelling will make him move. While some might refer to such a response as obstinate or stupid, it's the Clumber's own personal way of telling you that such tactics just won't

work. For centuries, the spaniel breeds have been known for their aversion to a heavy hand and, because they are so darned eager to please and do your bidding, such rough treatment simply isn't necessary.

"This affectionate nature makes it easy to train this breed because they respond to attention, petting and warm words of approval," Mrs. Marion says. "The trainer doesn't have to give the Clumber a heavy-handed approach. Occasionally, a Clumber may take on a bad habit, getting away with something early in his life that shouldn't have been allowed. When time comes for correction, it will not be a major project to straighten out the situation. With affection from the trainer your Clumber would rather respond to what is asked of him than continue in his old ways which are to your disliking. He likes to give you his attention and he likes also to have your attention. If you take advantage of his need to please and show him what you want from him, you will shortly find you will have a very happy relationship between man and dog." New owners should be advised that, like most sporting breeds, the Clumber goes through an adolescent period when he is inclined to chew and may be temporarily destructive. Crate training, during this crucial time, is a must.

With his gentle, kind and docile ways, the Clumber is an excellent choice for a family with children. The breed is large enough to stand up to rough housing and very patient with youngsters. Despite his great bulk, Clumbers have a reputation for being especially gentle with infants. Generally, Clumbers and kids hit it off great. The dog will spend many happy hours retrieving any object the child cares to throw. Indeed, Clumber Spaniels can become quite devoted to and protective of their pint-sized charges.

"A Clumber Spaniel puppy looks like a happy little bear," write Brian Ghent and Eric Gillibrand in *That's a Good Dog,* "and a full-grown Clumber is a great, bustling creature that reminds me of an Irish washerwoman, with the same tenderness of heart and loyalty of spirit." It's that tender spirit, that wonderful good-natured personality and the abiding and enduring loyalty that thrills Clumber owners. To know a Clumber Spaniel is to love him and it would take the most hard hearted soul not to be won over by the breed's great charm. I confess, I am one of those who have succumbed to that legendary charm and, as I conclude this chapter, you can sign me "A Clumber Spaniel Fan."

Chapter 14

The Coton de Tulear

The rarest of the Bichon group, worldwide, the Coton de Tulear hails from Madagascar. It's island home is located in the Indian Ocean, off Africa's east coast. The island kingdom is, perhaps, best known as the home of most of the world's lemurs. And yet, it is in this remote corner of the earth that the joyous, cottony coated dog developed.

The breed's history is poorly documented, but is, obviously, closely associated with the other Bichon breeds. Madagascar and the surrounding islands were first discovered by a Portuguese seaman, in the 1500's. A fleet of ships was bound for India and, as they passed the Cape of Good Hope, Diogo Dias' ship was blown off course by a violent storm. He landed on Madagascar. In the early 1600's, Portuguese missionaries came to the island, intent on converting the natives. They were unsuccessful. The French came to Madagascar, in 1642, and established a garrison. The Malagasy natives rebelled and massacred many of the foreigners. The remaining French were hastily evacuated and Madagascar became the haven of pirates who preyed on ships bound for India. The French came again in 1768 and, during the subsequent decades, succeeded in establishing themselves on the island. It was an uncomfortable relationship, punctuated by rebellions and outright war. Still, Madagascar remained a French colony until 1946.

Breed authorities tell us that the cottony coated dogs made their first appearance on the Mascarene Islands. Considering the region's history, we may speculate that the initial stock arrived from France. The dogs were principally raised in the port city of Reunion. They proved to be a popular trade commodity and were often taken to nearby Madagascar. Eventually, the little dogs of Reunion became extinct.

The dogs imported to Madagascar, though, thrived. They were embraced by nobles of the Merina tribe. The Merinas, of Indonesian descent, were among the original inhabitants of Madagascar, and were fiercely proud of their country. Malagasy society ran on a caste system with the Merinas divided into nobles and freemen. Coton de Tulear ownership was restricted to the nobility. In fact, they enacted laws making it a criminal offense for anyone other than Merina nobles to own the breed.

Today, the Coton de Tulear is rare in its own homeland. Merina officials and merchants still dote on the breed, but there are few kennels actively raising Cotons. The few breeders are very dedicated, jealously guarding and maintaining the breed.

In 1974, American Robert J. Russell first "discovered" the Malagasy breed. He journeyed to Madagascar to conduct studies for his doctorate in tropical biology. Each day, he passed the home of a Merina businessman. A long time dog lover, Russell was captivated by the lively, bouncing dog which frolicked in the front yard. He paused briefly each day to play with the little dog. Intrigued, Russell asked about the dog and learned that he had stumbled upon a Coton de Tulear.

Russell's fascination with the little dog led him to seek out the few remaining breeders on the island. Initially, he was discouraged for the breeders were reluctant to sell their cherished dogs to foreigners. They were doubly skeptical about allowing their treasured pets to leave the country. But Russell's persistence and sincerity finally paid off. He managed to acquire several Cotons and they accompanied him when he returned to the United States.

Robert Russell's parents fell in love with his new

dogs. The dogs' elegant appearance and loving, affectionate personalities won them over. J. Lewis and Roberta Russell established their Oakshade Kennels, in 1975, in Marlton, New Jersey. They billed themselves, and rightly so, as the "sole breeders of the Coton de Tulear in the Western Hemisphere." Others were interested in these new imports, too. In 1976, the Coton de Tulear Club of America was formed.

Oakshade has remained the cornerstone of the breed. They are very careful in placing puppies and aim to protect the breed. All dogs sold are expected to be full fledged members of the family. No puppies leave the kennel until they are at least five months old and have been fully evaluated. Show puppies sell for $2,500 and pet quality dogs command $1,325. Those who wish to purchase a pet must also pay for the cost of neutering and the operation is performed before the dog leaves the kennel. Despite the high price, the demand for Cotons is such that buyers routinely have to join a waiting list. There's an average wait of eight to twelve months for a puppy. A deposit of $1,000 for show quality pups and $525 for pet dogs is required before your name will be added to the waiting list. You should be aware that there is a 25% cancellation fee should you change your mind. While many breeders recommend crating puppies, for short periods of time, as an aid to training, this is not the case at Oakshade. "Confinement by cage for any reason is considered...as cruel and unreasonable treatment," a brochure from the kennel says.

The other Bichon breeds have grown and prospered in this country, attracting a host of loyal, dedicated breeders. Even the recently introduced Bolognese is attracting conscientious and experienced breeders. This, however, has not really been the case with the Coton. We occasionally see a litter of Cotons advertised nationally, but, by and large, Oakshade remains the sole source of the breed. After 17 years, it is still the only nationally advertised kennel devoted exclusively to the breed.

The Coton de Tulear is an attractive little dog. His sparkling dark eyes are rimmed in black. The nose and lips, as well as the foot pads, are also black. The skull is slightly rounded, with a moderately pronounced stop. The Coton's dropped ears are carried close to the cheek and covered in profuse flowing hair.

The breed has a long elegant neck and a compact body with a deep chest. The topline is generally straight. The tail may be carried either straight or curled over the rump. The Coton must weigh less than 15 pounds and should not exceed 13 inches at the withers.

The breed takes its name, of course, from the dry, cottony texture of the coat. It should never be silky in texture. The coat is long and flowing with a touseled natural appearance. A profuse moustache and beard add

This delightful Coton de Tulear is Sage, owned by Barbara Carlin, of Ft. Myers, Florida.

to the charming impression. The eyes are usually hidden beneath a heavy fall of hair. Breeders are intent on keeping the Coton a natural breed, with no trimming or scissoring allowed on dogs destined for the show ring.

The lovely Coton de Tulear comes in three color variations. White is the most commonly seen color. Dogs may be either pure white or have small patches of cream colored hair. Cotons also come in black and white. In this pattern, distinctive patches of black are set on a white background. A striking tri-color variation is also seen. The standard describes this color as "mostly white and cream, but tinged with beige areas; black hairs dust portions of the ears and sometimes the body and beard."

As with any long coated breed, the Coton's coat requires regular grooming. The cottony texture does tend to tangle and mat if left unattended. Daily brushing, making sure to get down to the skin, will keep the coat in good condition. For show dogs, the natural look is the order of the day. The Coton de Tulear should never be clipped and sculpted like its cousin the Bichon Frise. Pet owners do occasionally clip the long tresses, particularly on the face, to make the dogs easier to care for.

The Coton has been bred, for centuries, specifically to be a companion. He performs this job admirably. Owners report that the breed is affectionate and loving, with an outgoing, friendly nature. Generally, Cotons are calm, easy going dogs with an inquisitive nature. Owners frequently describe their dogs as "laid back."

This breed bonds closely with its owners. They are happiest when they can be near and love playing the

The cottony textured coat gave the breed its name. This is Barbara Carlin's Sage.

part of cuddly lap dogs. Many owners say that their Cotons follow them around, checking on them as they go about their daily tasks. These dogs really do crave and thrive on human attention and you must be prepared to spend time with them. They will certainly repay you with utter devotion. One characteristic is particularly endearing to owners. The Coton has a charming habit of smiling or grinning. Owners often describe it as "laughing."

An intelligent breed, the Coton de Tulear is eager to please and easily trained. An outgoing dog, this breed adapts readily to the show ring and enjoys obedience training. Around the house, dogs are usually quiet, but they will sound the alarm when a stranger approaches.

The breed should be considered a hardy and rugged little dog, not a mere ornament. Most owners report that their Cotons greatly enjoy a good rough-housing session and get along well with children and other dogs. One should ensure that the Coton is never paired with an aggressive dog, though. The breed has a submissive nature and may not defend itself if challenged.

The temperament and personality I've described are characteristic of a confident, well-adjusted Coton de Tulear. Unfortunately, some problems have surfaced in recent years. A number of owners have reported that, much to their disappointment, their Cotons are excessively shy, fearful and cringing. They startle and panic

easily, often running fearfully from strangers. Such dogs are apt to adopt a particular member of the family, fleeing from all others. Characteristically, the dogs often whine, hide under beds, couches or chairs, roll on their backs and urinate when excited or nervous.

Coton de Tulear Tips, a publication of the Coton de Tulear Club of America, reports that "...a few owners (less than 3%) have reported that their beloved Coton is excessively shy, nervous of all strangers and even some members of their human family. This observation disturbs us very much. It means that some Cotons and their families are miserable...."

While the Club places the number of afflicted dogs at 3%, some reports indicate that the number may be higher. Authorities on the other Bichon breeds tell us that socialization, from a very young age, is vital. They feel that it's the key to developing a sound, well-adjusted and confident dog. Exposing puppies to strange people and situations is the best policy. Unfortunately, the policies at Oakshade may prevent this approach. Since puppies are retained until at least five months of age, they have little exposure to outside influences. The kennel, admittedly, allows few visitors.

According to *Coton de Tulear Tips,* "the condition is curable." They recommend patience, gentle reprimands and obedience training. Indeed, vigilant owners do find that their dogs improve with time. Some have seen an improvement in six months while others say it's taken them two years for the dog to fully come into his own. It would be best to query breeders on what steps they have taken to properly socialize their pups. It can be a bitter pill to swallow, having paid a high price for a dog, waited months for his arrival and then discover that he is excessively shy and will require months of work.

It's truly a pleasure to welcome this Malagasy breed to the United States. The Coton has a charming and enchanting personality and a regal air. One hopes that he will attract a bevy of loyal and dedicated owners, intent on preserving the breed. Our thanks go to the Russell family for introducing us to the "Royal Dog of Madagascar."

"It may very well turn out," writes Bruce Wolk, in the July 1984 issue of *Dog World,* "that by allowing the establishment of a 'new colony' apart from Madagascar, the Coton de Tulear may have been ultimately saved from extinction. Madagascar has been in severe political turmoil. The Coton, a symbol of the past, might possibly become the target for a lot of unjustified anger and be destroyed." One hopes that this will never occur. The demise of the delightful Coton de Tulear would truly be the dog world's loss.

The impressive Ch. Summerwind's Charles Dickens CD, WC is the only Curly to win a Best in Show in the U.S. He is also a two time Westminster Best of Breed winner and a National Specialty winner. His proud owners are Michael and Sue Tokolics and Debbie Wales.

Chapter 15

The Curly-Coated Retriever

"If any breed of gundog deserves letters after its name this one does! In my opinion it should have D.S.D.X. (meaning Duck-Shooter's Dog Excellent), because over the centuries he has done his job magnificently, and it is a great pity that fashion is now phasing him out of existence. I can accept that no one these days has 'Major Taylor' handlebars on his bicycle, and that Mother no longer wears a bustle, but the way in which shooters have turned their backs on such a friend as the curly-coated retriever is little short of disgraceful," says Roy Burnell, Australian sporting dog authority, who has owned and hunted with Curlies since boyhood. *(Gundogs for Field and Trial, 1972)*

"Little or nothing seems to be known of the history of this dog so extensively bred throughout the United Kingdom," wrote Stonehenge, in 1878. His statement is certainly true, for there is little agreement on the origin of the Curly-Coat. This is undoubtedly due to the fact that the breed is the oldest of the retriever family. Most authorities concede that the Curly is descended from the extinct 16th century dog, the English Water Spaniel. Writing in *The Sportsman's Repository*, in 1820, John Scott tells us that this dog "burns with inextinguishable ardor in the pursuit, and which merely for the gratification of swimming after and bringing to shore a bird that he is neither destined nor desires to taste, will risk his life in the most dangerous abysses, or carry himself by repetitions of labour and fatigue to the very verge of existence."

Other authorities suggest that the Irish Water Spaniel played a part in the breed's formation. McCarthy, the originator of that breed, strongly denied the claim. Many authorities believe that the Lesser Newfoundland, Labrador or St. John's Newfoundland (all names for the same breed), the progenitor of today's Labrador Retriever, was a contributor to the Curly-Coat. This may be so for the breed was crossed with many of the retrieving breeds. Some suggest that crosses to retrieving setters were attempted, but the Curly shows little setter influence. Probably due to the coat type, many early writers suggested a cross to the Poodle. Other authorities vehemently deny this assertion.

We may never know the truth of the Curly-Coated Retriever's origin. But, by the mid-1800's, the breed was popular with British sportsmen. Gamekeepers treasured the Curly's unerring nose and persistence in the field. The advent of dog shows, in England, helped stabilize many a breed and thrust it into the spotlight. This does not seem to have been the case with the Curly. Classes for retrievers were first offered, at British shows, in 1860 and the breed was well represented. By 1864, classes were divided into various breeds. Vero Shaw, writing in 1879 tells us that "In spite of his very handsome appearance, the Curly-Coated Retriever has steadily lost ground in popular estimation since the introduction of dog shows, and the subsequent rapid advance of the Wavy-Coated breed."

Many prominent sporting men, including Mr. Shirley, who helped found the English Kennel Club, were untiring in their promotion of the Wavy-Coat (now known as the Flat-Coated Retriever). The public followed their lead, casting aside the Curly. With so much in the way of beauty and sagacity to recommend him," Vero Shaw wrote, "it is a decided pity that the Curly-Coated Retriever should be suffered to become extinct, an event which, taking into consideration the great dearth of good specimens, seems to be far from an unlikely one."

About the same time, an oft repeated rumor began to circulate, saying that the Curly Coat was known for being hard mouthed. Some say that the false allegation was spread by early Wavy-Coat breeders, in an effort to promote their own breed over the more established Curly. The majority of writers, who had had experience with the breed, vehemently denied the false claim. But, still it persisted. As late as 1903, in *Breaking and Training Dogs*, Pathfinder and Dalziel, express this prejudice. "No! Give me the flat or wavy-coated black sorts for choice. I do not like curlies of any colour. As far as my experience goes, the more the coat curls the more bounce and impetuosity in the dog, and the harder his mouth..." Such superstitions would often plague the Curly in the following years.

In 1889, the Curly-Coated Retriever was first imported to New Zealand. In both New Zealand and Australia, the breed was to be greatly appreciated. Many of the breed's finest specimens are still to be found in these countries. There, the Curly is appreciated as an all-round hunter, used on ducks and other waterfowl as well as upland game birds. He has even been pressed into service as a kangaroo hunter, a job requiring exceptional courage, which the Curly has in abundance. He has proved a wonderful guard dog on many isolated Australian homesteads.

While the Curly was slipping from general popularity, in Britain, there were those who still greatly admired the breed. One such gentleman was Prebendary Harry Jones. In *Dogs I Have Known*, published in 1893, Prebendary Harry Jones writes fondly of Nep, his Curly. "One day I was returning home from Charing Cross by the steamboat and saw a lovely brown retriever, with a tar-line around his neck, in the custody of two or three roughs, who said aloud and incidentally that they had fished him out of the river as he was being carried down by the tide.

"Nep caught my eye, and looked at me with such a petitioning glance that I went up and spoke to him. If ever a dog replied, he begged me to take him home. I remarked, half to myself (knowing that it is famous for its curly brown retrievers), 'That dog came from Maldon, in Essex.' Nep's keepers understood me, I suppose...to claim the knowledge, not of his breed but of his owner's address, and promptly replied, 'If the gentleman will give us half a crown for finding him, he shall have him.' So I tendered the half-crown with the condition that they should let me have the tar-line too, and led him off when we touched at the Thames Tunnel Pier—our landing place for St. George's. But Nep wanted no leading. At once, and permanently, he ac-

This incredible photo shows a gathering of nine Curly-Coated Retriever champions in Australia.

cepted me as his master, and never referred to any other ownership or incident in his former life.

"His passion though for the water exceeded that of the most ambitious water dog I have ever had or heard of. I took him down once for a few days into the country, where he rejoiced in the resources of a shallow muddy pond. All day long Nep busied himself in ploughing the bottom of it with his nose and bringing ashore every stone and saturated stick he could find, till the pool had quite a fringe of these rescued treasures. Of course this procedure made his face shamefully dirty, and he had to be prohibited, since next to mud he preferred sofas. He would however 'tub' himself, though with an eye to the sensation of moisture rather than cleanliness, getting his four legs into a vessel of water, ducking his head into it, and splashing himself with his fore paws. But he did not know how to wet his back, unless under propitious circumstances. Of these he promptly availed himself.

"Once, indeed, having gone out for a walk in the streets of St. George's, in the course of some aimless inquiries he came upon the river, where he stopped. I had given him up for lost till one Sunday a smiling policeman brought him back in custody. He (not the constable) had my name on his collar, and 'from information received' I gathered that he had been for days accepting the civilities of young mudlarks who had incessantly thrown sticks into the water for him during that period. He seemed to have eaten nothing, being as lean as a basket, and was wet to the bone. But the temptation had been too much for him. He had tasted a Paradise of splash."

The Curly-Coated Retriever has retained his great love of the water, the paradise of splash, throughout the centuries. But, that could be said of all retrievers. The breed's persistence, courage and special, hard to define, personality is what really endears him to his owners. The Curly has an uncanny ability to think for himself, with a splash of humor thrown in. Patrick R. Chalmers, writing in the 1931 book, *Gun Dogs*, gives us an insight into this remarkable breed.

"I was brought up with him, and he figures in all my earliest shooting memories. He was a powerful dog, and he seemed to enjoy the jumping of five-barred gates with a big brown hare in his mouth. For rough wear there never was nor ever will be one to beat him. He was tireless on the steep, blue August Grampian; he was unbeatable over the wide acres of arable Norfolk. No day was too long for him, no task too hard. And when the long days and the hard days followed each other like a skein of wild geese, would a week of them, or a month of them, get to the bottom of him? Never in his life or yours.

"But it was in water that he was the black pearl. His coat was made to get wet in, and afterwards to sit in, breast to the biting weather, the snow flurries freezing to his tight, elastic curls, and his ear and eye cocked, as keenly as those of his master, to hear the far-off gaggle on the gale.

"He had a wonderful nose, too, and some of the finest bits of retrieving that ever I saw have been the work of the Curly-Coat. Give him time and an active runner, a cock pheasant for choice, and he made magic

A wonderful head study of Ithaca, owned by Doris Hodges, of Phoenix, Arizona.

again and again....

"The Curly-Coat...is among sporting dogs, a character. And he is always remembered, in my recollections of him, anyhow, as a sort of freebooting wag...

"I can see a huge black beast. 'Pop' is his name, who has just swum the Esk river twice and again to find a mythical partridge that an imaginative sportsman declared to be downed. 'But I know its down,' urges the Gun. For the fourth time 'Pop' is bidden 'seek-a-toor,' and over he goes. Presently we see him pounce into a tussock and return. 'He's got something,' the observant says, as 'Pop' approaches, huge and black as a thundercloud, his great head held low, his tremendous jaws carefully closed, his yellow eyes uplifted in a hideous squint. 'Come awa' wo' it, noo' says his master, 'fine muckle dog!' Then the cavern yawns, and forth, as from the fabled mountain, hops a field mouse that scurries, unhurt, into the segs. The imaginative man is the first to laugh."

A pair of Curlies was imported into this country, in 1907. It was not until 1924, however, that the breed was registered with the American Kennel Club. In the U.S., the Curly has always been a rare dog. He has seldom been seen in field trials. In the late 1930's, however, J. Gould Remick, of New York, successfully competed, with a pair of Curlies. In *Retriever Gun Dogs,* William Brown describes one of the dog's performances, in the 1936 Midwest Club's Novice Stake:

"This Curly...is a reliable, dependable sort. He accepts his assignments willingly and accomplishes his tasks in a businesslike manner. No flashing burst of speed is his, no burning desire to sear the cover, no warm vivacity. But Jacob is gifted with exceptional marking talent and keen olfactory organs. is bold and methodical; comfortable in pace, he took directions commendably. Murdock *(note-his handler)* showed complete confidence in the dog and Jacob never failed him. This Curly is of a stamp that will be in the money when the faster, flashier kind make errors of commission or omission, for Jacob is not likely to commit a blunder and he compiled a perfect score on this occasion."

In the show ring, too, the Curly-Coated Retriever is a rarity. I can still remember the thrill of seeing the imported Ch. Black Rod of Siccawei stride across a ring. What a magnificent sight! I couldn't take my eyes off this superb sporting dog with the marvelous movement. Competition was so sparse, that he earned his majors by capturing the Sporting Group. "Limey," as he was known to his friends, became the first of the breed to earn a championship in two decades.

It took the breed more than fifty years, since its recognition here, to achieve a Best in Show. The honor goes to the lovely Ch. Summerwind's Charles Dickens CD, WC, owned by ardent Curly enthusiast Sue Tokolics. A National Specialty winner, Charles has proven himself in obedience, the field and on the bench.

The Curly-Coated is unique in the retriever clan. He has many noticeable type differences, apart from coat, from the rest of this group. He is the tallest of these breeds, with a shorter body and a more upstanding look. His proportions are decidedly elegant, compared to the almost squatty appearance of the other retrievers. Very good specimens have a wonderful symmetry that is a delight to behold. As Bede Maxwell says in her 1972 book, *The Truth About Sporting Dogs,* "He should not (maybe could not) look like a Labrador in outline, nor a Golden, nor a Flat-Coated. He is all his own dog!" And so he is.

Curlies come in either black or liver, the first being the more popular of the two. The ideal head is long, but never snipey. The ears, covered with short curls, are set rather low. The eyes are black, in black dogs, and brown in liver dogs, but should never be yellow. His deep body is rather short, compared with the other retrievers, and he presents an image of power.

Franco, a lovely son of Ch. Summerwind's Charles Dickens CD, WC, is owned by Sue Tokolics, of West Chester, Pennsylvania.

Well muscled throughout, the dog's body ends in a distinctive tail, covered with curls.

As his name implies, the breed's key characteristic is its curly coat. The body is covered by a mass of crisp, tight curls. The curls, often likened to astrakhan, cling closely to the body. Large loose curls are sometimes seen, but the small, tight curls are preferred. The ears and tail are also covered with curls. The hair on the head is short and should never form a topknot.

Coat faults are dealt with seriously and, unfortunately, are too often seen. Saddle backs, patches of uncurled hair or bald areas are harshly penalized. The Curly's coat was designed for protection from icy waters and such coat variations preclude protection. "There's no denying that there are coat problems in the breed," says Sue Tokolics. "They can be found in varying degrees, from minor to severe. In advanced cases, the dogs will have bare necks, rumps and back legs." Janean Marti agrees. "Some Curlies suffer from a symmetrical baldness problem that most breeders believe is hereditary and caused by an adrenal/endocrine system malfunction. The good news is, because the breed is rare and therefore has a limited gene pool, most breeders are very strict about checking for and eliminating problem dogs from their breeding program."

Certainly, the Curly-Coated Retriever is one of the easiest of all breeds to groom. The adult coat is never combed and requires little preparation for the show ring. Some breeders like to dampen the coat and massage it in a circular fashion. Sue Tokolics spritzes the coat with water, before taking the dog into the ring. The dogs do shed seasonally and, at that time, combing helps to loosen the dead hair and make way for the new. Curlies do have one grooming problem, however. Keeping toenails trimmed back is an ever present problem for most Curly owners. In this breed, the quick grows to the tip of the nail and is apt to breed profusely when trimmed. This makes the regular trimming of nails an ordeal for both dog and owner. "No one really knows why this occurs," Sue Tokolics reports, "but it seems to be a breed wide trait, encompassing all lines."

Curlies still earn the admiration of owners with their field prowess. Many breeders actively use their dogs for hunting and compete for working certificates. "Because they are so rare, the breed as a whole has not been divided between show and hunting lines," says Janean Marti, of Ptarmigan Curlies, in Cadott, Wisconsin. "The average Curly, with a minimum of training, will be able to give the average hunter a complete day of work on all gamebird species...I've hunted upland birds and waterfowl with my Curlies since 1977. I do recommend, however, that a hunter who wishes to purchase a Curly buy only from a breeder who hunts his dogs.

"As hunters, my husband and I most highly value the courage and persistence of the Curly in the field. A Curly just doesn't want to quit. As conservation of resources, including wild game, becomes more important, the innate perseverance of a Curly in finding crippled or downed game becomes extremely important. With the possible exception of one dog, I believe that my Curlies would actually die in their tracks rather than quit."

Sue Tokolics, who breeds both Labradors and Curlies, would certainly agree. "In the field, Curlies are very persistent. They just will not give up. There have been times when we have called the dogs off, believing that nothing was there. The Labs obeyed us, but the Curlies insisted on staying. Sure enough, there was a bird where the Curlies had said. The Labs simply missed it. It's difficult to get a Curly to give up."

And what about those old accusations that the breed is hard mouthed. "The old rumor of Curly-Coated Retrievers being hard mouthed has hopefully died away by now," writes Kathy Day, of Seattle, Washington, in the March 1979 issue of the *American Kennel Gazette*. "I have never seen a Curly with even close to a hard mouth and anybody who owns one of these hunting masters will echo me. Curly-Coated Retrievers are not flashy trial performers. Rather, they are steady day to day workers that seldom miss. The instinct is still there in great force..."

"This is not an easy breed to describe," says Janean Marti, "perhaps because they harbor a whole kaleidoscope of personality traits—a Curly is a very complicated dog! The very traits that endear the breed to me can also make for some trying times....

"Curlies are not only intelligent, but they possess the faculties to work out solutions to problems. Unfortunately, the solutions are most often designed to benefit the Curlies in the house, not the humans. For instance, it was no big deal when one of my nine Curlies learned that to open a door one must turn the knob. After all, what's a few teeth marks in an otherwise pretty brass knob? But, when Michael learned that it wasn't fun to let yourself outdoors without any playmates, he began lifting latches on kennels and turning other door knobs to enable all nine of my Curlies out in the yard to romp.

"This led to even bigger and better things. Four-year-old Jim Bob decided on a bit of one-upmanship and learned to open my car door. Now, even though we live in a rural area, far from most serious crime, I must lock my door. Otherwise, I'll go out into the driveway and find one Curly sitting in the driver's seat of my car,

A trio of Curly champions, Ch. Ptarmigan Rainy Day Jonah, Ch. Ptarmigan Distant Thunder and Ch. Ptarmigan Stormy Monday are owned by Doris Hodges.

his wet, muddy front paws planted firmly on the dashboard, the better to see his colleagues milling around. Those same colleagues have already run on my car's cloth upholstery, leaving their own marks of distinction."

Kathy Day echoes these sentiments. "They are generally happy, calm, loving dogs with a good brain and a desire to please. They are good at figuring out problems. Some can get out of any crate and others must be padlocked into their runs lest they work the latch open. Yet, once out, most merely seek human companionship and, therefore, are rarely lost."

"To live with a Curly," Janean Marti observes, "one must be willing to appreciate free thinkers....A Curly scorned will save a trick for a future day! Some people, who have owned other retriever breeds, find owning a Curly disconcertingly or charmingly different, depending not on the dog, but the human. The Curly does not have the typical Labrador or Golden Retriever attitude of hale, hearty, fellow-well-met. If the Lab and Golden enjoy a slapstick type of humor and activity, the Curly, as denotes his British ancestry, enjoys a witty sense of humor. This stems, I believe, from his long history of extreme self-confidence..."

"Curlies are known to be stubborn," Janean says, "yet obedience and other performance activity results indicate that they are often high scoring, attentive, trainable dogs. The success with Curlies in performance events lies in the fact that a Curly is loyal and dedicated to his owner. If the dog is given a chance to form a bond with the owner, he is willing to try anything that owner wishes him to do."

Sue Tokolics thinks there may be another reason the breed excels in obedience. "The Curly's memory is absolutely amazing. This is a great advantage in obedience for you do not have to continually refresh the dog's memory. I began obedience training with Charlie *(BIS winner Ch. Summerwind's Charles Dickens CD, WC)* when he was quite young. Then, he was sent out on the show circuit for quite a while. When he returned, I decided that it was time he earned his C.D. title. I was sure we'd have to start all over. Not so. I was absolutely amazed to discover that Charles remembered everything that he'd been taught. I find this to be typical. Once a Curly has learned something, he's not apt to forget it."

"Curlies can do quite well in obedience," says Kathy Day, "but must be well acclimated to show conditions so their curiosity doesn't lead them astray. When working with a Curly-Coated Retriever, the trainer must take into consideration their natural desire to clown around. I have seen quite a few Curlies do the down-stay on their backs with all fours waving away!"

"Given the chance for daily challenge," Janean Marti says, "be it obedience exercises, hunting or just plain exercise, the Curly is a very mellow, obliging house companion. It's quite simple to live with nine Curlies in the house, but we hunt in the fall and enjoy a daily romp everyday with our dogs.

"Non-doggy friends are amazed that our entire pack of Curlies will stand behind an imaginary dividing line and not enter certain parts of the house. For instance, the rule is 'no dogs in the kitchen.' That means that our nine Curlies stand in our family room, watch me make dinner while the air fills with tantalizing smells, yet never cross the line from family room to kitchen. The training required for this was fairly simple (since I'm a lazy dog trainer): If a Curly steps over the line, you simply say his name and 'no, no.'"

"This breed is very, very intelligent," Sue Tokolics says. "but they can sometimes be hard headed and stubborn. They are going to do things their way. Temperaments within the breed vary somewhat. Some Curlies have a softer, mellower temperament. A simple 'no' and they'll do what you want. Others are more stubborn and you have to be sterner with them. But, regardless of the difference you never need to be overly harsh. I tell my

This versatile Curly, owned by Doris Hodges, is in his element...the water.

dogs, very firmly, what I want them to do. I need only say it one time and they get the message.

"I feel it's important for new owners to realize that the Curly-Coated Retriever is slow to mature," Sue notes. "They mature slowly both physically and mentally. I don't believe that dogs are fully mature until they hit about four years of age. They will certainly hunt before this age, but it's then that the dog really comes into his own.

"They are very sweet, very affectionate dogs. They aren't fawning, however, like Labs," Sue says. "If I sit down, my Labs will try to crawl in my lap. My Curlies are content to sit beside me. They are a little more reserved than the Labs and so I recommend that people socialize their dogs.

"The Curly-Coated Retriever has an incredible devotion to his master. One of our dogs, Kenna, is my husband's dog. I don't know quite how to describe it, but you can look in her face and tell that she's utterly devoted to him. Charlie is my dog and he has that same look for me. I've never seen this type of look in my Labs or any other breed."

Janean Marti agrees. "My husband said it best. One night he was watching my first Curly, Ivor, as the dog put his head on the edge of the bathtub while waiting for me to complete a shower. 'That dog would do anything for you.' And it was true. Allowed to form a bond with me, Ivor decided that no matter what I asked him to do, he would try. Curlies make the best pets when allowed to share living quarters with their owners. They are not really the ideal kennel dogs unless they are given time to bond with their owners."

Perhaps it's that incredible devotion that really charms owners and endears the breed to them. Or maybe it's something else...something undefinable.

"The Curly-Coated Retriever is not a wonder breed," says Janean Marti. "It is a thinking man's breed. It's a breed that will be enjoyed by those who understand that creativity and intelligence are to be prized in a world increasingly dominated by generic brands. To be able to live with a Curly, you must want a dog that you are willing to develop a personal relationship with—a dog that will be a soulmate, if you will. If you are willing to treat a Curly not so much as a dog, but as a living, breathing animal on a plane not necessarily lower, but different, from the human place, then a Curly can prove to be the most wonderful and loyal of companions."

Chapter 16

The Dandie Dinmont Terrier

"The Dandie Dinmont Terrier is but little known in America to others than fanciers. It is difficult to understand why he is not more popular, for...he is one of the brightest, most active and vivacious of all the Terrier family. The liking for him invariably grows as one becomes more acquainted with his good qualities, for he embodies all that goes to make up a good, workmanlike Terrier, with an admirable disposition for a companion for lady or gentleman, or as a playmate for children..."

The above words were penned in 1891, by Dandie breeder John H. Naylor. Not much has changed in the century since Mr. Naylor's words first appeared, in G.O. Shield's *The American Book of the Dog*. This quaint little fellow, with the jaunty air and the wagging tail, is still little known outside dog show circles. That's a shame, for one look at the dark, shining eyes, peering from beneath the silken topknot, and you know you're in the presence of a special dog. "He is a rascal that will look up at you with mischievous eyes in a cherubic face and win your heart for all time," writes Mrs. William M. Kirby, in her 1964 book, *How to Raise and Train a Dandie Dinmont Terrier*.

Of all the British terriers, the Dandie has one of the most colorful and interesting of histories. Indeed, the somewhat eccentric human characters who nurtured the breed, in the early days, were as unique as the dogs they raised. The Dandie's past can be documented to about the 1700's. The breed was born in those beautiful, rugged hills which mark the border between Scotland and England. Tinkers traveled the roads between villages, offering their services to small farmers. These jacks of all trades could repair the farm wife's pots and pans, and carried an assortment of practical items, such as spoons or baskets, for her perusal. But, it was not only the farm women who hailed the arrival of the tinker. The men and children crowded around, to hear the news from other villages.

William Allan, born in 1704, in Holystone, was one such individual. Allan, familiarly known as "Piper," for his proficiency on the bagpipes, was an authentic character. He was one of those colorful eccentrics, who seem to romp through the pages of British history. A cheerful man, a lover of people, songs and music, Allan liked nothing better than a day spent fishing or hunting. His lifestyle and occupation afforded plenty of time for both.

It was not Allan's piping nor his songs or stories, however, that would earn him lasting fame. It was the little rough-coated terriers that accompanied him everywhere. Delightful companions and hunters, so well known did the dogs become that some would refer to all terriers of the kind as "Piper Allan's breed."

Stories of the exploits of the Piper's dogs and their success afield, form the basis of Dandie Dinmont legend. In those days of old, the gentry often called on the owners of Otter Hound packs, to rid their streams and rivers of the sly varmints. Fishing was not mere sport, but an important source of food, and the otter was viewed as a ruthless competitor. The hunters were paid a fee and also claimed the otter's furry coat as their bounty. Piper Allan often attended these hunts and his dogs were valuable adjutants to the larger hounds. When the otter darted into a hollow, beneath a tree's gnarled roots, the terriers flushed him out, or if he remained stubbornly underground, killed him in the lair.

One of Piper Allan's most renowned dogs was "Peachem" (identified by some as "Hitchem"). Allan had such confidence in the little tyke that he would proudly proclaim, in his thick brogue, that "when my Peachem gi'es mouth, I durst always sell the otter's skin." Word of Peachem's accomplishments spread, and there were many who wished to purchase the game little worker. Few offers were more tempting than the one broached by the Duke of Northumberland. He offered William Allan a small farm, rent free for the remainder of his life, if he would part with the dog. It must have been a heady proposal for an itinerant traveler, whose sole possessions were his dogs and what he could carry aboard his wagon. He did, after all, have a family to support. He considered the Duke's proposition for a day, then replied, "No, my lord, keep your farm. What would a piper do with a farm anyway?"

Then there was Charley. Lord Ravensworth had called on hunters, to rid his vast estate of otters. Piper Allan came along. His Charley thrilled the crowd with his performance. Lord Ravensworth was mightily impressed, too. He sent his steward to purchase the dog. Name your price, Piper Allan was told. But the Piper, flushed with the excitement and success of the hunt, turned around haughtily, waved his arm expansively and declared, "The whole estate cannot buy Charley."

Though William Allan's dogs achieved fame, he was not the sole owner of the shaggy haired terriers. It's believed that his dogs were typical of those owned by the gypsies and tinkers who wandered the region. Legend holds that once or twice a year, families would gather for outings. There was plenty of time to exchange stories and recap the hunting exploits of the dogs. But stories alone would not suffice. Whenever possible, the men would locate that most formidable of opponents, a badger. If no badger could be found, they would settle for a foulmart (the European polecat) or a hedgehog. The best hunters were highly valued and, no doubt, many a breeding was arranged and puppies exchanged around the nightly campfires. And so, with working ability their sole criterion, they fostered the dogs that would one day be known as Dandie Dinmont Terriers.

What about that name, though? How in the world did the daring little border hunters become known by such an unusual appellation? Enter Sir Walter Scott, the famed British author. In the early 1800's, Sir Walter journeyed through the hills, doing research for his *Mistrelsy of the Scottish Borders*. During his travels, he became well acquainted with the hardy people of the region. In 1814, his novel *Guy Mannering* was published. One of his memorable characters was a figure named Dandie Dinmont. The burly tenant of the farm known as Charlieshope was the proud owner of a

The irresistible appeal of the Dandie Dinmont Terrier. This dog is owned by Frances Brewer.

number of plucky little terriers, which Scott named Auld Pepper, Auld Mustard, Young Pepper, Young Mustard, Little Pepper and Little Mustard. The game little terriers, he said, "fear naething that ever cam' wi' a hairy skin on't." All those peppers and mustards romped right across the pages of the novel and into the hearts of British dog lovers. Soon, there arose a clamor for the "game wee dogs," just like those owned by Dandie Dinmont.

Sir Walter Scott's immortal character was an amalgam of different farmers he had met throughout the Border country. But, there were some who thought that Dandie Dinmont had been patterned after one John Davidson, a farmer residing at Hindlee. A colorful character, Davidson owned some of the little terriers and often named them Mustard and Pepper. He could regularly been seen on the hills, with his dogs, pursuing fox and badger. It was said that he originally procured his stock from the stomping grounds of old Piper Allan. Davidson certainly did nothing to dissuade those who thought he was the basis for Scott's character. In fact, after *Guy Mannering* was released, his neighbors and acquaintances took to calling him Dandie Dinmont. He loved his newfound notoriety.

Some have said that John Davidson actually originated the breed. Reverend J. Cumming said that he had discovered a note, penned in Davidson's hand, dated 1869, which read: "1800-"Tuggin" from A. Armstrong, reddish and wiry; "Tarr," reddish and wire-haired; "Pepper," shaggy and light from Dr. Brown of Borjenwood. The race of Dandie was bred from the last two. J.D." Most authorities, however, believe that Davidson was one of several people who bred the working terriers.

Whatever the truth, Sir Walter Scott's book propelled the dogs into national prominence. And, needless to say, it irrevocably changed the life of a farmer named John Davidson, henceforth known as Dandie Dinmont. He died in January of 1820 and retained his great love of hunting to the end. It is said that as he lay on his deathbed, he heard the sound of the hounds, as they lit upon the trail of a fox. Though deathly ill, he insisted on going to the window, so that he could watch the fun.

Dog lovers and dealers descended on the Border region, eager to procure one of the little terriers. Soon, the breed was a fashionable pet throughout Britain. The scruffy little dog that had been the companion of gypsies and tinkers, was welcomed into the homes of the aristocracy. For a time they were known as Dandie Dinmont's dogs, but soon the possessive was dropped. And so the Dandie Dinmont Terrier became the only breed in history to be named after a character in a book.

The first recorded showing of Dandies came in 1861, and the breed was recognized shortly thereafter. In 1875, the first Dandie club was started at Selkirk. Then, the breed really came into its own and began showing up regularly on the bench. In 1886, John Naylor (the man quoted in the lead to this chapter) and his wife imported the first Dandie Dinmonts to this country, from Scotland. Their Bonnie Britton was the first of the breed to be registered by the A.K.C. Breed progress was quite slow, but there was sufficient interest, by 1932, to form the Dandie Dinmont Terrier Club of America.

While the outline of most terrier breeds is decidedly angular, the Dandie's conformation is composed of curved lines. His strong, stocky body is borne on well boned, short legs, perfect for digging. His body is long and flexible enough to enable him to squirm into an underground den. A key characteristic of the breed is the curved topline. Lower at the shoulders, the topline arches over the loin and then slopes to the tail. The true curved topline, not one that's merely been trimmed on, is treasured by breeders. In length, the body should be an inch or two less than twice the dog's 8-11 inch height. Dandies generally weigh 18 to 24 pounds.

A Dandie's head, properly groomed and trimmed for the show ring, is unique. There's no mistaking him for any other breed. The head is large, with a full domed skull, which is capped by a topknot of long, silky hair. The prominent round eyes are dark hazel in color and always have an alert, wide awake look. The ears, with their tassel of hair, are set rather low. If the head is distinctive, so is the opposite end. The Dandie's tail is rather short, thick at the base and tapers gently to a point. He carries it gaily, above the level of the back, with what breeders call a "scimitar" like curve.

As in days of old, the Dandie still comes in two colors...pepper and mustard. The pepper varies from an almost bluish black to a silvery gray. Born black, the pepper color silvers as the hair grows out, giving it a pencilled look. The topknot is a pure silver color. The striking mustard color can vary from a rich almost reddish gold to a pale fawn. Born red, puppies gradually acquire the brilliant mustard color and the creamy topknot. The Dandie's coat is a mixture of both hard and soft hairs. The proper mix gives the coat a crisp, but not wiry feel.

Like most terriers, the Dandie's coat is plucked. Frequent plucking and removal of the longest hairs, helps to improve not only coat texture but also color. "Dandies do not shed, but daily combing is essential,

Beatrice illustrates the charm of a Dandie puppy. She lives with Mrs. Frances Brewer, in Colorado Springs, Colorado.

especially in the first year, so that the soft puppy coat never becomes matted and so that combing is always a pleasant experience," says Mrs. William Kirby, in *How to Raise and Train a Dandie Dinmont Terrier.* "It takes only a few minutes when done every day," she continues, "and the better the puppy is combed and brushed, the more colorful its adult coat will be. When the adult coat is in, daily combing takes out any loose hairs that want to come, allowing new hair to start growing in, which keeps the coat 'rolling,' as we say..." Properly preparing a Dandie for the show ring requires skill and practice. Most breeders are only too happy to instruct newcomers in the stripping and trimming methods.

"A Dandie is no dandy...he's a terrier," says the Dandie Dinmont Terrier Club of America (D.D.T.C.A.). "The Dandie combines the self-confidence and pride of a terrier without the high-strung temperament. His individualism is much to be admired in an age of conformity."

"Wherever he is known he is adored, for he has a charm and a fascination about him that is his alone," says Mrs. William Kirby, in *How to Raise and Train a Dandie Dinmont Terrier.* "Besides his quaint appearance, his wisdom and his pluck, his courage and his watchfulness, what endears him most to all who know him is his responsiveness. If you are tired of the indifference of certain breeds, you will be charmed by the warmth of the Dandie's nature and his constant awareness of you. Whenever you speak to him, there comes the eager, answering slap of his expressive tail, showing he is ready at all times to do what you want him to do. When you know him, only his loyalty will exceed your loyalty to him."

Dandie owners are uncommonly devoted to their dogs. A charming, gay, responsive and bright dog, living with a Dandie is just plain fun to live with. With his own family, he is a self-confident and very affectionate companion. Like many terriers, Dandies do have minds of their own. "The Dandie does not require constant attention. He is a restful companion," says the D.D.T.C.A. "However, he does need your love and, equally important, he needs and wants you to set the rules of the house and help to remind him of them consistently."

The Dandie, excuse the pun, is a dandy companion for children. He's always in the mood for a romp and more than happy to engage in roughhousing. Yet, he can be gentle, too. He becomes very fond of children and willingly protects them.

The Dandie is often reserved with strangers. It's not that he's shy. He just prefers to adopt a "wait and see" attitude. Don't try to force your affection on a Dandie. Instead, be patient. Soon, the dog's innate curiosity will get the better of him. Before you know it,

a little nose will be sniffing you. Those expressive eyes will look up at you and the tail will start to wag. You've made a friend.

Dandie Dinmont Terriers make ideal housepets.

"His unique appearance, the reserve of his demeanor and the fact that he is not a 'noisy' dog belies the fact that he is a true terrier," the D.D.T.C.A. says. Indeed, the Dandie is often called "the gentleman of the terrier group." This breed is not a yapper but, when aroused, the Dandie has an astonishingly deep, loud voice. Visitors are often surprised to find such a big voice attached to such a small dog. This, combined with the breed's natural alertness, makes the Dandie a good watchdog.

Gentlemanly though he is, one must always remember that the Dandie Dinmont is still a true terrier. While most dogs are now kept as companions and show dogs, this doesn't mean that the breed has lost it's hunting instincts. Let a mouse, rat or squirrel appear, and the Dandie Dinmont Terrier can move with surprising speed and dash. He demonstrates the same enthusiasm as the dogs which made old Piper Allan so famous. For this reason, a fence is a must for this breed. "The Dandie is by heredity an instinctive, independent rodent hunter," the D.D.T.C.A. reminds us. "So, the slightest movement may easily inspire swift, but unsafe, traversing of a busy street. As with a child, his safety is up to you."

The Dandie is not a quarrelsome dog who is prone to starting fights. "His motto seems to be 'live and let live,'" says the D.D.T.C.A., "however, if he is pushed too far or taken advantage of he will never back down." The Club adds that "he prefers to match his prowess against some fellow a wee bit bigger than himself." While he's not generally an instigator, the Dandie can be a formidable fighter, and a squabble between two of these dogs is apt to be a serious affair. For this reason, most breeders don't keep two males together and carefully choose which females to put out together.

"In closing, I must say that anyone wishing a hardy Terrier, one fit for all kinds of work, a companion for himself or children, cannot find anything better than a Dandie Dinmont. The more they become known, the more their merits are appreciated," wrote John Naylor, more than a century ago. Today's Dandie enthusiasts would be the first to agree.

Chapter 17

The Field Spaniel

The story of the Field Spaniel should be required reading for all dog breeders and judges, whether their interest be in Great Danes or Chihuahuas. It would serve well as an object lesson in how the quest for show ring success can destroy a breed. The sport of dog showing has many positive aspects and has done much to further our knowledge of dogs. At the same time, we must constantly be mindful of our responsibilities to the dogs we raise, and understand, implicitly, the qualities that enabled them to perform the functions for which they were originally bred. If our only goal is the garnering of trophies, accolades and the glory of show ring success, then we are vulnerable to the rollercoaster fads that come and go in the dog world. We must have, in our mind's eye, a strong vision of how the breed should look and an understanding the qualities that allow it to fulfill its duties. We must be faithful to that ideal, come what may, rather than running helter-skelter, in search of the next big winner.

Indeed it was the sole desire to own winning show dogs that led to the formation of the Field Spaniel in the first place. It was the show ring that catapulted the Field to the top of the spaniel world. But, it was also the desire for glory that spelled the breed's downfall. A fad, fueled by judges without the gumption to stand against the tide, soon turned a sensible working dog into a laughable caricature. As a consequence, the Field Spaniel plummeted from the pinnacle of popularity to the very brink of extinction. But, the story of the Field Spaniel is not all bleak. It is also a tribute to the skill, perseverance and commitment of breeders who managed to reverse a trend; who worked for years to restore a breed to its rightful and respected place in the family of dogs.

Today, the differences between breeds are so clearly delineated that it is difficult for us to imagine a different time. But, in the 1700's and 1800's, the classification of breeds, most particularly spaniels, was murky at best. The names, springing spaniel, cocking spaniel and field spaniel were in use, but they were not very precise. Much interbreeding between strains occurred during this formative period, until the differences could be clearly specified. These early spaniels were all utilitarian dogs, of course, meant to aid the hunter in his search for game. The most common spaniel colors were liver, liver and white, red, red and white, yellow, and black and white. Most hunters preferred dogs who contrasted nicely with the backgrounds of fields and woods, thus enabling them to be easily seen by the gunner.

With the advent of dog shows in England, in the 1850s, a new period was born. The British, dog lovers since time immemorial, found the new gatherings tremendously exciting. The gratification of molding a breed and producing a consistently winning strain was as appealing then as it is today. Men, who were actively breeding spaniels, were always eager for a new challenge. Why not breed a strain of raven haired spaniels, they wondered? It must have seemed a grand quest to produce a field dog in this rare shade.

The origins of the Cocker Spaniel and the Field Spaniel are inextricably intertwined. Both sprang from the same source, the medium sized spaniels that had been known, in the British Isles, for centuries. We do know that a Mr. Footman, of Lutterworth, Leicestershire, had some predominately black spaniels. At his death, these were acquired by Mr. F. Burdett, one of the pioneers in the plan to breed a black strain. He and other fanciers interbred these dogs with the Cockers they already owned. In those days, the primary distinction between the two breeds was one of size. Dogs over 25 pounds were said to be "Field" spaniels and those under that mark were declared "Cockers." In the early days, of course, this led to a great deal of confusion. Cockers and Fields often sprang from the same litter and the dog that was shown, this year, as a Cocker might enter the ring, next year, as a Field.

Much experimental breeding was used to produce this new breed, which came to be called, simply and modestly, the Black Field Spaniel. Some breeders made a cross with the Irish Water Spaniel, which intensified field and retrieving traits and added leg and bone. Many early Field Spaniels, before being trimmed for the ring, sported the Irish Water's distinctive topknot. The blood of what would become the Cocker Spaniel was, as we've seen, liberally applied. And crosses to the Sussex Spaniel added bone and power. Unfortunately, the delineation between the Cocker and the Field, based on weight alone, was to prove a great hindrance, as we've learned in modern times. When weight limits are applied, exhibitors may choose to starve or gorge their dogs to fit these arbitrary standards. We now know that it is much more sensible to ascribe a height restriction and, within that framework, seek to achieve balance. The early breeders of the Field Spaniel did not have such pragmatic guidelines. A 40 pound dog, standing 18 inches tall might be sturdily built and

have a balance and symmetry that was a delight to behold. That same weight, consigned to a 14 inch dog, presented quite a different picture.

We can get an idea of how those earliest Field Spaniels looked, by studying the wonderful portraits of both the Field and the Cocker presented in Stonehenge's 1882 book, *Dogs of the British Isles*. So similar are the two breeds, that we can see clearly that overall size is the only difference. Shown are the Field Spaniels Brush and his mother Nellie. They are remarkably like the Field Spaniels of today, appearing to be active, balanced dogs, a little longer than tall, with sensible length coats. Indeed, they lack only the chiselled nobility of the present day Field Spaniel's head.

Unfortunately, many of the fanciers who jumped on the Field Spaniel bandwagon were avid Sussex Spaniel breeders. They did much to further the Sussex and their impact on that breed was great. That they were enamored of Sussex type seems obvious. Their contributions to the Field were, in retrospect, to have devastating consequences. They set about to remake the Field Spaniel in a Sussex mold. Repeated breedings to Sussex and half-Sussex dogs produced a Field Spaniel of enormous bone, tremendous body length and a heavy head with a pronounced brow. While the smaller Sussex, with this body conformation, was active with a free, slightly rolling gait, this did not prove true with the Field. Because he was a larger, heavier dog to begin with, imposing the shorter Sussex height and length on the breed resulted in a very heavy, lumbering dog, that was all but crippled in movement. From a robust, active field dog, they had transformed the breed into what some future writers would liken to a "caterpillar."

The impressive Field Spaniel Ch. Richlynn's Jonathan Henry, owned by Becki Jo Wolkenheim, of Wales Wisconsin.

We, of course, have the liberty of playing Monday morning quarterback. This new fad in Field breeding was, at the outset, applauded in Great Britain. Mr. T. Jacobs, of Newton Abbot Kennels, bred both Field and Sussex, and was the prime advocate of this new type. These new Fields caught the eye of dog folks and they began to win at smaller shows, presided over by less experienced judges. The British dog world was soon abuzz with news of these new winners. The dog press initially hailed these new dogs and the tide rolled on, excitement mounting. When they appeared at larger shows, even the most knowledgeable judges lacked the moxie to put them down. Mr. Jacobs was hailed as one of the nation's most remarkable breeders; the one who had truly established Field Spaniel type. His

The lovely Ch. Pin Oak's Yankee Doodle Dandy. Clara, as she is known, is owned by Becki Jo Wolkenheim.

dogs soon captured top honors at the majority of British shows, and he compiled an impressive number of champions. There were some who dared to speak against this new trend and pointed out that Jacobs' dogs weren't exactly purebred. But, the tide continued to roll, and their comments were viewed as mere jealously. New fanciers bought and won with Mr. Jacobs' dogs, and the Field was soon the top winning spaniel in all of Britain.

"In spite of these cries I followed my own dictation," Mr. Jacobs wrote, in Vero Shaw's *The Illustrated Book of the Dog*, published in 1879, "my great aim was to improve the breed of Spaniels. Purity of breed I had foremost in my mind, which I do not consider I sacrificed when I mated my black bitches with a liver-colored Sussex....and noting their performances, I did not rest here, but thought there was still room for improvement, and by breeding these Blacks together, I have produced something that promises to eclipse everything I have yet seen. I am gradually creeping nearer the standard I have marked out for my beacon..." How sad that his "beacon" was not directed toward function, but rather toward victory in the show ring.

What's amazing, when one reviews the old writings on the breed, is that knowledgeable dog men realized, full well, that the trend in Field Spaniels was destroying the breed as a sporting dog. While they never

tolerated uselessness in other breeds, they made allowances for the Field Spaniel, so great was his show ring success. One of the most knowledgeable of America's dog men, James Watson, imported these long and low dogs to show in this country. His comments, contained in his 1916 edition of *The Dog Book,* will illustrate this point. "...in treating the field spaniel of the present day it is not necessary to go further back than the time when the modern type was established, mainly by Mr. T. Jacobs in the early '80's...when that gentleman revolutionised the variety...{prior to that} it ran higher on the leg and had a coat more inclined to wave or curl than had the dogs introduced by Mr. Jacobs, which set the fashion we have followed ever since....In English works on the dog a good deal is said about the old Burdett, Bullock and Boulton strains, and we have nothing to say against them in any way. Indeed, it is almost certain that as regards usefulness they were superior to the present-day dog, which, with all his show qualities in appearance, we cannot help concluding is not much adapted for use....

"The pre-Jacobites, if we must invent a word, were mainly like large cocker spaniels in conformation, and although we read in the older books of Stonehenge and other writers of his period of their lowness and length, that was only a comparative description. The prize winners were lower—in comparison with length—than the ordinary run of working spaniels of that period, but we should call them too high on the leg now. They also lacked the type in head called for in present-day spaniels, and we really think were more spaniel-like than our exaggerated type."

It is said that the continuing criticisms caused Mr. Jacobs to discontinue breeding. When some continued to call for longer legged Field Spaniels, more like the early type, Jacobs, in a fit of anger, auctioned off his entire kennel of both Fields and Sussex. Many of his Fields went to wealthy merchant Moses Woolland, who continued in Jacob's vein. His Bridford dogs acquired an amazing record of success that eclipsed even that of his predecessor. He was a firm advocate of the long and low type and, despite the mounting criticism, his dogs continued to win. Though slow to act, judges began to succumb to the pressure of the critics. In 1905, some say influenced by this criticism, Mr. Woolland, too, sold his dogs by auction. The Field Spaniel boom was over.

However, those who had been successful in the ring with the Field Spaniel weren't so quick to give it up. They saw, in colored Field Spaniels, their chance to once again recapture their status as top show spaniel. In the early days of the breed's formation, dogs had been culled according to color. Black dogs had been strictly selected for and, probably due to the Sussex crosses, liver dogs had been retained by breeders. All other

A wonderful head study of Ch. Richlynn's Jonathan Henry.

colors, as well as dogs trimmed with all but minimal white, had been destroyed. Dr. Spurgins, of Northampton, however, had bucked this trend. He liked the colored dogs and retained them in his kennels. In fact, Dr. Spurgins seems to have been one who stood up to the fads sweeping the Field Spaniel world. His dogs were not as extreme as those of Jacobs and Woolland, and he did not acquire or breed to their stock. In all, he was involved with the Field Spaniel for some 36 years, and it's a shame that his principles, rather than those of Jacobs, hadn't come to the fore. Had that happened, the history of the Field Spaniel might have been very different.

Dr. Spurgins bred Cockers, as well as Fields, and his dogs can be found behind many of today's Cocker lines. But, his primary focus seems to have been the Field Spaniel. While the majority of the dogs in his kennel were black or liver, he would occasionally have a blue roan or blue and tan. These odd colored Field Spaniels were not produced in any great number and few breeders had an interest in them. Now, however, as the breeders sought to revitalize interest in the ridiculed Field Spaniel, the colored dogs caught their eye. After all, it was the desire to breed a black spaniel that had led to the formation and show ring success of the Field originally. Wouldn't a colored Field Spaniel soar to the top, too?

There was one basic problem with this strategy, however. There simply weren't enough colored dogs to go around. Had breeders patiently worked with Dr.

Spurgins' stock and the occasional other colored dogs that had surfaced, they would, undoubtedly, have succeeded in producing a true strain of colored Field Spaniels. Yet, the Field Spaniel world had always been strongly swayed by the show ring and the gratification of instant winners. Field Spaniel owners did not have the patience to wait for that and crossed their dogs with Basset Hounds.

"Blue roans, blue and tan, red roans, orange roans, lemon roans, with or without tan, colours hitherto undreamed of appeared suddenly and in profusion," says Peggy Grayson, in the 1984 book *The History and Management of the Field Spaniel*. There was great excitement, in the dog world, over these new dogs and soon there were separate classes for these colored dogs at shows. "Although a large number of blacks were still being bred and regularly exhibited," Mrs. Grayson says, "the new colours quickly caught on, and litters containing every hue hitherto thought impossible began to turn up." Naturally, a cross to the Basset Hound did nothing to improve the breed's short legged stature. In fact, it introduced a number of new problems. Field Spaniels exhibited crooked front legs, bad feet and prominent haws. Such was the state of the breed as Britain entered the First World War.

World War I provided a clean sweep, of sorts, for the Field Spaniel. At the conclusion of the conflict, none of the big names who had so predominated the Field world, were still active. Show ring entries were scant and the Field was overlooked. But, while show fanciers had abandoned the breed, it was field people who would step in to save it. Hunters in the Midlands region had to contend with dense thickets of scrubby blackthorn that were difficult for most dogs to penetrate. They liked the English Springer Spaniel, but did not find him strong and powerful enough for their needs. The Clumber and the Sussex were too slow to please these sporting gents. They decided that, by crossing the Field Spaniel with the English Springer, they could arrive at a dog which ideally suited their needs. Beginning in the 1920s and continuing through the 1930s, they made many such crosses.

Suddenly, the Field Spaniel was popular once again. These new Springer inspired dogs were seen in the show ring and also starred at field trials. Many new fanciers were attracted to the breed and bought Field Spaniels specifically to compete in field trials. The breed achieved notable success. While grateful for the infusion of Springer blood, which they too added, show breeders worked quickly to carefully delineate the type differences between the Springer and the Field. They declared that the Field should be largely a solid colored dog, to differentiate it from the parti-colored Springer. Black, liver, golden liver, mahogany red and roans, with tan markings, were permitted but colors like black and white were out. For a time there continued to be a few parti-colored winners, but gradually the breed was transformed to the solid colors we see today.

Toward the end of the 1930's, in the years immediately before World War II, the Field Spaniel began to decline in popularity. While all breeds were hard hit during the War years, when most breeding was suspended, the Field Spaniel was particularly decimated. "The war

An adorable litter of seven week old Field Spaniel puppies. These charmers are owned by Becki Jo Wolkenheim.

almost knocked the poor old Field Spaniel down for good," Peggy Grayson says. Mrs. Grayson, who obtained her first Field in 1939, was one of a small stalwart band of fanciers who regrouped to save the breed. "The end of the war saw an all time low in the breed," Mrs. Grayson recalls, "....but we were not dismayed and determined that now the world was getting back to normal, somehow we would revive the interest in the Field Spaniel no matter how long it took us!"

It was a long hard road. There were few dogs to work with. The breed got a boost in 1949, when Champion Vandyke became the first Field Spaniel to top a sporting group. Plagued with a lack of uniformity, and the necessity for weeding out the consequences of the Springer crosses, which now began to crop up, this small band of fanciers persevered. One additional cross to a Springer was employed in 1958. What they accomplished has been remarkable, particularly considering the small genetic base they had to work with. Indeed, all of today's Field Spaniels trace back to only four bitches. Yet, succeed they have. Today's Field Spaniel is a beautiful animal, close to the original spaniel type, but with an elegance and nobility lacking in the former. One can't help but think that those earliest pioneers would be proud.

The Field Spaniel made his debut in the United States in the late 1800's. The first official A.K.C. registration came in 1894. We seem to have had both the original and the exaggerated type here, in those early years. The drawing of Champion Black Prince, owned by Clumber breeder A. Clinton Wilmerding, of New York, which appears in the rare 1891 work *The American Book of the Dog*, is a little lower stationed, but quite reminiscent of the early Boulton dogs pictured in Stonehenge's book. We can only guess that Prince must have been an English champion, since his illustration in

this book predates the first A.K.C. registration. However, the exaggerated type was to make its way to this country, too. As we've already seen, James Watson imported some low to the ground Fields. In 1888, Charles Mason published a now rare book entitled, *Our Prize Dogs*. One of the first American books to employ photographs, rather than drawings, Mr. Mason, an early prominent judge, traipsed through the benching area of eastern shows and wrote detailed critiques on each and every dog he saw. He faults many of the Fields shown during this period as being too near to Cocker type. We can see clearly, through his detailed descriptions, that dogs actually bred by Mr. Jacobs arrived and won at American shows. According to information compiled by the Field Spaniel Society of America, a fire in the 1920's obliterated the last Field Spaniels in the country. The breed remained, according to them, extinct until the 1960's.

All this was to change in 1967, however, when a prominent English Field breeder became interested in the Cocker Spaniel (the breed known to the Brits as the "American" Cocker Spaniel). Mr. and Mrs. Richard Squirer and Carl Tuttle, both Cocker breeders, were equally interested in the Field Spaniel. A swap was arranged. Soon, Pilgrim of Mittina and Flowering May of Mittina were on their way to Mr. and Mrs. Squirer. Brigiadier of Mittina journeyed to Carl Tuttle's Gunhill Kennels. A year later Jeannie of Mittina joined the Squirer family and Joanne of Mittina went to the Tuttles. All of these five dogs became American champions and have established the foundation for the breed in this country. By 1978, there was sufficient interest in the breed to form the Field Spaniel Society of America.

It's a shame that the Field is so little known, for he is a charming and affectionate fellow, who'd make a delightful addition to more American homes. This breed is very good natured, laid back and craves human affection. For this reason, the Field is best as a personal companion, where he can relish the activities of a family, rather than being consigned to a kennel. He takes special delight in the companionship of children. An active, curious dog, it's best to train your Field Spaniel for he needs something to do. Boredom is apt to present problems, as it does in so many other breeds. Like all spaniels, the Field has a sensitive nature and responds poorly to harsh treatment.

The Field Spaniel is an intelligent dog and he welcomes a chance to prove it. While some have said that the breed is more headstrong than other spaniels, he still has a powerful desire to please. This is ably demonstrated by the dogs in this country who have earned many obedience degrees, from novice through Utility, and have even captured High in Trial awards. "While alert and able to bark an alarm," the Field Spaniel Society of America says, "the Field *is not* a guard dog and may well usher an intruder to your family silver."

While Field Spaniels are predominately kept as companions and show dogs, one must not overlook their ability to work. It's true that they will never be field trial stars because they lack the speed and style required for that endeavor. Still, they approach their duties with a workmanlike attitude and are more than capable of giving a hunter a day's pleasure filling the game bag. Those who have hunted with the breed say that the Field has the keenest nose to be found on any of the spaniel breeds. The Brits, who've had more experience with the breed in the field than we, report that this breed is a little more difficult to train than other spaniels. Patience and consistency, along with a well scheduled routine, is required to produce a top notch field dog. The Field Spaniel is equally at home on land and water and will avidly hunt both fur and feather. In fact, if you intend to use your dog solely on birds, it's best to keep him from rabbits and other small game. The breed is so good on rabbits that it's difficult to call them off for they are apt to pursue them with a zest usually reserved for hounds.

Today's Field Spaniel is a very attractive dog. He has a distinctive head with beautifully chiselled features. The foreface is long and the skull has a slightly raised occiput. His eyes, which range in color from brown to hazel, are set fairly wide apart and are almond shaped. Expression is key to the breed. "The expression is mild and kind," Peggy Grayson says, in *The History*

and Management of the Field Spaniel, "not merry like the Cocker, not all eager and alert as the Springer, not thoughtful as the Clumber, and not faraway as the Sussex. The expression in the eyes is all important, for without those, we lose much of the essential Field."

This breed is slow maturing and may not reach its peak until the second year. The Field stands about 18 inches at the withers and weighs from 35-50 pounds. He is a strong, well-boned dog who looks as though he could go all day afield. His body is of moderate length and he is sensibly angulated. He has a level topline which ends in a tail carried level with or slightly below the line of the back. His coat lies flat, but may be slightly waved, and has a lovely glossy, silken texture. Coat length is moderate. The standard allows "black, liver, golden liver, mahogany, red, or roan; or any of these colors with tan over the eyes and on the cheeks, feet and pasterns." The Field Spaniel's movement has been described as flowing and majestic. Peggy Grayson says "that lovely, low, deliberate and majestic movement that is the hallmark of the Field Spaniel."

Despite the limited gene pool, the Field Spaniel is a hardy and healthy breed. A few problems have been encountered, but these are rare and a healthy interchange between breeders has helped to ward off potential problems. Field Spaniel breeders aim to keep it that way, too. They x-ray and perform eye checks on all breeding stock. A thyroid condition is fairly common and manifests itself in scaly skin and poor coat quality. A simple blood test confirms the diagnosis and an inexpensive daily medication soon controls the problem.

"Currently, the main concern of breeders is to keep the Field alive as a breed," C. Bede Maxwell wrote in *The Truth About Sporting Dogs.* "If they can succeed in doing that, his ancient virtues, still shackled to the blood and bone of him, will make new friends to support him as the years roll by." That was written in 1972 and, in the nearly 20 years since, the Field Spaniel has indeed won new friends who are passionately dedicated to his welfare. While still rare, the breed is making headway. They have even begun to, once again, capture the eye of judges and there have been several group placements. Now that sensible heads have prevailed, the Field Spaniel is truly back. Perhaps, we can all learn something from his story.

Chapter 18

The Flat-Coated Retriever

The British Isles have produced some of our most splendid sporting dogs. Notable among these are the retrievers. It is interesting to note that, with the exception of the Portuguese Water Dog, all the specialist retrievers hail from either Britain or America. Intelligent, easily trainable and always companionable, these dogs have become favorites in many countries.

The Flat-Coated Retriever ranks as one of the most versatile of the retriever breeds. Perhaps the lack of overall popularity has contributed to the breed's current healthy status. The Flat-Coat has retained both his looks and his inherent field ability. Vernon Vogel, of Bolingbroke Kennels, in Edinboro, Pennsylvania, rankles somewhat at those who consider the breed "rare." This long time breeder is enthusiastic about the Flat-Coat's versatility. "This is a multi-purpose breed that can compete in show, obedience, field trials or for working certificates," he says. "Our field dogs and our show dogs are one and the same. There's no split between types, as we see in so many sporting breeds." All Flat-Coat breeders aim to keep it that way, too. As Dr. Nancy Laughton says in her 1968 book, *A Review of the Flat-Coated Retriever,* this is "a gundog for the minority whose tastes and circumstances enable them to understand and appreciate him, but not—emphatically not!—just for the majority."

The Flat-Coat was developed during one of the most exciting periods in the evolution of modern dogs. In the 1800's, there was an explosion of interest in hunting dogs. During the early days of the 17th century, Pointers, Setters and Spaniels were used not only to locate, but also to retrieve, game. They functioned in an all-round capacity, much like the sporting utility breeds that have come to us from other parts of Europe (eg. the German Shorthaired Pointer, the Weimaraner and the Wirehaired Pointing Griffon). British sportsmen, however, found that their field dogs didn't perfectly fill the bill. Pointers and Setters tended to become less steady for field work when asked to do complicated retrieves. And Spaniels, though capable, tended to develop ear canker when used extensively for water work. What hunters wanted was a larger and faster dog that could be used exclusively for retrieving, both in and out of the water. They tried many different breeds and combinations in their attempts to come up with a dog geared specifically for retrieving. Setters, Pointers, Spaniels, Poodles and even sheepdogs were all used, in the effort to achieve that goal.

During this period, a new dog burst upon the scene that was to radically alter the course of breeding. Dubbed the St. Johns Dog, the Lesser Newfoundland or the Labrador, this new blood was to have a profound effect on the search for an ideal retriever. Ships bringing cod and lumber to England's ports, from Newfoundland, brought with them dogs ideally suited to water, having webbed feet and coats impervious to the water. Colonel Peter Hawkes, in his 1814 work, *Instructions to Young Sportsmen in All That Relates to the Guns and Shooting,* first described these imports. "The St. John's Breed of these dogs is chiefly used on their native coast by fisherman....Their discrimination of scent, in following a wounded pheasant through a whole covert full of game, or a pinioned wild fowl through a furzebrake, or warren of rabbits, appears almost impossible. The real Newfoundland may be broken in to any kind of shooting; and without additional instruction, is generally under such command that he may be safely kept, if required to be taken out with pointers. For finding game of every description there is not his equal in the canine race; and he is *sine qua non* in the general pursuit of wild fowl..."

Small wonder that these new dogs attracted such attention. Now, the St. John's dog was used as a basis for the continuing experiments to produce an ideal retriever. Crosses with setters were very popular. Writing in 1847, in *Dog Breaking,* General Hutchinson tells us that the best retrievers came from a cross of the St. John's dog with a setter. The esteemed dog writer, Stonehenge, also speaks

The beautiful American, Canadian Ch. Bertschire's Doc Holiday Am. CDX, WCX, Can. CD, owned by Mrs. Mark Cavallo, of Atlanta, Georgia. (Photo courtesy of Vernon Vogel.)

of these setter crosses. The popularity of the newly formed dogs coincided with the advent of dog shows. Classes for retrievers were offered in 1860 and the entrants were divided into classes for curly-coated, wavy-coated or smooth-coated dogs. The Wavy-Coats are the ones that interest us, here, for they were the forerunners of the Flat-Coated Retriever. By 1864, there was enough interest in the Wavy-Coats that they were accorded separate classes at shows.

The Wavy-Coat became extremely popular with gamekeepers and remains so to this day. These men recognized the breed's working attributes and held these dogs in high esteem. For a time, the Wavy-Coat was even called the "Keeper's Dog." The famous bitches, "Old Bounce" and "Young Bounce," who won in both show and field in the 1860's, were owned by the Redditch gamekeeper, Mr. D. Hull. The breed garnered much attention and became tremendously popular. Vero Shaw, writing in the 1879-81 work, *The Illustrated Book of the Dog,* said that "no breed has made more rapid strides in public estimation..."

It was Dr. Bond Moore who did much to stablize breed type. Moore maintained a kennel of Wavy-Coats at his home in Wolverhampton and his dogs were, as Vero Shaw puts it, "highly esteemed." As a judge, however, Dr. Moore proved to be quite controversial.

"As a judge of the breed...Dr. Bond Moore was quite at the head of affairs, though he was on many occasions considered arbitrary in his decisions," Shaw says. "As an instance, he has been known to disqualify a dog for having a few white hairs upon it, which...was at the time considered by many an unnecessarily harsh action. Dr. Bond Moore was, we believe, influenced in pursuing this course by a determination to adhere to a type he had laid down, and...had made up his mind to give no encouragement to any but the correct type of dog. There can be little question but that his example influenced other judges, and, possibly, this may have done much toward the improvement which the variety has made since its first appearance on the bench." Stonehenge did not concur. "Mr. Bond Moore who is considered to be the highest authority on the breed, would disqualify a dog for a white spot of the smallest kind on the breast or forehead. This is very absurd in a dog intended for use. Fancy dogs may be measured by any rule however artificial, but a shooting dog should only be judged in points which are relevant to his work."

Dr. Moore's work was carried on by another man, considered by many to be the true "father" of the breed. Sewallis Evelyn Shirley was a wealthy sportsman and served as a member of Parliament. He was to become a devoted Wavy-Coat enthusiast who assembled a top-notch group of dogs at his kennels in Ettington. He purchased progeny of Old Bounce and Young Bounce and some of Dr. Moore's dogs found their way into his kennel. Soon, his dogs became so noteworthy that some suggested the Wavy-Coat should henceforth be known as the Shirley Retriever. Indeed, like Mr. Moore before him, Shirley set the tone for the breed. He began to eliminate the wavy coat and sought to diminish the heavy feathering from the setter side of the family. It was due to his efforts that the "Flat," rather than "Wavy," coat became the desired norm. One of his most successful sires, Zelstone, has been dubbed by some writers as the "Adam" of the breed, so pervasive was his influence. However, Mr. Shirley's contributions to dogs extend much further than his sponsorship of the Flat-Coat. He will forever be remembered as one of those who formed England's Kennel Club, in 1873, and served as its first President.

In those days, the color of the Flat-Coat was universally acknowledged as black. Stonehenge says that the "colour is always black without white." Shaw tells of some "sandy" or golden colored dogs which popped up in Mr. Moore's breedings. While not used for show, these dogs were bred. While the history of the liver colored Flat-Coat is not well documented, there is evidence that the color has been around almost since the beginning. Idstone, writing in 1872, says that he doesn't like the color because "in fading it tends to take on the shade of a rusty nail." In 1900, the gamekeeper J.H. Abbott, ran a liver bitch, Rust, in trials conducted by the Retriever Society. When she captured the top award, critics grumbled about her color.

The Flat-Coat's future seemed assured. Wealthy British sportsmen had taken the breed to their hearts and made it the most popular of all retrievers. This was not to last, though. As the new century dawned, the Labrador Retriever became increasingly popular. The Lab displayed a great deal of style and dash in the field and began to eclipse the Flat-Coat. Breeders decided that the Flat-Coat needed a longer foreface and jaws in order to retrieve pheasants and hares. To achieve this aim, they crossed the Flat-Coat with the Borzoi. "The products immediately displayed narrow skulls and long forefaces, giving to the whole head a 'coffin-like' structure and aspect," wrote Major Harding Cox, in *Hutchinson's Dog Encyclopedia*. "The old established judges were unwilling to recognize this new type, but in time the resistance broke down. New judges took the place of the old, and the Flat-Coated Retriever became a breed with long narrow heads and weak muzzles. Some 'old time' breeders and exhibitors gave up the breed altogether, but a few held on and eventually succeeded in putting the 'coffin-headed' dogs in their proper place 'below the salt.' But the damage had been done, and it took

generations of careful breeding to eliminate the traces of this destructive experiment..."

While wealthy sportsmen and the general public may have surrendered their attentions to the Labrador, there were some who remained true to the Flat-Coat. Chief among these were the gamekeepers. They continued to hunt and breed their dogs. There were others, too, who remained stalwart fans of the Flat-Coat. One such breeder was Reginald Cooke, of Riverside Kennels. His seventy years of involvement with the breed, spanned both the ups and downs of the Flat-Coat. Born in 1860, Mr. Cooke became interested in the breed at an early age. At his death, in 1951, he had achieved a remarkable record. His kennels had produced two dual champions and 32 other champions and his dogs had earned an amazing 349 Challenge Certificates. He also passed on a valuable historical legacy for modern day breeders. He kept detailed records on his dogs and their accomplishments. These were bound in volumes, covering the period from 1903-1950. Mr. Cooke was unstinting in his devotion to the breed and his advocacy of true type. One of his most famous dogs was Ch. High Legh Blarney, immortalized by the celebrated dog painter, Maud Earl. When Blarney's owner died, in 1905, the dog was put up at auction. So great was Mr. Cooke's admiration for the dog, that he gave his agent a blank check to acquire him.

Despite the sponsorship of Mr. Cooke and a few others, World War I had a devastating impact on the breed. As Mr. Cooke recalled in *The Book of the Dog*, edited by Brian Vesey-Fitzgerald, "It is beyond doubt that the ranks of this breed were much depleted by the Great War, as to a very large extent it was in the hands of gamekeepers. These sportsmen joined up early...some,

American, Canadian Ch. Essex Summer Sorcerer Am., Can. CD is the son of Vernon Vogel's famous Ch. Mantayo Bo James Bolingbroke.

alas! never to return...and on leaving for the front either put down their dogs or sold them to people who had no interest in breeding; consequently the breed lost a full six years' fostering, as well as training, and has been at a disadvantage compared with other breeds which had the good fortune to be taken up by owners of large kennels, and make a better start at the conclusion of the War...."

As World War I ended, the gamekeepers returned and once again acquired their much loved Flat-Coats. It was during this period, Paddy Petch tells us in *The Complete Flat-Coated Retriever,* that the dogs were occasionally interbred with Labradors. The breed was still struggling and had competition not only from the Lab, but also the Golden Retriever, as interest in this breed was steadily increasing. Still, the Flat-Coat had his share of success in the field. It looked as though the breed was making a great comeback. Major Harding Cox, writing in *Hutchinson's Dog Encyclopedia,* says that at the 1932 Cruft's show, there was an entry of 170.

World War II was to interfere with the breed's promising rally. Once again, the game-keepers were among the first to volunteer for military duty. "If it had not been for such enthusiasts as Phizacklea, Cooke and others including Mrs. P.M. Barwise's Forestholm dogs and the Claverdon Kennel of Mrs. Nancy Laughton, the breed might have been lost forever, for they continued breeding, albeit in a very restricted manner," says Paddy Petch in *The Complete Flat-Coated Retriever.* "At the end of hostilities many of the former devotees returned from active service...and of course those men who were the backbone of the Society pre-War—the gamekeepers..."

Fortunately, the Flat-Coat has rebounded from its troubles. It has become increasing popular in England, where it is esteemed both on the bench and in the field. A top wins at Crufts has done much to spur interest in the breed. As Bede Maxwell writes in her 1972 book, *The Truth About Sporting Dogs,* "one can still find a surprising strength in terms of entries at the great British championship shows, and it takes very little probing to discover how rich the percentage of practical working dogs among the Flat-Coat entry. In this respect, it leaves the other retrieving breeds whole streets behind it..."

We do not know precisely when the first Flat-Coated Retriever came to the United States. In 1915, the American Kennel Club recognized the breed and Sand Bridge Jester became the

first dog to be registered. Over the intervening years, several attempts to sponsor the breed began. Some Americans paid very high prices indeed for quality Flat-Coats. But the gene pool remained small and the breed never really gained much of a foothold. Finally, in 1960, a trio of devoted Flat-Coat owners met in Chicago to form a club for the breed. These breed pioneers were Mr. and Mrs. Homer W. Downing, owners of the first U.D.T. Flat-Coat, Mr. and Mrs. Edward J. Moroff, owners of an outstanding field trial dog and Mrs. Sally J. Terroux, who is still active to this day and stands as this country's most enduring breeder. The Club they formed, the Flat-Coated Retriever Society of America, has done much to foster interest in this versatile breed.

Undeniably, the Flat-Coat is an attractive fellow. Like the other retrievers, he has substance and strength, but the setter side of his ancestry has imparted a racy elegance. His head is decidedly different from the Labrador or the Golden. It is finely chiseled, longer and

A wonderful shot of American, Canadian Ch. Hy-Tyme's Stephanie Am., Can. CD. (Photo courtesy of Vernon Vogel.)

has little stop. The eyes are almond-shaped and must be dark brown (not black) or hazel. Light eyes are a serious fault. Males stand 23-24 1/2 inches, while bitches measure 22-23 1/2 inches. Dogs generally weight 60-80 pounds, while bitches tip the scales at 55-70 pounds.

As the breed name implies, the ideal coat lies flat and straight. The Flat-Coat has a dense undercoat which affords ideal protection from the elements. In the mature, fully coated dog, there is thick feathering on the ears, chest, back of forelegs, thighs and the underside of the tail. Flat-Coat owners are intent on avoiding the elaborate grooming that characterizes so many show dogs. "The Flat-Coat is shown with as natural a coat as possible and *must not* be penalized for lack of trimming," the standard says. "Tidying of whiskers, ears, feet and tip of tail is acceptable. Shaving or noticeable barbering of neck, body coat or feathering to change the natural appearance of the dog, *must* be heavily penalized." The lovely feathered tail is carried level with the back.

The black or liver colored coat is easily cared for. A good brushing one or twice a week will keep the coat attractive. The dogs do shed seasonally and need more brushing at that time.

In describing the Flat-Coat, owners are apt to first mention the ever wagging tail. Indeed, it is the breed's buoyant, outgoing, enthusiastic zest for life that owners love. Best of all, he retains these characteristics even into old age. Paddy Petch describes the breed as "one of life's optimists, the epitome of the canine extrovert. He is always ready for a game, a walk or a drive in the car." While gentle and lovable, the Flat-Coat is an energetic dog. Owners often find that obedience training is an ideal way to channel the breed's boundless energy. With his natural intelligence and extreme desire to please, the Flat-Coat is a natural for obedience work.

If there's one thing all Flat-Coat owners agree upon, it is this breed's need for human companionship. "To develop to his fullest potential," Vernon Vogel says, "the Flat-Coat must have lots of *individual* attention. In a home with just a few dogs, the Flat-Coat can develop into an absolutely *super* dog. New owners must understand that this is a very people oriented breed."

Sally Terroux would certainly agree. In her 1968 book, *How to Raise and Train a Flatcoated Retriever,* she describes the breed as, "Definitely dependent in nature, they are ideal for people who truly enjoy and appreciate dogs; definitely not for the people who want a dog as a show piece, status symbol, or to keep in the back yard for the children to play with now and then, and stay out of the way the rest of the time. Flat-Coats are responsive, intelligent, interested in what is going on around them, and basically friendly towards all living creatures."

Doing what comes naturally. This versatile dog is American, Canadian Ch. Bolingbroke's Kiss Me Kate CDX, WC, bred by Vernon Vogel and owned by Linda Randall, DVM. (Photo courtesy of Vernon Vogel.)

The Flat-Coat ranks high as a children's companion. "They are gentle as lambs with small children, whom they look after with all the innate intelligence of the breed," says Paddy Petch, in *The Complete Flat-Coated Retriever.* Vernon Vogel agrees. "They are just wonderful with kids. They are very patient and will let kids crawl all over them and maul them. When watching them, you sometimes think they take too much from kids."

The breed makes a good family watchdog, alerting his owners with a deep bark. Sally Terroux characterizes the Flat-Coat as "a good watch dog though never a biter." In our highly litigious society, that may well be a positive attribute.

Writing in 1872, Idstone described the performance of his friend's Flat-Coat. "For retrieving water fowl he was excellent; and in the narrow water courses and among the reeds and osiers his chase of a winged mallard was a thing to see. They seemed both to belong to one element; and he would dive like an otter for yards, sometimes coming up for breath, only to go down again for pleasure." This description, penned so long ago, must sound very familiar to present-day owners. The Flat-Coat has retained his inherent love of the water. Indeed, most take to the water like ducks and the only problem owners have is coaxing the dogs *out* when the day is done.

Vernon Vogel, of Bolingbroke Kennels, is enthusiastic about the breed's love for water and natural desire to retrieve. Mr. Vogel has been involved with dogs since 1969. He first owned a Schnauzer but decided that he'd really like to have a larger dog for obedience. A friend suggested a Flat-Coat. After investigating the breed, he obtained his first dog in 1971 and joined the national club. His American, Bermudian and Canadian Champion Mantayo Bo James Bolingbroke made breed history by becoming the first liver dog to win a Sporting Group. In the best tradition of the breed, "Jamie," as he was called, exemplified versatility. He obtained his C.D.X. in both the U.S. and Canada and earned a Bermudian C.D. At nine years of age, he earned a leg toward his Utility title and received his Working Certificate at eleven. He was in training for his tracking title when he died suddenly. Jamie's legacy lives on, however. Although not used at stud until four, he sired over 40 A.K.C. champions and over 15 Canadian champions. His get also earned many obedience and working titles.

"The day Jamie worked in 32 degree water for 15 minutes to recover a retrieving dummy, I knew he was special," Vernon recalls. "At ten weeks of age, he was determined." Vernon describes the Flat-Coat as a natural retriever. "They seem to have an instinctive desire to carry things. This can be seen in normal family activities. When one of my dogs comes into the house, they will first greet me with a tail wag and then they'll run to pick up something. It could be a sock, a teddy bear or something else. They want to carry things around." As if to illustrate the point, Vernon tells of one of his bitches. "She's 11 years old now and she will still retrieve until she drops. I recall one funny episode when she was in season and waiting to be bred. She was standing, flagging her tail and waiting for the male, when someone threw something. She immediately chased it and retrieved the article. She held it in her mouth during the entire breeding."

The Flat-Coat has had success in field trials, but is hampered somewhat by being judged by Labrador and Golden standards. "People will often say that their dog is birdy and loves the water and, therefore, would be an ideal trial dog," Vernon Vogel says. "Field people point out that while this is a good sign, it doesn't necessarily mean that the dog will develop into a trial performer. The dog has to be willing to follow commands even when he would rather not. The Flat-Coat was developed as a personal hunting companion and will often think out and discover the easiest way to get the bird. That's not what's required in a field trial performer."

He may not be the flashiest trial performer, but as a personal hunting companion, the Flat-Coat is excellent. Keen and birdy, the breed earns high marks for his resourcefulness at retrieving. "The Flat-Coat is at his best when he is part of the family group," says Sally Terroux, in *How to Raise and Train a Flat Coated Retriever*. "In this he differs from some of the other members of the sporting group who are most efficient in the field when they are kenneled between hunting trips. The Flat-Coat is first and foremost a personal shooting dog and should be kept and regarded as such."

"As far as Flat-Coats go they are still dual purpose dogs and it would be a great pity if they ever lost their working ability and became beautiful but useless. However, there are many people whose interest in the working side is very strong, so at the moment the future looks satisfactory." Satisfactory may well be an understatement. Flat-Coat owners jealously guard the breed's many qualities. They want the breed to remain a lovable companion, an elegant show dog, an enthusiastic obedience worker and an outstanding personal hunter.

Chapter 19

The Irish Red and White Setter

The Irish Setter has been a popular breed, in this country, since its introduction in the late 1800's. The proud, mahogany coated beauties, their heads held high, have often captured top honors in American show rings. Indeed, these magnificent dogs with their flaming coats are the most popular of all Irish breeds. Most Americans, then, will be startled to discover that the Emerald Isle is home to another Setter...The Irish Red and White. While they don't rival their more popular brethern, they are gaining a steady following in Ireland and England and have recently made their debut in other countries. Almost forgotten, the Irish Red and White is experiencing a resurgence and that's only fitting. In the early days, the parti-colored dogs were the most popular Setters in their misty homeland.

The first Setters sprang, authorities tell us, from a cross between the spaniel and the pointer. This new style of dog was developed specifically to suit the hunting methods of the time. In the days before firearms, birds were hunted with nets. And so, sporting men taught their dogs to "set" or crouch down silently while the net was spread. In this position, the excited dog was less likely to spring the game. We don't precisely know when the transition from springing to setting occurred. That famous dog writer, Dr. John Caius, in his 1576 book, *Englishe Dogges,* was the first person to describe the Setter.

With apologies to Caius, I have rewritten his archaic text in modern English. "Another sort of dog be there, serviceable for fowling, making no noise either with foot or with tongue, while they follow the game. These attend diligently upon their Master and frame their conditions to such becks, motions, and gestures, as it shall please him to exhibit and make, either going forward, drawing backward, inclining to the right hand, or yielding toward the left....when he hather found the bird, he keepeth sure and fast silence, he stays his steps and will proceed no further, and with a close, covert, watching eye, lays his belly to the ground and so creeps forward like a worm. When he approaches near to the place where the bird is, he lays him down, and with a mark of his paws, betrays the place of the bird's last abode, whereby it is supposed that this kind of dog is called *Index,* Setter, being in deed a name most consonant and agreeable to his quality...."

We do know that setting dogs have existed in Ireland for centuries. Joan Brearley, in her *This is the Irish Setter,* says that in the 1500's "a Sir Robert Cecil was importing 'setting dogs' from Ireland which he presented with great ceremony to visiting diplomats."

As hunting styles and practices evolved, so too did the dogs. While sportsmen found that it was handy to walk up to dogs who had "set" when they detected the presence of birds, it had its disadvantages. In fields of heather, or other such flora, the dogs were hard to see. Gradually, probably in the 1600's, sportsmen trained their setters to stand and point. The Setter breeds and the Pointer from the British Isles were, as a rule, used in more open fields, while spaniels pursued game in woods and brushy thickets. This explains why the tails of the Pointers and Setters, hailing from British stock, were not docked. By contrast, the tails of spaniels, used in heavy cover and subject to injury, were usually cut shortly after birth.

By the 1700's, setters seem to have been well known in Ireland. Curiously, the Emerald Isle has always preferred setters over spaniels and pointers. One of the earliest documented lines of Irish Setters dates back to about 1770. Maurice Nugent O'Connor, of Mount Pleasant, King's County, took great pride in his dogs and was one of the first breeders to favor the solid reds. While writers have usually focused on his preference for the solid color dogs, we know that O'Connor also kept a strain of red and whites, as well. In the early 1800's, O'Connor presented some of his dogs to his friend, Robert La Touche, of Harristown, in County Kildare. La Touche continued the line after O'Connor's death in 1818.

O'Connor's strain aside, his solid colored dogs appear to have been the exception in the early 1800's. In Rawdon Lee's *Modern Dogs*, Mr. W.C. Bennett tells of his conversations with several old Irish sportsmen. All agreed that the red and white dogs "or more properly the white and red dog," were much more common and preferred for field work. In fact, one man reported that a gamekeeper once brought him a solid red dog as a curiosity.

"The other breed—the white and red," writes Colonel White, in an 1860 issue of *The Field*, "claims equal antiquity with the red, and many consider them to have been as good as the red in all respects and superior in point of nose. I have seen these dogs, magnificent in

The lovely Rua Snowdrop, bred by Mary Tuite and owned by Mrs. J. Read.

appearance and excellent in the field, but have not met with them lately, though no doubt they are to be found. I know they were highly thought of eighty or ninety years ago, because a certain General White—a grand uncle of mine, who died about 1802....used to bring his setters from Ireland, and I have heard my father say that the General's favourite breed was the white and red; in fact, I distinctly remember seeing some of the descendants...."

Milo Denlinger writes in *The Complete Irish Setter,* published in 1949, that red and white was the predominate color for the breed during the 1830s. Mr. Baker, of County Tipperary, and Yelverton O'Keefe, were but two of the many prominent red and white breeders. Sir Francis Loftus carefully recorded, in a diary, notes on the training, field accomplishments and personalities of his red and whites. Perhaps the most famous dogs of this type, though, were the celebrated Rossmore strain, found in County Monaghan. This line was said to have been maintained pure and unbroken since the 1700s.

Some time in the 1830's or '40's, the famous Edward Laverack, truly the father of the English Setter, journeyed four times to Ireland. His visits were, as he says in his 1872 book *The Setter,* "for the express purpose of ascertaining where the pure blood was to be found, with a view of crossing them with my Beltons." Unfortunately, Laverack was disappointed with the performances and appearance of most of the dogs he saw. "There is another color of Irish setters, *blood red* and *white,* quite as pure, indeed some people maintain, of greater antiquity and purity of blood, than the blood red," Mr. Laverack observes. "Both the blood red and the blood red and white, will throw each color, evidently denoting that they are of the same strain. I think that the handsomest Irish setters I ever saw were in the possession of the two Misses Ledwidge, of Beggarbush, near Dublin." In fact, later writers tell us that Laverack tried to persuade the women to sell him one of their males. They adamantly refused. Laverack must have had a good eye for a dog, for the strain maintained by these Irish women was to produce some of the Irish Setter's most notable early winners. "Of the two colours, blood red and blood red and white, I admire the latter the most, they being in my opinion the handsomer of the two."

Evidently, the red and white Irish Setters captured the attention of many people. They were particularly prized for their work afield. Nimrod, writing in his 1837 work, *Sporting,* tells of grouse hunting with these dogs. "....it was a very pleasing sight to witness them in their work," he writes. "A leash of highly bred red and white setters were let loose at a time, and beautifully did they range the fields, quartering the ground in obedience to the voice or the whistle."

We know that both the solid red dogs and the red and whites co-existed, but it was not a peaceful coexistence. A heated, often virulent debate arose regarding the correct color for an Irish Setter. Each side held passionately to their own opinions, denigrating the dogs of the opposite color. Those who favored the red and white dogs, pointed out that they were easier to see in the field, particularly against meadows dotted with brown heather. Indeed, several valuable red setters were accidentally shot while hunting. To prevent this, red setter advocates took to tying a bit of white cloth around the necks of their dogs. Many also felt that the red and whites were more adept afield. They credited the dogs with having keener noses, better speed and more endurance. In addition, they pointed out that the red and whites were easier to train. The red's proponents, certainly, did not agree with this assessment.

The color differences may, in fact, have been regional disputes. This appears to be the view of Mrs. N. Ingle Bepler. In the years 1890-1920, her Rheola reds dominated show rings. In her rare 1930 book, *Setters: Irish, English and Gordon,* she tells us that the solid red dogs came primarily from northern Ireland. To the south and west, she says, the red and white colored dogs predominated. On Ireland's west coast was to be found a color she described, colorfully, as a "show of hail." These setters were more spotted with quarter-inch white spots sprinkled on a background of red.

Things might well have remained the same with both colors having their respective admirers, had it not been for the advent of dog shows. Like the English, the Irish were caught up in the dog show craze. Suddenly, there was a new market for the pups produced by Irish breeders. No longer were they wanted solely as field dogs. People eagerly lined up to purchase show prospects and the solid red's breeders were enthusiastically involved in this new pastime. Their advocacy of the solid reds took hold and they persuaded many judges that this was the *only* proper color for the entire breed. Though small amounts of white were often found on solid colored dogs, even these were held in disrepute. Some breeders urged judges to disqualify dogs with even a trace of white. As Vero Shaw observed, in *The Illustrated Book of the Dog,* published in 1879, "opinions are mainly divided on the question of white. Whether this colour is permissible in a pure-bred Irish Setter or not was, at one time, a very important feature in discussions on the breed, and we have of later years heard it maintained that white marks should disqualify an Irish Setter in competition on the show bench."

In the early show days, the red and whites held their own. Several of the earliest winners were, in fact, parti-colored. One such dog was the celebrated "Wrestler," who topped not only bench entries but also field trials. He was said to be a handsome dog of tremendous energy and verve. He was also noted for his most extraordinary endurance. It's been said that on the day of a field trial, Wrestler would run 10-15 miles cross country to get to the field trial site. Far from being exhausted, he was still rarin' to go when the trial began.

But, eventually, the reds would win out. As their dominance increased, it became difficult for the red and white dogs, no matter how good, to get a look from a judge. Because of this, some shows began to offer special classes for the red and white dogs. But, it was no use. Solid colored advocates still objected, and soon the red and whites no longer appeared at shows. As Vero Shaw says, "for our own part, we must confess that our affections lie in the direction of a whole-coloured dog, and that we think the less white an Irish Setter has about him the handsomer he is. So much in modern times depends upon appearances, and there are so few opportunities for satisfactorily testing the merits of a show dog in the field, that the question of his beauty is of far greater importance than it was before the origin of canine exhibitions." Indeed, most judges agreed with Shaw. And, while he sought to retain the red and whites, saying, "We, therefore, are strongly in favour of due encouragement being given to the red-and-whites by the committees of dog shows throughout the country," few listened.

The same pattern held true in America. Red and whites had been imported in the mid-1800s and appeared at the first shows for the breed given here. In the 1870's, Irish Setter fans gathered for a show in Chicago's Exposition Building. There were special classes offered for both imported and homebred red and whites. The first Westminster Kennel Club show was held in May 1877. There was a whopping entry of 130 Irish Setters.

Fermanagh Mist, owned by Vincent Brennan, of Northern Ireland.

In the Imported Bitch class, Londoner T. Medley's "Belle," a three year old red and white bitch triumphed. In the class for "Native Irish Setter Bitches," the entry of 19 was topped by the red and white Kate, owned by F.H. Cozzens, of New York City. But, the red and whites weren't to have a future in this country, either. Taking their lead from the British, from whom the dogs were imported, the red and whites were quickly abandoned in this country, too.

It's a wonder that the red and white setters did not become extinct. A few staunch Irishmen clung to their preference, though, and the red and whites were maintained as a field strain. In the 1940s, a club was formed to promote working qualities. The Cuddy family, of County Cork, took up the breed and quickly became the most noted breeders. Today, their dogs can be found behind all strains.

Though the Irish Red and White Setter is still scarce, there has been increased interest in the breed in both Ireland and England. Until 1987, the breed appeared in the Any Other Variety Gundog class at British shows. Now, however, the breed has been accorded separate status and can compete for Challenge Certificates and earn championships. As with other British gundogs, in order to qualify for a full championship (as opposed to a Show Championship), dogs must successfully earn a working gundog certificate.

The Irish Kennel Club recently gave the nod to a plan which allows for selected matings to Irish Red Setters. The purpose of this plan is to increase the breed's genetic base, while still retaining the Red and White's essential characteristics. The first several of these crosses have now been completed. "All red and white pups, prior to registration, must be passed on as to color, etc.," writes English breeder Mary Tuite, of Rua Kennels, in East Sussex, England. "Only those who meet the exacting standards will be registered with the Irish Kennel Club."

Breed popularity does, indeed, appear to be on the increase. Every year, the Irish Kennel Club hosts a championship show at Ballsbridge. It is, appropriately, held on St. Patrick's Day. In 1990, there was an entry of 26 Irish Red and Whites. At the 1990 Cruft's show, in London, there were 42 dogs and 40 bitches entered. In 1991, as most of you know, Cruft's was relocated to Birmingham, where there was considerably more room. Prior to 1991, entrants to Crufts had to have garnered a first place win at either a championship show or field trial to qualify to compete. In their new expanded location, the rules were modified, to allow for both first and second place class wins. This, of course, allowed for more qualifying dogs and was reflected in the number of entries. 114 Irish Red and Whites showed up for this Centenary show. Red and Whites are shown in separate

An adorable litter of puppies born at Mary Tuite's Rua Kennel, in England.

classes as a distinct breed, not as merely a variety of the more popular Irish Red Setter.

The Irish Red and White Setter has the same long legged, athletic elegance as his solid colored brother. The standard calls for a dog who is "strong and powerful, well balanced and proportioned without lumber— athletic rather than racy." His head is broad with a well defined stop. The muzzle is clean and square. His skull is slightly domed, but lacks the pronounced occipital protuberance found in the Irish Red Setter. The eyes should be dark brown or dark hazel. The slightly arched neck is moderately long and lends an elegant air. In body, one looks for the same qualities as in the Irish Red Setter. Dogs stand 24 1/2 to 26 inches at the withers, while bitches should measure 22 1/2 to 24 inches.

Coat and color are, of course, important to both Irish Setters. The body coat should lie straight and flat, and be "not over profuse." The breed features long, silky feathering of a fine texture. "Base colour white with solid red patches (clear islands of red colour)," the standard states. It adds that "both colours should show the maximum of life and bloom; flecking but not roaning permitted around the face and feet and up the foreleg as far as the elbow and up the hindleg as far as the hock; roaning, flecking or mottling on any other part of the body is most objectionable and is to be heavily penalized."

Vincent Brennan, of Rock View Kennels, located in County Fermanagh, in Northern Ireland, is an enthusiastic fan of the Irish Red and Whites. He actively hunts his dogs and has been successful in showing them. "The Irish Red and White Setter has a calmer and better balanced personality than the Irish Red Setter and is easier to train as a gundog," Mr. Brennan observes.

Recently, Mr. Brennan exported one of his Red and White pups to Germany. There, "Duke," as he is known, is making quite a name for himself in gundog circles. In May, he was entered in a three-day field event

Vincent Brennan's Lough Erne Lady is a consistant winner in Ireland.

on the island of Fohr, a few miles from the Danish border. It was the 100th anniversary of the North Germany Hunter's Association. There were 44 dogs entered, comprising a mix of European sporting utility breeds, Pointers and all setter breeds. Duke was the first Irish Red and White to be imported to the country and, so, the first to compete in hunting trials. Out of a possible 70 points, Duke earned 68 and placed eighth overall. He was the second best male dog and topped the British gundog breeds. In September 1990, he was entered in Germany's toughest hunting certification, the HZP test. Out of a possible 180 points, Duke scored the full 180! One can only predict that, due to his auspicious performance, Duke will be but the first of many Irish Red and Whites to be imported to Germany. Vincent Brennan is, justifiably, proud.

Mary Tuite, in England, is also interested in the Irish Red and White Setter as a dual purpose dog. At her Rua kennels (Rua means 'red' in Gaelic), she breeds Irish Terriers, Irish Red Setters and, of course, Irish Red and White Setters. In 1981, one of her Irish Setters topped Crufts, defeating more than 10,000 dogs! Her ties to Ireland are strong and Mary also owns a home there. To ensure that her dogs have experience in the field, she has taken them to Scotland to hunt on the moors.

"Most of the dogs in England are mainly show dogs," Mary says. "I am the only breeder that continually perseveres in trying to keep a dual aspect, that is the ability to work and compete at field trials as well as in the show ring. At the field trials, they have to compete with the bird dogs (English Setters, Irish Red Setters, Gordon Setters and English Pointers). These stakes have entries of over 30 dogs." Her trips to Scotland have proved quite beneficial. "I have been very satisfied with the dogs working ability," she reports. "Being shot over regularly has certainly improved their steadiness on game.

"The Red and White Setter seems to be more aware of everything around it," Mary says. "In the show ring, for instance, they notice strangers with hats and glasses or the clicking of cameras. They do seem to show some nervousness at this, while the Irish Red doesn't seem to be so aware."

Thankfully, the Irish Red and White Setter is alive and well. In the past decade, several have been imported into the United States, but no serious attempt has been made to promote or sponsor the breed. With the new increasing interest in rare breeds, however, that is certain to change. A dog of uncommon beauty, the Irish Red and White shares the same charm that has endeared so many to the Irish Red. It's certain that we'll see more of this breed . The Irish Red and White seems destined to capture top awards at rare breed outings.

The impressive winner Ch. Tralee's Storm Warning, owned by Mary Roberts and Robert Milano. (Photo courtesy of Peggy Gill)

Chapter 20

The Irish Terrier

"My opinion of this breed is indeed a high one," wrote Lt. Col. E.H. Richardson, head of the British War Dog School, during the second World War. "They are highly sensitive, spirited dogs of fine mettle, and those who respect and admire the finer qualities of mind will find them amply reflected in these terriers. They are extraordinarily intelligent, faithful and honest, and a man who has one of them as a companion will never lack a true friend."

Those who know the Irish Terrier would echo Lt. Col. Richardson's comments. Indeed, dog history is replete with stories of the Irish daredevil, his antics and accomplishments. Wherever he is known, he captures the hearts of those he lives with. Jack London featured the breed in several of his books. And, those familiar with Albert Payson Terhune and his legendary books featuring Collies, may be surprised to find that he was a great admirer of the Irish Terrier. Writing in the *Herald Tribune*, he once penned this tribute to the breed:

"The Irish Terrier is perhaps the finest dog on earth. He does not throw away his priceless devotion and loyalty on every stranger who may chirp to him. But to the death he is the comrade and protector, and exuberant playmate and sympathizing comforter of the human who once has won his heart and respect.

"He is an Irish gentleman of the deathless old school; a fiery, true gentleman, from the tips of his braced toes to the rough thatch of his crown. He is more; he has a heart that is as white and clean as a Knight-errant's.

"He is no bully, but he will flinch not one hundredth of an inch from the fight that is forced on him, be the odds ever so impossible against him.

"There is a psychic side to the Irish Terrier, too, found in almost no other dog; a tinge of the mysticism of the land of his ancestry."

The land of his ancestry is, of course, the Emerald Isle. Originally, the breed was raised by Irish cottiers, or peasant farmers. They had a difficult time earning a living on their small acreages and life was often hard. Like the people themselves, their dogs were expected to earn their keep. The terriers which they developed were used as an all-round farm dog. They kept the pigs and chickens in their pens and out of the garden. At night, they served as watchdogs and they also kept rats from the potatoes, which were generally stored in earthen pits. They served admirably as companions and playmates for children.

In the main, the Irish peasant's farm was not fenced. This led to much interbreeding, we are told, between the dogs on various farms in each region. "As such terriers were indiscriminately bred," reports W.J. Cotton, of County Wicklow, in a letter which appears in Rawdon Lee's 1894 book, *Modern Dogs,* "and all ran wild, the dog with the most pluck exercised the largest influence on the breed."

The Irish Terrier was also expected to serve as an all-round hunting dog. His skills were born of necessity. The owner needed meat or fowl for the stewpot. The fox had to be deterred from the poultry pen. Rats had to be kept from the food stored for the winter. Otters had to be kept in check, in the streams, lest they take too many fish.

While these hunting skills were essential for the survival of Irish farm families, they also provided sport. The farmers worked long and hard and there wasn't much opportunity for entertainment. In hunting, the

A wonderful head study of Ch. Gilmere's Blarney Stone, owned by Paul and Peggy Gill, of Carlisle, Mass.

cottier could combine work and pleasure. Being human, they started to compete with each other. There was great pride in owning an accomplished terrier. Gameness, endurance, intelligence and hardiness were prized. The Irish Terrier displayed these qualities in abundance.

In England, terriers were often kept in Foxhound kennels. Not so in Ireland. When hound owners needed the assistance of one of these small dogs, they merely detoured to the closest farm. It is recorded that two local terriers helped Lord Massareene's pack, in County Louth, kill five foxes in a single afternoon. Three of them had gone to earth.

F. M. Jowett, in his early book, *The Irish Terrier,* tells us of dogs who flushed rabbits from hedgerows and then retrieved them to hand. He recalls the thrill of watching the dogs bolt otters from drains and tree roots, and tenaciously hold badgers.

The breed gained quite a reputation for its prowess on rats. In 1870, Mr. Ridgeway (one of the pioneers who helped write the first breed standard) recalled a day afield with his bitch, Antrim Jess. "A bank was being bored, and at one place a rat bolted. Jess had him almost before he cleared his hole. Then came another, and another, so fast that the work was getting too hot for the Terrier, when a happy thought seemed to strike her. While in the act of killing a very big one, she leaned down her shoulder to block the hole, and then let them out one by one, until she had killed eighteen rats." Her

quick thinking and intelligence amazed all who were present.

All of these endeavors are, after all, typical of the duties undertaken by terriers. However, we don't usually think of the little spitfires as gundogs. And yet, history tells us that the Irish Terrier often proved to be an admirable adjutant to the gun. Writing in the late 1800's, Mr. Thomas Erwin, of Ballymena, says "There are some strains of them that will hunt stubble, or indeed any kind of field or marsh, quartering their ground in their own style. When a lad I had a Terrier of this breed over which I have shot as many as nine couples of snipe, and have been home in good time for morning school. There was little time for missing on the part of either of us, and the dog did not make a single mistake." Jowett confirms this, telling us that the breed would hunt partridge "as well as Spaniels" and retrieve the birds to hand when they had been shot.

In 1873, classes were first offered for Irish Terriers at a Dublin show. Type varied considerably among those early entries, particularly with regard to size. The terriers shown ranged from less than nine pounds to 40 pounds. In 1874, fanciers declared that no dog under 12 pounds could be shown, and the following year, the minimum limit was raised to 16 pounds.

The breed made rapid progress. In 1879, the Irish Terrier Club was formed, in Dublin, and later that year fanciers in London organized a breed club. A real donnybrook erupted over the subject of size. Finally, it was decreed that Irish Terriers should not exceed 24 pounds. There was also great dissension on the subject of ear cropping, a common practice in those days. In 1888, the practice was outlawed.

In the early to mid-1900's, the breed became a popular show dog. But, he also found another laudable outlet for his many talents. During both World Wars, Irish Terriers served as messenger dogs for the military. Lt. Col. Richardson, head of Britain's war dog program, declared that "I can say with decided emphasis that the Irish Terriers of the service more than did their part. Many a soldier is alive today through the effort of one of these very Terriers. Isolated from his unit in some advanced position, entirely cut off from the main body by a wall of shells, and thus prevented from communicating his position or circumstance by telephone or runner so that help might follow, this messenger dog was often the only means his officers had of carrying the dispatch which eventually would bring relief."

Indeed, history records the accomplishments of the breed during the war. There was Tim, who "did his journey in seventeen minutes which would have taken a man three-quarters of an hour to do." And there was the heroic Paddy, who "was bringin a message when he was shot by a German who was entrenched in a farmhouse. He carried on and then dropped. Paddy was then reported dead, but his keeper determined to search for his body. He was found with the message on him and life still in him. He subsequently revived."

Not every Irish Terrier, of course, passed the military's stringent qualifications. Richardson says, however, that "the percentage of acceptance for service among the Irish Terriers was very high." Those dogs that were rejected, he says, failed "only because their bodies did not match the size of their valiant spirits." He praised the breed for its inherent intelligence and trainability. "It must be admitted that many of our best dogs were Irish Terriers...these little fellows were remarkably easily taught, and were tremendously keen on their work."

So what we have, in the Irish Terrier, is a dog of amazing versatility. One that is able to do the traditional work of a terrier, plus much more. A go-to-earth dog, a gun dog and a war dog...it seems there's little that the breed cannot do. Despite his small size, the breed has even been pressed into service as a big game hunter. An article, which appeared in *National Geographic*, tells of one such experience. "While on a hunting expedition in Africa a few years ago, some hunters were trying by means of a pack of dogs to dislodge a lion which had been brought to bay in a dense tangle of bushes. For a long time they have been unsuccessful, when without apparent reason the lion bolted from the covert. A

moment later the reason became apparent. As he dashed into the open his tail stood straight out behind, and on the end of it was a little Irish Terrier with his teeth locked."

It is that self-confidence, that innate sense of himself, that natural fire and poise that make the Irish Terrier a superb show dog. The breed is quite distinct among the terriers and difficult to confuse with another breed. Somewhat racy in outline and fast as the wind, he nevertheless combines that speed with a sturdy, substantial body. He is one of the taller members of the group and his body is moderately long. In fact, the short back, found in so many terriers, is extremely objectionable in an Irish. In comparing his body type to that of the better known Fox Terrier, fanciers are apt to say that the Irishman embodies the qualities of a hunter, built for speed and freedom of movement, while the Fox Terrier typifies a cob (a short, more thickly set horse). The breed's alertness and pluck shows in the high set, docked tail.

The Irish Terrier's head is long and his skull is rather narrow. As befits a working terrier, he has a strong jaw. This look of strength is accentuated by his beard, which is not as profuse as other terrier breeds. His eyes, so full of fire and penetratingly intense, are dark brown and rather small in size. His ears are small, V-shaped and high set.

The standard calls for a shoulder height of 18 inches and says that average weights for dogs are 27 pounds, with 25 pounds for bitches. In practice, however, the dogs seen in the show ring are apt to be larger. Dogs generally run 19 inches and weigh in at about 31 pounds, while bitches stand about 18 inches and weight approximately 26 pounds. Since there is no disqualification in the standard for size, heights and weights have tended to increase over the years. While the larger dogs look more impressive in the show ring, most breeders are intent on keeping the size down.

For those interested in the show ring, they are in luck. Quality within the breed is at an all-time high. There are currently many good Irish Terrier breeders and the products of their labors can be seen in the show ring, where depth of quality is readily apparent. One noted judge paid the breed a great tribute when she remarked that "Twenty years ago, I would have given my eye teeth to see the poorest dog found in today's Irish Terrier ring."

As with most terriers, coat is extremely important in this breed. The outercoat is dense and wiry, while the undercoat is finer, softer and lighter in color. The coat lies close to the body and should not be so long that it obscures the clean outline. Irish Terriers come in solid colors ranging from bright red, golden red, and red wheaten to wheaten. Small white markings on the chest are permissible, but not desirable.

Grooming an Irish Terrier, for the show ring, does require skill and practice. Trimming is apt to alter color, so it takes conscientious care to bring the entire body into uniform color simultaneously. However, because the breed carries less coat than many of the other terrier breeds, grooming is not quite as complicated. Like other coated terriers, Irishmen are hand stripped. Three strippings per year will keep a pet in presentable condition. Show dogs, of course, are stripped more often.

Writing in *House and Garden* magazine, in June 1930, Robert Lemmon says, "He has the quality of initiative developed to a high degree and tempered by an astonishing amount of brains. He has never suffered the fate which has overtaken some other breeds—sacrifice of native intelligence or stamina on the altar of show ring appearance. In fact, the process of refinement through which he has passed since entering the show game, has made him an even better dog inside than in his old days. He is still the gay, imaginative, do-or-die Irishman of yore."

"This breed is just so terrific. I'm extraordinarily enthusiastic about them," says Peggy Gill, of Carlisle, Massachussets. Peggy obtained her first Irish Terrier in 1978. Her husband, Paul, was involved with a local theater group and one of his fellow actors had an Irish Terrier. When the bitch had a litter, the Gills went to see the pups. The smallest, but most independent, pup in the litter won their hearts. For the next 12 years, Erin, as she was named, ruled the roost at the Gill homestead. Though shown only occasionally, Erin proved her worth as a brood bitch. Several of her descendants continue to captivate Paul and Peggy.

"This breed is remarkably intelligent," Peggy says. "In fact, I can unequivocally state that I've never met a dumb Irish Terrier." Robert Lemmon would agree. This breed, he writes, has a special characteristic "which might be termed the instinct for wise action. Time after time you will see a duly mature Irish Terrier choose instantly the right course for the circumstances

The lovely Ch. Gilmere's Katie Colleen, bred and owned by Paul and Peggy Gill.

of the moment. Call it intuition, intelligence, instinct or what you will, there it is."

"To live with an Irish Terrier, you simply must have a sense of humor," Peggy Gill laughs, "because these dogs certainly do!" Writing in the 1959 book, *Irish Terriers,* Edna Howard Jones says, "I do not think it can be too strongly emphasized that they are essentially happy natured dogs with a great sense of humour."

"Most Irish Terriers are kept as house dogs," Peggy Gill says. "They are just wonderful. They are very proud, self-confident dogs who are sure of themselves. They are honest dogs. They are bold, but not sneaky. You never have to wonder where you stand with an Irish Terrier. The dogs will always let you know.

"They are wonderfully gentle and loving with people. They just crave affection. They are sweet and attentive. I don't know about other breeders, but I notice a difference between males and females. My females are more affectionate. When I sit on the sofa, my females are sure to sit beside me, resting their heads on my legs. The males will stay on the floor. It's not necessary for them to touch me. If I should get up, though, they'll follow me from room to room. They are very attentive, but not fawning."

This attentiveness and devotion is common in the breed. Owners say that there dogs would do anything for them. "They are extremely sensitive to humans and very eager to please," Peggy Gill reports. This makes for easy training. "All it takes is a word to let them know what you want." Edna H. Jones, in *Irish Terriers,* says that "They hate to be in disgrace with those they love and properly handled from the beginning are the easiest dogs to train." Peggy Gill advises that "Irish Terriers must be handled gently. As puppies, they do not take well to harsh treatment. They really resent rough manhandling. This breed can turn nasty if they are manhandled."

While the breed is easy to train, housebreaking can sometimes present a challenge. "They don't usually bark and carry on when they want to go out," Peggy Gill says. "This sometimes makes housebreaking difficult for new owners. During this period, you need to watch the dog closely. You'll quickly learn to know your dog and be able to read his body language."

With children, the Irish Terrier becomes as a child himself. He delights in jumping, playing and romping for hours on end. He is playful, but not overly boisterous. He becomes very devoted to his young charges, guarding and protecting them. "Irish Terriers have a great love for children and are very gentle with them," Peggy Gill says. "My five-month-old nephew visits and all my dogs are wonderful with him. They seem to recognize that he's a baby and act very gentle. We have known of dogs that became very protective toward children and would fight to the death to protect them."

With his alert nature, the Irish Terrier makes a good watchdog. "They are very observant," Peggy Gill comments. "They are not yappers. They will, however, bark when something happens. They always announce the presence of someone at the door. They watch my manner when I answer the door and are very good at reading my body language. If it's someone I welcome, they acknowledge the person and then go on about their business. If it's someone I don't know, they will stay right by my side.

"This breed is very adaptable and resilient. Unlike other breeds, Irish Terriers are easily placed as adult dogs. They adjust very quickly to their new homes. Older people often contact us wanting a dog that's past the puppy phase. In fact, many Irish Terriers are sold to old timers who have had the breed all their lives."

While the Irishman is gentle and lovable with people, the same cannot be said of other dogs. Irish Terriers aren't bullies, but they won't run away from a fight, no matter how large the adversary. Fanciers are fond of saying that the Irishman fights no more than other terriers, he just loves it more!

"They are very territorial and don't like another dog invading their domain," Peggy Gill notes. "This makes it difficult for those of us who work to rescue unwanted Irish Terriers. Most Irish Terriers are house pets and few breeders have kennels. Since our dogs will not accept outsiders, we often have to board the dogs at a kennel. It can be very costly, but we do all we can to locate a new responsible owner.

"In the house, the dogs seem to work out their own hierarchy. All of my girls get along well together. My male will tolerate a male puppy in the house until he turns six months old. Like most breeders, I take precau-

The classic look of an Irish Terrier. This handsome fellow is Ch. The Irishman's Mr. Rockledge CD. He was bred by Marion Honey and is owned by Edna Mae Sullivan. (Photo courtesy of Peggy Gill.)

tions to prevent friction. These dogs tend to be very possessive of their food. I can put down and pick up food bowls with no problem, but don't let another dog come near that food bowl. Therefore, we don't feed two dogs in close proximity. Most breeders take care to prevent squabbles. A fight between two Irish Terriers is a very serious matter for they will fight to the death."

While most Irish Terriers today are kept as companions and show dogs, their hunting instincts remain pronounced. For this reason, a fenced yard is a must. "Most Irish Terriers live to about the age of 15," Peggy Gill says. "Invariably, when we hear of a dog who dies younger than this, it's from having been hit by a car. These dogs get out and their hunting instincts take over. They see a squirrel or something and they just take off. They become intense and are totally oblivious to an oncoming car."

And so, there you have it....the Irish Terrier, Erin's daredevil, the proverbial rough and tumble dog, who can seemingly do it all. His rarity doesn't bother breeders at all. They are devoted to their dogs and intent on protecting them from the fate that has befallen other, more popular breeds. It's a devotion the dogs repay daily with their love. As Peggy Gill says, "It's very hard to switch breeds once you've become accustomed to Irish Terriers."

Alkola Fujiyama was 1990's top puppy in England, and is owned by Lynne Robson, of Peterborough.

Chapter 21

The Japanese Spitz

"Wherever we go, these dogs command attention," says Lynne Robson, of Stibbington, Peterborough, England. "When we go on holiday, we usually take two of them with us and we find that we cannot walk very far without someone stopping us to talk about the breed."

Indeed, the popularity of dogs of this type is quite amazing. Many countries have embraced the white Spitz and made it their own. In Germany, we have the White Spitz, found in varying sizes, that has been known since the earliest of times. Sadly, this dog is now extinct. In Italy, the white Spitz is well represented by the little Volpino Italiano. Those who read the first volume of *A Celebration of Rare Breeds*, will be quite familiar with the U.S. entry, the American Eskimo. It's somewhat astonishing to see how far the White Spitz has traveled. In faraway Japan, the beautiful white dogs are known as the Japanese Spitz.

The Japanese seem quite confused as to the breed's origin. They offer several theories to explain the breed's presence in their islands. Queries to Japanese authorities have resulted in only the vaguest of information. I'll sketch these diverse Japanese theories for you, before offering my own opinion on the breed's past. Some believe that, in the "Taisho Period" of the 1920s, a number of white Spitz dogs arrived from foreign countries. Some of these animals came from the United States and Canada. About the same time, it is believed, the Samoyed also journeyed to Japan and was soon joined by the Russian Spitz via Manchuria. There is also believed to have been an importation of German White Spitz, which came from Poland. These dogs were all interbred and a new distinct breed emerged. The larger dogs became known as the "Samo" and the smaller ones were simply called the "Spitz."

Another theory ties the breed's importation to the great Japanese earthquake of 1923. Supposedly, a Canadian cargo ship was destroyed and a group of Spitz dogs was discovered in the wreckage. Then, in the 1930s, the Russian Spitz arrived in Japan. The two were interbred and the Japanese Spitz resulted. Advocates of this theory hold that no Samoyed blood was ever introduced.

The third theory holds that the breed has been in Japan for centuries. Originally, advocates of this scenario speculate, the ancestors of the Japanese Spitz, came to the islands from the Arctic regions and prospered.

At first glance, many dog fanciers are apt to believe that all the white Spitz breeds are descended from the Samoyed. It's an obvious assumption and one that I also made, initially. However, research and study of the various breeds reveals that this is wholly inaccurate. In 1989, I co-authored a book, *The American Eskimo*, with long time Eskie breeder Nancy J. Hofman. For this undertaking, we conducted extensive research into the history of the numerous varieties of the white Spitz. Our studies led us to conclude, unequivocally we believe, that all these breeds are descended from the German White Spitz. The similarity, both in type and temperament, among all of these breeds is uncanny and too amazingly uniform to be mere coincidence.

Since the publication of that book, we've heard from breeders around the world. Japanese Spitz, German White Spitz and Volpino Italiano owners are all struck by the remarkable temperamental likeness to the

American Eskimo. "I sent to America for your book on the American Eskimo," writes Lynne Robson. "One thing I had to do when I was reading your book was to keep reminding myself that I wasn't reading about the Japanese Spitz." Recently, Lynne has had the opportunity to see two American Eskimos, imported to England by Lynda Lynch. "I cannot believe that the Japanese Spitz and the American Eskimo are not somewhere related," Lynne says, "everything about them is too much of a coincidence." The American Eskimo bitch, Lynne reports, is "very similar to the only bitch that was imported to our country directly from Japan."

We may never know precisely how the white Spitz dogs arrived in Japan. However, we do know that the American Eskimo and the Volpino can trace their roots directly to Germany. And, it seems virtually certain, there lies the initial stock behind the Japanese Spitz, too. German studies on the Spitz trace the breed back to the Neolithic, or Late Stone Age, of approximately 5,000 B.C. Studying the remains of dogs from this period, noted German archaeologist Karl Ludwig Ruetimeyer concludes that the dogs were 11-14 inches at the shoulder. They were most likely used as watchdogs for primitive settlements.

The enchanting Alkola Chocho, at eight weeks of age.

"Dogs of the Spitz type became very popular in Germany," I wrote in *The American Eskimo*. "In fact, the word 'Spitz,' meaning 'sharp point,' is of German derivation. The first documented recording of the term 'Spitz' was made by Count Eberhard zu Sayne, in 1540. Count zu Sayne was a feudal land baron, who made his home in Germany's Rhine Valley. His holdings consisted of thousands of acres of land, very rich in game. Here, Count zu Sayne and his friends indulged in splendid hunts. There is evidence to suggest that feudal lords, like Count zu Sayne, may have presented Spitz dogs to their tenants. In the 1951 German book, *Dogs and Dog Care,* Ulrich Klever writes, 'Straying and chasing game are things he does not know, because in comparison with his master's house and property, noth-

ing is of any importance to him. When the hunting lords gave their tenants a Spitz, it was calculated generosity. They knew full well that a Spitz never chased game, no matter how rich a preserve he might have lived in.'

"Apparently, it was the habit among Count zu Sayne's servants to condemn those they did not like by calling them *Spitzhunds*. Perhaps the Count admired Spitz dogs, or he may just have wanted to insure harmony. At any rate, he issued an edict prohibiting the derogatory use of the word.

"We also find the term 'Spitz' in German dictionaries from the 1500's. Some early German fiction writers, from this period, mentioned the Spitz, portraying him as a valiant defender of the home. It seems safe, therefore, to conclude that the Spitz was well known in Germany during this period."

The breed continued to grow in popularity and could be widely seen in Germany by the 1700's. "The German Spitz became the cherished dog of the common man," I write in *The American Eskimo*. "On the farm, he was esteemed as a multifaceted, all-around watchdog *par excellence*. When the peasant was at work his Spitz would stay by the door, protecting the home. The owners could go about their daily tasks, secure in the knowledge that no stranger would be permitted on their property."

In the above mentioned book, we carefully detail the breeds' uses in Germany and the popularity of the Spitz in various German localities. We also document the spread of the breed to the Netherlands (where the wolf-gray colored variety would become known as the Keeshond), to England (where they would serve as the basis for the Pomeranian), to Italy (where they developed into the Volpino) and to the United States. It's interesting to note that wherever the little dogs have landed, they have become popular. Other countries have adopted the dogs as their own and given them their own distinctive names. In fact, the title "American Eskimo," was chosen, for the dogs in the United States, to distance them somewhat from the anti-German sentiment that prevailed around the time of World War I.

It seems logical to assume that the Japanese Spitz also traces to these farm dogs of Germany. We can't fix the exact date of arrival in Japan, but records seem to indicate that the dogs were being bred in the 1930s. It was not until 1954 that the first standard was drawn up and the dogs were given the official title of "Japanese Spitz." Today, the breed is well represented in Japan. While not as popular as the Akita or Shiba, he does have the support of a loyal group of Japanese fanciers. The breed first reached the West when it was imported by Scandinavian fanciers.

The Japanese Spitz first came to England in 1977, when Dorothy Kenyon, a Norwegian Buhund breeder, imported a bitch from a Mrs. Nystrom in Sweden. When Alvretens Jicho of Norsken was released from quarantine, her pictured appeared on the cover of one of England's dog papers. This stimulated great interest in the new breed and other imports followed.

That intriguing photo of Alvretens Jicho of Norsken immediately captured the attention of Lynne Robson. Like Mrs. Kenyon, Lynne was a Norwegian Buhund breeder. One of the bitches from her breeding still holds the record for the most Challenge Certificates ever awarded to a bitch. In the beginning, Lynne reports, Japanese Spitz were very expensive, due to the high cost of importing them and paying for England's six month mandatory quarantine. The breed also had small litters, typically of three or four pups and, with the excitement

over the new breed, there was a long waiting list for puppies. She finally got her break in 1984. A couple, no longer interested in the breed, sold her a bitch puppy with a very good pedigree. The little bitch's sire was the first Japanese Spitz to win a Reserve in the Utility group at a Championship show. Her mother was top bitch in England for several years.

"As a show dog, she never took to the ring," Lynne says, "but as a brood bitch she has been worth her weight in gold a hundred times over." In fact, Lynne's Alkola Japanese Spitz have become quite successful in the ring. Her foundation bitch had only four litters before being spayed and retired to house pet status. She has produced Ch. Alkola Yamabuki, Ch. Alkola Kikimas and Alkola Seiko, who needs only one more Challenge Certificate to complete his championship. This is quite an accomplishment when we remember that it is more difficult to finish a championship in England than here. There, dogs have to compete with and defeat finished champions to gain their title. The three dogs mentioned above all have earned Junior Warrant awards, the first three of the breed to do so. In addition, Lynne's foundation bitch produced the Top Puppy in 1987 and again in 1990.

"My family of Japanese Spitz has now grown to seven," Lynne says. "All are direct descendants of my foundation bitch. She is now over seven and is a housedog. She sleeps on her beanbag in our bedroom each night." Lynne bred Norwegian Buhunds for over 15 years, before acquiring her first first Japanese Spitz and still owns two champions, a mother and son, now thirteen and ten years old. "I have not been actively involved with the Norwegian Buhund for the last five years," Lynne says. "The Japanese Spitz seem to have taken over." Others have fallen victim to the charms of the breed, too. "Quite a lot of people add the Japanese Spitz to their kennels as a second breed," Lynne says, "but some have found, like me, that they have taken over, too."

Up until 1988, the breed was shown in England's "Not Separately Classified—Utility and Working" group. In 1982, at Crufts, a Japanese Spitz scored the first ever Reserve in the Group. Since then, two other dogs have achieved this honor in England, with another winning this award in southern Ireland. In 1988, the breed was accorded separate status and earned the right to compete for Challenge Certificates. These were first offered at Crufts in 1988. It was an historic occasion. Yonala Tiger Lily, bred by the late Mrs. Dot Collins and owned by Vee Stripe, captured the C.C. for bitches. Lily also became the breed's first champion, finishing her title in three straight shows. Taking the nod for the male C.C. was Sherivale Osaka of Valdonic, bred by Iris Bowker and owned by Val and Don Brookes. Later that

year, Osaka became the first male champion. Officiating at the show was breeder-judge Freda Spector, President of The Japanese Spitz Club. Sadly, she died this year. "The vacancy she left was very hard to fill," Lynne says sadly. "She had a very steadying influence on the breed. I never knew her to become annoyed or cross with anyone and she always appeared willing to help anyone who wanted to know anything about the breed."

Lynne Robson is very grateful to all those early pioneers who imported the first Japanese Spitz. With the quarantine laws, it's very expensive to bring a new breed into England. It takes a toll on the dogs, too, particularly with the Japanese Spitz who craves the attention of family. "It's not something the Spitz takes kindly to," Lynne says. "It is to these people that all my gratitude belongs," Lynne writes, "for importing this lovely breed into this country and giving me the the dogs I own today. Without the time and considerable money they spent, the breed would not even be in this country."

The American Eskimo is often called "The Dog Beautiful," and this would be an apt description of his Japanese cousin, too. The Japanese Spitz has a well built, compact body, with a broad and deep chest. He has a short level back with a good tuck-up. He is truly beautiful in motion, as he moves with light, lively steps. His skull is broad, with little stop, and narrows to a pointed muzzle, tipped by a black pigmented nose. His always erect ears are small and set high. They are carried facing forward.

What attracts most people's attention is, of course, the glorious coat. It is a straight, stand-off, profuse coat. The undercoat is soft, short and thick, while the outercoat is composed of longer guard hairs. This provides ideal insulation against both heat and cold. The coat is particularly pronounced about the neck and shoulders, forming an impressive ruff or mane. The tail is set on high and moderately long. It should always be carried curled over the back in typical Spitz fashion. The hair on the tail is quite long and truly gives a lovely finish to the dog. In color, the ideal Japanese Spitz should be pure white. Cream colored patches are seen occasionally, but are not desirable.

Size varies somewhat from country to country. The Federation Cynologique Internationale standard allows males to be 12-16 inches at the withers and females to be 10-14 inches. However, there has been a move recently to reduce size. The English standard for the breed was, until lately, the same as that of the F.C.I. They have now reduced the top heights for the breed by two inches, so that males must not exceed 14 inches and females 12 inches. "Many thought this was too much too soon," Lynne Robson says. "This resulted in quite a fluctuation in size, something we are still suffering from even now, although it is beginning to settle down."

Most people think that it's difficult to keep a white dog in pristine condition. And, they say, surely such a profusely coated dog must require hours of tedious grooming. Not so. "They are a very clean breed," Lynne Robson reports. "They don't like living in dirty conditions, although that does not mean that they do not like to run in muddy puddles, given the chance. However, their coats clean very easily if they are just allowed to dry out and then are brushed....They do not really need bathing except for our convenience, such as if you show your dog. Like many other Spitz breeds, they do not have a doggy odour."

A good brushing, once or twice weekly, will keep your Japanese Spitz in tip top condition. Thorough brushing is a must and one shouldn't skimp on it. It's important to brush carefully and to get right down to the skin. The marvelous bloom seen on show dogs is only achieved through conscientious brushing. Pay particular attention to the dense areas of the coat, such as the ruff or mane, the hind legs and the tail. Be sure to carefully check the armpits and the area around the ears. It's there that mats are most likely to form.

English breeders have found the Japanese Spitz to be a remarkably healthy breed, suffering from few problems. They routinely have eye checks done on their dogs in accordance with a plan outlined by the British Veterinary Association. To date, no problems have been detected, but breeders continue as a safeguard. Patella luxation, or slipped stifles, have been found in the breed. "This is when the grooves that hold the kneecap in place are either very shallow or non-existent," Lynne says. "As breeders, it is something we are very much aware of and it is something that a vet can check for very easily." While there is no official program for certifying dogs free of the condition, the Japanese Spitz Club has taken an innovative lead. "The Club's secretary keeps a record of dogs who have been tested and who have produced a vet's letter saying that they can find no evidence of the defect," Lynne says. Such a program is clearly a positive first step in eradicating the problem.

The Japanese Spitz makes a wonderful house dog. He is spirited, proud and very affectionate. Indeed, he bonds closely with his family and craves their attention and approval. For this reason, this breed is not particularly suited to life in a kennel. This little Spitz is intensely curious and has a lively, bouncy nature. They enjoy being included in all family activities. They do, however, have a slight stubborn streak and can be very assertive. Kind, firm discipline is a must to prevent the dog from getting the upper hand.

Like all the Spitz breeds, these Japanese dogs have a long history as home guardians. It is something they do instinctively. They are very territorial and

These are several of Lynne Robson's top winning Japanese Spitz. Lynne's foundation bitch, Astutus Kurakumo of Alkola, poses with three of her offspring: Alkola Seiko, Ch. Alkola Yamabuki and Ch. Alkola Kikimas.

consider it their duty to protect the family and its property. They have a very keen sense of hearing and, as puppies, are apt to be barkers. Most owners reprimand puppies for nuisance barking and the dogs soon learn to sort out real danger from the imaginary.

The Japanese Spitz is an incredibly smart breed with a real desire to please. "Like most Spitz breeds they are very intelligent," Lynne Robson says, "too much so at times. They tend to work things out for themselves." Indeed, owners say that these dogs have an uncanny ability to understand their every word. Their quick intelligence coupled with their agility and desire to show off, makes the breed a good candidate for obedience competition. One of Lynne's dogs went to a woman who's an enthusiastic participant in agility trials. "Although he will never match the Border Collies for speed," Lynne writes, "he is accurate and often gets clear rounds in competition."

This breed is apt to be reserved and quite aloof with strangers. Perhaps this suspicion of strangers is part of what makes the breed such an effective watch dog. Socialization, during puppyhood, is a must. With proper exposure, the Japanese Spitz can learn quite readily to accept and enjoy the advances of strangers. "The breed standard states that they are wary of strangers when they first meet," Lynne Robson says. "This was very much so, at first, especially with bitches. In

fact, you were very lucky to have a bitch that would keep its tail up in the ring. This, thankfully, is virtually a thing of the past. Now, we have reached the point where many just love everybody they meet. I am finding this more so now that I have reached my third generation....They need a lot of socialising at a very early age. I think people with small children have a definite advantage. They are extremely faithful to those they live with and get on very well with children. They also mix well with other breeds."

This dog from the Far East has made quite a name for himself in England and seems certain to become more popular. Fanciers from other countries are also becoming interested in the breed. Lynne Robson has already sent two dogs to Australia and another should be joining them soon. One of her puppies is just about to start a show career in Switzerland. Another of her dogs recently journeyed to a new home in Austria and has already picked up points toward both his Austrian and International titles. While the breed has yet to be imported, so far as I know, to the United States, some Americans have expressed interest in the breed. It's possible that success may be hampered by the breed's resemblance to the American Eskimo. However, one never knows, for there's tremendous interest in all the Japanese breeds here. One thing is for certain, wherever the Japanese Spitz goes, he wins hearts.

The Kai Ken foundation stud, Ch. Rikiro of Takahata Kensha. Rikko is owned by Mary Malone, of Alliance, Ohio.

Chapter 22

The Kai Ken

"I never met an animal I didn't like" might well be Mary Malone's motto. Those who read the first volume of *Celebration* may recall Mary and her menagerie of pets, which included the Shiba. Indeed, a veritable Noah's Ark resides at Mary and Jack's Mini-Meadows Farm, in Alliance, Ohio. As a child, Mary lived on a 300 acre farm and the country has always remained close to her heart. In 1967, she and Jack established Mini-Meadows. Over the years, Mary's menagerie has included: llamas, fallow deer, Norwegian blue fox, squirrels, ferrets, prairie dogs, pheasants, turkeys, guinea fowl, sheep, both miniature and standard horses, pygmy goats, donkeys, rabbits, skunks, raccoons, rheas, fancy chickens, mandarin ducks, Vietnamese pot-bellied pigs and, of course, dogs and cats. One never knows quite what to expect on a trip to Mini-Meadows. Mary is always eager to share her love for animals. This has made the farm a popular visiting place for school groups on field trips. One of her donkeys is the proud star of the yearly Christmas pageant.

It is the dogs, though, that have propelled Mary Malone to national prominence. Some twenty years ago, she began breeding Dobermans. But, the Akita soon caught her eye and began her love affair with the Japanese breeds. While showing and breeding her Akitas, Mary learned of the Shiba and soon "Bamboo," the first of many Shibas, came to stay at Mini-Meadows. Since that time, Mary has made quite a name for herself with this small Japanese breed. She has bred many Best in Show winning Shibas and takes great pride in her breeding program. She has also bred a Best in Show winning Cesky Terrier, another rare breed that the Ohio resident enthusiastically raises.

Now, thanks to Mary, Americans have the opportunity to see and learn about the rarest of all Japanese breeds...the Kai Ken. The first of these exotic dogs arrived at Mini-Meadows in January of 1990. Mary was fortunate to obtain the aid of John and Joan Wetzstein, of Corona, California, in her quest to import the Kai. Formerly residents of Tokyo, the Wetzsteins were critical in helping Mary to learn about the breed, establish contacts with breeders and translate information on the dogs. Mary plans to accompany the Wetzsteins, on a trip to Japan, to see the breed for herself, discuss them with Japanese breeders and procure additional stock.

The Kai was developed in the ancient province of Kai, on Honshu, in the area that now comprises the prefecture of Yamanashi. Some of Japan's most famous mountains encircle the one-thousand mile valley that is the Kai's original homeland. To the south, towers revered Mount Fuji and to the north Mount Yatsugatake soars. The Southern Japanese Alps border the valley to the west, while the Kanto range embraces it on the east. Here, in this wild and secluded valley, the Kai Ken prospered. Because of its sheltered position, the breed remained geographically isolated and did not suffer the crossbreedings that threatened the other native Japanese breeds. In fact, the primitive Kai may be the purest of all the breeds which hail from Japan.

Little is, as yet, known of the breed's history. We do know, however, that the Kai has been around for centuries. In Japan, the breed is respected for its prowess in hunting. In the earliest days, the dogs probably hunted in a primitive fashion. They routed game and held it at bay until a hunter could spear or dispatch the prey with a bow and arrow.

With the introduction of firearms, the breed's use

changed, somewhat. The dogs became the treasured aids of the matagi. These professional hunters, armed with flintlock rifles, ventured into the densely forested mountainous regions in search of game. The matagi were big game hunters who specialized in slaying deer and wild boar. They used small packs of dogs. Dogs used on deer were noted for their speed and were rangier in appearance. The wild boar hunting dogs had a stockier, more rugged look.

Wild boar hunting was an extremely dangerous occupation. The flintlock rifle could fire only a single shot and then had to be reloaded. While most matagi were excellent shots, it often took more than one bullet to bring down a boar. This placed the matagi in a precarious position. Wounded boars often charged the hunter as he reloaded. It was the task of the dog to divert the animal's attention until the hunter was ready to shoot again. The Kai gained an enviable reputation for his courage. It was said that such dogs would "not concede a step before danger." Indeed, many dogs bore scars from such encounters and some were, undoubtedly, killed in the confrontations. The Japanese tell us that three Kai Kens, working in concert, can bring down a wild boar.

Originally, it was felt that the Kai Ken had too wild and primitive a nature to be suitable for a pet. Those who dared to bring the dogs into their homes, however, found something quite different. They discovered that the Kai was a gentle, sweet, loyal and loving companion.

The Kai was not officially recognized, in Japan, until 1934. Like the other native breeds, the Kai is considered a national treasure. As such, it is to be respected and cherished. Even so, the Kai is still considered rare, even in Japan. The Kai Ken Aigokai, or preservation society, oversees registration of the breed. In over fifty years (from 1934 to the present), only 21,600 Kais have been registered by the organization, which is headquartered in Yamanashi.

Today's breeders still celebrate the Kai's diversity. They wish to retain the qualities esteemed by deer hunters, as well as those treasured by wild boar hunters. All of today's dogs trace their ancestry to two great foundation studs, Dairo and Kaikuro. Dairo was a famed deer hunter, while Kaikuro was a renowned boar hunter. Each had somewhat different characteristics. The dogs stemming from the Dairo line tend to be thinner and longer bodied with a very foxy look. The descendants of Kaikuro share his thicker, stockier frame and bear-type head.

The Kai Ken is a medium sized dog, larger than the Shiba, but smaller than the Akita. Males stand 19-20 inches at the withers, while bitches measure 18-20 inches. Weights average around 45 pounds. The Kai

An adorable Kai puppy bitch, from Mary Malone's Mini-Meadow Farms.

packs a lot of muscle into his sturdy frame. His neck is thick and powerful, as we would expect in a dog destined to hunt wild boar. He is slightly longer than tall, with a deep chest, straight topline and noticeable tuck-up. The breed's high set tail differs, somewhat, from the other native breeds. The standard allows for either a curled or sickle tail. "Unlike other Japanese breeds," Mary explains, "the tail of the Kai Ken does not curl so much that it wraps around inside. Instead, the tail is shaped like a sickle over the back. In fact, when chasing its prey, the tail straightens just like a wolf's tail."

The Kai has the same intriguing head type found in all the Japanese breeds. His skull is broad, with a well defined stop. His pointed muzzle is moderately thick and long. The nose should always be black and the tongue is usually spotted. The eyes are dark brown in color and have a slightly triangular shape. He has larger ears than other Japanese dogs of similar size. They are, of course, pricked and held strongly upright, inclining slightly forward.

One of the breed's key characteristics is its coat and color. The Kai carries a double coat, composed of a harsh, straight outer jacket, beneath which lies a soft, dense undercoat. His color is always brindle, leading the Japanese to dub the breed the "Tora" (or Tiger) dog. The standard calls for black, red or intermediate shades of brindle. "The breed is largely divided into three color categories," Mary reports. "the Kuro-Tora is a black brindle, the Chu-Tora is a medium brindle and the Aka-Tora is a red brindle." Puppies are usually born with a black fuzzy coat. The brindle bars begin to emerge as the straight adult coat comes in. A crisp, clear well defined brindle is greatly preferred. "Dogs lacking heavy brindle bar markings," Mary advises, "must be bred to heavier brindled dogs to keep the true brindle markings which are one of the most distinguishing characteristics of the breed."

Much to Mary's surprise, she learned that she was not the first to import the Kai Ken to this country. In 1951, several dogs were sent to Salt Lake City, Utah. No one knows what happened to these dogs and it's doubtful if any of their descendants survive. In obtaining her foundation stock, Mary Malone was fortunate, in being able to procure one of Japan's top stud dogs. Four-year-old Rikiro, better know as Rikko, sired over 100 puppies before being exported. He was particularly prized in Japan because he is a pure Kaikiro descendant. Ninety percent of all the Japanese Kais have pedigrees with Dairo in their bloodlines, Mary reports. "This fact and his strong sense of presence are what led to his being selected for the primary foundation stud dog of the Kai Ken in the United States." Mary also imported three bitch puppies, which she thinks will combine well with Rikko. She hopes to acquire more stock on her trip to Japan. She and the Wetzsteins have formed the American Aigokai, which serves as the official registry for the National Kai Ken Club.

In Japan, the Kai is noted for his extraordinary devotion to his master. Even when he goes to a new home, the Japanese say, he never forgets his original owner. With this as an inherent characteristic of the breed, Mary was naturally worried over whether Rikko would have an easy time adjusting to life in this country. He was, after all, already an adult and had been raised primarily by a man. "I felt that the adjustment to our culture, architecture, language and the aroma of our total country and people would be so different that he might have trouble adjusting," Mary says. "To my surprise and delight, this dog has bonded himself to me devotedly. When I open the door in the morning, he greets me with wagging tail and excited body animation, as well as a sing-song vocalization. In fact, he talks whenever he sees me. If, at a show, I ask someone to hold him while I run an errand, they say he sits and watches for me. When he hears my footsteps, or sniffs my presence in the air or zeros in on my voice in a crowd, he starts to fidget and look for me. Quite often he calls to me and listens for a response. The dog truly loves me, and I him in return."

The female puppies were all quite young when they arrived at Mary's home. "After twenty-four hours in a crate, they stepped out and greeted me with kisses and wiggles. They took the trip in stride....They have their own personalities and are very loving."

Mary has taken her Kai Kens to several rare breeding outings, where they have caught the eye of both judges and spectators. "Rikko is quite a beautiful mover," Mary says. "He enjoys showing tremendously, much more than I do, and he loves the attention he receives." Mary also believes the breed has a future as an obedience dog. They "appear to be intelligent enough for easy training," she says. "They watch people most intently, as though waiting for a sign as to what is expected of them." Once the breed is more numerous, Mary hopes that some owners will try hunting with their Kais. She is intent on preserving their natural instincts. In her experience, she has not found the Kai to be aggressive with other dogs. This probably stems from his use as a hunter in Japan, where the dogs are used in packs.

Undoubtedly, we will be hearing more from the rare Kai. This is a very natural breed, which requires little grooming. Like his relatives, the Kai Ken is a hardy, sturdy and rugged dog with a charming character and a natural beauty and dignity. The breed appears to be very people oriented and should prove a devoted companion dog. "I am absolutely delighted with this breed," Mary says. With his legendary loyalty and loving ways, it won't be long before other Americans can make the same statement.

The outstanding group winner Ch. Foxrun Stormdance, is owned by Barbara Capron, of Glenwood Landing, New York. (Ashby photo)

Chapter 23

The Lakeland Terrier

Lakeland Terriers are "active, alert, eager, energetic, hardy, intelligent, lively, loving, obnoxious, overbearing, quiet, rambunctious, serious, tenacious and 'typically terrier,'" says Cindy Clausen of Portis, Kansas. "While not the breed for all, anyone that enjoys terriers will *love* these dogs."

"Lakelands are the most marvelous pets in the world," enthuses Barbara Capron, of Foxrun Kennels, in Glenwood Landing, New York. "They just want to be with you all the time. My husband always describes them as a lot of dog in a small package. That's very true."

"I would not be without a Lakeland, they have something the others have not got, but that 'something' is still a mystery to me. It may be their character, their spirit or gameness, or perhaps a touch of 'The Devil' at times, but I really believe it is 'the look in their eyes.'" So writes Archie Kirk in the 1964 book *The Lakeland Terrier*.

If you've gotten the impression that Lakeland folk are uncommonly devoted to their breed, you're absolutely right! This little giant of a dog, with his cock-of-the-walk attitude, inspires fierce loyalty. Comical, affectionate, ready for anything and always entertaining, you'll remain young at heart when a Lakeland Terrier shares your home.

The breed evolved in England's Lake District, near the Scottish border. Home to some of the country's highest mountains, the area's terrain is rough and rocky. The term "fell," or high rocky ground, is often used in describing the region. Interspersed among the mountains are crystal clear lakes, which give the area its name. The weather can be unpredictable. Sometimes

the sun shines peacefully, but other times the area is wracked with driving blizzards or pounding rain, often accompanied by gale forces. To survive in the Lake District, both people and dogs must be hardy and rugged.

Today's Lakeland has retained his tough resilience. "Their extreme hardiness to adverse weather conditions never ceases to amaze me," says Cindy Clausen. "These dogs seem to thrive on our ever-changing Kansas weather, going from the highs of 100 degrees in summer to snow and wind chill of minus 50 degrees in winter."

When we think of foxhunting, we are likely to envision gentlemen in colorful regalia, astride their mounts, galloping o'er rolling fields. The hounds give fervent tongue as they chase old Reynard. Terriers, tucked into saddle bags, are released if the fox goes to ground. The little dogs bolt the quarry and the chase is on once again.

Foxhunting in the Lake District differs radically from the above picture. The Fell foxes are larger than those found in the south and their raids on poultry coops, or newborn lambs, endanger the survival of the self-sufficient farms. Farmers in the region bred dogs specifically designed for hunting in this exacting area.

The Lake District's rocky terrain isn't conducive to horses, so all hunting is done on foot and the terriers are never carried. Thus, a leggier dog is required. In her 1931 book, *Hunt and Working Terriers*, Jocelyn Lucas says that the dogs must be "sufficiently on the leg to be able to travel through the snow." *Hutchinson's Dog Encyclopedia* points out that dogs must, at times, "walk fifteen or twenty miles over the hills from the Kennels

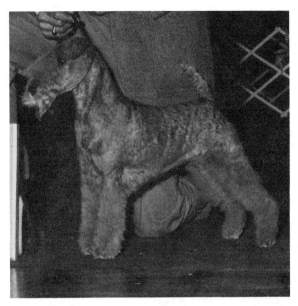

The multiple Best in Show winner, Ch. Foxrun Flash-dance, is owned by Barbara Capron, of Foxrun Lakelands. (Tatham photo)

to the Meet in the early hours of the morning; and then at night the same distance back has to be covered, and that is in addition to hunting all day, when no one can say what distances over the tops of mountains they will have to run." Jocelyn Lucas cites an additional reason for length of leg. "Another reason for the necessity of a long-legged dog in the fell countries, is that a terrier often has to drop down a cleft in the rock to get at his fox, and if he can't jump out, he has to climb by putting his back against one wall and his feet against the other. A short-legged terrier is at a great disadvantage in trying to get a fox off a ledge, and may get terribly punished."

Farmers also needed a dog with a narrow chest, ideal for squirming into the tight passages favored by the fox. They were fond of saying that their dogs could pass through any opening large enough to admit the head. Thus, they bred for narrow chests and shoulders and rather flattish sides. The Lakeland depended on depth of chest, rather than girth, for sufficient heart and lung room.

In other regions, terriers are used to bolt the fox. If this is not possible, they bark so that the fox can be dug out. This was impossible in the rocky Fell region. "There are so many earths that cannot be stopped, that foxes have to be killed underground if hounds fail to catch them..." Jocelyn Lucas says. "It takes a good dog to tackle them underground." Indeed, the Lakeland's gameness, his utter disregard for danger, is a hallmark of the breed. To survive the encounter, the dog had to have uncompromising courage and unswerving determination. Once underground, he was on his own.

Many remarkable stories are told of the Lakeland's hunting prowess. It is said that dogs often remained below ground for ten or twelve days before reappearing. One of the most amazing stories is recounted in *The Complete Dog Book*. We read that "in 1871, Lord Lonsdale had one which crawled twenty-three feet under rock after an otter. In order to extricate the dog it was necessary to undertake extensive blasting operations. Finally, after three days' work, they reached the dog, and he was gotten out, none the worse for his experience." No wonder the Lakeland earned the admiration of his owner.

The Lakeland's origin is somewhat murky. Lake District farmers were concerned solely with ability and any successful worker was incorporated into the breeding program, regardless of looks. Most authorities agree that England's rough coated Black and Tan Terrier, now extinct, played a large part in the breed's development. Early Dandie Dinmonts were probably used and a dash of Bedlington blood heightened gameness. We do not know if the Border Terrier, who has a similar background, was used or if the two breeds merely have parallel origins.

We do not know precisely when the breed came into being because, originally, these dogs were not known as Lakeland Terriers. Farmers identified their

Sir Dudley in what owner Cindy Clausen calls his "no frills, wash and wear, everyday clothes".

dogs by the village they hailed from, even though the terriers were identical. Thus, the dogs were known as Patterdale, Cumberland and Fell Terriers. The breed probably got its start in the early 1800s. Two well known breeders, John Peel and Tommy Dobson, were able to trace their dog's pedigrees back to 1850.

Terrier classes were first held at agricultural shows in the Lake District about 1896. First grouped all together, the classes were later divided into colored and white working terriers. In 1912, an effort was made to formally promote the breed. World War I put an end to the endeavor. Finally, in 1921, a group of fanciers met at Whitehaven, in Cumberland County, to renew efforts to foster the breed. There was much discussion as to the proper breed name and finally "Lakeland" was chosen as a compromise. A standard was drawn up and soon the dogs began to appear at shows.

By the 1930's, the Lakeland began to attract attention outside the Lake District. "Since the breed's introduction to the show ring, he has been smartened up with Wire Fox and Welsh Terrier blood," says Archie Kirk. This attempt to mold the dog for the show ring was controversial. Jocelyn Lucas, writing in 1931 says, "There can be little doubt that the Lakeland is one of the gamest and hardiest terriers to be found anywhere in the world today. Whether the show bench will have a detrimental effect on the breed remains to be seen, but, for some years at least, the working qualities of the breed should predominate. One can only hope that they always will do so."

We do not know exactly when the first Lakelands came to this country. People emigrating from the Lake District probably brought some of their working terriers with them. Other specimens were imported by terrier lovers. The American Kennel Club recognized the breed in 1934 and Egton What a Lad of Howtown was the first dog to be registered.

The Lakeland Terrier is a smart, dapper-looking dog. He is quite similar to the Welsh Terrier and some people confuse the two. The Lakeland, however, is a smaller dog than his Welsh cousin. His square-shaped body has the look of a finely tuned athlete. "He stands on his toes as if ready to go," the standard says. Indeed, his confident, ready to take on the world demeanor is hard to beat in a show ring. The Lakeland's head is rectangular in outline and his dark eyes are full of fire. The breed has a captivatingly intelligent expression, heightened by the endearing Lakeland habit of cocking the head to one side, as if trying to understand your

Andrew Krier poses with a Lakeland puppy. (Teresa Krier photo)

every word. The docked tail is set on high and carried in gay, upright fashion. Long hair, known as "furnishings," trims the muzzle and legs. The Lakeland comes in a variety of solid colors. Solid colors permitted are blue, black, liver, red and wheaten. The dogs may also be tan with saddle markings of black, blue, liver, grizzle or red grizzle. The tan should always be light in color, generally a wheat or blonde shade. While many colors are permitted, red, red grizzle, black and tan and grizzle and tan are the colors most often seen in the show ring. Heights vary from 13 1/2 to 15 inches and general weight is about 17 pounds.

Like all the rough-coated terriers, the Lakeland requires grooming. "There is nothing mysterious about this type of grooming and the technique is not difficult to master for the pet groomer," says Pat Rock, in the 1984 book *The Lakeland Terrier*. "If the coat is 'blown,' that is, grown out to its full length, the process of stripping is not uncomfortable to the dog. Stripping (with a special dull knife) or plucking (using the fingers to do the same job as the knife) is really just facilitated shedding. When the hairs are long enough, you do your dog's shedding for him, with the happy result that he never drops hair in the house and looks tidy and smart."

Pets should be brushed weekly and handstripped every two or three months. Some pet owners prefer to use clippers, but this does soften the naturally hard coat. Some owners compromise by stripping the back area and clipping the rest of the coat. Show grooming is an art, and it takes expertise and practice to turn out a

Lakeland. Show dogs must be completely handstripped and most exhibitors work over the coat twice a week. They jealously guard the furnishings, which may be easily lost without proper care. To protect these, most show breeders wash and oil the furnishings twice a week. Pat Rock's book, *The Lakeland Terrier,* contains an excellent chapter on grooming, which covers both pet and show preparation.

"The Lakeland loves people, especially children," says Barbara Capron. "Some of my puppies just have an instinctive affinity for kids and I try to place them in homes with youngsters." Indeed, the active Lakeland is a natural child's playmate, although youngsters should never be allowed to tease this breed. Barbara first met the Lakeland when she was a child. "There was a Lakeland Terrier in my neighborhood who used to come and visit all the time," she recalls. After a brief foray in Miniature Schnauzers, the New York resident acquired a show quality Lakeland bitch. Since then, she has realized her dream of showing and breeding top quality dogs. Two dogs from her breeding have gone on to win Bests in Show. One, Champion Foxrun Stray Beam, exported to Denmark, became the youngest dog ever to go Best in Show in that country.

"Lakelands are best when they are family dogs, kept indoors," Mrs. Capron says. "They love being a part of things. I do not consider them good kennel dogs. While I insist that new owners have a crate, most Lakelands would rather not be confined. They're just so incredibly curious that a dull kennel life doesn't suit them. For this reason, many handlers don't like the breed. Lakelands are active dogs, always on the go. However, they are not hyper.

"They are very courageous and tenacious little dogs. They are also quite comical. They just love to entertain you. Lakelands are like little clowns," Barbara laughs. In *An Introduction to Owning a Lakeland Terrier,* the pamphlet distributed by the United States Lakeland Terrier Club, Jo-Lynn Hefferman describes the breed as "an entertainment committee of one." She advises that "a sense of humor is mandatory on the part of a Lakeland owner."

Lakeland owners appreciate the breed's intelligence. "They are smart as a whip and they love to please," Barbara Capron says. "You only have to show them something once and they'll never forget it. That is, of course," she laughs, "if they want to do it. They do have a stubborn streak." Jo-Lynn Hefferman adds that the "Lakeland is endowed with his fair share of terrier independence and inquisitiveness. He is exceptionally quick to learn, but can be a true challenge to obedience train."

"Some Lakelands are effusively friendly with strangers, some more reserved," Pat Rock writes in *The Lakeland Terrier.* "A Lakeland will not automatically become your slave. His loyalty and devotion is given only when he feels it is deserved, and then more as a chum, not a subordinate."

While not quarrelsome, the Lakeland is all terrier. This can make it difficult to keep a number of dogs in the home. "They tend to get very jealous," Barbara says, "so you have to pick and choose who you can put together. Like most breeders, I don't allow males together. Bitches, however, can often be worse than the males. Unfortunately, the ones who are the best show dogs and have that marvelous air about them that says they're the hottest thing that's ever been born, also tend to be the most aggressive." Surprisingly, many Lakelands get along well with other non-terrier breeds.

Cindy Clausen, of Portis, Kansas, is an enthusiastic Lakeland owner. "The qualities that I like best about the Lakelands are their longevity (12 to 15 years plus) and the fact that they remain active during their lifetime."

It's a good thing Lakelands are so long lived, since they have a way of worming themselves into your heart. As Cindy Clausen says, "In the fourteen years I've owned Lakelands, there have been very few dull moments, but countless new and interesting ones." With his zest for living, the Lakeland adds much to the lives of those fortunate enough to own him. "Once you've owned one," Barbara Capron says, "I don't think any other breed will do."

Chapter 24

The Longhaired Whippet

In the latter part of the last century, the first Whippets made their way to America. English mill workers brought the "poor man's racehorse," as the breed was known in England, to the mill towns of Massachussets. Lawrence and Lowell became the center for early Whippet activities. So popular did the fleet newcomers prove to be, that the American Kennel Club registered the breed in 1888, three years *before* it was recognized by the English Kennel Club. One hundred years later, once again in Massachussets, a new and very controversial chapter in Whippet history is being written. Walter Wheeler, of Sherborn, has set out to revive the longhaired variety of the Whippet.

For most of us, the Whippet is characterized by his classic graceful lines and short coat. Indeed, the short, sleek, easy to care for coat is a primary attraction of the breed. The idea that a longhaired version of the Whippet is being actively produced has struck many Whippet fanciers as nothing short of blasphemy. To them, the Whippet always has been and always will be a short haired dog. A longhaired Whippet is now disqualified under the A.K.C. breed standard, they contend, and surely must have been arrived at by surreptitious crossbreeding.

Not so, says Harvard graduate Walter Wheeler. Mr. Wheeler obtained his first A.K.C. registered dogs in 1937 and finished his first champion in 1941. Since 1957, he has specialized in Whippets and many notable smooths have come from his Windsprite Kennels. Indeed, Mr. Wheeler still actively breeds smooths at his Sherborn home. And yet, the existence of both long and wire coated Whippets has always intrigued the Massachussets breeder. He saw his first "fuzzy" puppy, in a smooth litter, born more than thirty years ago. The breeder told him that the puppy would be put down if it matured with a long coat. Rather than being appalled by the puppy, Mr. Wheeler was intrigued with this fuzzy throwback. Over the years, he's become a pedigree detective, tracking the relatives of that first fuzzy puppy, as well as other Whippets reported to have produced longhaired progeny. Utilizing such information, he has worked to isolate the recessive longhaired gene. By inbreeding and tight linebreeding, he has succeeded in establishing a strain of Longhaired Whippets.

Was there, at one time, a longhaired version of the Whippet? No, many smooth breeders contend. However, it seemed to me that, if Mr. Wheeler's contention that this was a throwback was accurate, there must be some written record to substantiate his claims. I began searching to see if there was any verification of Mr. Wheeler's contentions.

Contemporary books on the breed say little about the existence of any but short coated dogs. In fact, C.H. Douglas Todd, writing in the 1961 book *The Popular Whippet*, says, "*if* the Whippet of today is the result of recent and various 'crosses,' as is suggested by so many writers, surely we would occasionally hear of some breeders getting peculiar specimens in litters now and again. Something akin to a 'throwback'—a puppy with a long coarse coat for instance...During all my experience in the breed I have never bred one of these 'throwbacks' nor have I ever heard of anyone who has..."

Yet, once we begin exploring the historical record of the breed, contained in old volumes, a different picture emerges. Clearly, dog writers from an earlier era were well aware of the existence of both a longhaired and a wire-haired Whippet. The chapter on the breed, contained in Robert Leighton's 1906 classic *The New Book of the Dog,* was penned by F.C. Hignett. A longtime fancier, Mr. Hignett says that he was well acquainted with the Whippet for at least fifty years.

"Formerly there were two varieties of the Whippet," Mr. Hignett says, "long and short coated, but the former is rarely met with nowadays, either at the exhibitions or on the running track; in fact, a long-coated dog, however good it might be as regards anatomy, would have a poor chance of winning a prize at a show, for its shaggy appearance would most likely hide the graceful outline which is a much admired and characteristic feature."

Other writers from the same period concur with Hignett's observations. Writing in the 1907 Melbourne Sporting Library edition of *Dogs,* Freeman Lloyd tells us that "Whippets are exceedingly sharp and smart dogs, very delightful to look upon. There are smooth and rough in coat. The former are the more popular."

Mr. Lloyd discusses coat types briefly in *The Whippet and Race Dog,* published in 1894, the first book devoted exclusively to the Whippet. "For the sporting Whippet I should be inclined to pick the rough-haired variety...I would rather go in for the hard-coated variety—one with a grizzled face and a fairly dense coat—I think these are more suitable for the work, and can stand the weather better than the animal that has to be clothed in winter and even pampered in the summer. Therefore, were I going in for a brace of rabbitting Whippets I should choose...a coat of the texture described. It should be borne in mind that a dog required for the wear and tear of rabbit-catching should above all have a good constitution, for working in short furzes soon takes it out of the canine." Furzes are prickly, thorny evergreen shrubs which grow in dense thickets. One can easily see, therefore, why Mr. Lloyd would have preferred a coated, rather than smooth, dog for such sport.

In a small, yet prophetic passage, Freeman Lloyd foresaw the dominance of the smooth Whippet. He predicted that both the Longhaired and Wire-haired Whippet, would fade from public favor. "I am not of the opinion that the rough variety or the broken-haired kind will ever find so much favor in the eyes of judges as the smooth ones....Therefore, for show Whippets, I would advise the smooth coats, for with a little 'elbow grease' they can be made to shine like satin."

Sadly, the wire-haired Whippet is now extinct in America. In the 1920's and 1930's, however, the wire-haired dogs were seen often on California racing tracks. Many years ago, well known Whippet breeder Christine Cormany penned a short article on this variety for *Kennel Review.* Her father, James F. Young, was an avid and successful racing enthusiast and his Wire-hairs were star performers. Mrs. Cormany says they "were the best racers and won the most races over the smooths." One of Mr. Young's most notable winners was a small 15 pound wire-haired bitch named "Kerryline." In her three year career, she was entered in 60 races. She won a remarkable 58 of them.

Included with Mrs. Cormany's article, were three photos of her father's wire-haired Whippets. They are very attractive, clearly demonstrating the elegance of the Whippet, with a Scottish Deerhound type jacket. In

The gorgeous Windsprite Winton Wind, owned by Walter Wheeler, of Sherborn, Massachusetts. (L.M. Gray photo)

A white and red Longhaired Whippet, Ch. Windsprite Autumnal Yarrow, is owned by Walter Wheeler, of Windsprite Kennels. (L.M. Gray photo)

recalling the appearance of the Wire-hairs, Mrs. Cormany states that they were about 22 pounds, with colors running to black, silver and fawn. "As far as I can recall," Christine says, "we never had a white, brindle or parti color....The conformation of the rough-haired variety often compared favorably with the smooth." According to Mrs. Cormany, her father entered his dogs in bench shows on rare occasions. The dogs would be shown only "when a race meet was in conjunction with an All Breed show and we would support the entry of Whippets."

And what became of Mr. Young's wire-haired racing wonders? "When racing declined in southern California and we found ourselves forced to move from the wide open spaces to a refined city life, rather than have the some 25 odd dogs exploited, they were nearly all put to sleep (roughs and smooths) and thus ended the era of the rough haired Whippet."

Walter Wheeler bemoans the loss of those Wire-haired Whippets. "What a pity that someone could not continue the line." The loss of those dogs, in all likelihood, spelled the extinction of the variety. This is because, Wheeler notes, "wire-hair is a dominant, and cannot be carried in the genotype of animals to pop up as a throwback many generations later, as the recessive longhair does." Wheeler believes that the Wire-hairs owned by Cor-many's father were imported from Ire-

land. "Hopefully, there are those on the Emerald Isle who still breed the Wire-haired variety."

Opinions vary on the origin of the Whippet. Some contend that, like his cousin the Greyhound, Whippets have been around for centuries. Others believe that the breed is a fairly recent creation, produced by crossing the Greyhound with the Italian Greyhound and adding a dash of terrier blood. Freeman Lloyd says that terrier crosses added "the wonderful tenacity of the terrier that helps him in his very severe trials...." Indeed, the 1985 version of *The Complete Dog Book* notes that "Though his main forte is as a racedog, he is a rabbit courser of great ability." No matter what the truth of his origin, English Whippet fanciers, in the 1800s, certainly did much experimental breeding in their effort to obtain speedy dogs.

The earliest Whippets were undoubtedly used as hunting dogs, coursing rabbits for their owners and filling the stew pot. But, soon, in the mining and milling communities of Lancashire, Durham, Northumberland and Yorkshire, this workaday coursing was turned into sport. Well, from the dogs' point of view it might have been sport, but early meets weren't really very sporting at all. Wild rabbits were caught in nets and transported to an enclosure. Unfamiliar with the terrain and shaken by its capture, the terrified rabbit was loosed. A pair of Whippets stood by, held by an official slipper. When the rabbit had run some 60 yards, the dogs were released and quickly snapped it up. The first dog to kill the rabbit was declared the winner. With no possibility of escape, the rabbit really didn't have a chance. Soon, the cruelty of such exhibitions generated an outcry from British humane authorities and the meets stopped.

These early meets gave way to the immensely more popular sport of Whippet racing. There on a straightaway track, four or five Whippets headed for the finish line. The miners and mill workers developed a rather elaborate system of handicapping. The dog's starting position was determined by his weight, age and

139

previous winnings. A specified number of yards was deducted, so that each dog could contend fairly and the race would be competitive. Each dog wore a different colored collar to allow spectators to follow the race. When the dogs were positioned at their respective starting points, the owner or trainer would run to the finish line. There, he would take up a position from which he could yell, wave a towel or rag and encourage the dog. Dogs were held, by the nape of the neck and the tail, by slippers. Since a good start could mean the difference between a win and a loss, experienced slippers were in great demand. They aimed to swing the dog as far forward as possible, actually throwing him onto the track. It took great skill to fling the dog forward and still make sure that he alighted on his feet, ready to go.

The judge took up his position at the finish line, and when all were ready, the starter fired a pistol. The 200 yard race was on. "It takes a very good dog or bitch, the female is generally the more speedy," Freeman Lloyd writes in the Melbourne Sporting Library's *Dogs*, "to run 200 yards in twelve seconds. That would be sixteen yards, twenty-four inches per second, which means 'flying' for so small a dog." As they crossed the finish line, the dogs latched onto the towels waved by their owners or trainers and were often spun into the air. It was a quick way of slowing their speed at the often cramped finish line.

Whippet racing became immensely popular and great sums were wagered on the contests. Many a miner found that owning a winning race dog was a wonderful way to supplement his meager earnings. Indeed, he might earn more than he did in the mines or mills. During hard times, the race track winnings might be a family's sole means of support. Because of the money involved coupled with the sense of keen rivalry and competition, Whippets were very carefully cared for and trained.

Puppies grew up in the house, usually playing in the kitchen, with the housewife and children. When the man returned home from work, he would take the dog out for road conditioning. At night, the dog often slept in the children's bed, snuggling happily under the covers with them. The dog which developed, therefore, was far more than a mere track competitor. He was also a full fledged family member.

Writing in Robert Leighton's 1906 work *The New Book of the Dog*, Whippet breeder F. C. Hignett gives us details on the care and training of the race dog. "The training of Whippets is by no means easy work, and is more expensive than most people imagine. To begin with, the very choicest food is deemed absolutely necessary, in fact a Whippet undergoing preparation for an important race is provided with the most wholesome fare. Choice mutton chops, beef steaks and similar

dainties comprise their daily portion. Of course, exercise is a necessity, but it is not considered good policy to allow a dog in training to gambol about whether on the roads or in the fields. Indeed, all dogs which are undergoing preparation for a race are particularly deprived of their freedom, in lieu of which they are walked along hard roads, secured by a lead; and for fear of their picking up the least bit of refuse each is securely muzzled by a box-like leather arrangement which completely envelops the jaws, but which is freely perforated to permit proper breathing. Any distance between six and a dozen miles a day, according to the stamina and condition of the dog, is supposed to be the proper amount of exercise, and scales are brought in every few days to gauge the effect which is produced. In addition to this, private trials are necessary in the presence of someone who is accustomed to timing races by the aid of a stop watch...."

Indeed, it was undoubtedly the thirst for racing success that led to the demise of the longhaired Whippet. "Rough coated dogs were a common sight in the old days when the look of the animal was secondary to performance," Pauline Wilson writes in her 1979 *Whippets, Rearing and Racing*, "However, it was soon realised that the smooth coat was more compatible with racing." Although the longhaired coat provided protection, under natural coursing conditions, it added wind resistance on the race track where a fraction of a second could spell the difference between victory and defeat. It seems logical to conclude that longhaired puppies would have been destroyed. The desire for short coated dogs passed on to the show ring. The earliest Whippet show dogs were, in fact, those individuals who were not fast enough to win on the race course. Clearly, the smooth dogs caught the judges' eyes, for no coat obscured the refined elegance of their outline.

While longhaired Whippets may have been shunned by 19th century English judges, they are attracting the attention of both spectators and judges at rare breed events in this country. There has also been increasing interest from abroad. The top winner for 1988, Ch. Shandor's Prince of Windsprite, owned by respected A.K.C. and International judge Edith Nash Hellerman, attracted many to the variety. The formation of the Longhaired Whippet Association (LWA), in 1981, has done much to foster interest in the breed.

"Beneath its protective yet decorative coat, the Longhaired Whippet is identical to the smooth Whippet, except that its skin has greater substance and suppleness to support the longer hair," the L.W.A. standard says. "This small, very athletic and graceful sighthound expresses its competitive spirit in its alert demeanor, and can race, course and hunt in a wide variety of terrain and weather because of its size and coat."

The flashy black and white Ch. Windsprite Autumnal Quest. This lovely bitch is owned by Walter Wheeler. (L.M. Gray photo)

Colors may range from the stark, bold beauty of black and white to the exotic pastel shades of lilac and blue. Whether your taste runs to the bright vibrant tones of red or the ethereal beauty of a solid white, you'll find something to delight you. The standard states that "Any color and marking is allowed...Each should enhance the beauty of the total dog."

The Longhaired Whippet is the same size as his smooth coated counterpart. Males measure 19-22" at the withers and females run 18-21," with a 1/2" grace interval above or below these figures. However, with the added coat, the Longhaired Whippet often appears larger than his

It is the soft, silky coat that has attracted so much attention in rare breed circles. Indeed, this characteristic has given rise to the nickname "Silken Windsprites." The undercoat should be thick enough to afford protection, but should not add a bulky look. The longer guard hairs may be wavy or sometimes slightly curly. A profuse ruff about the neck accentuates the head. An excessive coat, which impedes movement, is not desirable. Breeders prefer to show their dogs with a minimum of grooming, but some "discreet" trimming is allowed. "Some dogs grow the most profuse coat in the areas where the least coat is needed to reveal the Whippet contours beneath," Mr. Wheeler says. This is particularly true with males, who sometimes carry profuse hair on the withers, croup and beneath the loin. This tends to obscure the graceful curving topline and the characteristic tuck-up so essential to the Whippet. "Unfortunately, many fanciers cannot visualize the anatomy beneath the coat of a longhaired dog. Therefore, some Longhaired Whippets, especially males in the winter months, will require discreet 'shaping' to show their structure to those incapable of seeing it under a natural coat." To enhance the natural body contours, Mr. Wheeler recommends that dogs be tidied up with thinning shears before being shown.

The Longhaired Whippet comes in a kaleidoscope of hues. Indeed, the varied palette of colors makes breeding Longhaired Whippets particularly interesting.

smooth cousin. "Since any measurement taken in the show ring will include coat, breeders must realize that the Longhaired Whippet, in order to look the same way as any given smooth, must be slightly smaller of build beneath its coat than the smooth," Mr. Wheeler says.

Not content to rest on his laurels, several years ago Mr. Wheeler initiated a new phase in his Longhaired Whippet breeding program. Using small specimens from his Longhaired litters, he set out to produce a Miniature variety of the Longhaired Whippet. The Mini-Whippets range in size from six to ten pounds, with eight pounds being the average. "Small animals are permitted as long as type, soundness, stamina and temperament are retained," the standard says. In 1982, Mr. Wheeler's Miniature *Verdin* made her show ring appearance. "At the rare breed show, Verdin touched the ground only when in the ring," Mr. Wheeler reports. "Admirers begged to be allowed to carry her about and for several hours, in a state of absolute bliss, she passed from the caressing arms of one Longhaired fan to another." Since those early days, the Miniature Longhaired Whippets have become increasingly popular.

The Longhaired Whippet shares the same wonderful temperament that has made the smooth so popular. "Never aggressive with its own kind, it also should display a love for and devotion to its human associates. An aloof, undemonstrative temperament is not typical," the standard specifies. "Through the years," Mr. Wheeler says, "I've always selected gene pool members for not only their physical qualities, but also for intelligence, tractability, stability and lack of accident proclivity." In addition, Mr. Wheeler stresses "devotion to and dependence upon human beings in general and a chosen owner in particular." Those who have purchased dogs from Mr. Wheeler often praise the breed's easy going, mellow temperament.

What's in store for the Longhaired Whippet? Only time will tell. Presently, there rages an extraordinary controversy over the longhaired dogs. Smooth fanciers are adamant in their belief that the longhairs should not be considered Whippets at all. Indeed, the virulent altercation is so rancorous that it's more akin to all out war. In an attempt to counter Mr. Wheeler's efforts, smooth Whippet fanciers have amended the breed standard to include a disqualification for coat length. Bo Bengtson, highly successful smooth Whippet breeder, undoubtedly speaks for many when he wrote, in *Dog World*, "One would have thought the controversy over the longhaired so called 'Whippets' would have died a natural death by now...

"It should be clearly stated," he continues, "that according to a panel of breed experts in America, England and elsewhere, including the American Whippet Club, the American Kennel Club and all other nationally recognized dog clubs, there is no such thing as a longhaired Whippet; nor has one ever existed since the breed was first recognized a century ago...

"...The longhaired 'Whippets,'...have more of a Sheltie or Borzoi-type coat—totally different from anything acceptable in a purebred Whippet. The A.K.C. breed standard now includes a disqualification on coat length.

"While longhaired dogs may be attractive in their own way," Mr. Bengtson admits, "they do not conform to what has been accepted as the classical Whippet type since the breed was first recognized. One would hope that those who like the longhaired dogs will have enough faith in their intrinsic quality for them to 'stand on their own legs' and possibly at some future time become accepted as a new breed, instead of borrowing the Whippet's name."

Walter Wheeler, father of the modern Longhaired Whippet, poses with Ch. Windsprite Frost Knight. (Lily Rose photo)

Mr. Wheeler certainly wouldn't agree with that suggestion. Assigning a different breed name would be to deny the Longhairs' ancestry. And the history of the Whippet has been an enduring passion of his, long before his project with the Longhairs began. It's too soon for us to tell whether the Longhaired Whippet will gain a permanent place among the breeds and varieties known in this country. Certainly there are many smooth Whippet breeders who would like to think of Mr. Wheeler's work as a passing fad. The exotic dogs do seem, however, to be gaining a foothold within the ever growing rare breed movement. Clearly, the Longhair will never overtake the smooth Whippet in popularity, but he may find his niche among dog lovers. With his luxurious silken coat, elegant build and endearing personality, the Longhaired Whippet seems destined to be a show stopper at rare breed events.

Chapter 25

The Miniature Chinese Shar-Pei

Who can deny the irresistible appeal of a Chinese Shar-Pei puppy? The twinkling eyes, the wagging tail, the playful zest, the excessive skin and wrinkles, wrinkles, wrinkles. Indeed, it's the captivating look of the Shar-Pei puppy that has drawn so many to the breed in the first place. They soon discover, however, that the real value of the Shar-Pei lies in its great charm. The intelligence, loyalty, clown-like impishness, protectiveness and utter devotion of the Chinese Shar-Pei is what's made the breed so popular.

Is it possible to capture and retain those puppy attributes in an adult dog? Some breeders think so. In the past two years, an effort has begun to breed a Miniature version of the Shar-Pei. It's a controversial undertaking which provokes the ire of many established Shar-Pei breeders. It is not sanctioned, as yet, by the Chinese Shar-Pei Club of America. Often the victim of exploitation, many fear that this is just the latest in one more fad to sweep through the breed. When the craze is over, they say, the breed will once again be discredited and they'll be left to pick up the pieces. While there are certainly charlatans who have jumped on the Miniature bandwagon, there are also some established breeders who have been involved with this new movement. Slowly and conscientiously they have been working to bring down size, while still retaining all the best qualities of the Standard sized Shar-Pei.

In describing the Miniature, perhaps it's best if we begin our discussion by talking about what a Miniature Chinese Shar-Pei *is not*. A Miniature is not a sickly puppy who, because of his infirmities, fails to achieve full adult size. The runt in an otherwise normal litter is not a Miniature. Dogs of normal size who simply have short legs are not Miniatures, either. And, most emphatically, a Miniature is not the result of a cross with a Pug, aimed at quickly bringing down size in a single generation.

A true Miniature is a pint-sized replica of the larger Shar-Pei. He packs all the qualities found in the larger dog, including bone size, into a smaller frame. He should still be a stocky, sturdy dog with a solid, well built frame. Despite his small size, he should still be well-balanced and muscular. Faults in the construction of fronts, rears and toplines are not to be excused simply because smaller size is what's sought. His head should retain all the quality epitomized in the best of the standard sized Shar-Pei. It should have the legendary "warrior" scowl and the hippopotamus like look. The muzzle should still be broad and blunt, with little stop. "Meatmouths," dogs with extremely full, blocky muzzles may be found in these smaller dogs, too. And, like his larger brother, the Miniature should have either the short, bristly "horse" coat or the slightly longer "brush" coat.

Size among the Minis has not been definitely established. Some hold that any dog 17 inches or under qualifies as a Miniature. However, this is just a scant one inch below the recognized limits for a Standard and seems a little high for a dog destined to be considered a Miniature. Most Miniature breeders consider that their dogs should be 16 inches or under to qualify for the Miniature label. Weight is, of course, proportionally lower, too. Ideally, the Miniature should be half to three-quarters the size of the Standard-sized Shar-Pei. That said, it's very important to emphasize that quality, breed type and soundness should never be sacrificed in the quest for reduced size. In the Miniature variety, a greater emphasis is placed on wrinkling than in the Standard Shar-Pei. This is in keeping with the attempt to retain the breed's puppy-like characteristics.

Size has often varied significantly in the breed, but the Chinese Shar-Pei has, before the present move, been considered a medium sized dog. Though there have been several changes in the standard, over the years, the given height has not wavered. The standard specifies that the Shar-Pei should stand between 18 and 20 inches at the shoulder. The preferred weight is listed at 40-55 pounds. In truth, there are now Shar-Pei in the show ring who exceed the upper limits designated by the standard. Miniature breeders point out that oversize dogs are regularly exhibited and few are routinely penalized for their extra size. Indeed, it seems that these larger dogs, often looking more impressive, frequently capture top awards.

For Linda Coffee, the introduction to Miniatures came quite by accident. For the past eight years, she has bred Standard sized Shar-Pei at her Arlington, Texas home. "I kept my first Mini simply because she was the best dog in the litter," Linda says. "I had no idea that she would grow up to be a Miniature." Linda's eye proved correct, for the bitch finished her championship in short order, in competition with Standard sized dogs. "I am still actively involved with my Standards," Linda says. "I like it when those searching for a Mini ask if I also have Standards. I try to stress that I am interested, first and foremost, in a *quality* Shar-Pei, whether they be Standards or Minis."

Mrs. Coffee began in dogs, years ago, with Poodles and Cockers. She admits that she was drawn to

the Chinese Shar-Pei by its uniqueness. She gladly cast aside her clippers and grooming shears for the Shar-Pei's easy care coat. "What impressed me initially about this breed is its tremendous intelligence and its wonderful qualities as a companion. They really are terrific dogs. Their lovingness, protectiveness and desire for companionship simply is unequaled."

Linda Coffee's first Minis were descendants of Shir Du Bang. "He was a small dog and the size seems to have come down through the line," she says. Linda has concentrated on that line and recently introduced an outcross line which has proven successful. "My aim is to bring down size gradually while maintaining the same quality I have in my Standards," Linda says.

Linda's first Mini, 16 inch Rosie, finished as a Standard. Since then, she has succeeded in reducing size in subsequent generations. "My second generation dogs are coming in at 14 to 15 1/2 inches and the third generation is 12 to 13 1/2 inches." Linda has been kind enough to provide weights on her Miniatures. The 16 inch dogs tip the scales at 36 pounds; 14 1/2 inch dogs weigh 30 pounds; 13 1/2 to 14 inch dogs weigh just 25 pounds. "When compared with the 50 pound average weight of a Standard," Linda observes, "this makes the smaller Minis half the weight of the Standard Shar-Pei."

Naturally, with their smaller size, it can be difficult for the Mini to compete with his larger brothers. When Linda enters her Minis in regular classes, she usually confines herself to the puppy or bred-by-exhibitor classes. "Minis that mature at 16 inches or less are about the size of a 3 1/2 to 4 month old Standard Shar-Pei," Linda says. "That makes it difficult for them to compete in the open classes."

Recently, two clubs have been formed to meet the growing interest in Miniatures. They offer special classes for Minis only and enable breeders to compete and compare dogs. Eventually, Mini breeders hope that their dogs will be recognized as a separate variety. That will, undoubtedly, take some time and Mini breeders will have to demonstrate that this is no passing fad. They will have to prove that they are indeed capable of breeding sound, typey dogs.

Currently, there is a great deal of prejudice among Standard breeders toward those who actively seek to produce Minis. The animosity runs deep and often approaches outright hostility. Standard advocates insist that the the Shar-Pei is a medium sized dog and that tradition should not be lightly cast aside. "While I don't agree, I can certainly understand their view," Linda Coffee says. "Minis are becoming extremely

This photo clearly illustrates the size difference between the Standard and Miniature Shar-Pei. Note the more profuse wrinkling on the Mini. (Photo courtesy of Linda Coffee.)

A charming litter of puppies sired by Linda Coffee's Baggin's Big Boy.

popular and I too worry about them. There are very few breeders out there who are offering guarantees for both size and quality. There have been people who are simply defrauding the public by selling sickly or runt puppies as Miniatures. Often, these dogs, at maturity, turn out to be Standard sized."

What's Linda's advice for those who want to purchase a Miniature Shar-Pei? "Investigate, investigate, investigate," she advises. "There are responsible breeders out there, but it may take some work to find them. Don't blindly accept the first puppy offered because someone says they are sure it will be a Mini. Be sure to ask for a written guarantee that specifies both adult size and ensures quality. Don't hesitate to ask plenty of questions and steer away from anyone unwilling to answer them. Ask about the breeder's record and try to ascertain how much experience they have with the breed."

Many people have been attracted to the Mini because they like wrinkles and wish to have the perpetual puppy look. Indeed, most Shar-Pei breeders, Standard or Mini, are besieged with calls requesting the most wrinkled puppy possible. This is particularly true with Minis in which emphasis is placed on retaining wrinkling. Potential owners must realize, however, that choosing the most profusely wrinkled puppy is no guarantee that they will get a well wrinkled adult. Not all Shar-Pei lines develop the same with regard to wrinkling. Some profusely wrinkled puppies have all their wrinkling at a very young age. As they mature, they grow into their coat and wrinkles, and can appear quite smooth by the time they are adults. Other puppies start out with only moderate wrinkling. Yet, as they mature, the wrinkles continue to develop as they add extra skin. If wrinkling is one of your top priorities, it's best to proceed cautiously and investigate bloodlines.

Ask to see relatives of the dogs: parents, siblings, aunts, uncles, cousins, etc., in an attempt to discover which lines retain adult wrinkling.

The Miniature Shar-Pei shares the same wonderful personality traits that have captivated so many people. Mini breeders, however, say that there are some pleasant differences. "The Minis are truly delightful," says Linda Coffee. "They are more laid back than the Standards. Minis seem to retain their playful puppy temperaments even into adulthood. Like most concerned breeders, I place great emphasis on temperament. I simply will not tolerate an aggressive dog, whether it's a Miniature or a Standard. I have children and my dogs are raised with them. I just don't think you can compromise on temperament."

All those interested in the Chinese Shar-Pei, be it Standard or Miniature, should be aware of the breed's medical problems. A limited initial gene pool, coupled with the breed's distinctive appearance, has led to several largely pervasive conditions within the breed. Before buying a dog, be sure to quiz breeders about the problems within their bloodlines. Any breeder who denies having any medical problems should be viewed with extreme skepticism.

This stunning male is a rare blue color. He is Nortex Bleu Baggins, co-owned by John and Denise Smith and Linda Coffee.

The charming, sixteen inch tall Ch. Baggins Leading Lady. "Rosie," as she's known, is the dam of two champions from her only litter. She is owned by Linda Coffee, Baggins Kennel, Arlington, Texas. (Hagerman photo)

Entropion is a fairly common problem in Shar-Pei, although many breeders work diligently to diminish it. The eyelid of an entropic dog rolls inward, causing the eyelashes to scratch the cornea. If caught early enough, the eyelid can be "tacked," which may prevent the condition from developing. If this does not work, surgery can correct the condition. If left untreated, the eye will ulcerate and the dog may eventually become blind.

Some large muzzled dogs, called "meatmouths," may suffer from a condition which breeders call "tight lip." The dog's lower lip tends to roll over the teeth and eating becomes very painful. In severe cases, surgery is necessary.

Many Shar-Pei suffer from skin disorders. Most will blow their coats as puberty approaches. Generally, the Shar-Pei can be expected to blow its coat twice annually. Breeders describe the coats as having a "moth eaten" appearance. Pregnant and nursing bitches almost always suffer from ratty looking coats, but this should not be cause for alarm. Buyers are counseled to ask breeders about other skin conditions they may have encountered. Ask specifically about the diet the breeder recommends. Many breeders feel that diet has a strong influence on coat. After trial and error, they have arrived at a formulation which they feel helps to control the problem. Some breeders feel strongly that the coat improves when soymeal is eliminated from the diet.

The Standard sized Shar-Pei is prone to hip dysplasia. Most dedicated breeders x-ray their stock before breeding. It's too soon to tell if the Minis, with their smaller size, may suffer less from this condition. At this point, it's better to be safe than sorry, so be sure to ask if the breeder x-rays his stock.

While there are, admittedly, problems in the breed, they are not overwhelming. Many owners have found that they are willing to deal with the difficulties, in exchange for the pleasure of sharing their lives with a Chinese Shar-Pei. In this chapter, I have tried to focus exclusively on the Miniature Shar-Pei. Those seeking more information on the breed in general, its history and temperamental qualities, can find a more detailed discussion in the first volume of *A Celebration of Rare Breeds*. It will provide a good general introduction to the breed.

What does the future hold for the Miniature Shar-Pei? Only time will tell. There's certainly a desire among the public for a pint-sized Shar-Pei, who retains the many endearing qualities that epitomize the breed. Much will depend upon the dedication and commitment of those breeding Miniatures. They have a tremendous task ahead of them, both in their own personal breeding programs and in educating the public about this variety. If their quest for a Miniature is motivated by profit, they will surely fail. This will be just one more passing fad within the breed. One hopes that they will work slowly and conscientiously to reduce size in a sensible manner. To succeed, they must maintain quality, soundness and temperament, while striving for smaller size. If they can do this, there's no doubt that this variety will prosper.

Chapter 26

The New Guinea Singing Dog

It's dusk at Sharon McKenzie's South Carolina home. Without warning, a dog begins to howl. The sound is weird, with an eerie plaintive, yet strangely melodious quality. Another dog picks up the cry and then yet another joins in. The dogs' voices unite and seem to blend in a curious canine chorus. It's a riveting sound, unlike that of any other animal. Natives of New Guinea called them "Singing Dogs" and believed that the originator of the universe had bestowed this special carol on the animals. Once they barked like other canines, but the great god had given them the singing voice of a bird. Natives sometimes joined in, yodeling in imitation of the dogs. Some even said that they could understand what the dogs were singing. They knew well the unearthly song, believing that the dogs could see ghosts that were invisible to men. Or, conversely, some thought that the dogs themselves embodied the spirits of the departed. The song of Sharon McKenzie's dogs continues for several minutes then stops abruptly, as quickly as it had begun. Sharon is one of a few select Americans who is privileged to own a trio of the rare New Guinea Singing Dogs.

The Singing Dogs have lifted their voice in song since time immemorial. New Guinea, the world's second largest island (Australia is considered a continent and Greenland has dibs on first place), has long intrigued scholars. First discovered, in the 1500's, by the Portuguese, the island attracted the attention of other countries, too. The Dutch arrived in the 1600's and gave the island its name. The British came in the 1700's. The people, flora and fauna of the island attracted the attention of anthropologists, biologists, explorers and adventurers. They set sail to discover the nature of this remote island. Our most comprehensive view of the part that dogs played, in the primitive culture of the island's people, comes from anthropologists, many of whom traveled throughout the country and lived with its people.

During the early days, the dogs were common throughout the island. In the highland areas the dogs occasionally kept company with man, but more often they lived wild and free. In the lowland villages, they were more apt to take up residence with the many humans inhabiting the area. It is from these lowland tribes that we gain a true understanding of the Singing Dog's place in these primitive societies.

The popularity of the dog, in lowland villages, seems to have varied considerably. Researchers tell us that some villages had no dogs at all, while in other locales they were extremely popular. The dog seems to have been prevalent among the Garamundi people. F.E. Williams, in his 1936 book, *Papuans of the Trans-Fly,* says that with this tribe "the dogs would seem to outnumber the humans. In visiting the island of Ianforok I found myself in a house with eleven men and boys and between thirty-five and forty clamorous dogs; and throughout the village were to be seen litters of pups at every state of infancy."

The respect and treatment accorded dogs also seems to have varied widely from village to village. In 1880, d'Albertis camped among natives on Hall Sound and the Fly River. The people d'Albertis saw called the dog *waia,* and considered it a pet. Women, he reported, "often carry about dogs and little pigs, of which they seem to be very fond." Four years later, Otto Finsch journeyed to New Guinea and recorded similar observations. "Little pigs as well as young dogs are favorites of the Papuan lady's world," he says. He saw women suckling young puppies, just as they did their own children.

Men also treated dogs kindly. Among the Orokaiva clan, a respected man was one who "did not beat his wife and children," Williams tells us, in his 1930 work *Orokaiva Society*, nor "ill-treat his dogs and pigs." However, this kind treatment was not always the case. Life for the dogs of the Moorheads was not pleasant. The dogs were left to fend for themselves and often had to resort to stealing food from the tribe. They often received kicks or blows. But, even amongst these folks, Williams found a dog lover or two. In *Papuans of the Trans-Fly*, he says that occasional Moorhead men "show great fondness toward them. I have seen a youth...boisterously welcomed by his dogs; and he did not fail to return their show of affection."

Among some New Guinea tribesman, the Singing Dog appears almost to have been revered. Like our American Indians, these island people were totally dependent on their environment. They lived in harmony with nature. Their religious beliefs attempted to explain the origin of the many elements so important to their lives. The dog played a key role in their beliefs.

The Elema tribe believed that a god, named "Kambel," was the creator of their world. This mythical figure had a pet dog, known as "Natekari." It was Natekari who introduced the Elemas to the many plants that grew in their world. It seems that Natekari caught and devoured a cassowary, a fleet bird similar to, but smaller than, an ostrich. He later regurgitated the bird and from that very spot some important food plant, such as taro, grows. Natekari was also responsible for guiding the Elema to the pure springs that provided water. It was Kambel that changed Natekari, and all subsequent dogs, from barking to singing animals. He did this by substituting the dog's tongue with the quill of a cassowary.

Several ceremonies seem to tell how the natives first learned to use the Singing Dog in hunting. In one of these dramas, humans attempt to find game in a tree, but are unsuccessful. A dog, on leash, is led to the spot and succeeds in routing the game.

The Orokaiva tribe believed that it was the dog who had brought fire to their people. Williams writes, in *Orokaiva Society*, that dogs were a common sight "crouching in the ashes of a hardly expired fire....Indeed, the dog is said to have a special prerogative over the fire by virtue of the legendary fact that he first brought it to the Orokaiva."

It appears that, among most tribes, the Singing Dog was a highly valued animal. The dog was so important to one tribe that they erected a special shrine to him. Offerings were frequently taken to this sacred spot. Writing in *Papuans of the Trans-Fly*, Williams says that "If long neglected, it is thought by these people that dogs fall victims of disease."

Apparently, the dog was also used in trading with other tribes. "The natives value their dogs highly," reports A.F.R. Wollaston, in his 1912 book *Pygmies and Papuans, The Stone Age Today in Dutch New Guinea.* "as they well may do, for they provide the whole of their meat supply, and they use them to exchange for articles of which they have great need. The people of Parimau have a small piece of iron about the size of a chisel, used for carving their canoes and paddles, for which the enormous price of three dogs had to be paid...to the people of the Wakatini."

The most common and most appreciated use of the Singing Dog was as an aid in the hunt. Little is known of the training methods employed by the natives. However, numerous references tell us that proficient hunters were highly valued and that it required time to adequately train a good hunting dog. We do know something of the style of hunting used in New Guinea. Generally, dogs pursued game and held it at bay until the hunter could arrive. The animal was then either speared or slain with a bow and arrow. As a reward for his help, the dog received a portion of the meat.

Hunting appears to have been a year round endeavor. In *Orokaiva Society*, F.E. Williams says that "When an individual travels in the bush he goes armed with his spear and followed by his dog so as to lose no opportunities." While the dogs were undoubtedly used on many types of game, travelers tell us that wallaby and bush pigs were their primary targets. In *Papuans of the Trans-Fly*, Williams reports that "Dogs of the common Papuan variety are fairly numerous, especially....where wallaby hunting is a more important phase of the food-quest.....It is undeniably a game little animal, an excellent hunter of small game, and equal to bringing a bush-pig to bay."

Scientists often learn much about primitive cultures by studying the ways in which they bury their dead. The descriptions of dog burials leave little doubt that New Guinea natives loved and respected their canines. Dogs were buried in graves, the same as humans, and often mourned for several days. Yam fragments were scattered on the grave as a sign of respect. When a particularly good hunting dog died, his owner broke his arrows and placed them in the grave with the dog's body. A mourning period was observed, during which the owner would abstain from hunting.

"One day one of our 'boys' shot a dog," A.F.R. Wollaston recalls in his 1912 book, *Pygmies and Papuans, The Stone Age Today in Dutch New Guinea,* "which had been in the habit of stealing food from our camp. When the natives knew that it was dead, all the

Swamp Fox Owen Stanley, a male Singing Dog owned by breed pioneer I. L. Brisbin. Note the black muzzle and characteristic white, plume-like underside of the tail. (I. L. Brisbin photo)

people of the village began to wail in the same manner as they do when a person dies, and the owner of the dog smeared himself with mud and mourned bitterly.

There are many reported cases of the Singing Dog being used for food. It appears, however, that this was primarily for ceremonial occasions. "In slaughtering," Williams reports in *Orokaiva Society* and again in his 1940 book, *Drama of the Orkolo, The Social and Ceremonial Life of the Elema,* the dog was "seized by the hind legs and dashed against a tree, a method which seems brutal but is instantly effective."

Otto Finsch, who journeyed to New Guinea in the late 1800's, tells us that dog meat was served only at big feasts. Seligman details several instances of the use of dogs. He says they, along with pigs, were served at wedding celebrations. He also tells, in detail, of the initiation ceremony. The tribe Seligman visited had a matrilineal culture. When a boy approached manhood, he was initiated into the household of his mother's family. This assumption of clan responsibilities was referred to as the *itaburi*. It was appropriate at such a time to have a celebration and feast. The boy's father would kill a dog and take it to the young man's maternal uncle.

Otto Finsch's report was penned in 1884 and Seligman's writings date to 1910. Perhaps the situation

had changed by the time Williams visited New Guinea. In 1936 he wrote that the "eating of dogs is usually regarded with abhorrence...Nowadays the idea is universally deprecated both because of the value of the dog as a hunter and because of the sentimental scruples of its owner."

Sadly, purebred Singing Dogs are no longer found in the New Guinea lowlands. The introduction of foreign dogs, which interbred with the native population, destroyed the pure lowland Singing Dog. In fact, it was often the very researchers, who report in such rich detail, who hastened the demise of the lowland dogs. It appears that the New Guinea tribes, unfamiliar with barking canines, were initially frightened by the strange dogs that accompanied foreigners. In recounting his experiences, Wollaston writes in 1912: "Dogs are usually more useful on smaller ships than cannon, for nothing helps so wonderfully to clear the deck of natives as a number of barking dogs."

The introduction of foreign culture was to alter forever the role of the Singing Dog. From the European settlements, these new intruders swept throughout much of the country. Native policeman were given barking dogs to serve as their aids. The Europeans also introduced the native peoples to poultry. The Singing Dogs seemed to have had a penchant for chasing and destroy-

A wonderful head study of Hager II, owned by Phil Persky, of New York City.

ing these birds. Due to this, the dogs were often rounded up and killed. It also appears that foreign dogs were seen as a status symbol, by those natives intent on embracing the new culture.

The picture of the highland Singing Dog which emerges is incomplete and sometimes contradictory. In part, this is because few researchers ventured into the remote mountains. In general, the highland dogs lived wild, shunning man. Since they were nocturnal, they were rarely even seen. The dogs fed on rodents of various kinds and ground nesting birds.

The highland natives, however, were aware of the dogs. Accomplished hunters and trackers themselves, the tribesmen often saw pawprints. H. Clissold, who wrote an article on the highland dogs, for *South Pacific Post,* says that the "natives fear them and will leave an area where a spoor is seen or a cry is heard as quickly as possible." In spite of this, puppies were occasionally stolen, ostensibly for food. "When they capture one they mark the nearest tree with symbols so that its mother will know what happened to it."

One researcher, however, does say that highland dogs sometimes lived in association with man. M.J.

Meggitt studied the Enga, a highland tribe. According to him, the Enga kept only a single dog. "They were highly prized....," he writes in a 1958 issue of *Oceania,* "and a good bitch cost as much as a stone ax, a net bag or a small barrow.

"Ownership, care and training of dogs are men's business," Meggitt continues. "Men inherit their father's dogs. A man who kills another's dog, accidentally or on purpose, compensates the owner with an ax, a small pig or another dog." Indeed, such killings are said to have led to a number of feuds. "Dogs past their prime may be eaten, but there are so few of them that they are a negligible source of meat. A good hunting dog to which a man has become attached and given a name is not eaten. It is buried in the same way as a child. It is even mourned for several days."

The earliest known Singing Dog to leave New Guinea, left the island in 1897. Unfortunately, it was dead. As those familiar with Audubon's work will know, naturalists often killed their specimens and then studied them. Sir William MacGregor shot the dog on Mount Scratchley, at an elevation of 7,000 feet. He sent both the skeleton and the skin, preserved in alcohol, to the Queensland Museum. There it lay in storage until 1911, when C.W. DeVis assembled and studied the specimen. He described the dog as 11 1/2 inches at the shoulder and primarily black in color. White markings trimmed the nape of the neck, the throat and chest and the tip of the tail.

In 1911, Professor Wood Jones reviewed DeVis' findings, dissenting with his conclusions. In 1928, Queensland Museum Director H.A. Longman again examined the specimen and published his own findings. Until the 1950's, this sole skeleton comprised the scientific community's entire knowledge of the New Guinea Singing Dog.

In 1954, Ellis Troughton, Curator of Mammals for the Australian Museum, travelled to New Guinea. He spent some time collecting mammalian species around Mount Hagen. Troughton heard reports of Singing Dogs in the vicinity of Mount Giluwe. He succeeded in obtaining a pair of dogs, which were brought down to a government station. Unfortunately, Troughton failed to realize what extraordinary escape artists the dogs were. They broke free and destroyed many of the government's carefully managed poultry. A political brouhaha ensued and the dogs were given to local natives, who killed and ate them.

In 1956, Medical Assistant Albert Speer and Assistant District Officer J. P. Sinclair heard reports of the Singing Dogs. They managed to obtain a pair from the isolated Lavanni Valley, in the southern highlands. (Some reports say the pair came from the Shangri-La Valley.) The dogs were sent to Sir Edward Hallstrom, who had set up a native animal study center in the western highlands, at Nondugl. Hallstrom kept the dogs for a time, studying their habits and comparing his observations with the previous studies. In 1957, he sent the dogs to the Taronga Park Zoo, in Sydney, Australia.

When the dogs arrived in Australia, they were examined by Ellis Troughton. He believed they were a separate species and dubbed them *Canis hallstromi*. This designation would be contested by later researchers, who believed that the dog did not deserve separate categorization. The prevailing belief today is that the Singing Dog should be called *Canis familiaris hallstromi*. Shortly after arriving at the Zoo, the female gave birth to a litter. The majority of Singing Dogs, found throughout the world, stem from this pair.

In 1963, a field representative for the Bishop Museum, in Honolulu, captured a female Singing Dog. Mr. H. Clissold trapped the dog at 13,400 feet on Mount Giluwe. Clissold and his team brought the dog down to a lower elevation where it excited the local natives. They said it was very bad luck to capture a Singing Dog for it embodied the spirit of a dead person. The two men who had actually trapped the dog, they predicted ominously, would not live out the year. As if to confirm their suspicions that this was a bad omen, a heavy downpour began at the same time the bitch was captured. The torrential rains continued for a week, subsiding only after Clissold left.

Writing of his experiences, in the *South Pacific Post*, Mr. Clissold describes his first night with his new Singing Dog. She was very vocal, he reports, "the sobbing wail, rising and falling on a strong wind was unearthly. From the distance, she appeared to utter two or three anguished sobs deep in the throat and with rising volume and pitch, tremble along for a short time to fade away and be lost in the wind. It is the saddest, loneliest and most hair-raising sound it has ever been my misfortune to hear. After three hours of partial sleep, I went to her crate. Shining the torch between the slats the only visible thing was a pair of luminescent green eyes...a most ghastly sobbing wail came at me....fear rippled up and down my spine and my hair tingled. The dog blinked and the tension broke. I spoke and she looked up at me, not with eyes bitter or evil but with a world of sadness and longing. No doubt she could smell on the wind the scent of the mountain on which she had lived."

I'm not positive, but I believe that the bitch Clissold obtained was presented to the Taronga Park Zoo. We do know that she produced at least one litter and several of the puppies were distributed to zoos around the world.

In the late 1970's, researchers captured a pair of dogs in Irian Jaya's Eipomak Valley. These dogs were presented to the Kiel Institute für Haustierkunde, in what was then West Germany. The dogs have produced progeny and a few have come to the U.S. and Canada. At least one other dog has been captured in New Guinea.

The Singing Dog first came to this country in 1958, shortly after the first captive breeding was done. The Taronga Park Zoo sent a female, and later a male, to the San Diego Zoo. Puppies from their litters were distributed to zoos in this country and abroad.

Until recent years, the dogs have been confined exclusively to zoos. Thanks to the efforts of Dr. I. Lehr Brisbin, Jr. all that has changed. Several years ago he learned of the New Guinea Singing Dog and was able to

One of the Singing Dogs imported by Sheryl Langan from Australia. This rare dog now makes its home at Driftwood Ranch, in Canada.

acquire several for his research facility at the Savannah River Ecology Laboratory, in Aiken, South Carolina. "With the exception of the pioneering efforts of Dr. Ulie Seal and his wife in Minnesota, few if any singing dogs had ever been adapted to life as a house pet or to live in a closely socialized state with their owners," Dr. Brisbin writes in the *Feral Canid Research Newsletter,* which he publishes. "Since that time however, a number of new singing dog owners have reported remarkable breakthroughs in their ability to socialize these animals and adapt them to home care conditions in their households." Indeed, thanks to Dr. Brisbin a number of owners are enjoying the companionship of Singing Dogs.

One owner, who has successfully socialized her Singing Dogs, is Sharon McKenzie. An Akita breeder, Sharon had long been interested in primitive breeds. For years, she'd longed to have an Australian Dingo. Several years ago she saw an article about Dr. Brisbin's work and contacted him. Four years ago, she received a male Singing Dog. He was soon joined by a female. Since living with her rare dogs, Sharon has become very enthusiastic about the breed.

"This is a very primitive breed, unchanged by man's whims," Sharon McKenzie says. I feel that people familar with other primitive breeds—the Akita, Shiba, Telomian, Basenji, etc.—will have the easiest time adjusting to the Singing Dog. They really are intriguing. They keep you on your toes because they always find something new. There's never a dull moment with one of these dogs around."

"They are very special dogs," says Sheryl Lan-

Singing Dogs are intensely curious, as demonstrated by Phil Persky's Jaya.

gan, of Beaverlodge, Alberta, Canada. Sheryl raises Arabian horses, Akitas and Shibas at her Driftwood Ranch. She also has eight timberwolves and two tundra wolves. Sheryl had long been interested in Singing Dogs, but it was the predicament of the breed that finally spurred her to action. The Taronga Park Zoo announced that it was cutting back on its stock of Singing Dogs. The situation was critical and, if homes could not be found for the dogs, they would be euthanized. Sharon contacted the Zoo immediately. "It was an expensive proposition," she says. The freight alone was exorbitant and the dogs needed special crates. Four Singing Dogs arrived in Vancouver, 1000 miles away from Driftwood Ranch. A friend volunteered to pick up the dogs, get them through customs and bring them to Beaverlodge. It was quite a journey for the dogs. They left Sydney in the summer and arrived during winter and a temperature of -40 degrees. Thankfully, the dogs adjusted well, although they spent the remainder of the winter in a heated building. Other Taronga Park dogs made their way to this country. "They are very intelligent, but they have many feral instincts," Sheryl says, "and owners must understand this."

Sharon McKenzie concedes that Singing Dogs are not the easiest breed to live with. "Some would say that these dogs have flaws that make them difficult to keep. I don't look at it that way. After all, the qualities that make them challenging to us are the very same attributes that have enabled them to survive in the wild. I don't look at them as flaws, but as little eccentricities. Singing Dogs are very curious and can become easily bored in the house. When this happens, unless they are supervised, they can be quite destructive.

"The Singing Dogs like high places and they are great jumpers. My female can jump from a standstill to the top of the refrigerator in a single leap. I finally had to put a cactus plant on the refrigerator to keep her from doing that. They will jump to any high place. I don't mind it when they sit on the back of the couch, but I don't like it when they jump on top of the television or bookcases. I put cactus plants or leave a stack of books on surfaces to discourage them. It looks cluttered, but it works."

"While Singing Dogs are not barkers," Sheryl Langan observes, "they certainly aren't silent. They have a very high pitched yodel. This is fine if you live out in the country, but may not be appreciated in the city." Sharon McKenzie says that the dogs are, in fact, capable of barking. "It's a deformed, almost choking sound and they usually employ it only when they are alarmed or under stress."

"They are very active dogs," Sheryl Langan says. Sharon McKenzie agrees. "They are not as active as the terrier breeds, but they are quite energetic. It's incredible to see how agile they are. You wouldn't believe how they run, turn and maneuver. Their hunting instincts are still very strong. Any quick darting movement will catch their eye. They are likely to go after something, grab it and ask questions later. This can make it difficult for those who own cats."

Training the New Guinea Singing Dog is, admittedly, a challenge. "They are very sensitive dogs, yet quite headstrong and stubborn," Sharon states. "Normally, you would think that this type of dog would take a very firm, strong hand. That's most definitely *not* the case with this breed. Singing Dogs are very very sensitive. If you try a hard-handed approach, they will yelp and scream and you will find a quivering mass at your feet. Some people, who don't understand their primitive natures, are apt to view them as wimps. They can certainly be trained, but it requires a great deal of patience. You must rely on voice control only. Even after training, you have to understand that Singing Dogs are not working dogs. They will never mind you like the more popular obedience breeds."

Some literature states that Singing Dogs are easy to housebreak, while other writings say that it's a difficult task. Sharon McKenzie helps us sort out these discrepancies. "They are not easy to housebreak as young puppies. I suspect that this is because they don't yet have full control over those muscles at an early age. I've found, though, that if you wait until they are six months old, they are fairly easy to housebreak."

"Singing Dogs are very gentle and friendly with people, though inclined to be a bit shy with strangers at first," writes New York owner Phillip Persky. "They are not at all aggressive with people," Sharon McKenzie says. "I've never heard of a case of a Singing Dog biting anyone. They are quite submissive to humans. Their response to strangers varies somewhat. One of our strains is more outgoing, while the other appears to be more shy."

While submissive to humans, the Singing Dog's response to other dogs is quite different. "They are most definitely *not* pack dogs," Sharon says. "They are dog aggressive. They tend to pair bond and will fight with an adult dog of the same sex. You absolutely cannot run these dogs together in groups. They will even challenge larger dogs. They aren't stupid, though. If it appears that a larger dog will fight, the Singing Dog will back down. If not, they will jump them." Phillip Persky adds that, despite "their small size, they are fierce fighters.

"They are also notorious escape artists," Mr. Persky reports, "and can climb and jump with cat-like agility, so enclosures must be secure." Sheryl Langan agrees. "They are extraordinary jumpers and capable of climbing trees. They must be housed very carefully." The Langans have tops on all their six-foot runs.

From the wilds of New Guinea to the streets of the Big Apple. Hager II and Jaya with Phil Persky. (Tara Darling photo)

"They are consummate escape artists," Sharon McKenzie confirms, "and any enclosure must have fencing on both the bottom and top. They are great diggers and can climb fences as easily as a squirrel. They can get through a space you wouldn't have thought a snake could get through," Sharon laughs.

Some reports say that the dogs have only one season a year, a trait found in many very primitive breeds. Others writers tell us that, in captivity, the dogs come in season twice a year. Once again, Sharon McKenzie helps us sort out the truth. "Bitches really have only a single season per year. Yet, if they are not bred, they will come back into season about six months later. If they *are* bred, they won't come into season for a year or, if they do, they will not allow the male to breed them.

"This is the only breed I know of in which bitches are dominate," Sharon observes. "Bitches dominate at all times. They always eat first and the male will stand by until they are finished. They always get first crack at where they would like to sleep. Bitches really call the shots."

The breed appears to be healthy and hardy with few problems. One of Dr. Brisbin's dogs lived to 15 years before he was euthanized. Best yet, Singing Dogs retain their playfulness throughout their lives. The breed also seems to have adapted well to commercial dog food, not the normal fare in zoos. When Sheryl Langan received her Singing Dogs, they came complete with the Taronga Park Zoo's feeding instructions. These called for beef on the bone, dog biscuits, two rabbits and two large rats each week. Sheryl's dogs have adjusted well to the meat and poultry based diet she prefers. Sharon McKenzie has had success with a dry high protein food with no soy additive.

The New Guinea Singing Dog has a fox-like appearance. His head is wedge-shaped, with a broad skull and prominent stop. Wrinkling is sometimes seen in puppies, but disappears as the dogs mature. The standard says that "the corner of the lips at the back of the mouth turn upwards to form a characteristic grin." The Singing Dog has small triangular-shaped erect ears which are very mobile. The dark eyes are also small and triangular in shape.

Singing Dogs are agile and athletic and should be in trim condition. They have moderate bone and are very well muscled. They are slightly longer than tall, with a level or slightly roached topline. They have moderate angulation and tuck-up. The bushy tail is carried low when the dog is relaxed, but is usually raised over the back when the dog is alert or excited. "The underside of the tail *must* be either white or very light in color and the tip should be white, as these aid in its function as a signaling device in the wild." Males should stand 14-16 1/2 inches at the withers while bitches measure 13-15 inches. Average weights range from 17-25 pounds. There is one difference in this breed that fanciers should be aware of. Due to the small genetic base, monorchidism occurs at a relatively high rate. Currently, the standard allows monorchid dogs to compete, but states that they are not preferred.

The Singing Dog has a dense double coat. The undercoat is soft and downy, while the outer guard hairs are shiny and stiff. "Overall texture is plush and reminiscent of a mink when the dog is in full coat," according to the standard. Red colors are preferred for the dog

should resemble a red fox. The bright red shades may range from an orange buff to rust red. Sable colored dogs are often seen and usually have black tips on the ends of the hairs. The standard does allow black and tan dogs, but these are not preferred and few have been seen. White markings are fairly common and accepted, as long as they don't exceed one-third of the total body area. Young puppies often have black masks, but these usually fade by the time they reach adulthood.

Little is known about the number of Singing Dogs still in New Guinea. Dr. I. Lehr Brisbin visited Papua, New Guinea in 1988. "During an informal survey," he told the American Association of Zoological Parks and Aquaria, he "was only able to learn of two remote areas where populations of this canid may still exist in an unhybridized state. These include the highest alpine grasslands of Mount Giluwe and Mount Wilhelm," in the central highlands. "Although no visit could actually be conducted to either of these two areas, a reconnaissance of the alpine highlands in the region of the Tari Gap, where pure populations had previously been thought to occur, indicated that hybridization with village dogs had already occurred within the population found in this latter area."

Recently, Dr. Brisbin has received some exciting news. An official with the Nature Conservation and Forest Protection District informed him that there was the possibility that wild Singing Dogs might still exist in Irian Jaya, an area under Indonesian control. "We certainly hope that this report can be confirmed in the near future, and that some day soon an expedition can be sent to that region to collect new animals for our captive breeding program."

With cutbacks in many zoo budgets, the future of this extremely endangered canine may well rest in the hands of dog lovers throughout the world. Most zoos prefer to focus on more exotic animals and some, like Taronga Park, have cut back on their Singing Dog holdings. But, with the aid of Dr. Brisbin and other fanciers, a new chapter is now being written in this breed's long history. The New Guinea Singing Dog certainly isn't the easiest breed to live with, but for those who are up to the challenge, the reward is rich. They are saving a true canine treasure.

Chapter 27

The Puli

"Once an American farmer went to town to fetch the vet to his cows which had bloat, taking his Puli with him. Next time, when the cows were once again bloated and its master was not at home, the Puli ran into town and kept barking at the vet's house until he understood what the matter was and quickly drove to the farm to save the cattle." This charming story from *Hungarian Dog Breeds*, by Pál Sárkány and Imre Ocsag, tells much about the Puli (Poo-lee), Hungary's native sheepdog. Alert, intelligent, able to evaluate a situation and choose an appropriate course of action, the Puli never shirks his duties. And so it has always been.

We may never know the true origin of the Puli. Many experts believe that he had his beginnings in Asia, probably Tibet. Although fanciers have long been intrigued by the similarities between the Tibetan Terrier and the Puli, it is, perhaps, the larger, longhaired guardian from Tibet, the Kyi-Apso, that had a part in the breed's heritage. Photos, taken recently in Tibet, show a Kyi-Apso with an unkempt coat falling naturally into a corded pattern. While the Kyi-Apso is a larger breed, we know that, in the past, Pulik (the plural of Puli) of a larger size were often seen in Hungary. Adolf Lendl, the great Hungarian dog authority, did extensive research to discover the origins of the breed. His findings point clearly to a Tibetan origin. In addition to the physical resemblance between the dogs, he also discovered certain cultural similarities between the pastoral practices of the Tibetan herdsman and his Hungarian counterpart.

Whatever his origin, the Puli has long been associated with Hungary. Some speculate that the breed accompanied the Magyars, who migrated and settled present day Hungary more than 1,000 years ago. Others believe that the breed predates the Magyars, initially arriving with the Huns and Avars. No matter which theory you subscribe to, it appears obvious that the native sheepherder has long been known in Hungary.

It was on the *puszta*, the great fertile plains of Hungary, that the true value of the Puli was recognized. Indeed, he formed an integral partnership with the *juhasz*, or shepherd, in the struggle for survival. The steppes were a forbidding place, where bitterly cold winds were the norm. The thick, heavy coat of the Puli provided protection from the elements. Life for the *juhasz* and his dogs was a spare and solitary existence. The shepherd, with the help of the Puli and Komondor, managed large herds of semi-wild, long-horned cattle and flocks of sheep. The entire enclave, dogs, people and stock, moved frequently to take advantage of fresh grazing lands. There were no fences, and Hungarian sheep do not show a natural tendency to flock together. Therefore, a herding dog was absolutely essential. This was the niche filled by the Puli.

A shepherd and his family (if he had one) were isolated from other humans. They lived in small hut-type homes, which could be hitched up and drawn by horses, when the time came to move to fresh grazing lands. Due to the isolation, shepherds developed a close kinship with their dogs. While the large Komondor roamed the range at night, to ward off predators, the smaller Puli was often taken into the crude hut at day's end. The shepherd shared his spartan diet with his dogs, tossing them stale brown bread and ladling out portions of mutton stew. At night, the Puli listened intently to the soft strains of the *czigana*, or gypsy music, that the herdsman played on his flute. Small wonder that the

The impressive Ch. Jatekos Bika of Pebbletree, winner of nine Bests in Show and two time National Specialty winner. Bika was the top Puli in 1981, 1982 and 1983. Owned by Dee Rummel.

juhasz and his dog developed a deep and close bond. The Puli had plenty of time to observe his master and, from this close association, there developed an almost uncanny ability to read the shepherd's wants. Some say that the Puli seemed to understand every word spoken by his master.

Puppies learned their duties at an early age. Their instincts were strong, almost intuitive, and the shepherd did little actual training. Pups were introduced to the flock from their earliest days. They observed adult dogs at work and quickly learned the fundamentals of herding. Some say the dogs were so adept at the task, that the shepherd had only to name a particular animal, and the Puli would cut it out from the rest of the herd. With no fences to restrain the flock, it was imperative that adventuresome, errant animals be brought quickly under control. For this, the Puli employed a unique herding style. Jumping on the back of the runaway, the Puli dug in his claws and "rode" the sheep until it stopped running. Then, quickly, he would alight and herd the sheep back into position. Courage, agility, speed and determination were essentials for the task.

At the end of the grazing season, the flock was driven to market. This task would have been impossible without the Puli acting as a drover. At these market round-ups, animals were butchered, sheep sheared and the quality of the flock assessed. The dogs, unkempt and matted, were sheared at the same time. At these periodic gatherings, the shepherds found time to talk about their lives and sing the praises of their dogs. Some records indicate that they even held sheepdog-type trials. The dogs would herd a flock of sheep in and out of water so that the shepherds could compare their performances. A top working dog was a source of great pride. Some say that a shepherd would give as much as an entire year's wages for a good worker. Often, the dog was not available at any price. However, he could be used for breeding or it might be possible to purchase a puppy. "A shepherd who took pride in his job would boast of his clever Puli, who was more than just a dog in his eyes," report Pál Sárkány and Imre Ocsag, in *Hungarian Dog Breeds*. "But again a Puli was immediately downgraded into being a dog, and was easily gotten rid of, even killed, as soon as he proved unsatisfactory in everyday working tasks."

And so the Puli developed as Hungary's great herding dog. To maintain the abilities of their working partners, shepherds ruthlessly culled their stock. At round-ups, they sought to acquire new bloodlines, when needed, to infuse into their strains. They took great care not to allow the crossing of Pulik with Komondorok, which might lessen the effectiveness of each breed. The Magyar shepherds cared little for appearance. Obviously, the herding dogs needed a dense coat capable of withstanding the elements. There was no time to coddle any poorly coated specimens. The sole criteria for the dogs' usefulness was their working ability. Lazy, slow, weak-willed and less intelligent dogs were simply of no use to shepherds. Through the centuries, the Puli developed as the lively, always eager for action, supremely bright and easily trainable dog that was needed to insure survival of the flock and herd.

Though well known on the *puszta,* it would be centuries before the breed came to the attention of Hungarian dog lovers. The breed was first mentioned, by name, in 1751. In the 1800s, several writers mentioned the sheepdogs, but no clear distinction was made between the Puli and the Pumi. The breed was first seen at a Budapest show in 1855. In 1899, Pulik again were exhibited at a Szeged show, though there was still not a great deal of interest in the breed. This was to change in 1914, however. Two dog lovers were named to positions at the Budapest Zoo. Dr. Emil Raitsits, the Zoo's resident veterinarian, and Adolf Lendl, the Director, decided to establish an exhibit of Hungarian pastoral dogs. This led to the formation of a breeding kennel. From 1914-1930, this remained the sole concerted breeding operation, outside the *puszta,* for Pulik. Raitsits and Lendl made many excursions into the countryside, to purchase stock from shepherds and peasants.

Due to the pioneering work of Raitsits and Lendl, many Hungarians came to know and appreciate the native sheepherder. Two World Wars, however, brought devastating hardships and the dogs, like their owners, suffered. Thankfully, the breed has rebounded and remains quite popular in his homeland.

We do not know precisely when the first Pulik came to this country. California resident Nicholas Roosevelt, U.S. Minister to Hungary, brought a pair of dogs with him, when he returned from Budapest. While this duo was later sold, he did acquire other pups and helped spread word of the breed on the West Coast. Louis Kiss, of New York, imported several dogs from Hungary. His Törökvész Sarika had the honor of being the first Puli registered with the American Kennel Club, in 1936. A year later, Mr. Kiss registered the first litter.

In 1935, an experiment by the United States Department of Agriculture was to provide a new source of breeding stock. Intent on introducing a herding farm dog to assist Americans, the U.S.D.A. imported four Pulik from Hungary. One additional dog, born in this country, was loaned to the project. World War II,

however, put an end to the experiment and the program was disbanded and the dogs sold. Thankfully, they went to people who were seriously interested in the breed and these dogs can be found behind many of today's winners.

In 1951, several fanciers met at the Westminster Kennel Club show and banded together to form the Puli Club of America. The national club has done much to promote interest in the breed and provide information to new owners. Though still considered rare, Pulik have captured the attention of many judges, and the list of Group and Best in Show winners is impressive. Hungary's native sheepdog has found a host of loyal admirers in this country.

The many qualities of the herding dog of the *puszta* can still be seen in today's shaggy coated Puli. Under his wealth of hair, he is a sound, balanced dog, capable of tough, rigorous work. The Puli is medium in size, with moderate bone. The standard calls for males to ideally measure 17 inches at the shoulder, while bitches should be 16 inches. However, they are not to be penalized if they deviate an inch above or below the ideal. Weight usually averages between 25-35 pounds. The Puli has a square compact body with a level topline. His head is hardly discernable beneath the fall of hair. The skull is slightly domed and has a moderate stop. Look closely, and you'll see dark brown, almond-shaped eyes peering from beneath the thick hair. Undoubtedly, the hair protected the eyes from dust and grass seeds on the range. It's also difficult to see the Puli's V-shaped ears, so closely do they blend in with the coat. The tail is curled jauntily over the back or carried on either side of the thighs. The Puli's tail is often a barometer of his feelings. When alert and excited, the tail is usually curled over the back. When he is in new surroundings or temporarily unsure of himself, he often drops his tail. When he is tired, bored or feeling poorly, the tail is also apt to be down. When he's happy, though, the tail will come up in merry fashion. When herding, the Puli occasionally extends his tail outward, aiding him in maintaining balance.

I must take a moment to talk about the joys of watching a sound moving Puli in action. The Puli's gait is nimble, athletic, quick, bouncy, animated, gay and absolutely unforgettable. Whether you are a breed fancier or not, I hope you will take some time, at your next dog show, to watch Pulik judging. If you're fortunate, there will be several good movers and a ring large enough to accommodate them. Settle back and enjoy. You're in for one of the great delights in all of dogdom.

The one striking Puli feature that intrigues most people is his coat. "There is no mistaking him for any other breed if his profuse coat is allowed to cord naturally, often reaching the ground," says the Puli Club of America. "He is best described as 'mop-like' or a 'shag rug' whether corded or brushed." The Puli has a dense double coat, which entirely covers the body, from nose to tail. The undercoat is soft and wooly, while the outercoat is longer, more profuse and sometimes wavy. The coat provides ideal protection from the elements and, when corded, provides a hirsute suit of armor. This, undoubtedly, provided valuable protection in encounters with predators.

In most countries, the Puli is required to have a corded coat, in order to compete in the show ring. Americans allow for either a corded or brushed coat. No matter which type of presentation you prefer, your Puli should always be bathed and groomed. "Without care and grooming, the coat will soon become badly matted and no Puli can be a healthy dog if his coat is neglected," the Puli Club of America advises. "Both types of coat must be kept clean and well bathed....The Puli should be bathed if he becomes dirty, which a weekly inspection of the coat and skin will reveal. A corded coat takes much longer to get thoroughly wet than a brushed coat, and if a mature coat, it will require a longer time to dry. Cords do not come undone when the Puli is bathed, but will tighten up with age and washing."

The brushed coat emphasizes the typical "shaggy dog" look. Most breeders begin to familiarize their puppies with grooming from an early age. The coat should be brushed thoroughly, making sure to get all the way down to the skin. Regular brushing will prevent the hair from forming into a thick matted wad. Many breeders use a skin conditioner to add luster and prevent split ends. Special attention should be paid to the elbows, the muzzle, behind the ears, under the hind legs and the base of the tail. It's here that mats are likely to go unnoticed. Always be sure there are no mats in the brushed coat before bathing. Show dogs with brushed coats are usually groomed on a daily basis. A good brushing, once or twice a week, will keep the pet in presentable condition.

When mature, a Puli with a corded coat, looks for all the world like a walking mop. The cords have a distinctly felt-like texture. Puppy coats show a tendency to tuft or bunch. The cording results from a natural tendency of the under and outer coats to entangle together. When this begins to occur, the coat must be separated into emerging cords, or it will mat. As the dog matures, the cords will increase in length, reaching their full glory when the Puli is two to three years old. Mature Pulik may have coats which reach the ground. The appearance of the final corded coat depends primarily on the texture of the hair. Some Pulik have what's described as a "ribbon" type coat, which consists of wide plaits, while others have a "string" coat which resembles heavy twine.

Ch. Pebbletree's Jatekos Primas, HIC at his first Herding Instinct test. This lovely dog is owned by Dee Rummel, Pebbletree Kennel, Whitewater, Wisconsin.

The Puli Club of America has produced a brochure providing detailed grooming procedures and breeders are happy to assist new owners in learning about proper grooming. To the great embarrassment of dedicated Puli owners, some novices have gained the mistaken impression that the breed does not require bathing or grooming. Nothing could be further from the truth. Whether you prefer the shaggy or mop-like look, be prepared to devote the time needed to maintaining your Puli in proper condition.

"Puli coloring is distinctive and cannot be compared with the color of any other breed," the Puli Club of America says. "Individual Puli colors result from different proportions of hair mixtures which usually are in combinations of black to reddish black, gray or white. Shading may be varied but the color must appear solid or uniform." Black is the most popular of the Puli colors. "Ordinarily it is called black, but it a black so unlike that of any other breed as to warrant explanation," *The Complete Dog Book* emphasizes. "It is dull, in some cases bronze-tinged, in others just barely grayed like a weather-worn old coat faded by the sun. An outdoor life on the hillside, in all weathers, but particularly under a constant and glaring sun, robbed the black of its intensity and its sheen. This was the black prized as typical of the breed in its homeland."

The Puli also comes in several shades of gray. The ultimate shade depends on the admixture of gray-black or gray-silver hairs. Gray Pulis may go through many color stages. A dark gray coat may lighten to a silver shade and then revert back to its darker hue. "One must remember that both black and gray puppies are born jet black, with a sleek, satin like coat," says esteemd breeder Sylvia Owen, in *The Complete Puli*. "However, the soft downy hair on their tiny pads may be a light gray; these are the pups that will eventually become solid gray. At about two to three months old their face and legs turn gray, several shades of gray often give an impression of a parti-colored youngster between six and twelve months. The coat is not likely to grow into one of solid uniform gray until maturity, between 18 months and two or perhaps three years of age. Some remain streaked or patchy longer than others before attaining the desired uniformity of color. This can be perplexing and it pertains to grays only." Such frustrations aside, the varying gray shades are quite attractive.

Most rare of the Puli colors is white. A stunning, pure white Puli is a sight to behold. These dogs should be absolutely white in color, without shading. Fawn or light tan markings on the ears or along the back are sometimes seen, but are undesirable. Golden and buff colored Pulik appear occasionally, but are disqualified in the show ring.

A corded Puli in motion. This is Dee Rummel's top winning bitch Ch. Jatekos Bika of Pebbletree.

There's never a dull moment when you share your home with a Puli. As with all breeds, temperaments vary somewhat. Some Pulik are outgoing hams, who delight in showing off for applause. Others are quieter and more reserved. All Pulik, however, seem to have a real sense of humor, a clownish attitude that makes them a joy to have around.

To understand the Puli, one must acknowledge the breed's extreme intelligence. Perceptive and quick to read your cues, your Puli has confidence in his own judgement. The Hungarian shepherds selected their dogs for intelligence and the ingenuity and resourcefulness required in herding. Their dogs were uncommonly devoted to the flock. Though your Puli may be a house dog, rather than a worker, he will transfer his age-old faithfulness to his human family, where his good natured devotion endears him to owners.

The Puli does, however, have a mind of his own. Even young Pulik can be surprisingly willful. Perhaps, with his keen intelligence, he just thinks he knows better than you. Many breeders suggest obedience training as an excellent way to channel the breed's boundless energy. Obedience training builds a rapport between dog and owner, and provides an outlet for the Puli's talents. A bored Puli is apt to get into trouble, so be sure to provide your puppy with toys. You will find that he

Ch. Pebbletree's Hangos-Huba CDX became a champion with back to back Group Firsts. Owned by Wilma Peterson, Jan Arnold and Dee Rummel.

can amuse himself for hours playing with them. While he can be a quiet housedog, it's in his nature to be active and involved in all that's going on around him. He's happiest when he's a full member of the family.

"When a Puli puppy becomes adjusted to a happy home life, he readily adjusts to obedience training," says Sylvia Owen, in *The Complete Puli,* "but the manner in which he is treated at home affects his whole being, and his personality develops fully through love, trust and understanding. Not everyone is suited to own a Puli, for although willing to please, he has a mind of his own and can be willful and stubborn at times just to find out if he can get the better of you. For best results be patient, firm, but gentle, and be lavish with praise when your Puli performs successfully."

"As the Puli is an extremely intelligent dog, he is not submissive," Ellanor Anderson says in *How to Raise and Train a Puli.* "As a puppy, he will try to outwit his new owners and establish his own rules. However, being adaptable and loyal, he gradually will establish his relationship with the family and agree to follow the house rules. He will decide in his own mind which member is the head of the family and that person's wishes will be law to him....He is happy and at his best only when he is accepted as a respected working member of the family."

Like all the herding breeds, the Puli requires socialization. He is naturally wary of strangers, preferring the attentions of his own family. While he should never be shy or cringing, don't expect your Puli to greet strangers like long-lost friends. He'll take his time in warming up to newcomers, making up his own mind when it's time to approach them. He will take his cues from you and, once you both accept someone, he's likely to recognize them as family friends. This natural wariness serves the Puli well, in his role as watchdog and guardian of the home. He will let you know when any stranger approaches.

The Puli has proven himself a great dog for both city and country homes. Being very devoted, your Puli isn't likely to wander. By nature, he is quite adaptable and not aggressive, making him very accepting of other family pets. Pulik who have been raised with children are uncommonly devoted to them. The dog and child often become great pals.

"The Puli uses his head more than any other breed I know," says Sylvia Owen. Those who wish to share their homes with an intelligent, versatile, perceptive and devoted companion, with a dash of the clown, would do well to further investigate the Puli. Chances are you'll discover why Hungary's legendary herding dog, is treasured by so many American owners. "This is a dog of great personality and desirable characteristics," Sylvia Owen observes. "To those who know, the breed is unique!"

Chapter 28

The Pyrenean Shepherd

"A good, handsome dog, with elegant form, perfect instincts and mental qualities capable of absolute perfection with skillful training—this constitutes, without a doubt, one of the most perfect creations of nature," wrote Noël Wanlin. " All of these magnetic qualities come together in our French shepherd breeds..."

Owners of the Pyrenean Shepherd would wholeheartedly agree. Americans are learning about the little high mountain herder which breed authority Guy Mansencal calls "the last French breed to discover." President of the Reunion des Amateurs des Chiens Pyrenees (R.A.C.P.), parent club for both Pyrenean Shepherds and Great Pyrenees, Mansencal says, "...The Pyrenean Shepherd has remained THE farm dog, the 'all-purpose maid' who tends horses, cattle, pigs and poultry, and is an incomparable guardian announcing intruders and visitors."

Little is conclusively known about the age and origin of the breed. That's because no depictions of the Pyrenean Shepherd appeared until the 1800's. In his 1927 book, *Les Chien Pyrenees,* celebrated French dog authority Bernard Senac-Legrange speculates that the breed dates back to the Bronze Age (2,000 B.C.-1,000 B.C.). That small herding dogs have been known in the Pyrenees for centuries, there can be no doubt. Undoubtedly, the Pyrenean Shepherd shares a close kinship with the Catalonian Sheepdog (also known as the Gos d'Atura), found on the Spanish side of the Pyrenees. He may well also be related to other European sheep herding breeds.

Paul Megnin, in his 1904 work, *Nos Chiens,* describes the Pyrenean Shepherd as extremely courageous and adds, "It is a splendid mountaineer, used to drive flocks of sheep which, each season, pass the summer in the mountains and descend into the plains in the winter."

Indeed, it was this seasonal migration that created the need for a sheepherding dog. During winter, French sheep are kept at lowland farms. When spring arrives, the entire flock is moved to fresh highland pastures where they will remain until fall. It's the little Pyrenean Shepherd who is responsible for keeping the flock moving. In this country, most sheep are raised for meat and wool. In France, the focus is on milk (for the famed cheeses) and wool production. Since sheep must be milked twice a day, it is necessary to have a herding dog to assist with the everyday roundups.

The large Great Pyrenees and the small Pyrenean Shepherd are working counterparts in the French peasant farmer's struggle for existence. The Great Pyr, who bonds closely with the flock, guards them from predators and thieves, particularly at night. The little Pyr Shepherd, by contrast, works very closely with the human shepherd, and their close bond was essential. Indeed, his responsiveness is legendary, leading French peasants to say that "he never questions why."

The Great Pyrenees achieved national recognition in 1675, when the young Dauphin (later to become Louis XIV), befriended one of the dogs while on vacation. He took the dog with him, when he returned to the Louvre, and soon the Great Pyr became the favored dog of French nobility. However, the tousle haired herding dogs remained obscure outside their native lands. It was not until the late 1800's that French dog fanciers took an interest in the breed. This was primarily through the efforts of Bernard Senac-Lagrange. In the 1890's, he formed a club to sponsor the Pyrenean breeds. His wife, using the Luckville prefix, bred the little herders for many years. This early club was disbanded with the advent of World War I.

Like the other French herding breeds, the Pyrenean Shepherd was pressed into duty in the war effort. Despite his small size, the breed's bravery, intelligence and ease of training more than made up for his petite stature. He saw service mainly as a messenger and liaison dog. Front line soldiers were often trapped and cut off from their command posts, with no way to send word for urgently needed help. But, a dog, trained to avoid strangers and able to dart through the hail of gunfire and shells, could often get a desperate call for help to the proper authorities. Dogs, destined for such duty, had to be agile, quick, stable, very courageous and able to improvise resourcefully on the spot. The Pyrenean Shepherd displayed these qualities in abundance. Many were lost in the war in a valiant effort to assist their masters.

Following World War I, fanciers regrouped. In 1921, they met to discuss the breed and formulate a standard. 1923 saw the creation of the Reunion des Amateurs des Chiens Pyrenees and three years later the breed was officially recognized by the French Kennel Club.

World War II made breeding difficult. In most of the country, food rationing was in effect. Once again, numbers of Pyrenean Shepherds were assigned military duties. When Hitler swept across France, the Pyr Shepherd became a valuable adjutant to the Resistance fighters. Thankfully, the hostilities did not extend to the Pyrenees Mountains themselves and the stronghold of the breed remained untouched.

But, while world wars did not take their toll on the breed, progress certainly has. Fewer farmers live in the old style in the high Pyrenees. These days, most shepherds move their flocks by truck which is certainly more efficient, but less picturesque, than the old ways. The Pyrenees Mountains have become a popular resort area and each year thousands of pilgrims make the journey to the renowned religious site at Lourdes. Still, there remains a cadre of shepherds who cling tenaciously to the old ways, breeding the Pyrenean Shepherd for use on their farms. These dogs, French authorities tell us, are of often of high quality, exhibiting excellent type and soundness. While they do not have official papers and pedigrees, the French do take advantage of this valuable source of new blood. Dogs, fresh from the mountains, are examined by a team of authorities to insure that they are truly purebred. Provisional registration follows and, after a designated number of generations, the descendants of these mountain dogs may be fully registered. Employing this method, allows French breeders to invigorate their stock, by returning

to the breed's original homeland. Thus, working instincts and the accompanying temperament remain strong in the breed.

Today, in France, the breed is in good hands. The dogs compete quite successfully in shows, where they often top the herding group and have been known to carry away Best in Show awards. The highlight of the year, for French fanciers, is the large show put on by the Reunion des Amateurs des Chiens Pyrenees, the equivalent of our national specialty. Here there are classes for both Great Pyrenees and Pyrenean Shepherds. At the conclusion of the celebration, both breed winners compete for Best in Show honors. Pyr Shepherds also compete frequently in specially designed French herding dog trials. These are real showcases for the breed's working talents and, in the late 1970's, a Pyrenean Shepherd was France's top herding dog for several years running. In fact, prior to 1983, in order to complete a championship, a Pyrenean Shepherd was required to pass a herding test. The standards are now more flexible, however. A dog who has gained the required wins for a show championship may compete in tracking, agility, ring sport, search and rescue, herding or any of a number of types of working trials. While the breed has been used for manwork, French breeders point out that he does not respond well to the normal Schutzhund type training. This breed requires a softer touch, they say.

We don't know precisely when the first Pyrenean Shepherd came to the United States. A few scattered dogs may have emigrated to this country with their French owners. The first serious attempt to establish the breed came in the 1970's, when Washington resident Linda Weisser imported several dogs. She formed a club for the breed, but it did not last and she soon stopped breeding.

In 1983, Patricia Princehouse, of Chardon, Ohio, imported Urrugne de l'Estaube, who was to become a champion and two time National Specialty winner. Patricia and her parents, Joseph and Frances, are Great Pyrenees breeders. Patricia joined the Reunion des Amateurs des Chiens Pyrenees and soon began receiving their club bulletin. She admits that she was captivated by the faces that she saw in each issue. While on a trip to France she obtained Urrugne, better known as Blythe. "I bought a puppy for all the wrong reasons," Patricia Princehouse admits in *The Sheep Pen*, official newsletter of the Pyrenean Shepherd Club of America, "because it was so cute, because it was unusual....although I had some concept of breed type, I knew next to nothing about the breed's temperament or herding dogs in general."

Blythe soon captivated the entire Princehouse family. "Blythe grew and impressed everyone with her beauty, sparkling personality, obedience and skill with the sheep," Patricia writes. "It very quickly became

A lovely drawing of a Pyrenean Shepherd, by artist Amy Fernandez.

clear that this was not a breed for everyone and placing puppies in the ring homes would be difficult. So breeding was not on the agenda." All that was to change, however. Miss Princehouse heard that a Canadian, with a dubious reputation, had acquired some Pyr Shepherds and she was alarmed. She set out to educate the public about the breed. Picking up the remaining fragments of the earlier club, she and others formed the Pyrenean Shepherd Club of America in 1987. Since then, several other Pyrenean Shepherds have joined the Princehouse home.

The smallest of the native French herding breeds, the Pyrenean Shepherd comes in two varieties: the rough faced and the smooth faced. The rough coated dogs, who sport bewhiskered chins and bushy eyebrows, are the most common. According to Patricia Princehouse, the rough faced dogs are seen in two types. The *poil de chevre,* or "goat-haired," dog carries a minimum of fringes, while the *poil de montagne*, or "long-haired," dog has more abundant furnishings on the legs, and his hair, if left unbrushed, will cord over the rear. Certain type differences also exist within the two varieties.

Rough-faced Pyrenean Shepherd males typically measure 15 1/2 to 19 inches tall, while females are 15 to 18 inches. Writing in the February 1989 issue of *Dog World*, Miss Princehouse describes the rough-faced

dog as "longer than he is tall, and well rounded in the rear, with good tuck-up. His rear is higher than his withers; however, he should never display a roached back. His hocks are well let down, and his feet are oval in shape."

Rough faced dogs come in a wide range of colors. The most common is what's described as "fawn," although this shade may vary from a pale blonde to a deep golden copper. Some fawns sport a black mask and they may also have charcoal highlights (black hairs distributed through the coat). Next in popularity are the greys, which can run from a slate to charcoal in the darker hues and from silver to pearl gray in the lighter shades. The breed is also occasionally found in black, brindle, blue or merle. While solid shades are preferred, some black and white dogs are seen. Whites and black and tans are disqualified.

The rarer smooth-faced dogs are larger than their rough-faced counterparts. Males measure 16 to 21 inches, while bitches stand 15 1/2 to 20 1/2 inches. Miss Princehouse says that the smooth-face is "as smooth as a Collie or Australian Shepherd....His back is level and his body square. He is higher on hock and possesses more cat-like feet." While the same colors are permissible in smooth-faced dogs, they are generally found in blue merle.

The Pyrenean Shepherd employs an effortless,

efficient gait. Fanciers say that you really have to see one of these dogs in action to appreciate it. Patricia Princehouse writes, in *Dog World,* that the "feet barely leave the ground when trotting, but rather appear to 'shave the meadow' as the dog goes along."

Guy Mansencal cites the axiom "A minimum of height and weight, a maximum of nervous influx," to describe the Pyrenean Shepherd. "This indicates that the dog must always have a little yard or patio at its disposal," he writes. "All dogs can adapt to apartment life. But, if the Pyrenean Shepherd, a veritable live wire, cannot find an outlet for his energy he will rapidly become a nuisance. In his original lifestyle, this dog would go ten, twenty, even twenty-five miles a day. If you cannot give him at least one hour a day of exercise, *do not choose this dog for a companion.*

"Do not destroy that which nature, the elements and the work of dedicated breeders have created," Mr. Mansencal warns. "But, if you have a yard, and a little free time, you will have a fabulous companion—sporting, intelligent, beautiful in motion, with that unparalleled Pyrenean Shepherd allure. You will be proud of your dog."

"They are very lively dogs, very quick and very mischievous," says Pyr Shepherd fancier Joe Gentzel, of Jefferson, Georgia. Mr. Gentzel has bred Great Pyrenees since 1972. Initially, it was because of the close working association between the Great Pyr and the Pyr Shepherd that he became interested in the herding dogs. He saw his first Pyrenean Shepherds six years ago when he journeyed to France for the Reunion des Amateurs des Chiens Pyrenees annual show. Soon, the first of several dogs were on their way to his Georgia home. "In temperament, the Great Pyrenees and the Pyrenean Shepherd are exact opposites," he says. "Some have called them hyperactive, but I don't believe that's the case. They only appear so when contrasted with the very laid back Great Pyrenees, not when compared with other herding breeds. They are very entertaining. They are real comedians and will keep you on your toes. They are very strong willed and have minds of their own. It takes a firm, but kind, hand and you must establish yourself as the boss from an early age or they'll take advantage of you. They are very clean dogs and easy to keep," Joe observes. "They need lots of exercise, but don't require as much space as a Great Pyrenees.

"The speed and agility of the breed is phenomenal," Joe reports. "It's amazing to see just how quick and athletic they are. Our dogs often play with our Great Pyrenees puppies. It's really comical to watch. They dart in, leap over the puppies and pounce on them. The Great Pyr's can't touch them unless they decide that it would be fun to be caught.

"They are incredibly and absolutely devoted to the family," Joe explains. "They don't give their love easily so it's kind of an honor to be accepted and loved by a Pyrenean Shepherd. Their complete and total devotion has really won me over. Much as I love my Great Pyrenees, I have to say that I will always have a Pyrenean Shepherd."

Indeed, it is the breed's close bond with their master that so impresses most owners. However, it is also a cause for concern. "Unlike some of the more outgoing breeds, the Pyrenean Shepherd does not transfer his affections easily," says Patricia Princehouse. Joe Gentzel agrees. "They form incredibly strong bonds. The bonds begin to form from an early age, often as soon as three or four months. For this reason, one should think very seriously before buying one of these dogs. This is emphatically not a breed to be discarded once you're tired of them. Since these dogs have a lifespan of between fifteen and twenty years, you should carefully consider before buying this breed. These dogs may experience problems when changing homes. It's one of the things that worries me about the breed in this country. I fear that adult dogs may have a difficult time making a transition to a new home."

If you should decide on this breed, be prepared to devote plenty of time to your dog. The breed craves human companionship and reaches his full potential only when he has lots of attention. For those he trusts, he will give his all and devoted owners find the breed very willing to please.

While friendly, charming and playful with his family, the Pyrenean Shepherd is distrustful and suspicious with strangers. "By nature they are quite standoffish with strangers," Joe Gentzel says. "They're very aloof and reserved. Even with those they know, but who are not an actual part of the immediate family, their reaction can be strange. We have two grown sons who no longer live at home. They visit often and the dogs know them well. Still, they totally ignore them when they visit. They're not part of the immediate family and the dogs just won't have anything to do with them."

While socialization is a must for all herding breeds, it is critical with the little Pyrenean Shepherd. "Although the Pyrenean Shepherd is not an outgoing breed, consistent early socialization to strange people and new situations can turn this mountain recluse into a fairly sociable and certainly well behaved member of society," Patricia Princehouse writes. "Because of their wariness with strangers, they need intensive socialization," Joe Gentzel advises. "I'd suggest that people get a dog as young as possible and work on socialization like you never have before. Their natural aversion to strangers can present a problem in American show rings. With socialization, they will learn to tolerate the touch of a judge, but they don't really like it. Still, we have been able to show our dogs. Even with proper socialization, you must be realistic in your expectations.

This breed will be extremely devoted and friendly to you, but they won't take up with your friends, your neighbors or the neighborhood kids."

Pyrenean Shepherds bond closely with the children in the family, too. Indeed, they can become devoted playmates. "They are wonderful with kids," Joe Gentzel says. "We have a two-year-old. When he was at the crawling stage, our Great Pyrenees, especially the males, were somewhat skeptical about this little thing. What did he want from them, they seemed to wonder. Not the Pyrenean Shepherds. They weren't the least bit bothered and my son and the dogs are great friends."

The breed can get along well with other dogs, though you must let them know that you love and care for them or they're apt to become jealous. "They can get along quite well with other dogs," Joe Gentzel observes. "But, if you allow it, they will rule the roost. With other breeds, they're apt to be top dog, but they don't do it aggressively. They just charmingly and benevolently take over. Our two Pyrenean Shepherd females have always gotten along well. However, they are both grown now and we've seen some evidence of jealousy. We're hoping to discourage it, but there's the possibility that we may have to separate them."

The breed also seems to willingly accept other animals. "They get along well with our cats," Joe says. "Our cats aren't at all wary of dogs, of course. They will often go out into the kennel and curl up with the puppies. At first, our Pyrenean Shepherds were a little wary of them. But, it didn't take them long to learn that the cats belonged here. They have accepted them fully and we've had little trouble."

With his fiercely devoted nature, the little Pyr Shepherd makes a suitable watchdog, despite his small size. "They are incredibly terrific watchdogs," Joe Gentzel enthuses. "They are absolutely fearless and, with every breath in their bodies, will defend their homes. After knowing both the Great Pyrenees and the Pyrenean Shepherd, I can well imagine how wonderfully these two breeds must have complimented each other in a working situation. I can assure you that if anything approached the flock, the little Pyrenean Shepherd would have been first on the scene and would not back off from any intruder. Certainly, the Great Pyrenees is a magnificent guardian and would be there in the event of a real threat. But, while the Great Pyr is rousing himself from sleep under a tree to run toward the intruder, the little Pyrenean Shepherd would already be there. And he'd not only be sounding the alarm, but beginning the fight!" Small wonder that all the French authorities characterize the breed as extremely courageous.

In France, the Pyrenean Shepherd is still used actively as a herding dog and he would seem ideal for American farms, too. The French are high in their praise for the breed, noting that he combines strength, agility and speed with great endurance. "Small and lightweight but rugged, the working Pyrenean Shepherd is traditionally required to herd sheep from dawn til dusk in all kinds of weather in the steep mountain ranges of the Pyrenees," Patricia Princehouse writes in *Dog World*. "Often this work demands that the Pyrenean Shepherd run for hours on end, circling the flock, rounding up wanderers, moving from one valley to another in search of better pasture. The Pyrenean Shepherd is equal to the task. *He thirsts for action.*" Indeed, this lively always eager dog is typical of what American shepherd's term a "hot blooded" temperament. Traditionally, they feel that dogs with this attribute make the best workers.

"I know very little about herding," Joe Gentzel admits, "but I've seen evidence of the ability in my own dogs. They try to herd everything, including themselves," he laughs. "We've certainly given them no training in this regard, so it must be a very strong part of their natural instinct." Indeed, time does not seem to have diminished this innate desire for work.

The Pyrenean Shepherd is still quite rare in this country, but he seems to be off to a good start. The Pyrenean Shepherd Club of America has done much to educate people about the breed. They've adopted a strict code of ethics and taken great care in the placement of puppies. Many challenges still lie ahead of them, but if they mirror the devotion that their dogs display, the breed will have a rich future in the United States.

Ch. Barraglen's Brankie Birk in a collage of poses. This lovely Skye Terrier is owned by Ann and Ross Bower, of Grant's Pass, Oregon. (Delcoure photo)

Chapter 29

The Skye Terrier

One of the most touching stories in the annals of dog literature involves a little drop-eared Skye Terrier. I'm sure that you all know the extraordinary story of Greyfriar's Bobby, but I'll summarize it here for no chapter on the breed would be truly complete without its inclusion. It seems that John Gray, a tenant farmer and shepherd, lived on a small farm, about 20 miles from Edinburgh. When he died, in 1858, he had little to show for his years of hard work and so, penniless and friendless, he was interred in a simple grave at Greyfriar's Churchyard. But, Gray was not entirely friendless, for he had shared his life with a Skye Terrier called Bobby. No sooner had Gray's body been laid to rest, than Bobby took up his vigil. He lay astride the grave, protecting his master's body even in death. Folks in Edinburgh were touched by the little dog and no doubt felt sorry for him. Several times Bobby was physically removed and offered fine homes. But, always, the little tyke escaped and could be found at the grave at Greyfriars. For the next 14 years, from 1858 to 1872, he maintained his constant vigil. The townsfolk saw to it that Bobby was fed and word of his devotion spread, touching the hearts of many. The Lord Provost awarded him a permanent license and collar. Upon his death, Baroness Burdett-Coutts erected a monument to the dog in Edinburgh. Even today, visitors journey to this memorial, a drinking fountain with a central column where the stone Bobby sits. Word of Bobby's devotion spread, in 1912, when Eleanor Atkinson wrote her now classic story of him. In 1961, Hollywood immortalized Bobby in a charming, tearjerker.

The Skye Terrier, or "The Heavenly Breed," as early fanciers dubbed it, comes from the Isle of Skye, northwest of Scotland. It is a windswept, rock strewn island with crannies, cairns, dens and burrows where vermin can hide. The people of Skye developed a breed which was long and low and could squirm and wriggle into the tight passages in pursuit of game. A long, thick coat provided protection from the elements and a face fringe helped to screen the eyes. Those original Skyes were probably smaller, scruffier and less profusely coated than today's elegant breed.

We do not know precisely when the first Skye Terrier was brought from his misty homeland to the English mainland. It appears, however, that he he was one of the first terriers to make his debut in England. "A beggarly beast brought out of the barbarous borders from the uttermost countryes northward," Dr. Caius wrote in *English Dogges*, first published in 1567. He added that these dogs "by reason of the length of heare, makes showe neither of face nor of body."

As early as the 16th century, the Skye appears to have been a fashionable pet, widely known among the nobility. The famous Flemish artist, Peter Breughel, included a Skye Terrier in his depiction of Adam and Eve in the Garden of Eden, painted in the 1500's. By the 1800's, the Skye was the most widely known of all terriers. A very good depiction of the breed is contained in the 1839 work *Natural History of Dogs*.

The breed received a tremendous boost when Queen Victoria acquired her first Skye in 1842. For the remainder of her life, she was never without at least one Skye Terrier. One of her early dogs, Islay, was of the popular drop-eared type. The Queen was presented with a Skye, in 1874, by one Mr. Pratt, who was quite a famous breeder. Every day, Pratt took six of his terriers for a walk in London's Hyde Park. He and his pack of dogs became widely known. A visitor to the city from Norway, in 1885, was so impressed with the sight of these remarkable dogs that, when he returned home, he made an excellent sketch of the team. He wanted to share it with the owner of the dogs that had so captivated him. But, where to send it? Finally, he posted it, addressed simply to "The Man with the Dogs," London. So well known was Mr. Pratt and his canine ensemble that the letter was delivered posthaste.

Another of Queen Victoria's dogs was a bitch named "Rona II." She was obtained from the esteemed breeder Rev. Dr. Rosslyn Bruce. When he presented a litter of puppies to the Queen, Bruce reports, she examined them with all the skill of a show judge, carefully selecting the one that would be hers. He was impressed with her knowledge of the breed. Rona II and her royal owner would be immortalized in a well known painting by William Nicholson.

Naturally, with such royal patronage, the Skye Terrier became a popular breed. In 1896, the Princess of Wales (later Queen Alexandria) was presented with a Skye puppy. Soon, the breed was the most popular of British terriers. Landseer's paintings of the breed also did much to spur interest. When the first stud book was established by England's Kennel Club, the Skye was duly registered. By the 1900's,

This is just one of the beautiful champion Skyes from Ann and Ross Bower's Barraglen Kennels. (Barrett photo)

the Skye was an extremely popular show dog. At a Manchester show, in 1902, there was a staggering 110 Skye Terrier entries. They continued their reign as top terrier until shortly before World War I. Some say that the trend for excessive coat length resulted in the breed losing favor with the general public. Others contend that it was simply that there were new breeds which caught the public's eye.

The Skye Terrier was first registered with the American Kennel Club in 1887. The breed made quite a splash in the ring, and soon became one of the most popular of show dogs. There were a number of early kennels who competed, with keen rivalry. One of the earliest Skye breeders was Lawrence Timpson, of New York City. Writing in G. O. Shields' *The American Book of the Dog*, published in 1891, Mr. Timpson says, "Their disposition resembles very much that of the Highlanders themselves—in their love of home, and in war by their dash, pluck and dogged courage and endurance, and by a loyalty and devotion to their mas-

ter, through fair and foul weather..." Mr. Timpson added that "The Skye is a peaceful, well-conducted little citizen, and attends strictly to his own affairs, unless those...are interfered with by others...."

The breed, Timpson writes, has "...a sound constitution, which enables him to go almost anywhere, do almost anything, and rough it with his master in any climate. He is a born sportsman, always ready for a quiet bit of sport in a barn, or along the hedgerows, displaying the utmost keenness and sagacity in the pursuit of all sorts of vermin...." His love of the breed is evident in his concluding remarks that one "can have no better companion that this friendly, cheerful little fellow."

The Skye Terrier Club of America was formed in 1938. While Skyes certainly aren't the most popular show dogs today, their glamorous looks never fail to catch the judge's eye. There have been many notable Best in Show winners, including Walter and Adele Goodman's Ch. Glamoor Good News, who topped Westminster in 1969, breeder-owner handled. While numerically few, the Skye has attracted a host of hard core, extremely dedicated and loyal owners, who take tremendous pride in "The Heavenly Breed."

While rare in the obedience ring, the few Skyes who have come out have done quite well. When asked if Skyes can show in obedience, Ann B. Bower, of Barraglen Kennels, emphatically replies, "Absolutely, yes!" The Grants Pass, Oregon, fancier should know well. Her Ch. Talakan Tapestry O'Barraglen completed her C.D. in 1988 and was the Delaney System's top obedience Skye for the year. The next year, she completed her C.D.X. in three straight shows. Taps, as she's called, has proven her versatility. Not only is she both a bench champion and an obedience title holder, but, in 1989, she was the number one Skye Terrier dam with five champions to her credit. "It's unfortunate that more Skyes aren't shown in obedience," Ann says. "Several judges told me that in all their years of judging, mine were the first Skyes they'd seen in an obedience ring." Ann has become unabashedly enthusiastic about obedience. Now, one of Taps' daughters is carrying on the family tradition. She's already earned her C.D. and is in training for her C.D.X.

"Since there are so many different ways of training," Ann observes, "let me state here that we only train with kindness and food rewards. If obedience is fun for your Skye, he will enjoy it and perform his exercises well. If, in his eyes, it is not, you may have great difficulty in getting any degree.

"Living with a Skye is a delightful experience," Ann says. It was happenstance that the Bowers obtained their first Skye Terrier. They had bred Scotties for more than twenty years and didn't know much about Skyes. But, one of their regular boarding clients wanted a Skye and turned to the Bowers for help. "We did a lot of reading, contacted some breeders and ultimately found a nice four-month-old puppy for them. Since they travelled frequently, the puppy stayed with us a lot and I simply fell in love with the dog. The result, of course, was that we agreed a Skye Terrier was important in our lives and we subsequently acquired Taps."

According to Ann, Skyes "can be very determined at times. Our Skye's are sensitive, intelligent, comical and just plain fun. They will alert us to cars in our driveway, people arriving and leaving and will let us know when the children are walking home from the grade school just down the road...They bark only when they consider it necessary...for such things as announcing a stranger, to get a special treat, at dinnertime or because they need to go out. Once told, they expect their person to deal with the problem with, of course, Skye backup.

"Of the Terrier group, I would say that Skyes are the 'most laid back' breed," Ann says. "They are not a dog who stands with madly wagging tail, inviting a stranger to come over and pat or play with them. They are not a 'sparring' terrier either and are somewhat aloof and reserved. A Skye is not a dog for everyone. They need a loving home with a person who understands their personality and enjoys it. This should be someone who will never let them be 'top dog,' but who will understand them and know how to discipline them correctly should that be necessary."

While Skyes certainly need discipline, a heavy handed approach is never correct, since this breed is very sensitive. "A Skye needs no more than a harsh reprimand to make him understand you are displeased," writes Richard Rutledge, in the February 1987 issue of *The American Kennel Gazette*. "He aims to please, particularly in house-breaking. While it is easy to spoil the intelligent dog, the Skye should not be allowed to take over. It is no exaggeration to say that a Skye Terrier should never be struck or hit for any reason."

Mr. Rutledge describes the breed as "intelligent, spirited, tenacious, courageous" and "showing great stamina. A true terrier! As the list continues, however, a distinction sets in. The Skye is cautious, especially with strangers, and reserved, often assuming a stern stand-offish appearance. He resents attention being forced upon him, preferring to make advances on his own.

"The Skye's loyalty is legendary," Mr. Rutledge notes, "and the one-to-one relationship is a strong bond often difficult to break." Ann Bower agrees. "They make a superb friend through thick and thin and are excellent guardians of those who are important to them. I am never afraid wherever I am as long as one of our Skyes is with me. They are exceptionally devoted to those they love and will 'pine' when separated. They are NOT good kennel dogs. They really need to live with those they love. While Skyes can and do live outside, our dogs have always been and will always be house dogs. We have them because we love them and that means sharing our home as well as our hearts!"

Indeed, those who share their home with a Skye will find him a charming, affectionate and comical companion. "Skyes in our home prefer sofas and lounging chairs to the floor except when they are playing," Ann Bower says. "Watching Skye puppies play is really comical...They settle the dominance department with each playtime by 'jumping' on another puppy's head. That puppy then rolls over and grabs the whiskers, muzzle, ear or whatever is available...It's an up-down seesaw until both tire and it is very amusing to watch. Even as adults, this type of play can continue....

"Whether we have been gone for ten minutes or ten days, our Skyes greet us with unbridled enthusiasm," Ann laughs. "Taps will run and get a toy, playing coy with us and trying to keep it out of our reach. What she really wants is for you to grab it, play pull with her, take it away and throw it for her to fetch. When she retrieves it, she will flop over on her back and ask for a tummy scratch which was what she really wanted in the first place. Lady Di, on the other hand, jumps up, checks me out (to make sure I haven't seen another dog) and, with her tail madly wagging, places 'kisses' on any part of the anatomy she can reach. Then, she rushes off to find herself a toy which she carries proudly as she prances around the room. Birk rushes in, jumps up, checks us out and promptly flips over on his back for a tummy scratch. Once that has been attended to, he finds himself a toy and goes on a 'Skye tear' around and around in circles at a dead run through the house, ending up with his toy in one of the lounge chairs." After a hard day, arriving home at the Bower's house must be quite a delight!

In the 1862 *Book of Home Pets*, Beeton says, "It would be well worth enquiring how it is that this dog is so constantly losing himself. That this is the case, anyone taking ordinary notice of window-bills and placards must have discovered. It can't be that the dog's extraordinary value tempts the dog thief, for many dogs allowed as much freedom as the Skye are of much more value, and are seldom 'lost or stolen.'...he is a dog of so much intelligence and of such an enquiring turn of mind that he is impelled to investigate any and every odd matter than may turn up in the course of a morning's walk."

Little has changed since 1862. Today's Skye still has a curious and inquiring mind and, if not properly confined, will venture off on his own. "Never own a Skye if you do not have a fenced yard," Ann Bower warns. "This is a very important requirement. A Skye will chase a bird, rabbit, etc., anything that he sees or smells and one can get either lost or out on a road where he might be seriously injured by a car.

"Skyes are special to me because I find them so unique. They are very sensitive to mood and expression and they are real charmers," Ann enthuses. "They are striking looking and although a show coat does take a lot of care, it is very rewarding to see a beautiful Skye in full, glorious coat."

Indeed, it is the Skye's spectacular appearance that first attracts many people. Hands down, he is the most glamorous of all the terrier clan. He is a dog of great style and elegance who exudes dignity. His strong, muscular body is well boned and muscled. The breed is slow maturing, with dogs not completely mature until about age two. His body is all low, long and sinewy with great agility. In proportion, the Skye Terrier should be twice as long as he is tall. Dogs generally stand 10 inches at the withers, while bitches are one half inch

less. The tender softness of his brown eyes is obscured by a veil of protective hair. The breed comes in both prick eared and drop eared styles. The prick ears are placed high on the skull, while the larger drop ears fall flat against the head. In the past, drop eared Skyes were the most popular. Nowadays, it is the prick eared dogs that are in vogue, no doubt because the cascading hair which falls over the ears makes such a stunning appearance. The Skye is one of the few terriers that does not carry his tail elevated. Instead, it should form a graceful extension of the back and should be carried no higher.

The Skye's coat is, of course, quite distinctive. It is a double coat, composed of a short, soft, wooly undercoat topped by a straight, flat, hard outercoat. On the body, the coat is parted from the head to the tail and hangs straight down each side. While the coat should be at least 5 1/2 inches long, and no extra credit is given for greater length, many show dogs do boast first rate, floor length coats. The hair on the head is shorter and softer in texture and forms a veil over the forehead and eyes. On the ears, the coat falls from the tips and outer edges, forming a fringe, which accentuates the ears' outline. The Skye is a solid colored dog, though varying shades of the same color are permissible. The standard permits "black, blue, dark or light gray, silver platinum, fawn or cream." Black points on the ears, muzzle and tip of tail are desirable.

The standard wisely includes a discussion of puppy coats. "The puppy coat may be very different in color from the adult coat," it says. "As it is growing and clearing, wide variations of color may occur; consequently this is permissible in dogs under 18 months of age. However, even in puppies there must be no trace of pattern, design or clear-cut variations with the exception of the black band of varying width frequently seen encircling the body coat of the cream-colored dog...."

Those interested in the breed should be sure to make time for regular grooming. With their double coats, Skyes do shed and routine brushing can keep this to a minimum. Without routine upkeep, the Skye's coat will become badly matted. For this reason, some pet owners prefer to keep their dog's coat clipped. Pet Skyes should be bathed as needed. "Depending on where one lives, city versus country, climate, etc., about once a month to six weeks should be just about right," Ann Bower says. "Never brush or comb a Skye coat dry," she advises. "You should always spritz it with water, diluted conditioner or some such thing before beginning."

Show grooming is, of course, much more involved. "I enjoy brushing my dogs...it's very relaxing to me," Ann says. "I may tend to do more than is required. I don't clip my dogs since it really spoils a Skye's look and takes away one of his most striking features. Skyes

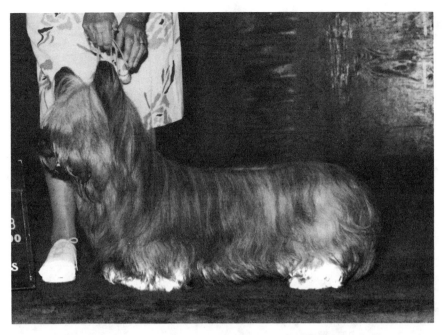

The long and low look of the Skye Terrier is illustrated by Ch. Barraglen's Brankie Birk, owned by Ann and Ross Bower. (Ross photo)

out in about half an hour unless the dog is matted. Once or twice a week brushing will keep a coat in very good condition usually, but each dog is different so each individual owner must adapt to his particular dog's coat.

"If Skye's are shown in conformation, then their coat must be parted from the fall to the tip of the tail," Ann continues. "Some exhibitors do not bother to part the tail itself, but the rest of the coat must be parted. If you are showing in obedience, do *not* part the coat since this may tend to make a long dog look as if he is sitting crooked."

While the Skye has a loyal cadre of followers, he is not widely known. Indeed, there are many non-show people who have never seen one. That's a shame because the Skye Terrier, with his wonderful personality has much to rec-

are always bathed before every show. A mild, but cleansing shampoo, is used, followed by conditioner which, depending on the type, can be rinsed out or left in. Then the coat is blown dry in winter or air dried in summer. Most of your show grooming involves brushing (not combing). You should use a soft pin brush. Bathing and conditioning a show coat on a heavily coated Skye takes about three hours from start to finish, including drying time. A Skye can be completely brushed

ommend him. "The breed is alert and intelligent," writes John Marvin in the 1964 *Book of All Terriers,* "and with its great heritage, it deserves greater popularity than it now enjoys." Many Skye owners would second that opinion, although they, like most dog owners, don't want the breed to become too popular. Be forewarned, though, the Skye is likely to charm himself into your heart.

Obedience star Neva Ava Mia By Dazen is owned by Ruth E. Adams, of Indianapolis, Indiana.

Chapter 30

The Spinone Italiani

"The Spinone Italianis are the greatest dogs in the world," says Dave Badollet, of Indianapolis, Indiana. Paolo Sacchetti certainly agrees. "This is a breed which cannot be equaled in its kind, loyal disposition..." Jim Channon writes charmingly, "In the home, a Spinone is a companion—a guardian of the house—a friend that I can talk to when I am alone—a buddy and a pal who is quite willing to put up with my ways, take long walks in the country with me, or play and romp like a young colt.

"He is a gentle nursemaid and playmate to all children. He is an intelligent pupil—willing and quick to learn. True, he is sometimes like a spoiled brat. When scolded he becomes a con-artist—knowing that by looking at me with his sad eyes and touching me with his paw, my heart will melt and all will be well again."

If you've gained the impression that owners are passionate about this breed, you're absolutely right. Enthusiasm runs high among those who have had the opportunity to know and hunt with the breed. They appreciate the many qualities of Italy's all-round pointer and they are determined to see it take it's rightful place, in this country, with the other dual purpose hunting breeds.

The Spinone has been in the A.K.C's Miscellaneous Class for many years. Other breeds have progressed, earning the A.K.C. imprimatur of recognition. The Spinone, however, has remained consigned to this designation, and efforts to promote the breed have been largely unsuccessful.

Several attempts have been made to introduce the breed. In the 1930's, a number of Spinones were imported. The American Field registered 18 in their 1935 stud book. Mr. Emil Perona exhibited the lovely specimen, "Mery," at the Westminster Kennel Club, in the 1930s. Despite the valiant start, the effort to draw attention to the Spinone failed. In the early 1970's, Spinones were once again imported. I can recall seeing a lovely bitch named, if memory serves, "Duck Soup," at eastern shows. Still, the breed did not gain a foothold. This time, however, things appear to be different. With the tremendous interest in rare breeds, the Spinone's time may well have come.

Rarely has there been a breed whose origins and early history are so fraught with controversy. In researching this chapter, I have come across statements ascribing the Spinone's origin to Italy, France, Spain, Russia and Greece. It would take an intrepid detective to sort through all these theories and it's still unlikely that there would be a definitive answer. This may be, in part, because the Spinone is, undoubtedly, a very old breed.

Those who advocate an entirely Italian origin for the breed, often cite quotes from many writers between 100-300 A.D. In checking out these references, however, it appears that they apply to hunting dogs, in general, rather than specifically to the Spinone. Others have credited him as descending from the Spanish Pointer, but this now extinct breed played a pivotal part in the formation of all modern pointers. Some have claimed that he is descended from the Russian setter. Still others guess that his origins lie in an Italian coarse-haired setter, which was crossed with a white variety of Mastiff. And many believe that the wiry coat came from the Italian hound breed, the Segugio.

Many writers have noted the resemblance of the Spinone to the Griffon breeds of France. Some even claim that the Spinone is the progenitor of the Griffons.

While this seems doubtful, it is certainly true that the Spinone and the Griffon type hunting breeds, such as the Wirehaired Pointing Griffon, have much in common, both in conformation and style of hunting.

An intriguing theory comes from British writer David Hancock. Writing on the Scottish Deerhound, in *Dog World,* he discusses the evolution of the rough coated breeds. "The Celts were famous for their coarse-haired running dogs, both trackers and gazehounds. Celtic expansion along the main river routes in central Europe led to settlements being established in 200 B.C. from northern Spain in the West to the British Isles in the North to the Adriatic in the South. It is significant that coarse-haired hunting dogs are found wherever they settled: the griffon hound breeds of France, the rough-haired Styrian hounds of Austria, the Wolfhound of Ireland, the Spinone of Italy, the Wirehaired Pointing Griffons of Hungary, Germany and Czechoslovakia and many of the terrier breeds, perhaps influencing the rough-haired Segugio of Italy and the Bosnian hound, too."

Whatever the truth of his origin, dogs of this type became established in Italy. A dog of Spinone type appears in a fresco painted by Andrea Montagna, which hangs in the Duke's Palace in Mantova. The artists Tiziano and Tiepolo featured the breed in their paintings, also.

The breed's history in modern times is a little easier to track. By the 1800's, the Spinone appears to have been widely known in Italy. The same wiry-coated pointing dog could be found in various parts of the country, although each district applied its own name. The dogs came in either roan-brown or white or white-orange color. The white or white-orange Spinones were most prevalent in and around Alba, in the Piedmont district. In some areas the dog was known as the *Spinoso* or *Spinone.* The name comes from a thorny bush, the *pino,* which often grows in impenetrable thickets. Only the thick skinned, wiry coated hunting dogs could succeed in flushing the game from such surroundings.

In 1828, Crippa wrote the first reference to the breed, telling of this wiry coated hunting dog and comparing him favorably to the setter. In 1887, Delor penned the first complete description of the breed. It was he who suggested that Spinone was the appropriate name for the breed and should be used universally throughout the country.

Widespread and popular though the breed was, interest began to wane in the late 1800's and early 1900's. In speaking of the white Spinone, Robert Leighton, in his *The New Book of the Dog,* written in 1906, says that they are "difficult to procure, but this is not perhaps a matter for regret, for in Italy, as everywhere else on the Continent, the indigenous shooting

A trio of rare Spinones. (Left to right) Dina Vera Dell'Adige Romano, Neva Ava Mia By Dazen and Purosanque's Bianco Praetorian Luigi. All are owned by Ruth Adams.

dogs are fast making room for English Pointers, Setters and Spaniels."

While Leighton may have applauded the popularity of the British breeds in Italy, not all Italian dog lovers shared his view. Many were very concerned about the Spinone. The Italian sporting journal, *Il Cacciatore,* appealed to its readers to save the breed. They damned those "connoisseurs of foreign breeds" whose abandonment of the Spinone was leading to the breed's demise. Finally, the Italian Kennel Club took an interest in the breed and it increased in popularity.

The breed was to face an additional challenge. World War II devastated Italy and many breeds, especially large ones, suffered. The Spinone might well have become extinct were it not for the efforts of Drs. Ceresoli and Brianzi. In 1949, Ceresoli toured all of Italy to make a survey of the remaining Spinones. The breed had become so scarce, in some areas, that breeders had resorted to crosses with other hunting breeds. Boulet, Wirehaired (or Korthals) Pointing Griffon and German Wire-haired Pointer blood had been introduced. Ceresoli declared that the white or white and orange dogs had been less tainted by other blood.

Using Dr. Ceresoli's survey, Dr. Paul Brianzi and others began to reconstruct the breed. It was through their efforts that the breed survived. Brianzi formed an organization, the Friends of the Spinone, which did much to revive the breed. Interest grew rapidly and Spinones began to appear regularly at dog shows throughout the country. Many field days were held to compare the dogs' hunting instincts. They provided a rich opportunity for newcomers to learn about the breed. There were still some controversies. Hunting advocates debated whether the Spinone should be faster in the field. Would they have to diminish size to increase speed? Show fanciers had their questions, too. Were the roan-browns equal in quality to the orange-whites?

Today, the Spinone thrives in Italy. He is a very popular dog on the show bench. The roan-browns of today have increased in quality and can now rival the orange-whites. The breed is well known to sportsmen, not only in Italy, but in other Continental countries. By and large he is a personal hunting companion. Even in Italy, his slow manner of hunting keeps him from being popular in field trials. Regrettably, there has been a split in type between the show and working animals. As has happened with so many hunting breeds in America, the type differs between field and show dogs.

The central Europeans have always favored dual-purpose sporting breeds, rather than the specialized dogs employed in Great Britain and America. The Continental sportsman has no desire to keep a pointer, setter, spaniel, retriever and hound. He wants them all wrapped up neatly in a dog which can fill the bag, be it in pursuit of feather or fur. For this reason, the European dual purpose sporting breeds were created specifically to be "jacks of all trades."

These breeds have been handicapped when they arrive in our country. Americans have tried to make them fit the conventional Pointer-Setter mold. They've compared them to the big-running, horizon busting Pointer-Setter breeds and declared them lacking. In truth, they have been comparing apples and oranges. The European dual purpose sporting breeds have never

been intended to hunt with the speed and style of the Pointer or Setter. They are a breed apart and should never be pushed unfairly into this mold. If they are slow, by comparison, that's fine for the European sportsman hunts on foot, not from horseback. He wants a dog that's slower, steadier, more thorough and always within sight. The Spinone fills this bill ably. He's not meant to be a field trial dog, but a personal hunting companion *par excellence,* who can point and retrieve game from field and perform on waterfowl, too.

"First and foremost, he is a hunting companion," writes Jim Channon. "Before a Spinone came into my life, I would take my gun in hand on opening day of bird season and go off half-heartedly, hoping to scare up a pheasant or two. Now, with one of my companions along, I eagerly look forward to hunting—knowing that I will have the full enjoyment of watching my Spinone work and knowing, too, that there will be the limit in my pouch. Seeing my Spinone quarter a field is my joy! This joy reaches its climax when they come on point—steady and true."

In comparison to the more common sporting breeds, the Spinone is slow. But, he is also methodical and thorough and nothing escapes his attention. If you want a field trial dog, the Spinone is not for you. However, if your concern is a pleasant day spent hunting, a bag full of birds and a dog who will do his absolute utmost to please you in any way, then the Spinone can fill that bill, and very well, thank you. He always keeps his master within sight and does not range far in front of the gun. While hunting, the breed maintains "tight contact with his hunter-master," says Paolo Sacchetti. "I would unequivocally say that this is the best quality the Spinone has. All of the hard and elaborate work of the day's hunt is dedicated to the master."

The Spinone performs very well on most types of upland birds. He's wonderful on ring-neck pheasants, woodcocks and grouse. While his nose is especially good, his limited range makes him less useful on bevy birds, like quail and partridge, which scatter widely in wide-open country. His wiry jacket is especially well suited to birds that inhabit swampy, boggy, marshy areas, such as rails and jacksnipe. In such areas, his abilities as a water dog are much appreciated. He'll gladly enter areas that Pointers or Setters would eschew.

The Spinone is a large, robust dog. Males generally stand 23 1/2 to 27 1/2 inches at the withers, while bitches measure 23-25 1/2 inches. The standard lists male weights at 70-82 pounds and female weights at 62-71 pounds. However, dogs can exceed these weights. The height specifications, however, are strictly adhered to and oversized or undersized dogs are disqualified. In comparison to our recognized breeds, this makes the Spinone approximately the size of the Weimaraner.

Two of Ruth Adams' Spinone bitches. Dina is liver and roan, and Mia is white and orange.

The Spinone's body is square and he has a broad, deep chest. His head is large and somewhat long with a slightly domed skull. The eyes are large and round, with eyelids that fit tightly, showing no haw. In darker colored dogs, the eyes are light brown and in white or orange-white dogs, they are yellow. Expression is very important and the look should convey the impression of sweetness. The eyes are capped by full, bushy eyebrows. Nose pigment corresponds with the dog's color, ranging from a rosy-fleshed pigment in white dogs to a brown in roan colored specimens. The square shaped muzzle is obscured by a moustache and beard. The docked tail is carried down or horizontally.

One of the Spinone's key characteristics is his coat. His skin is thick and leathery and the coat is wiry, rough and close-fitting. A soft, silky or curly coat is a disqualification, and rightly so. Average length of the body jacket is 1 1/2 to 2 1/2 inches. Spinones come in several colors. They may be solid white, white with orange markings, or white peppered with orange. In the brown spectrum, Spinone's may be white with brown markings or white speckled with brown hairs (called brown roan). Tricolored dogs or solid colors other than white are disqualifications.

The Spinone is a hardy dog and an easy-keeper. Grooming consists mainly of a good, thorough brushing done weekly. For show purposes, the owner may elect to do a little stripping on the head. Ears should be cleaned weekly and eyes wiped daily. With his beard, the Spinone is apt to be a sloppy drinker and eater. Ruth Adams, of Indianapolis, Indiana, has a fine solution. One of her Spinones, "Mia has learned to wait for me to wipe her beard after taking a drink. One particular time, she took six drinks, stopping each time for me to wipe her beard."

The Spinone is rarely seen in show rings in this country. That's a shame, for his appearance would, no doubt, spark interest in the breed. "He is a born showman!" Jim Channon says. "When he hears applause, he just knows it is for him, so he holds his head a little higher and struts along a little more proudly."

Ruth Adams spotted her first Spinone at an Indiana show. "I saw my first Spinone at the Hoosier Kennel Club...in Indianapolis. I was attracted by his size and beautiful white coat. But, up close, it was his eyes that so fascinated me. There was just something extra special about this particular dog." Ruth is especially interested in obedience. She persuaded the dog's owner, to let her take the Spinone home and train it. "The owner agreed to let me take Ferdie home and train him through a ten week obedience class. Although he was over two years old with very little exposure to obedience and limited socialization, this dog learned quickly and confidently. We finished our class in first place with a score of 198 1/2!" Ruth had finished two obedience titles on Doberman Pinschers. "It was the Spinone Italiani that drew me back to obedience," she says. "Not only did he train easily, but Ferdi fit well into our household with eight and nine year old Dobes. Needless to say, I was 'hooked' and just had to have one of Ferdi's puppies."

Soon, Neva Ava Mia by Dazen, better known as Mia, joined the Adams household. This Spinone bitch has thrilled audiences with her dazzling obedience performances. Not only is she only the third Spinone to earn a Companion Dog title, but she is the first to capture the coveted *Dog World* award for her high scores. She finished her legs with three scores of 196 1/2 and one 197 1/2. Mia is now in training for her C.D.X. "We are very interested in having people know what a great obedience candidate this breed really is," Ruth says. Mia has also impressed knowledgeable sportsmen with her field instincts. She has completely won over the Adams household. Ruth has purchased another bitch, Dina Vera. As a special gift, Mia's breeder presented Ruth with a male, Luigi. We're sure these dogs will be seen in Midwestern obedience rings.

If the Spinone's looks and hunting prowess is what attracts newcomers, it is his terrific personality that makes them into diehard fans. One of the most enthusiastic Spinone advocates is Jim Channon. In a charming and eloquently written piece, entitled "What is an Italian Spinone," which appears in the club newsletter, he wonderfully describes the breed. "...He is a bundle of energized gold—willing and ready to take on any task with unfailing spirit and enthusiasm. He is an official greeter to all comers—but must be assured by his master that he is greeting a friend. He is a comfort seeker—would rather sleep on the bed than the floor. He thinks couches were made for him....

"He is a prankster who will take one of our possessions and hide it—knowing full well that he will be asked to seek—than given praise when he retrieves it from where he has had it secreted. He is a clown—a court jester—ad-libbing with tricks for attention. He is headstrong, but docile! Cautious, but daring! He is the wind when he runs—a symphony of movement. A free soul, loving the world he lives in.

"He is a joy to know. A happiness to possess. A fulfillment of one's desires. He is the owner of our home and me....He is a Spinone—and that sets him apart from all others. If he must be catalogued in the canine world, then we all must admit—he is a king!"

Chapter 31

The Sussex Spaniel

Fashions come and go, seemingly without logic or reason. The breed that is popular one day may be cast aside the next, only to elevated once again. The Sussex Spaniel is that unusual canine who seems always to have been rare. A review of the writings on the breed will substantiate this point:

1872-"...the Sussex has never been produced in great numbers, nor ever been common, but kept in the hands of a few families."; 1879-"...strange to say, notwithstanding its beauty, and capacity for rough work, it has never been common..."; 1891-"...it appears as if by a matter of a few years when the few purebred specimens that we have will die off, and the breed become practically extinct..."; 1900-"I have also, occasionally, seen a Sussex spaniel, which are rare dogs..."; 1912-"It is to be regretted that we have to speak in the past tense with regard to the Sussex spaniel, a true-bred specimen of which it would be difficult to find at the present time."; 1977-"Persistence is the word to apply to the Sussex...a persistence to remain part of the world's dog scene, to hold back against the forces that would hurl him into extinction....one prays for his survival..."(Quotes from Idstone, Shaw, Wilmerding, Lane, Watson & Maxwell)

And yet, survive the Sussex Spaniel has. The breed has suffered from innumerable hardships. The ravages of distemper, rabies and hepatitis have taken their toll. World Wars have reduced breed numbers to a few dogs. Breeding difficulties and a preponderance of males over females have threatened to wipe the breed out. Yet, the little Sussex has conquered all that the world has thrown at him. Amazingly, despite all the problems, he has clung tenaciously to his type...the distinctive head, the unique ears, the low-slung body, that fabulously whirring tail and, most particularly, his color...have all survived, gloriously. Drawings from the 1800s still compare favorably with the best of the dogs seen today. But, purebred dogs do not survive on their own. The Sussex has been fortunate to have a small band of breeders, often only one or two at a time, who cared deeply about the breed. It is to these individuals that we owe thanks for keeping one of dogdom's most remarkable breeds alive.

One of the oldest of the spaniel clan, the Sussex's beginnings can be traced to the late 1700's. Sportsmen in Sussex County, England, wanted a hunting dog to work in the game laden fields surrounding their estates. To understand the spaniel which they fashioned, specifically to suit their needs, we must know something of the conditions in which the dogs were expected to perform. It's true that game abounded in the woods and fields of Sussex County, but it was darned hard to get at. The vast woods were underlaid with briars and brambles, almost impossible for humans to penetrate. The fields were studded with thick hedgerows which provided ideal hiding places for birds, rabbits and other small game.

What the gentleman hunters of Sussex needed was a small, powerful dog who would not be deterred by the extreme conditions. A slow dog, keen-nosed, persistent and long on endurance was needed to flush the game from the thick cover. He must have a heavy coat to protect him from the bruising underbrush. Since the dogs were hunted in teams, a pleasant sociable temperament was a must. Like all hunters, they wanted an easy to train dog. Spaniels, long known for their extreme

The impressive nine month old future champion Ziyadah Black Tower, owned by Marcia and Andrew Deugan.

stabilizing the breed, there can be no doubt that Relf played a pivotal part in evolving and maintaining the Sussex. Early on, most Sussex Spaniels were liver or black in color. However, when a Rosehill bitch was mated to a dog owned by Dr. Watts, of Battle, a little pup was whelped with a peculiar golden tinge. Every now and then, in subsequent breedings, this golden liver color emerged. That Fuller and Relf liked the color is obvious, for they retained pups showing this characteristic. In the fifty years that Rosehill was in operation, the golden liver coat became the keystone, the one identifiable mark that stamped the dog as a Rosehill. Ultimately, it would also prove to be the hallmark of the entire breed.

We don't know how many spaniels were kenneled at Rosehill. Reports say that a rabies epidemic spread through the kennel and many dogs died. Regrettably, a number of others had to be destroyed. When Mr. Fuller died, in 1847, only nine dogs remained. In appreciation for his years of service, Mrs. Fuller allowed Albert Relf to select two dogs for his own. The remaining spaniels were sold at public auction.

Relf selected a male, George, and a bitch, Romp. From these two, he continued the Rosehill strain. For the next forty years, until 1887, he continued to hunt with and breed the strain. Indeed, without him, the purebred Sussex Spaniel might have vanished. He kept his keen interest in the breed to the very end.

In the 1870's, there was a move afoot to rescue the Sussex Spaniel. But, purebred dogs were extremely hard to find. Fanciers journeyed to Sussex, probably to Mr. Relf's kennel and others, in search of purebred specimens. These they found extremely difficult to locate. In a letter by Mr. A.W. Langdale, which appeared in Vero Shaw's 1879 work, *The Illustrated Book of the Dog*, he tells us that pure Sussex Spaniels were few and when he could find them, their owners would not part with the dogs. "I have rambled all over Sussex and Kent in search of a *bona fide* specimen, and although I have been favoured with a view, have never yet been able to obtain one, and call it my own."

"About the year 1870," Shaw says, "...a few gentlemen, actuated by feelings of interest in the Sussex Spaniel, set themselves to work to rescue the breed from the annihilation which threatened it...there were several types of Sussex Spaniel in existence—not that all were pure-bred by any means; so perhaps it would be more

desire to please, provided an excellent foundation. Though most spaniels hunted silently, the Sussex sportsmen found that, by giving tongue, their dogs could more effectively rout the game. This ability proved particularly valuable since, in the dense brush, the dog was often out of his master's line of sight. The enviable sporting dog they created would bear the name of their county. He would be known, forevermore, as the Sussex Spaniel.

While several hunters used the newly evolving spaniels, the dogs of one particular Sussex County estate would gain a lasting reputation. Rosehill Park, at Brightling, near Hastings, was owned by Mr. Fuller. An avid sportsman, Fuller turned his attention to the Sussex Spaniel, in about 1795. During the hunting season, he could be seen daily in the fields and woods with his dogs. He once described the breed as "a hunting dog kept exclusively for the use of Gentlemen."

Mr. Fuller employed Albert Relf as kennelmaster for his dogs. While credit is often given to Fuller for proper if we said that there were several specimens of the breed in whose veins a large amount of the old Rosehill blood ran, but who bore the taint of foreign crosses in a small degree."

The foreign blood that Shaw mentions was that of the Field Spaniel. Unfortunately, crosses to the Field yielded an unattractive brown cast to the coat. Since the golden liver was recognized as the touchstone of purity, they became discouraged. Shaw includes a letter from T.B. Bowers, in which he remarks that "pure specimens became exceedingly rare, when, I believe, some who had specimens crossed them with other strains of Spaniel, and, being disappointed with the result, gave up the attempt to resuscitate the breed."

There were, however, one or two fanciers who persevered. Thomas Jacobs, of Newton Abbot, became interested in the breed. In 1879, he established a kennel of Sussex and enjoyed much success. In 1891, his kennel was dispersed. The best of his dogs went to Moses Woolland, who exhibited the breed in both the field and on the bench. He gained quite a reputation for his work with the breed.

As the new century dawned, the Sussex Spaniel was still in a precarious state. Mr. Jacobs' kennel was broken up and dispersed in 1905. Campbell Newington and Colonel R. Claude Cane, attracted by the Woolland dogs, still continued to breed the Sussex. Colonel Cane speaks of the difficulties, in Robert Leighton's *The New Book of the Dog*, first published in 1906. "My own kennel...has been going for some fifteen years....I have not found them very easy to breed, the bitches being very uncertain, and the puppies delicate and hard to rear when one does get a good litter; but in spite of this I still retain enough enthusiasm to stick to it, especially at the present time, owing to Mr. Woolland's retirement, the breed seems to be left almost entirely to Mr. Newington and myself....This delicacy I attribute mainly to excessive inbreeding, which is, I fear, almost unavoidable, as there are so few pure-bred specimens left."

The breed didn't make much progress until after World War I. Then, slowly, a few breeders began to take up the cause of the Sussex Spaniel. One such individual, Joyce Freer, was to have a profound effect on the survival of the breed. Joy, as she is know to her many friends, bought her first Sussex in 1924. This male would grow up to be the illustrious Champion Brosse. So taken was Joy with the golden liver dog that the following year she purchased a bitch, Judy. These two would form the foundation for her Fourclovers Kennel.

By the late 1930's, the number of Sussex breeders had, once again, diminished. Joy Freer became concerned. As World War II loomed, her concern turned to alarm. As the Germans blitzed England and people took to underground bunkers, most breeding

activities were halted. Brits turned their attention to the war effort. Most devastating, however, was the lack of food. Strict rationing went into effect. Rather than see their beloved pets die slowly of starvation, many dog lovers, reluctantly, had the dogs put to sleep.

Joy Freer, however, decided to try to hang on. As she told Sussex owner Bruce Wolk, for a 1984 article, "The Spaniels of Joy," which appeared in *Dog World,* "It wasn't so much a question of gathering up the remaining fragments of the breed, as of finding a means of keeping my own kennel going and getting food for them." Fortunately, the Freers lived in the country and raised pigs. But, obtaining food for her beloved pets still wasn't easy. "We had a ration of meat meal to feed the pigs," she recalled, " I mixed a little of this with boiled potatoes and pieces I could find, including trimmings from boiled hams the grocer saved for me and everything and anything." When Mr. Wolk investigated, he discovered that Joy had often gone without food to ensure her dogs' survival.

Joy succeeded in providing for her eight Sussex Spaniels. She even managed to breed a litter each year. The puppies were given to those who loved the breed and could take care of them. At war's end, Joy was the sole remaining breeder of Sussex Spaniels in the world. And only four of her dogs were of breeding age. All dogs, today, can trace their roots to the dogs nurtured, during those hard times, at Fourclovers Kennel.

In the late 1800's, the Sussex Spaniel made his debut in the United States. In 1878, it became the fifth breed registered with the newly established American Kennel Club. The breed was used primarily as a gundog, although it did make occasional appearances on the

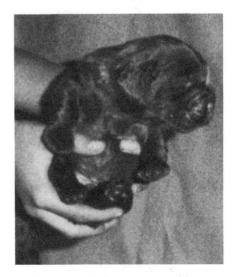

A five day old Sussex puppy, born at Ziyadah Kennels, Reg., in Bonita Springs, Florida.

bench. In the mid-1880's, A. Clinton Wilmerding imported several dogs from Thomas Jacobs' kennels at Newton Abbot. He showed and hunted his dogs. "In the field this dog is a strong and cheerful worker, of great pluck and energy," Mr. Wilmerding wrote, in G.O. Sheild's 1891 work, *The American Book of the Dog.* "...In many parts of our shooting territory they should be particularly useful and valuable, in spots where the Setter or Pointer cannot penetrate; the Sussex being powerful and short of leg, will fearlessly press his way through the densest briers and undergrowth, and ultimately reach and flush the fur or feather secreted therein..."

Indeed, wherever the Sussex was used, he earned the admiration of hunters. Writing in 1891, J.F. Kirk compared the performance of the breed with that of the more popular Field Spaniel. "I have seen a Sussex Spaniel bitch, measuring only fifteen inches full height at the shoulder, and forty inches from tip of nose to set-on of tail, able to get over a six-foot fence with ease, and work a tubby-built eighteen-inch dog to a stand-still in half a day's work. Why? Because she had grand supple shoulders, powerful loins and quarters, well-bent stifles and hocks, the possession of which gave her what Fox Terrier men call 'liberty,' while he, though of great muscular development and short coupled, was tied and cloddy in action."

Despite Mr. Wilmerding's promising start, the breed did not catch on. By 1912, James Watson reported that it was extremely difficult to find a representative of the breed. But, one or two at a time, a few Sussex Spaniels were imported. In 1922, this testimonial to the breed appeared, in the magazine *Outdoor America.* "The Cocker, while starting out full of energy and vim, cannot stand for a day's work in our heavy-timbered country, which is, of course, interspersed with scrub, spruce thickets, brier patches, and swamps. Having a copy of *Stonehenge on the Dog,* edition of 1887, in which we read up on the various breeds of sporting Spaniel, we decided that we would like a Sussex. So in 1922 a bitch was shipped to me, bred before shipment to the premier Sussex of Britain at the time. She arrived, and in her season presented me with three puppies. The beauty of the Sussex is beyond question, and its ability as a fit companion for the bird-hunter is unquestioned. As a retriever from land or water it is the equal of a Labrador."

As World War II put a halt to British Sussex Kennels, it did the same in this country. At the start of the War, the breed banner was carried only by Tarralong Kennels. When the owner's husband enlisted in the service, the kennel was disbanded. All the dogs were neu-

tered and placed as pets.

In the 1970's, however, there was a revival of interest in the Sussex in this country. Margaret Reid, of Wilred Kennels, had owned a Sussex which died in 1957. It took her thirteen years to find a replacement. In 1970, she succeeded in importing two from Scotland.

In the same year, George and Marcia Deugan, of Ziyadah Kennels, imported their first Sussex. The Deugans raised German Shepherds and Golden Retrievers, but were looking for a smaller breed to show along with their other dogs. They became intrigued with the Sussex. "It seemed that the Sussex breed needed us," Marcia says. The first of the dogs arrived at Ziyadah in 1970 and the next year was joined by two others. Their first litter was born in 1972. Three other English imports have subsequently joined the Deugan household.

Since then, the Deugans have enjoyed much success with their Sussex Spaniels. Their Ch. Sedora Galega was the first American champion to be crowned since World War II. Always owner handled, Galega placed five times in the Group, a record for the breed at the time. Their Champion Oakmoss Witch, C.D. became the first female Sussex champion to earn an obedience title. In the past twenty years, the couple has owned or bred over 19 champions. Currently, 17 adults make their home at the Deugan's Ziyadah Kennels, in Bonita Springs, Florida. More important, however, is the attention they have drawn to the breed. They have started many new fanciers on the road to success with the Sussex.

"At present, there are about 206 Sussex in the U.S.," Marcia reports. "Only about 60 are of 'show' age—the rest being either too old or too young." Indeed, the breed is quite long lived. The oldest dog owned by the Deugans is now 15.

In 1981, the very first Sussex Spaniel Club of America was formed. It was just over one hundred years since the breed had first been recognized by the Ameri-

Group placing Ch. Ziyadah Black Tower. (Graham photo)

Quality endures! Ziyadah's Boyd Tarleton at 12 years of age. Owned by Marcia Deugan, Ziyadah Kennels, Reg.

can Kennel Club. It has not always been an easy road, though. " Due to the small breed base after World War II, there have been many problems in getting puppies. Females tend to skip seasons, abort or re-absorb litters. Puppies require much care when born. We have invested much time, effort and expense in trying to solve these problems, and finally things seem to be improving. "

The best way to describe a Sussex Spaniel is long, low and level. This dog's massive muscular body is borne on short, heavily boned legs. Dogs stand 13-15" at the shoulders, while bitches measure 12-14". The Sussex's body is twice as long as his height. The breed has a unique head which is broad and characterized by heavy brows. The hazel eyes radiate warmth and intelligence. The dropping ears are the longest of any of the spaniel breeds. The Sussex carries his head low, barely above the level of the back. Due to his short legged stature and body width, he has a slightly rolling gait. Fanciers often liken it to that of a "drunken sailor on dry land."

No Sussex chapter would be complete without mention of the breed's constantly wagging tail. C. Bede Maxwell aptly describes it as "the most active tail in dogdom!" Indeed, it has always been so. Baron v. Bylandt, in his classic 1905 book on dogs, specifically mentions the Sussex tail and its "beau movement de la queue."

It's difficult to describe the color of the Sussex's coat in words. Not even color photos do justice to it. It is a very rich golden liver, but with a decided burnished sheen. Some have called it a golden chestnut. It is absolutely unique and found in no other breed of dog. In her 1972 book, *The Truth About Sporting Dogs,* C. Bede Maxwell says "Sussex color is the badge, the glory, and should always be *golden.* It is not exactly the gold of a 'freshly-minted sovereign'...but rather of an *old*-minted sovereign, with patina to suit." Proper color is most important for, as we have seen, down through the centuries it has been the one absolute mark of purity. The Sussex's flat lying coat makes for easy care. Unlike so many other spaniels, the breed is never shaved or excessively trimmed.

"Sussex are a lovely breed," says Marcia Deugan. An intelligent breed, always eager to please, the Sussex makes an enviable companion. Idstone, writing in 1872, says that the breed has "extreme intelligence and entire freedom from any indication of frivolity." While the breed does have a reputation for innate dignity, the Sussex joyously entertains his owners. "They have an endearing habit of nose-wrinkling and talking back-woo, woo, wooing," Marcia Deugan says. "They also 'kipper,' which is walking around on their front legs with their rear legs out in back and dragging or just moving back and forth in this manner. When the two are done together, they present quite a sight."

Comfortable and loving with their owners, Sussex Spaniels are apt to be a bit reserved with strangers. "They are a very people loving dog. They do well only as members of the family," Marcia says. "They are quite like a Golden Retriever in temperament, but more reserved with strangers." Most Sussex, Marcia observes, prefer "to meet strangers on their own terms and in their own good time."

Writing in 1879, Vero Shaw remarked that "the Sussex is the Spaniel which of all others should occupy the place of honour in a book on dogs." How right he was! It's amazing that the breed has survived down through the centuries. Somehow he has managed to make it, due to the efforts of a few brave and wonderful pioneers. The future looks bright for the Sussex Spaniel, now that people are becoming better acquainted with the breed. May we always see this unique golden liver dog stride across the ring.

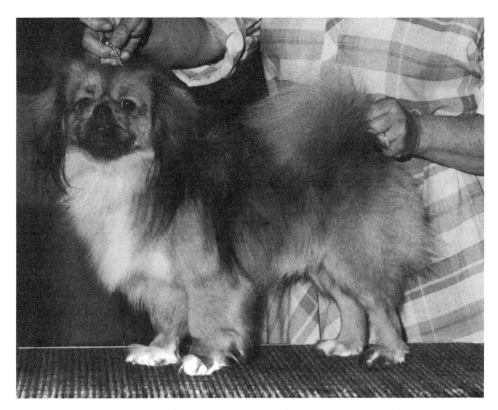

The lovely group placing Am. Can. Ch. Braeduke Pipa Northwood, owned by Pamela and David Bradbury, Northwood Kennels, of Grand Junction, Michigan. (Smith photo)

The beautiful parti-colored Tibetan Spaniel bitch, Ch. Northwoood The Magic Dragon. Puff is owned by Pamela and David Bradbury.

Chapter 32

The Tibetan Spaniel

"I consider Tibetan Spaniels to be absolutely ideal house pets," says Ann Rohrer. "They are really sensational little dogs. They are very, very loving. They bond closely with their owners and are extremely loyal. They want to be near you and enjoy sitting close by your side. One of the things that impresses me most is their intuitive understanding of their owner's moods. They have an almost uncanny ability to know when you want them to be near and when you'd rather be left alone. They are just perfect companions. In many ways these little dogs remind me of the larger Tibetan Mastiffs."

Ms. Rohrer should know since both Tibetan Spaniels and Mastiffs share her California home. She has also owned Tibetan Terriers. Ann's fascination with the Tibetan breeds dates back to the 1960's when she was posted to Nepal. From an early age, Ann found herself intrigued by the Orient. In the 1950s, she finally got the chance to see several Asian countries first-hand. As an officer in the Air Force and, later, an employee of the foreign aid program, she traveled throughout the continent. She lived and worked in Korea, Japan, Burma, Taiwan, Laos, Afghanistan and, of course, Nepal.

I'm always intrigued by Ann's stories of her travels. For an arm-chair traveler like me, her tales of exotic lands and their people are spellbinding. We collaborated on the 1989 book, *The Tibetan Mastiff, Legendary Guardian of the Himalayas,* and became fast friends. It was such a delight to vicariously share her experiences in Nepal. Ann made many friends among the large group of Tibetan refugees who had fled to Kathmandu, following the Communist Chinese take-over of their country. She found the Tibetans to be kind, cheerful and always charming. What interested me most, of course, were the stories of their dogs. The burly Tibetan Mastiffs which guarded monasteries and vil-

lages and could be seen accompanying the traders' pony trains. There were the little Lhasa Apsos that snuggled among multi-colored yarns, as Tibetan women worked at looms, in the rug factories. The sad Tibetan man, jailed and in dire need of money, who grieved when he sold his precious Tibetan Terrier to Ann. And, of course, the Tibetan Spaniels. I shared her excitement, on a trek to the Thangboche Monastery on the slopes of Mount Everest, when she chanced to see a little Tibetan Spaniel, carried in a basket strapped to his owner's back. And I smiled as she described a frantic Tibetan man racing through the streets, trying to corner his escaped black and tan Tibetan Spaniel.

The Tibetans in Nepal cherished their little Spaniels, according to Ann. "My Tibetan friends...referred to these dogs as *zim-kyi*, or 'bedroom dogs,'" she says. "The Tibetans treasured them, and they were not often seen loose in the villages. Although I tried, it was almost impossible to see a Tibetan Spaniel, much less acquire one. It took more than a year for me to get an invitation to the home of a Tibetan friend, just to see his dog. He wouldn't even consider selling her to me. As he put it, 'I might as well sell you one of my children.'"

One can see clearly, from this story, that the Tibetan people are uncommonly devoted to this breed. Indeed, the Tibetans have a long history of kind treatment to dogs. In fact, most view their dogs as good luck charms. This may stem from one of the stories of Buddha. In a triumph of love over violence, Buddha is said to have tamed a lion, who thereafter followed "at his heels like a faithful dog." Most Tibetans view their dogs as good luck charms and it's a special honor to receive one. Such gifts are generally reserved for traveling dignitaries, visiting monks or to insure safe passage on a difficult pilgrimage. The Tibetan calendar even includes a "year of the dog," which is also considered the "year of good harvests."

Tibetan life revolves around Buddhism, first introduced to the country in the 11th century. Before the Communist takeover, the Dalai Lama served as both the religious and secular leader of the country. He is still revered by Tibetans living under China's oppression. Almost every Tibetan village had a monastery, supported by contributions from the people. It was a common practice to present the monks with the best dogs and the smallest specimens were especially prized. It is for this reason that the most exquisite examples of the breed were found at monasteries. The breed was also a favorite with Tibet's wealthiest families. Visitors tell us that the 13th Dalai Lama was particularly fond of a pair of small Tibetan Spaniels.

Tibetan Spaniels were kept primarily as companions. "Owing to the constant society of human beings, these little dogs develop extraordinary intelligence and learn all kinds of little tricks," wrote Mrs. Geoffrey Hayes, in a 1932 issue of the British publication *Our Dogs*. "They hold the position of court jester in a country of few amusements." Indeed, an early story, circulated by those eager to promote the breed, held that the little dogs were trained to turn Tibetan prayer wheels bearing the script, "Omi padme om." A charming and colorful story, but one that we now realize is untrue.

The dogs, however, were more than mere ornaments. They also proved to be quite adept watchdogs. Often, they would position themselves on the monastery walls, keeping up a watch for intruders. With their keen eyes and acute hearing, they were often the first to sound the alarm. This alerted the very business-like Tibetan Mastiffs, stationed below in the courtyard. Ann Rohrer reports that this symbiotic partnership still continues. "Invariably, one of my four Tibetan Spaniels will perch on the back of a chair or sofa, keeping careful watch over outside activities. Should someone approach my driveway or veer too close to the fence, the alarm is sounded. Immediately, my Tibetan Mastiff, with her booming voice, and the other Tibetan Spaniels join in sounding the alert."

Nobody has conclusively pinned down the breed's origin. "The Tibetan spaniel is the *true* ancestor of all Pekinese *(sic)*, Japanese and English toy spaniels of that there really can be no doubt and as such they are doubly interesting," wrote Mrs. McLaren Morrison, the first western authority on Tibetan breeds. She may well have been right. Experts have long theorized on the link between Tibetan and Chinese dogs. We know that there was a long tradition of trade between the Tibetans and the Chinese. Often caravans travelled the arduous Silk Route and other byways linking the two countries. The Tibetans were required to pay tribute to the Chinese Emperor and it is reported that this practice continued

until 1905. No doubt dogs were included with the riches presented.

The testimony of Tibetans, themselves, supports the relationship between the dogs of both countries. Many early travelers to Tibet tell us that the people referred to the Tibetan Spaniel as a *Gyakyi* (*Gya* is the Tibetan word for "Chinese," while *kyi* means "dog"). Some early travelers also observed that the dogs found in monasteries near the Chinese border had shorter muzzles, while those found west of Lhasa had more natural length muzzles. This led them to speculate, probably correctly, that purer specimens of the breed were found in the regions to the west. We also know that the Tibetan Spaniel traveled to other countries via "tribute." Other Himalayan nations paid tribute to Tibet. In the late 1800's, Englishman John White obtained his first Tibetan Spaniel at the royal palace in Kathmandu. There, the dogs were known as Nepalese Palace Dogs.

Apparently, the first Tibetan Spaniels arrived in England in the late 1800's. Records indicate that, in 1898, Mrs. McLaren Morrison exhibited a pair of the dogs. Mr. John C. White, mentioned above, also returned with several Tibetan Spaniels. Unfortunately, these dogs had no lasting impact on the breed. In the 1920's, however, Dr. Greig, of Tibetan Terrier fame, acquired some little Tibetan Spaniels. She sent these dogs to her mother, in England, who began breeding and showing them. World War II, however, decimated the breed. Only one dog from the Greig breedings, *Skyid,* would remain to have an impact on British bloodlines.

Credit must go to Sir Edward and Lady Wakefield for re-establishing the breed in England. In 1938, the Wakefields received a Tibetan Spaniel bitch from the trade agent at Gartok, Tibet. This important bitch, *Mughiwuli,* produced two litters for the couple. Two of her progeny, *Gartok* and *Potala,* were retained by the Wakefields. Later, as a present from the Maharajah of Sikkim, they acquired a lovely bitch named *Dolma.* These dogs, together with *Skyid,* formed the basis for English Tibetan Spaniel bloodlines.

In later years, additional imports would infuse new blood into British lines. Mrs. Ann Wynyard, successful breeder and author of *Dogs of Tibet and the History of the Tibetan Spaniel,* managed to acquire a pair of litter sisters from Poona, India. Arriving in England in 1968, they established what Mrs. Wynyard calls the "Anglo-Indian" line.

An additional source of new blood was discovered, quite by accident. After seeing one of Ann Wynyard's advertisements in an issue of *Country Life,* Sue Hacker, then living in Nassau, contacted the British breeder. She informed Ann that she owned a Tibetan Spaniel bitch, *Honeybun,* acquired from a wealthy Chinese family living, while she was living in Hong Kong. A dog from Ann's kennel was soon on his way to Mrs. Hacker, to be bred to Honeybun. From this breed-

Am. International Ch. Northwood Tricky-Woo. Breeder/owner Pamela Bradbury.

ing, Mrs. Wynyard acquired a bitch puppy, who was to become *English Champion Ama Kuhla*. Mrs. Wynyard christened this her "Anglo-Chinese" line.

The first American litter of Tibetan Spaniels was born in 1965, bred by a Mr. Harrington, from stock acquired in Tibet. Unfortunately, nothing further was heard from these dogs. The breed got its real start when Leo Kearns, sexton of the Trinity Lutheran Church, in Connecticut, acquired *Doghouse Dream Baby*, in 1966. Two years later, he purchased *English Champion Yakrose Chiala of Amcross*. The dogs were bred and the first litter was whelped in 1968. The pups proved popular with the parishioners who purchased them, and Mr. Kearns imported a dozen other Tibetan Spaniels, in subsequent years.

In 1971, there was sufficient interest to organize The Tibetan Spaniel Club of America. The first specialty match was held the following year. Mrs. Jay Child is credited with exhibiting the first Tibetan Spaniel ever seen in an American show ring, when her *Ciceter Norbu* made its debut in 1971. Interest in the breed grew slowly but steadily and, in 1984, the American Kennel Club granted recognition to the breed.

The Tibetan Spaniel is unique and quite different in appearance from the other small Tibetan breeds. In fact, his outline and coat are more reminiscent of the Tibetan Mastiff. He stands on short, moderately boned legs and is slightly longer than tall. With his sensible length coat, this leaves a rectangle of daylight visible beneath his body. The front legs may be slightly bowed, but this should never be exaggerated. Tibetan Spaniels stand about 10 inches tall and weigh from 9-15 pounds.

The little dogs carry their head proudly, with a regal arrogance. Typically, the head is small in comparison with the body. The skull is slightly domed and the medium length muzzle is blunt, well cushioned and free of wrinkling. The oval-shaped eyes are dark brown and

the ideal bite is undershot.

The Tibetan Spaniel comes in a range of hues and may be either solid or parti-colored. The double coat is soft and silky and lies flat against the body. A mane accentuates the neck and shoulders. The tail, which curls over the back, is richly plumed.

Breeders wish to insure that the Tibetan Spaniel remains a natural breed. The standard includes the following note on presentation: "In the show ring it is essential that the Tibetan Spaniel be presented in an unaltered condition with the coat lying naturally with no teasing, parting or stylizing of the hair. Specimens where the coat has been altered by trimming, clipping or by artificial means shall be so severely penalized as to be effectively eliminated from competition. Dogs with such a long coat that there is no rectangle of daylight beneath, or so profuse that it obstructs the natural outline, are to be severely penalized. Whiskers are not to be removed. Hair growing between the pads of the underside of the feet may be trimmed for safety and cleanliness...."

"Tibetan Spaniels are very easy to groom," Ann Rohrer says. "The coat doesn't mat. They are well-feathered and only the hair behind the ears tends to tangle. It's so easy to take care of this because you can work it out with your fingers as you pet the dog. And the dogs are shown completely natural. You just brush the coat and fluff it up a little." The dogs do shed their undercoats annually. "Tibetan Spaniels are very clean dogs, by nature," Ann says. "They will often clean themselves like cats."

"To know them is to love them," Mrs. McLaren Morrison said in the early 1900's. Little has changed. "They are very affectionate, family-oriented dogs," Ann Rohrer observes. "They are real home bodies, not adventurers. They are sensitive dogs and must be treated kindly. They have long memories and will recall a past injustice. They are absolutely perfect with children. Babies are theirs, and they will hover as close as possible to them. They also seem to have a special affinity for older people."

Most Tibetan Spaniels are somewhat wary of strangers, which makes them ideal watchdogs. "It takes a few minutes for them to warm up to people," Ann reports. "Their response to strangers varies. Once they adjust, some are quite outgoing and want affection. Other dogs will totally ignore visitors."

As Ms. Rohrer has said, the Tibetan Spaniel bonds closely with owners and is utterly devoted to the family. It's a mutual arrangement for most owners are uncommonly devoted to their dogs. Fortunately, for lucky owners, the breed is hardy and long-lived. "They will often live into the late teens," Ann states, "and they seldom show their age." Indeed, the purchase of a Tibetan Spaniel promises to bring years and years of love. Each year, more and more Americans are discovering this enchanting Tibetan good luck charm.

The beauty of the Welsh Springer Spaniel. This is Ch. Tydaky's Wildfire, owned by Jennifer and Maurice Krohn. (Susan Riese photo)

The impressive Ch. Rysan's First Round Kayo was bred and is owned by Richard and Sandra Rohrbacher. (Susan Riese photo)

Chapter 33

The Welsh Springer Spaniel

It's as though Mother Nature took autumn's glowing red and splashed it on a canvas of pearly white. This striking combination, contrasted against the green of woods and fields, is a sight never to be forgotten. For hundreds of years, hunters have thrilled to the sight of red and white Welsh Springer Spaniels, eagerly quartering the fields ahead of them. Why, then, has this ancient dog, so undeniably beautiful, remained so rare?

In truth, the Welsh Springer Spaniel has suffered from comparison to other breeds. Due to the similarity of their breed names, the Welshman is often confused with the English Springer Spaniel. While the English Springer Spaniel is well known in show circles, where he often tops sporting groups and wins many Bests in Show, the Welsh has been largely ignored. His recognition by, and popularity among, the general public is scant in comparison to his English cousin. When writers begin their descriptions of the breed, they usually say that the Welsh is midway in size between the English Springer and the Cocker Spaniel. Such constant comparisons do not do the breed justice. The lovely Welshman is truly all his own breed, unique in type, color and personality.

Like the Sussex Spaniel, with his golden liver color, the hallmark of a Welshman is his red and white coat. Throughout the centuries, the breed has clung tenaciously to this essential characteristic. The color harks back to the very earliest days of all spaniels. Centuries ago, red and white was the predominate spaniel coloration, and dogs with this coat pattern have been known in the British Isles for more than 400 years. Dr. Johannes Caius, in *Englishe Dogges*, penned in 1570, says of Land Spaniels, "The most of their skynnes are white and if they be marked with any spottes they are commonly red." From the work of early authors and artists, we know that the red and white spaniels were widely dispersed throughout Britain.

By the 1700's and 1800's, however, things had begun to change. Liver colored and black and white spaniels became increasingly popular. Indeed, it seemed, in England proper, that the red and white dogs had almost disappeared, as new breeds captured the public fancy. The Clumber, the Cocker, the Sussex and the Field Spaniel were on the rise. Type was to change, too. With the advent of dog shows in England, in 1859, fanciers had a chance to look over many of these newly evolving breeds. "Long and low" became the watchword for many of the spaniels and, as competition flourished, breeds were altered to meet this new demand. Absurd fads swept the spaniel fraternity, as epitomized by the case of the Field Spaniel. Sportsmen decried these developments, insisting that many of these new long and low dogs couldn't hold their own in the field. Indeed, the active, quick, red and white dogs of ages past had been all but forgotten.

However, in the outlying districts of the British Isles, the red and whites had not been forgotten. This was particularly true in Wales. Hunters in the Neath Valley, in South Wales, had used red and white spaniels for centuries. Many families in this area maintained their own kennels of field dogs, passed on from father to son for generations. The Welsh red and whites, known locally as "Starters," were all-round gundogs, capable of working on birds, ducks or rabbits. They also proved to be splendid companions, watchdogs and playmates for generations of Welsh children.

Who can say how long the Starter would have remained an obscure dog, known only to those who ventured to the Welsh valleys? All this was to change, however, in the late 1800's. Sportsmen, angered by the developments in spaniel breeding in England, formed The Sporting Spaniel Society. It was their aim to encourage and maintain the spaniel as a true working dog and to counter the excesses produced by the show ring. A number of influential dog men joined the club and, because of their standing, they persuaded several clubs to offer classes specifically for "working type spaniels."

A new star burst on the scene. The setting was the Birmingham show in December of 1899. Mr. Purcell Llewellin, the dean of field winning English Setters, judged an entry of 24 working spaniels. A magnificent red and white male, entered as a Welsh Cocker, caught his eye. He awarded Corrin, owned by Mr. A.T. Williams first place. This success was quickly followed by other notable wins. Corrin blazed a remarkable trail in subsequent shows and soon all England was talking about him. He came to be considered the very best of all working type spaniels in the country.

Naturally, Corrin's success did much to pique interest in the red and white Welsh dogs. Where did this splendid dog come from, fanciers wondered? Mr. A. T. Williams, of Ynisygerwn, located in Wales' Neath Valley, was able to supply the answers. Ownership of

these dogs had been a Williams family tradition. Corrin's owner could trace his family's involvement with the breed back to 1750. In articles, published in England's leading papers, he told an eager audience that his grandfather, in the years 1805-1850, had personally trained and hunted with a team of 12-14 dogs. His father kept a team of eight dogs, with which he continually hunted, from 1845 to 1894. In his kennels, Mr. Williams kept three to eight dogs for hunting. It should be pointed out that the Welsh red and whites could also be found in other Neath Valley kennels. However, because of Mr. Williams' writings on the breed, and Corrin's achievements, his dogs garnered much attention. Indeed, it was Mr. Williams who would become known as the "father" of the breed.

Eager to learn more, sportsmen journeyed to Wales to see Mr. Williams' dogs and those of other breeders. Baron Jaubert, after one such visit, recalled his experiences in the *Illustrated Kennel News*. "We had an opportunity of seeing these spaniels hunt the steep slopes of the Neath Valley. The ground was a bed of matted bracken, which hid completely the fallen stones, and made walking very difficult. In a country like this the two teams we saw in the field trials worked for six consecutive hours. The dogs swarmed round their men as lightly and gaily as if in a stubble-field; they showed as much energy at the close of the day as they had done

A lovely Welshie head. This is Pat Pencak's Goldsprings Kopper.

at the beginning. They proved themselves to possess excellent noses and great keenness. They reconciled—a necessary point in teams—the greatest activity with perfect immobility at the flushing of game or the sound of a gun. The sixty-six head of game to four guns certainly gave us more pleasure than four hundred head would at a battue. We began the day with the...prize winner Corrin, who, despite his ten years, showed an energy and a dash as great as those of the puppies—a proof that the breed is sound."

A clamor arose to have the breed recognized. There was much heated debate, for the established spaniel community did not welcome

Cwrt Afon Deri typifies the breed's sweet expression. This charmer is owned by Pat Pencak, Meadow Way Welsh, Sparrow Bush, New York.

this newcomer. Many spoke out in support of the Starter, though. After visiting several kennels, Baron Jaubert wrote, "...their kennels confirmed my impression that they were a distinct variety, very consistent in type, very uniform, and sharply defined by shape and coat...." With the sponsorship of Mr. Williams, other Welsh breeders and the members of The Sporting Spaniel Society, the breed was finally recognized in 1902. It was christened the Welsh Springer Spaniel. Corrin continued to win under the new breed name. He earned his championship at the esteemed Crystal Palace show.

We do not know precisely when the first Welsh Springer Spaniel came to this country. Evidence, however, points to an introduction some time in the early 1700's. The author of *A Sportsman's Companion,* the first dog book written in this country, describes his favorite type of spaniel thusly: "They are commonly red and white....have a resemblance to the Setters, but not so large, though much larger than the little spaniels (cocking) with a fan-tail and pretty large ears: This kind of Doge ranges well, and will make a sudden stand, or short pause on point, and, as you come up, bounce in upon and spring the game." Artistic evidence confirms the existence of these dogs, in America, at this early date, too. A painting, by Justus Kuhn, done in 1712

pictures six-year-old Eleanor Darnell with her red and white spaniel.

The American Kennel Club recognized the Welsh Springer in 1906. It was some time later when they added "Spaniel" to the breed's official name. Despite the 1906 recognition, it was not until 1914 that the first members of the breed were registered. Faircroft Bob, owned by Missouri resident Harry B. Hawes, had the honor of being the first dog admitted to the A.K.C.'s registry. Mr. Hawes registered six Welsh Springers over the next few years. A few other dogs came to this country, but breed progress was very slow.

In 1950, however, an event occurred which was to give great impetus to the breed here. Dorothy H. Ellis, owner of Downland Kennels, in St. Mary's, Brambee, Sussex, England, made a crucial decision. She had learned that the Westminster Kennel Club had decided to waive it's usual regulation requiring all dogs entered to have won a blue ribbon at an A.K.C. show. They would allow puppies, who had never before been shown to enter. She decided to bring several of her young dogs to the United States. The British press quickly picked up the story and, as Miss Ellis arrived at the airport, she was greeted by reporters. After a grueling twenty hour journey, with stopovers in Ireland and Canada, she arrived in New York.

Meghen Riese cuddles one of the puppies born at her parents' Statesman Kennels, in Lithia Springs, Georgia.

Dorothy and her dogs checked into a hotel. "Just as soon as we were settled in," she recalled, in the 1967 Yearbook of the Welsh Springer Spaniel Club, "swarms of newspaper men came round, asking questions and flashing their cameras and it was not until I read their reports the following day that I understood why so much attention was being given. I was the first exhibitor from Britain since the war! It appears that the British Embassy was making sure that I sold my dogs and brought my dollars back to England, and a splendid job they did!"

The newspaper articles brought much attention to Mrs. Ellis and her contingent of Welsh dogs. A television appearance followed and, by the time Westminster began, Dorothy and her dogs were celebrities. Ambassador of Downland won Best of Breed and was rousingly applauded as he strode across the group ring. As Mrs. Ellis says, his appearance "created a sensation."

Mrs. Ellis stayed to show her dogs at the Hartford and Boston shows. These puppies soon found their way to American homes. Indeed, it was Miss Ellis' spur of the moment decision, to compete at Westminster, that is credited with reviving interest in the breed. Soon other imports followed and a small but enthusiastic group of fans took an interest in the Welsh Springer Spaniel. By 1964, there were more than 20 families who owned the red and white dogs. In 1964, they banded together to form the Welsh Springer Spaniel Club of America.

Since then, the breed has grown slowly and steadily. While the breed is still too often overlooked in group judging, some Welsh have made their presence felt. Perhaps it is because of their small numbers, that the breed teems with quality. The American breeders who have carried forth the Welsh banner are to be congratulated. At times, theirs has been a lonely vigil.

The Welsh Springer Spaniel is a strong compact dog built for field work. He must be lively and active, yet have great endurance. His moderate body length should balance nicely with the length of leg. His loin should be muscular and slightly arched. His lightly feathered tail is set on low and never carried above the level of the back. The Welsh stands about 18-19 inches at the withers. Since the earliest times, the coat has been a distinctive breed characteristic. It should always be a dark, rich red and white. The thick coat lies flat and has a silky texture.

The Welshman's head is a distinctive attribute and clearly sets it apart from the English Springer. It is of moderate length with a slightly domed skull and well defined stop. The eyes are hazel or dark. The ideal Welsh head is shallow flewed and slightly tapered, but should never be snipey. The end of the muzzle should always be squared. This breed belongs to the group of short eared spaniels. The ears are set on low and well feathered.

Writing in 1904, Mr. A. T. Williams, the father of the breed, said that the Welsh at "the mere sight of a gun, instantly brims over with delight. His greatest pleasure is to set to work immediately, and force out for the gun whatever there may be in the shape of game or

Ch. Loch-Haven's RD Rudy is the much loved companion of Elsie J. Bowles, of Rockwood, Tennessee.

190

rabbits." While most Welsh Springer Spaniels are kept as companions today, those who do take to the field with their dogs, can well appreciate Mr. Williams' comments. The breed still possesses the eager enthusiasm of those original dogs.

The breed wins high praise for his keen nose and little escapes his attention. He is suited to all types of terrain, with his sure footedness and his coat to protect him from briars and brambles. His coat color makes him easy to spot, even in dense thickets, and his tail is an indicator of the proximity of game. Inevitably, it wags faster and faster when he has found something. He is a rather close worker, but what he lacks in speed, he makes up for in thoroughness. The Welsh Springer is an all-round gun dog, that may be used on birds of all kinds as well as small game, such as rabbits. He has also proved adept at water work and most dogs of this breed will even enter icy water willingly. The breed is known for its great endurance and chances are you'll be ready to call it quits long before your dog is.

Due to his genuine love of hunting, the Welshman, if not properly schooled, is apt to become a lone hunter. Some have said that the Welsh is more headstrong and difficult to train than the English Springer. Those who have actually used the breed, however, take exception to this. In his lovely 1977 book, *The Welsh Springer Spaniel*, William Pferd III includes the comments of long time Welsh breeder Jack Dumbleton. "I'm not a fancy hunter," Mr. Dumbleton says. "I do it for leisurely enjoyment and I train my own dogs. I think the Welshman is a very easy dog to train if you set up a routine and spend a little time at it each day." True to his spaniel heritage, the Welsh requires a firm, but kind, hand. As with his other relatives, he resents harsh treatment.

Australian sporting dog authority Roy B. Burnett writes of the breed, in his 1973 book *Gundogs for Field or Trial*. He says that "if handled correctly, a Welsh springer spaniel, although somewhat more headstrong than an English springer, will make an even more spectacular worker because of his animated interest in game. Because the breed is excellent in water work and capable of handling rough terrain, it is a puzzle to me why the breed did not 'invade' Australia and become a most popular breed." One must wonder, as well, why the Welsh did not become more popular here.

Writing in the *American Kennel Gazette,* in 1977, the esteemed writer and judge C. Bede Maxwell says that "Welsh Springers are...rich in character. They are Celts to the heart and incline to the unruly in youth,

The extraordinarily beautiful Ch. Statesman's Exuberance, SH. Exuberance was bred by Gary and Susan Riese and is owned by Bill and Peggy Ruble. (Susan Riese photo)

but mellow with years. They are happy, as the continual activity of their tails can prove." Indeed, that tail does wag endlessly and the Welsh Springer seems to delight in all around him. He is an intelligent dog, who becomes very devoted to his family and makes a good watchdog. The breed is known for its gentleness and kindness with children, which he will joyously play with for hours on end. A proper Welsh Springer Spaniel demonstrates the characteristic merry spaniel temperament. He gets along well with other dogs and family pets. An aggressive temperament should not be seen and never excused.

With his handy size and vigorous, hardy nature, the Welsh Springer Spaniel is equally suited to city or country life. This is a charming breed, with a zest for life, and it's a shame that the Welshman isn't more widely known and appreciated. As Mr. Williams wrote, in 1903, "there is no better, nor more amiable and trustworthy companion and friend." Present day Welsh Springer Spaniel owners would certainly agree.

A wonderful family portrait. These rare Griffons are Fraulein von Herrenhausen, Ch. Sampson von Herrenhausen, Kalispell Ingo vom Glacier and Falcon von Herrenhausen. (Photo courtesy of Therese Good.)

Chapter 34

The Wirehaired Pointing Griffon

The Wirehaired Pointing Griffon is the rarest of the sporting dogs recognized by the American Kennel Club. And yet, the Griff, as the breed is commonly called, is one of the most talented members of the group. It seems incongruous that he should be so little known, for the Griff was the first of the European utility sporting dogs to make an appearance in the U.S. While the German Shorthaired Pointer, the Vizsla, the Weimaraner and, to a lesser extent, the German Wirehaired Pointer, have all attracted enthusiastic audiences, the Griff has remained elusive and little known. Show ring appearances are so rare that many judges have never seen a Griff. The breed is often shunned and even maligned by the field trial fraternity. And yet, those who have had a chance to work with the breed are uncommonly devoted to the Griff. They know that hidden beneath that scruffy exterior, lies a veritable treasure of a dog. And, slowly, largely by word of mouth, many are coming to recognize the Wirehaired Pointing Griffon as a superb all-round gundog and companion.

The story of the Wirehaired Pointing Griffon is also the story of a remarkable man, Eduard Karel Korthals. It is the story of a dream that took twenty-two years to reach fruition. Korthals faced many obstacles in achieving his goal. His family, unsympathetic to his dream, all but disowned him. He was forced to move to France, and later to Germany, to support himself and continue his work with his dogs. Bird dog owners often scoffed at his claims and attempted to denigrate his work. Then, when he had attained his goal, political implications threatened to thwart him once again. And yet he persevered, tenaciously adhering to his strict principles and never losing sight of his dream. In the end, he was vindicated. Whenever we see a Wirehaired Pointing Griffon staunchly on point, every muscle quivering, or watch one of these dogs plunge joyfully into an icy lake, we should say a silent prayer of thanks to one of dogdom's most remarkable individuals.

Eduard Korthals was Dutch by birth. At his home in Scooten, near Haarlem, his father was a wealthy banker. In his spare time, Korthals senior engaged in cattle breeding. As the scion of a well to do family, young Eduard had plenty of opportunity to indulge his passion...hunting. The area around his home was rich with game, found both in open pastures and woodlands. There was plenty of opportunity for waterfowl hunting, too, in the lowlands. It's reasonable to assume that Eduard often traveled to Belgium, France and Germany, to pursue his avocation. Indeed, hunting and dogs seemed to be all that interested the young Dutchman. He had little enthusiasm for either banking or raising cattle, which caused much friction between father and son.

Young Eduard became intrigued with the idea of creating a new sporting breed. The dog he envisioned would have a keen nose, soft mouth and great endurance. He wanted a single dog that could satisfy all a sportsman's needs, whether he chose to pursue upland game or hunt waterfowl. It was imperative that this new dog have a hard coat to protect him from cold water and dense brush. Of all the breeds that he saw (remember that the British Pointers and Setters were well known on the Continent during that period), the one that most interested Eduard was the French griffon. And so, based on this old French dog, Korthals determined, in 1873, to begin work on creating his conception of the ideal sporting dog.

To fully appreciate Eduard Korthals' decision, we must look at the events which were taking place among hunters, in France and Germany, at that time. Wealthy men had always indulged their fondness for hunting. In the 1870's, there was a great surge of interest in all-round hunting dogs. In Germany, sportsmen had begun to fashion dogs that would later become known as the German Shorthaired and Wirehaired Pointers. There was much interest in the old griffon breeds in France. Sportsmen feared that these great dogs would lapse into extinction. Most of the French griffons were being used as hounds, but some hunters had become interested in using them as bird dogs. In 1872, a wealthy merchant from Elbeuf, Emmanuel Boulet, set out to fashion such a gundog. In later years the breed he created, based on the griffon, would become known worldwide as the Woolyhaired Griffon. In France it is known as the *Griffon á poil laineux-Boulet*. The famous industrialist, A. Guerlain, of Crotoy, worked to evolve the *Griffon d'arrêt Picard*. Among the griffon hound advocates, Count Christian d'Elva began to work with the Grand Basset Griffon Vendéen. The work of these gentleman, with their desire to construct breeds which bred true to type, was no doubt also fueled by the new French interest in dog shows. The first had been held just a few short years before, in 1863, and the shows became pleasant gathering places to see dogs and exchange ideas.

It is evident that Eduard Korthals was influenced by the great excitement of this period. In 1874, he acquired a seven year old bitch named Mouche, from M.G. Armand, of Amsterdam. There were no stud books and so no verifiable pedigrees at the time, but Korthals described the gray and brown bitch as a griffon. He was impressed with Mouche's keen field performance and set about building his breeding program around her. During the next three years, he acquired five other dogs in northern France and Belgium. Janus had a softer, woolly type coat, Junon was shorthaired and Hector, Satan and Banco were all rough-coated. He was ready to begin his initial breedings. The first really significant breeding was when Korthals mated Huzar (Janus x Mouche) to Junon. From this breeding came Trouvee, a very hard coated bitch, who was tremendous in the field. Bred to Banco she produced an outstanding litter. Eduard retained three littermates from this breeding—Moustache I, Querida and Lina—and they became known as the fountainheads of his breeding program.

But a storm was brewing at home. Eduard's father had become increasingly distressed with his son's obsession with hunting and dogs. He banished him from the family home and the young man made his way to France. While it must have seemed a disaster at the time, the move actually proved a boon to Korthals' newly evolving breed. In France, he found employment as the advance agent for a nobleman, the Duke of Penthievre. In his new job, Korthals had a chance to travel throughout the country and abroad. It also allowed him plenty of time for hunting. Wherever he went, he championed his new breed to other sportsmen and word of his grand experiment spread. He was unstinting in his quest for excellence. All puppies were tested, in the field, at nine months of age. Those who didn't live up to Korthals' demanding criteria, were destroyed.

Around 1879, Eduard Korthals moved to Biebesheim, Germany. He accepted a position as kennelmaster for the noted sportsman, Prince Albrect zu Solms-Brauenfels, a member of the royal house of Hanover. Prince zu Solms was widely known as an accomplished hunter. His kennels were said to house Germany's finest collection of Pointers and Setters. He was deeply involved with the development of the German Shorthaired Pointer. In the early 1870's, German hunters had set out to produce an all-round field dog and Prince zu Solms aided them in their efforts. But, for a time, the German breeders became more interested in looks than field ability. The Prince urged that breeders concentrate on field work, telling them that this was the only way they could arrive at the birdy, versatile dog they wanted. As Bede Maxwell says in the 1982 book, *The New German Shorthaired Pointer*, "He gave breeders a direction best now ... translated into the familiar 'form follows function.' He told them that the only way to develop the wished-for utility dog-of-all-virtues was to take and use only the dogs who performed best in these requirements, not

Fritz, owned by Mark Hoge, of Eugene, Oregon, on point. (Photo courtesy of Barbara Smith.)

One of Terri Good's Griffons hunting near her home in Ravalli, Montana.

to worry at this early stage about outward appearances. These would with time take care of themselves." While a few breeders followed his advice, most cast aside his admonitions. And when many of the early dogs performed poorly in the field, the Prince abandoned his interest in the breed.

It is easy to see, therefore, why such respect and friendship developed between Eduard Korthals and Prince zu Solms. They were kindred spirits, with the same ideas about the formation of a new breed of hunting dog. Eduard was pleased with the results of his breeding program, but the dogs were getting a bit inbred. It was time for new blood. He purchased a bitch, Donna, with a rather longer and softer coat than the one that he hoped to develop. She was, however, an excellent field dog with many of the working qualities that he aimed for. She was bred twice to Moustache I, and two of her daughters, Augot and Clairette, proved ideal representatives of the new breed. Six years later, Korthals leased a bitch, Vesta, to incorporate into the strain. Vesta proved dominant for her hard, rough coat and passed it along to all of her descendants. The seven dogs Korthals used in his breeding program would become known as the "Korthals Patriarchs."

In 1887, Korthals composed the first standard for the breed. The following year there was sufficient interest in the new dogs to form the International Grif-

fon Club, which Eduard headed. The Club decreed that only those dogs who could trace their ancestry directly to the seven Patriarchs would be deemed purebred. The popularity of the *Griffon d' arrêt á poil dur*, as Korthals had dubbed the breed, spread. In 1895, German and Belgian clubs for the breed were established and a French club soon followed. It was not all easy going, though. In Germany, Korthals met great resistance, and petty politics almost held up recognition of his new breed.

When Korthals approached the German Canine Board to seek recognition of the breed, a great controversy arose. Germany had recently lost the Franco-German war, which concluded in 1871, and there was much animosity toward the French. Then, here came Korthals, asking them to recognize a breed with a profoundly French name, although part of its development had taken place in Germany. Why not call the breed the German Pointer or the Korthals Pointer, the Board suggested? Absolutely not, Korthals said. The breed was entirely based on the French griffons and was not of German lineage. He was offered the option of changing the breed's name or foregoing recognition. Korthals had come a long way and he firmly believed that the proper name for his creation should be the *Griffon d' arrêt á poil dur*. He was adamant.

No doubt Korthals' stubbornness provoked the ire of many a nationalistic German. A vigorous campaign of disparagement began. Rumors and letters to sporting papers declared that Korthals' dogs were not purebred and certainly not griffons. The only way he could have produced such remarkable field dogs, critics argued, was with a continual infusion of new blood. Korthals tried to ignore the rumors, but, finally, in 1888, he took pen in hand to answer his critics. His gentlemanly letter, remarkable considering the pressures that threatened to engulf him, appeared in a German magazine.

"Sir, In answer to numerous letters in various newspapers, wherein the honorable writers express a belief that my *Griffons d'arrêt a poil dur* are not purebred, but are produced by a series of admixtures, I feel I must declare afresh that I have always been careful to preserve the breed in absolute purity, and that in breeding nothing but *Griffons d'arrêt* I have never introduced the blood of any other breed. I trust, sir, that this communication will suffice to dispel the doubt which seems to exist concerning the purity of my *Griffons d'arrêt a poil dur,* whose advancement is achieved by selection, training and method of upbringing."

The controversy continued to swirl. But, while the German dog owning bureaucracy debated the issue, the dogs continued to ply their trade in the field. And people were impressed. The Count of Flanders purchased one of Korthals' dogs. The Grand Duke of Russia purchased a number of Griffs. As word spread of the dog's field prowess, the Germans relented at last. In fact, the German Emperor commissioned a special medal and personally presented it to Eduard Korthals, acknowledging his success in creating a useful new breed. In 1896, Korthals died, but he went to his grave knowing that he had achieved his long held dream. To honor him, many countries assigned the breed the name of Korthals Griffon.

The Wirehaired Pointing Griffon was first exhibited in England in 1888. It was often the practice, in the years before the quarantine was enacted, for German dog lovers to exhibit their breeds in Great Britain. The catalog of the Barn Elms show indicates that those first Griffs were owned by none other than Prince zu Solms and the entry identified the dogs as "late the property of M. Korthals." From this we can see how fully the Prince had embraced Korthals' creation.

The first Griff to be imported to this country was a bitch named Zolette who was registered in 1887. Unsure of how to classify this new breed, the A.K.C. registered her as a "Russian Setter (Griffon)." Zolette traced her ancestry directly to the Korthals Patriarchs. In the early 1900's, more Griffs were imported into both this country and Canada. French Canadians, with their strong ties to France, where the Griff was extremely popular, were great supporters of the breed. By 1916,

the Griff sported an entry of sixteen at the Westminster Kennel Club. Shortly thereafter, the Wirehaired Pointing Griffon Club of America was formed and an official standard was adopted. Breed progress was still slow, but received a boost after World War II. Many soldiers had a chance to see the dogs in action, in Europe, and brought Griffs with them upon returning home.

From the start, there was some controversy regarding this new import. Among private hunters, the breed was appreciated for its excellent field performance. Magazines of the day applauded the Griff because of his "reputation under the gun." One stated that "it is a rugged and prolific breed, a bold, strong dog of decided character, notable for his faithfulness, his devotion to his master, his intelligence and great sagacity, his endurance, and his all-round utility."

Among the traditional field trial fraternity, used to hunting with the far-ranging Pointers and Setters, though, the all-round abilities of the Griff were not appreciated. In fact, notable bird dog men were absolutely amazed that the comparatively slow paced Griff was attracting such attention. Totally unable to fathom the desire of the average hunter for a jack-of-all-trades, they denigrated his performance. Leading the charge against the Griff was A.F. Hochwalt, one of America's leading sporting writers and an authority on bird dogs who is best remembered for his books *The Modern Pointer* and *The Modern Setter.*

After viewing the dogs in the field, Hochwalt granted that their water work was good. But if you want a water dog, he asserted, why not get a Labrador or a Chesapeake? As for field work, "it would never please the man," Hochwalt said, "who has hunted the big open country of the south on horseback" nor those who hunt "the lordly prairie chicken on the wide plains."

Hochwalt and his ilk, the field trial men of the era, were totally unable to conceive of a non-specialist dog. It confounded them that the general public joyously adopted the Griff, eager for a dog that they could follow afoot. "The Wirehaired Pointing Griffon is not suited to field trial competition," he wrote, "unless it can be improved by selection and mating to the best and fastest and most stylish of the field dogs."

Speaking of Hochwalt's comments, esteemed sporting dog writer Bede Maxwell says in her wonderful 1972 work, *The Truth About Sporting Dogs,* "It is to laugh at were one not the more disposed to cry. Who *wanted* the versatility bred into the European? Practical hunting men did, all skills in one dog to feed. Field trial pressure toward specialization, turning back the clock, narrowed aims, so that nowadays judges complain (in print)...that many dogs under judgement do not swerve to hunt cover; pressure of whip, shot, electronic jolts in training condition them only to keep going, avoid search

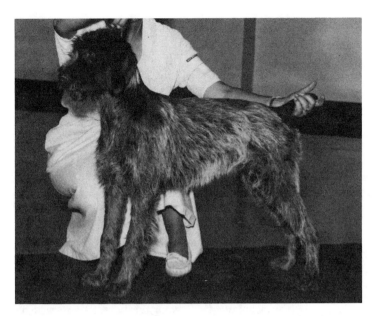

An impressive six month old puppy owned by Therese Good.

in likely places where birds may be, finding virtually only those they fall over or blunder into at the gallop."

It has been over a century since Eduard Korthals fashioned his versatile hunting dog. And yet, the Wirehaired Pointing Griffon still retains, in abundance, those qualities that the young Dutchmen first dreamed about. Today's Griff is an eager, hard working gundog, quite adept at scouting for and pointing upland game. Staunch on point, the Griff marks falls well and handily returns the bird to the waiting hunter. Those who hunt waterfowl, find much to admire about the breed. The Griff's steel-wool outer coat and dense soft undercoat grant him virtual impunity against cold weather, icy water and dense cover. Brushy land, that would thwart the average Pointer and Setter, is just the Griff's metier.

The Griff has long been damned for his slow pace. But, for the average hunter who doesn't want to take to the fields astride a horse, this slower pace is ideal. And, what the Griff lacks in speed, he more than makes up for in thoroughness. He may be slow, but he's deliberate and nothing escapes his attention. Generally, the Griff stays within shotgun range. This easy pace has other advantages. Since the owner stays in close contact with his dog, it is easy for him to control and manage the Griff, casually training him to the hunter's ideal.

Another valuable advantage of the breed is its wonderful temperament. As John Falk says in his 1976 book, *The Complete Guide to Bird Dog Training,* "By and large, the griff is so eager to please that he will practically knock himself out for a few words of praise, a pat on the head, and a bit of affectionate encouragement. Finding a hunting breed that seeks a closer relationship with master and family would be difficult indeed."

Used primarily as a meat-and-potatoes hunter, revered by the person interested in filling the hunting pouch, the Griff's style really isn't suited to traditional field trials. He lacks the speed, style and dash of the Pointers and Setters. Griffoniers, as fans of the breed call themselves, have managed to find other ways to demonstrate their dogs abilities. Trials run by the North American Versatile Hunting Dog Association (NAVHDA) are patterned after competitions held, in Europe, especially for versatile breeds. The Wirehaired Pointing Griffon has made quite a name for himself in such outings, often winning top honors in his class.

Kalispell Ingo Vom Glacier, owned by enthusiastic Griffonier Therese Good, of Ravalli, Montana, has been a star performer in NAVHDA trials. Terri and her husband are avid hunters and Kalie, as she's known, has more than earned their respect. "Our dogs are expected to earn their keep," Terri says. "The Griff's natural pace is slower," Terri admits, "but that's what attracted me to the breed in the first place. My German Shorthaired Pointer was always three mountain ranges ahead of me. Sometimes, by the time I arrived on the scene, the birds had already taken flight. I knew that I wanted a closer working dog."

Mrs. Good perused books, looking for details about various breeds of bird dogs. "There was a description of the Wirehaired Pointing Griffon. It wasn't very flattering. It said this breed certainly wouldn't win any beauty contests. That didn't deter me, I was interested in performance. When it described the breed's hunting ability, it said something about the dogs being so slow they were only good for people on crutches or cripples," Terri laughs. "This must be the breed for me, I thought."

Their Kalie has more than lived up to Terri Good's wishes. She has proven to be an able, adaptable hunter. In addition to her accomplishments in NAVHDA trials, she has proven the versatility of the breed. On a game preserve frequented by the Goods, Kalie pointed and retrieved to hand twelve pheasants in a two hour outing. She often accompanies them on duck hunts, where she waits patiently beside her owners in a blind. On a five day trip recently, she hunted both pheasants and geese.

"Some breeds are one-man dogs," Terri says. "They will only hunt for their master. We have found that the Griff isn't like that. Recently, a friend of ours wanted to hunt at a special game preserve. The only hitch was that dogs were required. We took along Kalie and a Vizsla. Kalie worked with the other hunter, although she'd never been out in the field with him before. Our dogs are trained to retrieve to hand with a 'fetch' command. We told the friend to give Kalie the 'fetch' command and, sure enough, she delivered the birds directly to him.

"Another thing we like about the Griff is that they mix very well with other breeds in the field. There are some breeds that just don't do this. You'll end up with fights. But, the Griff's very easy going and we've had no trouble running our dogs with other breeds.

"The Griff is a very hard working gundog, with tremendous desire" Terri says. "Recently, we went to Washington for a NAVHDA trial. The day before the meet, Kalie cut her foot on something. We had a devil of a time locating a veterinarian. Finally, on the vet's front lawn, he treated Kalie. He shaved the area, gave her antibiotic shots, administered a local anesthetic and stitched up her foot. The whole operation took about twenty minutes and all the time, she just stood stoically until he was through. The vet couldn't believe how calm and easy going she was. We feared that she wouldn't be able to participate in the trial, but we thought we'd give it a try. The next day, she hunted like a fiend and placed second in her class."

"The temperament and personality of the Griff can only be described as unique," says Barbara Young-Smith, President of the American Korthals Griffon Association. "Some people like to call him a clown, others a little old man with a sense of humor. He certainly has a high degree of intelligence, and most people feel he understands every word they say. That is why most Griffon owners rarely have another kind of dog. They've been bitten by the beard."

All Griff owners are united in agreement that the Wirehaired Pointing Griffon makes a pleasant and entertaining home companion. "Griffs get along very well with people and enjoy kids," Terri Good says. "They are great companions, being very gentle and responsive. Some breeds are one-man dogs who will respond only to the person that feeds them. The Griff's not at all like that. They are true family dogs and the more people in the family the better they like it."

"The Griffon is extremely affectionate and devoted to his family, but can be a watch dog if called upon," Barbara Young-Smith, of Eugene, Oregon, says. A quality which makes the breed such a charming companion is its almost insatiable desire to please. This attribute makes the Griff an extremely easy dog to train. As John Falk says, this breed "devotes every blessed ounce of himself to a single goal: Pleasing the man who owns him. For, temperamentally, the griff is like nothing so much as an overgrown kid, starved for affection, and, literally breaking his neck at every chance, in order

The versatile Am. Can. Ch. Baron von Herrenhausen makes his home with Barbara and Mark Smith, in Eugene, Oregon.

to win his 'hero's' approval." It's a good bet that, should you acquire a Griff, your dog won't be starved for affection. That's because the breed is just so darned much fun to have around.

When buying a puppy, Terri Good suggests that you ask breeders for information on temperament. "In general, the temperaments in this breed are wonderful," Terri says. "But, there are variations. Some breeders prefer a bolder temperament. Personally, I like a softer dog. The more you can tell the breeder about your lifestyle and what you want in a dog, the better. That will assist him in matching you up with a puppy of the right temperament."

Most books, describing the Wirehaired Pointing Griffon, start off with the statement that this breed won't win any beauty contests. Perhaps it's the general disdain for wire-coats, but I find the bewhiskered, moustached breed attractive. Males generally stand 21 1/2 to 23 1/2 inches and females must be between 19 1/2 and 21 1/2 inches. Weights generally run between 50-65 pounds. The Griff is moderate in his proportions, a little longer than he is tall. He must convey an impression of vigor combined with power. His long head is trimmed with an abundant moustache, and his yellow or light brown eyes peer out from beneath his bushy eyebrows. His well muscled body ends in a docked tail which is carried either straight out or raised.

The Griff's coat is one of the breed's distinctive characteristics and, since it affects his work, great emphasis is placed upon it. In color, the Griff may be steel gray with chestnut patches, a grayish white with chestnut or dirty white mixed with chestnut. He should never have black markings. The undercoat is soft and downy and is capped by a hard, dry, stiff topcoat. Fanciers liken this steely jacket to the bristles of a wild boar. Proper texture is of great importance. A Griff with a good hard coat will pick up but few burrs and thorns when hunting. A soft coat is a magnet for any foreign matter that the dog brushes against.

Grooming the Wirehaired Pointing Griffon is a snap. A weekly brushing will keep the pet's coat in prime condition. And, even without this, your Griff will probably look fine. Those who use their dogs for hunting, should give the coat a once over when they return home. This will ensure that nothing has stuck or lodged in the coat. There is no trimming or primping with the Griff. The scruffy, unkempt look is precisely what's desired in the breed.

The Wirehaired Pointing Griffon is rarely seen in show rings in this country. Now, however, some enterprising Griffioniers, including Terri Good, are beginning to change that. Hunting is still of prime importance to Terri, but last year she decided to give the show ring a try. She was one of five owners who participated in the 1991 Westminster Kennel Club show. The small band of Griffoniers rented a Greyhound bus, removed some of the seats, loaded their eight dogs and headed for the Big Apple.

"We wanted people to have a look first-hand at the Griff," Terri says. "What's impressive about the dogs we took along is that all are truly hunting dogs. Seven of the dogs have earned and won prizes in NAVHDA trials. The eighth dog, owned by a Canadian, hunts regularly but hasn't yet gotten to a NAVHDA trial. It's going to be entered in one this fall. We wanted to prove that we had versatile dogs who were hunting dogs first and foremost, but could also compete in the show ring. I daresay that my Kalie was probably the only dog there posed with a 'whoa' command."

Many people came to see, pet and examine the Griffs. "Many people had heard about the breed," Terri says, "but few had ever seen eight Griffs assembled in one place before. I am so very proud of our dogs. With all the attention, the stress of travel and the crowds of people about, they behaved marvelously. They maintained their good humor and never gave us any problems. We wanted to get the message across that these Griffs are truly versatile dogs and can do it all."

Hopefully other folks will get that message, too. As they come to see and understand the breed, they will be able to appreciate just how fully Eduard Korthals succeeded in his grand design to create an all-round hunting dog. And perhaps, at your next dog show, you'll be gifted with a sloppy kiss from a bewhiskered clown. "Owners take great pride in this breed and his abilities," says Barbara Young-Smith. The Griff is to be savored and enjoyed, she says, "like a fine rare wine. The Griffon is truly one of a kind." Let's hope that many more American owners are "bitten by the beard."

The impressive Standard Xolo Weissleader Saguaro Sam, owned by Pat Weissleader and Karen Johnson.

Chapter 35

The Xoloitzcuintli

The Xoloitzcuintli has been called "the first dog of the Americas." And so he is. This rare dog is our glorious, living link to the fabulous pre-Columbian civilizations of old. He can proudly count the Toltecs, the Aztecs, the Mayans, the Zapotecas and the Colima Indians as his masters. It's truly amazing that this living relic is still with us today. And what's even more incredible is that the Xoloitzcuintli has remained unchanged for so many thousands of years.

Before we proceed, let's clear up a few things. The first is the breed's foreign sounding, tongue twisting name. It's a combination of two Aztec words. "Xolotl" was one of their gods and "itzcuintli" was merely the word for dog. The correct pronunciation is *show-low-eats-queen-tlee,* but fanciers often call the breed "Xolo," *(Show-low)* for short. Secondly, many wonder at the relationship between the Xolo and the Mexican Hairless. The Mexican Hairless is but a former name applied to the Toy version of the Xolo.

One of the key characteristics of the breed is, of course, its hairlessness. We don't know exactly when or how the breed became hairless. Some believe it is a mutation which took hold. Fleas and ticks were a real concern in hot, humid Mexico and Central America, home of the Xolo. In those days, many dogs probably died from blood loss due to heavy infestations. It's entirely possible that dogs with no coat, to harbor such pests, may have survived in greater numbers. We do have evidence to suggest that the ancient Indians preferred hairless dogs. The Franciscan monk, Bernardino de Sahagun, traveled to Mexico with Cortez in the 1500's. When he returned to Spain, he recounted his observations of *Nueva España* (as the Spanish dubbed

Mexico) in the many volumed *La Historia General de las Cosas de Nueva España.* He mentions that there are dogs "born without hair." Interestingly, he also tells us that there are dogs born with hair, "but when they are small, their bodies are anointed with a resin, called *Oxitl,* due to this the hair falls out, leaving the skin of the body shiny and smooth." This would clearly indicate a preference for hairless dogs.

The work of archaeologists proves conclusively that the Xoloitzcuintli has been around for thousands of years. Artifacts discovered at Colima sites, in western Mexico, show clearly that the Xolo was often immortalized in clay sculptures. Hundreds of these artifacts depicting puppies were unearthed at Colima sites dating from 2,000 A.D. New evidence suggests, however, that the Xolo may be even older. In Tlatilco, Mexico, researchers unearthed a figure showing a woman suckling a dog. They date this figure at 3,700 B.C. This amazing sculpture is the earliest known depiction of a dog ever found in the Americas and is quite consistent with the depictions found in Colima ruins. It predates the Colima finds by 1,700 years.

Many writers tell us that the early Indians loved and respected their dogs. This was particularly true among the Toltecs, who ruled central Mexico from the 10th to the 12th centuries A.D. "The ancient Toltecs considered the love of a dog for its master the most perfect manifestation of unselfish love," writes Edmund Bordeau, in *The Soul of Ancient Mexico.* "The dog played an important role in the life of Mayans or Toltecs of the upper classes. There were few animals in Mexico before the arrival of the Spaniards: horses, donkeys and cows were unknown until after the conquest. However,

201

the dog was domesticated and held in high esteem, and was it's master's constant companion wherever he went...."

These ancient Indians saw life as a struggle between the forces of good and evil. "In most of the civilizations of Mexico and Central America, the dog was the symbol of love," says Dr. Bordeau. The Xolo was one of ten symbols of good. Indeed, the Indians ascribed several roles to the dog. He was certainly a valued protector of the home. Not only did he warn of predators and human intruders, but he was also a living good luck symbol, which could scare away evil spirits.

As with all hairless breeds, the Xolo's skin is warmth to the touch. Due to this, the dog's were considered as "healers" by the Indians. As all who have used a heating pad can attest, the warmth is often a comfort for aches and pains. In ancient days, the Xolo filled this role and he's credited with curing everything from simple headaches and toothaches to rheumatism and insomnia. Supposedly, when one slept with or cuddled one of the dogs, the ailment was transferred from the human to the dog. The dog would then stand or lie in a stream or mud hole (doubtless a relief to him in the blazing sun and high humidity) and he would be cleansed of the disease. In some remote parts of Mexico and Central America, this superstition is said to persist to the present day.

The dogs had other mystical uses, too. Writing in the April 1935 issue of the *American Kennel Gazette,* breeder-owner Ida H. Garret says that the dogs were used for prophecy. "Colors range from blue to tans and browns..." she writes. "But many of these dogs, although not born that color, turn speckled and spotted at about from four to six months of age. These two and three colored speckles are pink at birth, like a human baby. The speckles and spots sometimes develop into the most fantastic designs, such as sunbursts,

Five month old Razzmatazz Tangerine is owned by Mary Merlo, of Mastic Beach, New York.

circles and squares, stripes and often pictures....There is an ancient superstition in respect to these hieroglyphics on the skin of the hairless dog, the belief being that the fates of entire tribes could be foretold by 'prophets' who were able to read them." The solid colored dogs, she says, also had special meanings.

We do know that Xolos were slaughtered and used for food. Some authors imply that the dog meat was a staple of the Indian diet, while others believe that dogs were eaten only as part of ceremonial feasts. We do know that the Indians had many other food sources including deer, fowl and rabbit, so it's entirely possible that the dog was only used for special occasions. For such celebrations, different colored dogs were often selected, as each color had some significant meaning. Some historians also believe that the eating of a Xolo conferred a sort of spiritual protection on all those who partook of the meal.

The burial practices of the ancient Americans tell us much about their regard for the dog. When a man died, his dog was sacrificed and its body was placed in the grave beside his master. In death, as in life, the two were constant companions. The dog continued his traditional guarding duties even in death, safely guiding his master into the afterlife. When an Aztec died, his soul entered "Mictlan," the underworld and, for the next four years, he had to overcome a series of trials and hardships before he could finally rest in paradise. There were rivers to be forded and forests to be conquered, with the Xolo helping to guide the way. Dr. Bordeau, however, gives us another compelling reason for the dog's presence. When a man died, he faced the Indian's version of our Saint Peter and was expected to give an accounting of his life. According to Dr. Bordeau, "the dog was always present to testify in the master's favor, telling how kind the master had been all his life, thus proving him to have been a good man."

When Cortez arrived in Central America and Mexico, in the 1500's, he found many Indian dogs. Those who traveled with him have described both coated and hairless dogs, specifically mentioning the Xolo by name. At first the Indians were impressed with these foreign white men, believing they were gods. They thought their own dogs, the Xolos, were the embodiment of gods and they ascribed the same standing to the Spanish dogs. When one dog strayed from the Spanish camp and wandered into an Indian village, the natives treated it with great respect. They prepared a sumptuous feast for the dog, which included deer, birds of several types and rabbits. They prepared rich chocolate for it to drink. Then, they placed the dog on a fine blanket, which was carried on the shoulders of four Indians. Followed by a procession of 300 natives, they set out to return the dog to its master.

The Indians were soon to discover, however, that Cortez and his dogs were anything but gods. The Spaniard, aided by his dogs, killed untold numbers of Indians, in the most cruel and vicious manner possible. Many Xolos were also killed by these human and canine newcomers. Some say that the Indians kept their Xolos hidden within their homes to save them from a certain death. This also kept them from interbreeding with the Spanish dogs. We may never know how many Xolos were killed in *Nueva España,* but the number must have been high.

We don't know when the first of these South of the Border dogs first came to the U.S. They may well have been in the southwest before there was a United States. During the 1880's, the Xolo made its debut in show rings here. These early dogs came directly from Mexico and the breed was dubbed "The Mexican Hairless." The most prominent breeder, during this period, was probably Elroy Foote, of New York City. His 18-pound "Me Too" was considered the finest dog of the day.

There were a few other breeders, too. In a 1935 article on the breed, which appeared in the *American Kennel Gazette,* breeder-owner Ida H. Garret tells of an 1890's breeder. She says that "there was a breeder of hairless dogs on Long Island, New York, who, in the course of a few years, netted a small fortune in the breed. In 1899, this breeder told me that most of her patrons purchased puppies because they believed them to be a panacea for human ills. She said that many of her patrons reported to her that the mere action of allowing the dog to sleep with a nervous person or one suffering from insomnia, acted as a soporific."

During the 1930's, at least one Xolo attracted great attention. He was a little fellow known as "Bonzo." What a remarkable life this guy led. During his early days, he was the constant companion of the notorious Mexican bandit, Pancho Villa. On his deathbed, Villa gave the dog to one of his henchman. He, in turn, presented Bonzo to the great dog fancier, writer and lover of rare breeds, Freeman Lloyd. Bonzo adapted well to life in New York City and Lloyd was devoted to his new Mexican pet. But, somehow, Bonzo was lost. Luck, however, was with him. Famed opera singer Mary Garden found the little guy and fell in love with him. For many years, he was her devoted friend and Bonzo lived a life of luxury. Ms. Garden took him everywhere and he sported a diamond studded collar valued at $12,000. He remained with the singer for the rest of his life and died in her sumptuous suite at the Waldorf Astoria.

The A.K.C. recognized the breed as the Mexican Hairless. The initial standard was rather vague. With regard to size, it stated only that the dogs were "about

The exquisitely elegant toy Xolo Razzmatazz Neptuna. "Tippy" is owned by Amy Fernandez, Razzmatazz Kennels, Forest Hills, New York.

the size of a small Fox Terrier." Sadly, the breed never attracted a real following. There were years when nary a dog was registered. In 1959, the breed was dropped from the A.K.C.'s list of recognized breeds.

The breed did not fare well in old Mexico, either. In fact, the dogs were so rarely seen that the breed was believed to be close to extinction. Thanks to two dog lovers, though, the Xoloitzcuintli was rescued. Our thanks go to Norman Pelham Wright and Countess Lascelles de Premio Real for revitalizing the breed. Mr. Wright was the Director of the British Chamber of Commerce in Mexico City. This amateur botanist, archaeologist and zoologist, loved Mexico, its history and its culture. An avowed dog lover, he also served as President of the Mexican Kennel Club. Mr. Wright was intrigued with the Xoloitzcuintli, the ancient dog of Mexico. He organized an expedition to the state of Guerrero. Countess de Premio Real and several others went along. In the remote River Balsas region, near Pungarabato, they found Indians who still bred the Xolo. They were able to secure a number of specimens which were used in carefully monitored breeding programs. The Countess still breeds Xolos to this day.

The breed attracted public attention when famed artist Diego Rivera became enamored with the dogs. "Señor Xolotl" was one of his favorites. Rivera included Xolos in several of his famous murals.

The Mexican Kennel Club formally recognized the Xoloitzcuintli in May 1956. Only Standard and Miniature Xolos were permitted to be registered. The breed is also recognized by the Federation Cynologique Internationale and can compete in international shows. Unlike the U.S., the Canadian Kennel Club never dropped the Xolo from its roles and dogs are eligible to compete for championships in that country, as well. In 1989, a toy Xolo made breed history by becoming the first Canadian champion. In the United States, the breed competes in rare breed events.

In 1986, a small group of fanciers joined to form the Xoloitzcuintli Club of America. The enthusiastic members have done much to promote interest in the breed. They sponsor several shows each year. The X.C.A. also publishes the very informative *Xolo News*. It's a must for anyone interested in the breed.

An exotic eye-catcher, the Xolo is an elegant, sleek looking dog. He has a proud aristocratic bearing. Novices often compare the breed's looks to the Doberman Pinscher or the Manchester Terrier. Although refined and svelte as adults, Xolos don't begin life that way. Puppies tend to be short-legged, blunt-nosed and wrinkly, qualities they lose as they approach adulthood. Xolos come in two coat styles and three sizes. There are both hairless and coated dogs. Toy Xolos may not exceed 13 inches at the withers. Miniatures stand 13-18 inches and Standard sized Xolos measure 18-23 inches.

The Xolo head is lean and smooth. The skull is somewhat broad, with a slight stop and a longish muzzle. When alert, wrinkles accentuate the brow. The large erect ears are thin and delicate. The almond-shaped eyes range in color from yellow to black, but the darker colors are preferred. The nose is dark in darker colored dogs. Bronze dogs have brown noses and spotted dogs may have spotted noses.

The Xolo has a long, elegant smooth neck, which blends gracefully into a level topline. The hindquarters are well muscled, with the low set tail carried gaily, but never raised over the back.

Hairless Xolos are, well, hairless. Total hairlessness is preferred, but some dogs do have a fine wisp on the skull, nape, feet and tip of the tail. Total hairlessness is preferred. Coated Xolos have short, smooth coats. Their tails are fully covered with hair. Thin or bare patches are objectionable. The Xolo's skin is smooth and satiny with a distinctly warm feel. The skin is quite thick and helps to protect the dog against sunburn and

Ch. Weissleader's Casey, bred by Pat Weissleader and owned by Jennifer Locke.

injury. Owners report that Xolos are very resistant to fleas, ticks and other insects. This breed comes in any color or combination of colors. The darker colors (black, slate and blue) are the most common. Lighter colored dogs (red, liver and bronze) are also seen. Black and tan and brindle dogs exist, but are very rare. Small white markings, typically found on the chest, are common.

Hairless dogs do feel the cold, so it's best to provide them with a sweater in winter. Owners recommend rubbing oil or lotion into the skin to keep it soft and supple. A weekly bath will help to prevent the formation of blackheads and pimples. Owners of coated Xolos usually brush their dogs weekly with a curry brush.

As with all hairless breeds, hairless Xolos are usually missing their premolars. Their canine teeth often extend forward, like tusks. Coated dogs have normal dentition and this makes them invaluable in breeding programs. Chinese Crested breeders have found that, by making full use of coated dogs in their breeding programs, they have been able to improve the teeth of their hairless dogs.

Xolos are the perfect solution for those who love white velvet sofas and white wall-to-wall carpeting. There will never be any telltale dog hairs left lying about and since there is no coat, there are no fleas or ticks. Furthermore, Xolos are the perfect solution for people who are allergic to dog hair. Xolos are very tidy, by nature, and will often clean themselves like cats. They are also a cinch to housebreak.

As in days of old, the Xolo is still esteemed as a home guardian. Whether you own a Standard, Miniature or Toy Xolo, he will feel that it's his responsibility to protect the family from harm. This breed is very alert. One owner reports that her dogs are so vigilant that they will even sleep on their feet. The dog may drop its head and sway, but the minute he hears something, he's instantly alert.

With his family, the Xolo is sweet and loving. These dogs bond very closely with their owners and are very sensitive to their moods. Some dogs have been known to pine away when their owners go on vacation. Due to the close bond, most owners do not believe that Xolos make good kennel dogs.

"Xolos are very sociable and should be considered full family members," says Patricia Weissleader, of Lizardhaven Kennels, in Desert Hot Springs, California. Pat has owned Xolos for years and is very active in rescue work. She helps locate new homes for displaced or abandoned dogs. "Almost every time that I hear of a Xolo digging or climbing fences, it's because the dog is not given sufficient attention to make him feel like a real part of the family." Indeed, this is a breed that thrives on close contact. "If you have only one dog it may want to sit near you as much as possible," Pat adds.

Most owners report that Xolos are calm and easy to live with. "Living with a Xolo is like living with another person—some will be like children and some can be a maiden aunt, checking everything out and looking at you with disapproval if you fail to conform to the expected routine," Pat Weissleader says. "Most Xolos sleep in their masters' beds, sit on furniture and have free access to the house—and why not, when they behave so nicely?"

Within the home, the Xolo is likely to be a performer and a bit of a clown. They delight in charming owners with their antics. "Some Xolos will be very kitten-like, as puppies, and will keep their playfulness throughout their lives. Because of their excellent health, very old dogs may be mistaken for puppies," Pat reports. The dogs of Lizardhaven have a wealth of tricks to keep Pat entertained. Her rare orange skinned hairless male, Chalcedony Rose, adopted a little stuffed teddy bear when he was just a few weeks old. For hours on end, he will toss the toy in the air and pounce on it when it lands. "He is very distressed if he cannot find it," Pat says. "He will toss in the air so that it lands in my lap when he wants me to play. He has played with it for three years now without chewing it up."

Owners unanimously agree that Xolos are very intelligent dogs. They are willing to please and easily trained, doing well in obedience. "They want to know the rules and they pick up the household routine very quickly," Pat Weissleader says. New owners are often surprised at how quickly the dogs adapt to new surroundings. "New owners say, 'It seems like the dog was always here,'" Pat says. "They had expected a period of training and errors before the dog settled in."

Being very sociable animals, Xolos get along well with children and other dogs. "Most Xolos love other dogs, cats, kids and any living thing you want to add to your household," Pat reports. Indeed, the dogs seem to enjoy having other companions. "Xolos like to touch and, if you have several, they will often nap in a pile. If you are sitting down, the pile will be on your lap," Pat laughs. "Many people with infirm older dogs will get a Xolo pup as a companion for the dog. The Xolo seems to understand and allow for any handicap and usually the older dog gains a lot of vitality."

Most Xolos are quite wary of strangers. Some are uncomfortable when visitors arrive, but others learn to accept strangers. However, most dogs are loathe to lavish affection on anyone but their owners. Because of this attitude, it's best to make an effort to socialize your Xolo from puppyhood. This is particularly important if you wish to show your dog.

The breed has several other interesting and unusual characteristics. "Xolos rarely pant unless they are extremely hot and tired," Pat Weissleader says. "They do sweat over parts of their body, though. A few Xolos will break out in a clammy sweat, along their back and spine, when upset."

Some writers have reported that Xolos actually have the ability to cry. Others contend that this is mere fiction. "Most scientists believe that no animals cry from emotion," Pat says. But the California breeder has seen dogs that "do weep when you scold them and I know this for certain since I had one." Pat is quick to point out that most Xolos do *not* exhibit this mystifying behavior.

Xoloitzcuintli owners are an enthusiastic and dedicated bunch. Thanks to their hard work, the breed is becoming better known in this country. All admit, however, that this is still a very rare breed. "If Xolos were not classified as domestic dogs," Pat Weissleader says, "they would be eligible for endangered species status. I only know of about 500 in the world." Thanks to devoted breeders, however, the Xoloitzcuintli, Mexico's national dog, survives. "They are at once the most beautiful and the ugliest of dogs," wrote Ida H. Garret in the 1930's, "but always exotic, interesting and clever."

APPENDIX

AFFENPINSCHER
Affenpinscher Club of America
Bonnie R. Beskie
Lincoln Tower, Suite 400
Rochester, NY 14604

AMERICAN WATER SPANIEL
John Barth
Swan Lake Kennels
Pardeeville, WI 53954

AZAWAKH
Azawakh Club of America
Debra Rookard
318 Dacula Road
Dacula, GA 30211

Gisela Cook-Schmidt
P.O. Box 1146
Twenty-nine Palms, CA 92277

BEDLINGTON TERRIER
Bedlington Terrier Club of America
Norman A. Rappaport
25 Delaware Trail
Denville, NJ 07834

BELGIAN MALINOIS
American Belgian Malinois Club
Mary Janek
Rt. 1, Box 32-A
Farmland, IN 47340

BOLOGNESE
Bolognese Club of America
Box 1461
Montrose, CO 81402

BOURBONNAIS POINTER
Beth Cepil
Box 3849, RD 3
New Tripoli, PA 18066

BRIARD
Briard Club of America
Ms. Frances Davis
915 Buttonwood Trail
Crownsville, MD 21032

CANE CORSO
Michael & Kathy Sottile
P.O. Box 250307
Montgomery, AL 36125

CAUCASIAN OVTCHARKA
Caucasian Ovtcharka Club of America
P.O. Box 745
Painesville, OH 44077

CHART POLSKI
Betty Augustowski
1115 Delmont Rd.
Severn, MD 21144

CLUMBER SPANIEL
Edythe T. Donovan
241 Monterey Avenue
Pelham, NY 10803

COTON DE TULEAR
Coton de Tulear Club of America
Laurie L. Spalding
7042 Bevis Avenue
Van Nuys, CA 91405

CURLY-COATED RETRIEVER
Curly-Coated Retriever Club of America
Gina Columbo
24 Holmes Blvd.
Ft. Walton Beach, FL 32548

DANDIE DINMONT TERRIER
Dandie Dinmont Terrier Club of America
Mrs. Larry D. Cummins
3524 Aquila Avenue North
New Hope, MN 55427

FIELD SPANIEL
Field Spaniel Society of America
Becki Jo Wolkenheim
P.O. Box 187
Wales, WI 53183

FLAT-COATED RETRIEVER
Flat-Coated Retriever Society of America
Margot Hallett
170 Estabrook Road
Hampton, CT 06247

IRISH RED AND WHITE SETTER
Vincent Brennan
Rock View Kennels
Drumroosk Kinawley, Enniskillen
Co. Fermanagh, N. Ireland

Mary Tuite
Hillbrow House of Rua
Little London Road, Horam
Heathfield, East Sussex
England TN21 0BL

IRISH TERRIER
Irish Terrier Club of America
Judy LaBash
7047 Harrington Road
Lexington, MI 48450

JAPANESE SPITZ
Lynne Robson
Castle Farm Cottage
Great North Road
Stibbington, Peterborough
England PE8 6LN

KAI KEN
National Kai Club
P.O. Box 217
Maximo, OH 44650

LAKELAND TERRIER
United States Lakeland Terrier Club
Phyllis W. Belden
P.O. Box 87
Norge, VA 23127

LONGHAIRED WHIPPET
Longhaired Whippet Association
Walter Wheeler
P.O. Box 21
93 Eliot St.
Sherborn, MA 01770

MINIATURE SHAR-PEI
American Mini-Pei Club
P.O. Box 977
Weatherford, OK 73096

Linda Coffee
5809 Emerson Ct.
Arlington, TX 76016

NEW GUINEA SINGING DOG
New Guinea Singing Dog Society
Philip Persky
245 Eighth Avenue
New York, NY 10011

PULI
Puli Club of America
Carolyn Nusbickel
8087 Goshen Road
Malvern, PA 19355

PYRENEAN SHEPHERD
Pyrnean Shepherd Club of America
9560 Robinson Rd.
Chardon, OH 44024

SKYE TERRIER
Skye Terrier Club of America
Donna Dale
8217 Warfield Road
Gaithersburg, MD 20882

SPINONE ITALIANI
Ruth E. Adams
6106 N. Linton Lane
Indianapolis, IN 46220

SUSSEX SPANIEL
Sussex Spaniel Club of America
Joan Dunn
N3 W31535 Twin Oaks Dr.
Delafield, WI 53018

TIBETAN SPANIEL
Tibetan Spaniel Club of America
Shirley Howard
29 W. 028 River Glen Rd.
West Chicago, IL 60185

WELSH SPRINGER SPANIEL
Welsh Springer Spaniel Club of America
Edwin J. Cummings, III
RD 1, Box 164
Accord, NY 12404

WIREHAIRED POINTING GRIFFON
Wirehaired Pointing Griffon Club of America
Barbara Smith
90566 Coburg Road
Eugene, OR 97401

XOLOITZCUINTLI
Lorraine Chester
1821 North Camino Avra
Tucson, AZ

Amy Fernandez
100 Greenway South
Forest Hills, NY 11375

OTHER BOOKS FROM O.T.R.